"John Walton is one of the leading Old Testament scholars of our generation. I am always informed and stimulated in my own thinking whenever I read his work. He is rightly sensitive to the ancient context of the Old Testament as he pursues its continuing significance for our lives as Christians. *Old Testament Theology for Christians* presents his most wide-ranging analysis yet. I recommend this book enthusiastically to all who want to think seriously about the Old Testament."

Tremper Longman III, Robert H. Gundry Professor of Biblical Studies, Westmont College

"John Walton, a longtime leader in Old Testament and ancient Near East studies, sets himself to a large task in his latest book: to use historical inquiry to discover the Bible's enduring theological revelation for the church today. He does this by what he calls 'cognitive environment criticism,' which allows him to integrate history and theology within a confessional context so as to read the Old Testament 'from an Israelite perspective' with a focus on God's plans and purposes. Walton's weighty goal, coupled with his capacious approach, means that readers of all stripes will find much here to both agree and disagree with. What cannot be debated in the least, however, is that Walton has covered immense ground, categorized a vast range of data, and offered us a treasure trove of information and reflections that will repay reading and rereading."

Brent A. Strawn, professor of Old Testament, Emory University

Old Testament

THEOLOGY

for Christians

From

ANCIENT CONTEXT

to

ENDURING BELIEF

JOHN H. WALTON

IVP Academic

An imprint of InterVarsity Press
Downers Grove, Illinois

InterVarsity Press
P.O. Box 1400, Downers Grove, IL 60515-1426
ivpress.com
email@ivpress.com

InterVarsity Press® is the book-publishing division of InterVarsity Christian Fellowship/USA®, a movement of
students and faculty active on campus at hundreds of universities, colleges, and schools of nursing in the United
States of America, and a member movement of the International Fellowship of Evangelical Students. For
information about local and regional activities, visit intervarsity.org.

Cover design: Cindy Kiple and David Fassett
Interior design: Daniel van Loon
Images: blue background: © kostins / iStockphoto / Getty Images
    flames: © sbayram / iStockphoto / Getty Images
    smoke: © ozandogan / iStockphoto / Getty Images

ISBN 978-0-8308-5192-8 (print)
ISBN 978-0-8308-8904-4 (digital)

Printed in the United States of America ∞

InterVarsity Press is committed to ecological stewardship and to the conservation of natural resources in all our
operations. This book was printed using sustainably sourced paper.

Library of Congress Cataloging-in-Publication Data
A catalog record for this book is available from the Library of Congress.

| P | 23 | 22 | 21 | 20 | 19 | 18 | 17 | 16 | 15 | 14 | 13 | 12 | 11 | 10 | 9 | 8 | 7 | 6 | 5 | 4 | 3 | 2 | 1 |
| Y | 36 | 35 | 34 | 33 | 32 | 31 | 30 | 29 | 28 | 27 | 26 | 25 | 24 | 23 | 22 | 21 | 20 | 19 | 18 | 17 |

CONTENTS

ACKNOWLEDGMENTS

A BOOK SUCH AS THIS ONE that covers a lifetime of thinking is inevitably informed through interaction with a multitude of authors, colleagues, and students. As ideas merge in the mind over time, direct links are lost, but my indebtedness remains in many ways.

My students have especially shaped my thinking over the years, and this book could not have come about without all of that interaction. By far, however, the most significant contributor to my thinking remains my son Jon (pen name J. Harvey Walton). He read each section as it was written (and rewritten). He edited, argued, offered thoughts, and, yes, taught me, all along the way. It is one of my dearest privileges in life to have a conversation partner who so thoroughly understands my views and is willing to interact with them and to push them beyond where I imagined they could go.

I am also grateful to Jennifer Hale for editing and indexing the manuscript.

ABBREVIATIONS

ANET	*Ancient Near Eastern Texts Relating to the Old Testament.* Edited by James B. Pritchard. 3rd ed. Princeton, NJ: Princeton University Press, 1969
CAD	*The Assyrian Dictionary of the Oriental Institute of the University of Chicago.* Chicago: The Oriental Institute of the University of Chicago, 1956–2006
CANE	*Civilizations of the Ancient Near East.* Edited by Jack M. Sasson. 4 vols. New York, 1995. Repr. in 2 vols. Peabody, MA: Hendrickson, 2006
COS	*The Context of Scripture.* Edited by William W. Hallo. 3 vols. Leiden: Brill, 1997–2002
CT	Coffin Texts
DDD²	*Dictionary of Deities and Demons in the Bible.* Edited by Karel van der Toorn, Bob Becking, and Pieter W. van der Horst. 2nd rev. ed. Grand Rapids: Eerdmans, 1999
NIVAC	New International Version Application Commentary
PT	Pyramid Texts
SBLWAW	SBL Writings from the Ancient World
TDOT	*Theological Dictionary of the Old Testament.* Edited by G. Johannes Botterweck and Helmer Ringgren. Translated by John T. Willis et al. 8 vols. Grand Rapids: Eerdmans, 1974–2006
UL	*Utukku Lemnûtu*
ZIBBCOT	*Zondervan Illustrated Bible Backgrounds Commentary.* Edited by J. Walton. Grand Rapids: Zondervan, 2009

1

INTRODUCTION
and
FOUNDATIONS

Hermeneutical Considerations

I have been expecting to write this book since the beginning of my career, but I have also been dreading the prospect and largely avoiding it. Writing a book on the theology of the Old Testament is, in some ways, the height of presumption. Walter Kaiser demonstrated his recognition of these difficulties when he wisely included the disclaimer "toward" in the title of his own contribution, *Toward an Old Testament Theology*. When we throw our hats into the ring of comprehensive theologies, it is not because we have everything figured out. We simply have a few more tidbits to add to the discussions of those who have gone before us; we have a few insights (often instigated by interactions with students) to pass on to students. So we adopt the role of an aqueduct—taking what we have been given and passing it on to those who might benefit from it. The impetus, then, for writing a book like this is not to claim the final word; it is written in the exercise of stewardship. This stewardship calls us to give an account of ourselves after a long career of study and teaching; it causes us to ask the question, What have we got to show for it all?

Most of this introduction will talk about the methods and assumptions that drive this book. But before engaging those topics, we should talk about

the "elephant in the room"—why we should even bother spending time in
the Old Testament. This question is eloquently introduced in Yvonne Sherwood's summary:

> At the heart of Old Testament study in its infancy . . . is a profound anxiety
> about the status, and content, of the Old Testament. The Old Testament is a
> compendium of cannibalism (Voltaire), an exhausted child's primer torn out
> of our hands by the coming of Christ (Lessing), a document that fumes with
> anger and xenophobia (just like the Jews) and that is "marked by enmity to-
> wards all peoples and [that] therefore evokes the enmity of all" (Kant). Bound
> up with images of the primitive, the savage, the childish, it is the dark hin-
> terland of its purer, better sequel, the foreign country in need of civilization,
> colonization. At best, the "statutory" Old Testament foregrounds in childish
> stutters, or as in a mirror darkly, the "universal human reality" and the "pure
> moral religion" of the New—at worst (as Schleiermacher was to put it in the
> nineteenth century) it displays a restrictive monotheism that "by its limitation
> of the love of Jehovah to the race of Abraham displays a lingering affinity with
> fetishism." The sense of revulsion with this canonical fossil reaches its logical
> culmination in Harnack's suggestion that the Old Testament (now not merely
> the Old but the Exhausted, Paralysed, Infirm Testament given to senile mut-
> terings) be forcibly retired, or merely printed after the New, as an appendix.[1]

Modern readers may not feel free to express frustration with the Old
Testament so frankly, but they may well be confused by obscure prophecies
about people who no longer exist, obtuse laws that the New Testament identifies as obsolete, and graphic narratives of sex and violence that are simply
disturbing when read in the context of that which is supposed to be God's
Word. Just how, we may ask, can the Old Testament possibly stand as God's
Word to us? What truth does it have to offer, and how do we get to that truth?
And therein lies the focus of this book. We are going to attempt to discover
how God's revelation of himself to Israel can be understood and embraced
as God's revelation to us. But we have to lay the groundwork carefully.

While Old Testament theology books will differ from one another for a
variety of reasons, most of these differences arise from the presuppositions
that underlie the investigation and the resulting perspectives brought to the

---

[1]Yvonne Sherwood, *A Biblical Text and Its Afterlives* (Cambridge: Cambridge University Press,
2000), 31.

text. In the next few pages I would like to lay out some of the more important presuppositions and perspectives that have shaped my particular approach.

Interpretation that is authority-based, theocentrically focused. The approach in this book is centered on biblical authority. I use the term to refer to a complex profile encompassing a variety of descriptors (such as inspiration and inerrancy), as well as an understanding that the nature of the Bible calls for our response, i.e., submission to its authority. We accomplish this task by being readers who are competent, who handle the text ethically, and who strive to be the virtuous people the text calls us to be.[2] Having said that, however, it is important to recognize that determining what the Bible says with authority can be a complicated endeavor, and it requires careful nuancing with a fine-tuned hermeneutic.

We must understand that there is likely to be a difference between what even the most theologically astute Israelite believed and what the text teaches. Authority is found in the latter, rather than the former. God's authority is vested in the human communicators whose words are contained in both the Old and New Testaments. And if we truly believe that both Testaments present us with God's authoritative revelation, we then have the task of discerning the nature of that authoritative message, the message inherent in the Old Testament in its context. That is, the Old Testament had authority before the New Testament ever came along; it served its purpose of revelation to its contemporary audience.

This approach identifies the locus of the Bible's authority in theocentric revelation, in identifying its main purpose in the revelation of God's plans and purposes to us. This revelation is not its *sole* purpose, but it is its primary purpose. In other words, the authority of the Old Testament is not only found in how it points to Christ. It *does* point to Christ, of course, but that is not *all* that it does. Being trinitarian, we can conclude that the revelation of any of the three persons of the Trinity is legitimate subject matter.[3]

---

[2]John H. Walton and D. Brent Sandy, *The Lost World of Scripture* (Downers Grove, IL: InterVarsity Press, 2013), 283-91. This "virtuous" descriptor should not be reduced to morality or to the keeping of rules. "Virtuous" describes the sort of person we are in the depths of our identities, not just how we act.

[3]Christocentrism can too easily marginalize the other members of the Trinity. At the same time, it would be inadvisable to imagine that Yahweh is the name of "God the Father" alone. The revelation of God in the Old Testament is not person specific, and neither should our perception be. Just as we would not restrict "Yahweh" to God the Father, concomitantly, we should not restrict him to

As the text reveals God to us, we submit to its authority by embracing the understanding of the plans and purposes of God that is therein revealed. We accept the opportunity to participate in his great enterprise. We cannot customize the message to our own tastes, or it will become nothing other than our own concoction, a picture of God defined by our own image. The very idea that Scripture is inspired eliminates the claim that humanity merely fabricated the God of Scripture. No, when we affirm that Scripture has its source in God, we insist that the profile of God we adopt is not of our own making. We must therefore interpret Scripture in a way that preserves that truth.

For these reasons, our interpretation of Scripture needs to be founded in a hermeneutic that links the authoritative message of the text to the author's intention. The author has been vested with the authority of God.[4] We cannot get to the message that God has for us without going through the human authors chosen for that communicative task. At the same time, we cannot get inside the human author's head, and we are not committed to all his beliefs, whatever they may have been. We only have to believe that the (implied) author is an effective communicator and that we can therefore receive that communication to the extent that we are able to take our place in the implied audience.[5] Commensurately, we agree that the revelation of God to the Israelites had authority both in the time that it was given and in a continuing sense today. Identifying the specific theology taught by the Old Testament is therefore important to our understanding of God, though it is insufficient for the development of a full-fledged systematic or dogmatic theology today. Nevertheless, it has a formative and normative role to play in our own understanding of theology for our time and culture.

Ancient context, ultimate christological goal (we are not the implied audience). Any people of any time or culture can defensibly consider

---

God the Son. A healthy approach to the christological reading of the Old Testament is found in Richard Hays, *Echoes of Scripture in the Gospels* (Waco, TX: Baylor University Press, 2016).

[4]I am going to continue to use the customary language referring to the "authors" of Scripture heuristically, despite my insistence that there really were no "authors" per se, in the way that we think about them, in the ancient world. This discussion can be found in Walton and Sandy, *Lost World of Scripture.*

[5]By referring to the "implied" author, I am acknowledging that we can only profile the author through the communication that he has given us. We cannot know him independently of his literature. In the same manner, the implied audience is descriptive of the one that the author believed he was addressing—the audience the author had in mind.

themselves among the implied audience that *God* envisaged. But we are not in the implied audience of the human author. Another way to say this, and one I use all the time, is that the Bible is therefore *for* us but was not written *to* us. To fully comprehend the way that it is *for* us, we have to do whatever it takes to join the author's implied audience. In that cultural and literary context we will find the authoritative teaching of the text. What the ancient author gave his audience had authority for them, and that authority has not diminished through time or at the hands of future revelation. What had authority for them continues to have authority for us to the extent that it transcends the framework of the old covenant, and we must therefore glean its truth by using their lenses rather than by imposing our lenses on them. The ancient context may at times be obscure or opaque, and it offers challenges that can be difficult to overcome. But we must attempt to understand the ancient context to the best of our ability. Exercising cultural imperialism or theological anachronism can only result in a loss of access to the authoritative communication.

It is no excuse to point to the Christians who, for two thousand years, did not have access to the ancient world. While those who came before us may have made little attempt to understand the text in such a context, our responsibility is to use every tool at our disposal to do the most careful exegesis that we can, which is what the earlier Christians also sought to accomplish. Ethical interpretation is dependent on the full and informed use of the tools we have; it is not dependent on the identity of the tools.

We not only have to recognize the ancient context (so that we do not impose our modern thinking on the text); we also have to resist only reading the Old Testament text in light of the New Testament. It is not uncommon among Christian interpreters to superimpose a christological interpretation on the Old Testament and to use that perspective to glean the authoritative message. But through this approach an overriding message is preferred over whatever the Old Testament author may have been communicating to his audience. We will discuss this further in the next chapter, but for now I will describe my underlying presuppositions and methodology as "christotelic" rather than "christocentric." In the christotelic approach, we recognize that all of God's revelation reaches a new plateau in Christ, so all of it can be seen as heading in that direction. In that way we can talk about the Old Testament as pointing to Christ. Consequently, the approach used in this book first seeks authority in what the Old Testament authors were communicating, independent of Christology and derived from context. Christology can prove valuable for unpacking further understanding concerning God's plan and his kingdom, but it does not obviate that which was inherently taught in the Old Testament context that had nothing to do with Christology (and I would contend that there is much in the Old Testament that is not christological in nature). At the same time, all of the Old Testament is herding us toward Christ. Christology, then, cannot be left out of the equation, but it does not replace what the Old Testament authors were doing.[6] Therefore, throughout the bulk of this Old Testament theology, the focus will be on the Old Testament context and will make little reference to Christology, though at the end attention will be given to that aspect as the telos.

Consistent theological impulse. The variety of genres in the Old Testament gives us content packaged in many different literary forms. We are obliged to attend to those forms and to understand them as best we can in their ancient guise, yet we also recognize that genre is only the packaging, not the product. Whether we are dealing with narratives, proverbs, prophecies, laws, or hymns, the forms and genres of the Old Testament are being employed for theological purposes. When historical events are being portrayed, theological perspectives offer the most important lens for interpretation. Events are not just *reported* by the authors; they are *interpreted*—and theology is the goal. When legal sayings are being collected, it is not the structure of society that is the focus, but insight on how Israel was to identify itself with the plans and purposes of Yahweh, its wise and holy covenant God. This literature, then, helped Israel to know how to live in his presence.

Said another way, if the overarching role of the Old Testament is to give revelation from God, then readers (ancient or modern) must give ultimate attention to the revelation from God that is offered, regardless of the genre that is used to offer it. Whatever the genre and/or illocution

---

[6]As Richard Hays unfolds the intertextuality of the Gospel writers, who based their understanding of Jesus on a figural interpretation of the Old Testament, he offers a model that gives full value to what the Evangelists are doing and how we can read the Old Testament christologically without, at the same time, forfeiting the authority found in the contextual reading of the Old Testament. Hays, *Echoes of Scripture in the Gospels.*

used by the author, the text is being given another illocution by God—that of revelation. For example:

✦ We are not focused on the main purpose of the text when we try to reconstruct the history of the times. The theological point is more important than historical reconstruction and is valid even if we cannot reconstruct the events with confidence. In other words, the *interpretation* of the event by the Old Testament is more important than the *fact* of the event (though an event still serves as the referent).

✦ We are not focused on the main purpose of the text when we are doing apologetics for the historical accuracy of the events discussed. Often, since the text is indicating the role of God in events, the main point of God's involvement cannot be demonstrated. Even when we are able to prove that an event happened (tests for this are likewise questionable), the involvement of God is beyond demonstration—it calls for belief.

✦ We are not focused on the main purpose of the text when we try to build a legal system for today out of the laws of Israel or the legal sections of the Pentateuch. These legal sayings must be understood theologically, not just sociologically.

✦ We are not focused on the main purpose of the text when we try to construct what the end times will look like. Prophecies are more interested in revealing God than in revealing the future.

We could go on, but hopefully the statements above are sufficient. The theological nature of the text must have our primary attention.

Divine presence and relationship with God is foundational. I do not believe there is a center of Old Testament theology that every book addresses, but I do believe that there is a theme that spans the entire scope of Scripture (rather than pervading every book of Scripture) and provides the glue that holds it all together. In this book I will propose that from the very beginning it was God's intention to dwell among his people and to be in relationship with them: "I will be their God, and they will be my people" (e.g., Lev 26:12; Jer 31:33; Ezek 37:27; 2 Cor 6:16; Rev 21:3). The Bible traces this theme from the first chapter of Genesis to the last chapters of Revelation as it moves from Eden, through the tabernacle and temple, to the incarnation, the indwelling at Pentecost, and finally to new creation. Scripture is interested in conveying to God's people enough of what he is like (revelation) that they will know how to relate to him as they live in his presence and participate in the kingdom of God.

This point is as important for what it says as for what it does not say. For most of the Old Testament, this theme is building toward redemption in Christ without specifically referring to it. It is commonplace for the Bible in general and the Old Testament in particular to be referred to as "redemption history" or "salvation history." If in using that terminology it is implied that all of what God is doing throughout history and Scripture is focused on our personal salvation from our sins, then the terminology is too reductionistic. We can be (and will be) eternally grateful to God for providing deliverance from sin and justification before the Father through Christ. We dare not neglect this important point. But what God is doing is bigger than our personal salvation, so we also dare not make Scripture all about us.

More recently, some have been attempting to clarify "redemption history" by adding into its definition God's plan to redeem and restore the cosmos.[7] This broader description is more workable because it takes the focus off personal salvation; it includes the concept that God has been working to restore the entire cosmos (us included) to the condition that he always desired for it. This undertaking indicates what God's intentions have always been. We can focus on the steps he has taken (what he has done to restore all creation to himself) or on the intended product (God dwelling among his people in relationship with them). But even with the larger focus in mind, we also need to keep an eye on that which is God's ultimate desire for his creation.

Properly understood, then, salvation includes the restoration of all creation to God through Christ. The result is new creation. In this book we will be investigating what God has already undertaken as well as trying to understand the product as seen in the Old Testament.

Critically aware but evangelically founded. The interest of critical scholarship is that the biblical text be understood in all of its sophistication and depth. Such scholarship includes issues of literary analysis (including genre, rhetorical strategy, and discourse analysis), historical analysis, history

---

[7]J. Richard Middleton, *A New Heaven and a New Earth* (Grand Rapids: Baker, 2014).

of religions, composition of texts, attention to context (both literary and cultural), study of manuscripts, and the transmission of texts, just to mention a few. I am committed to all of these levels of study and will attempt to reflect the results of those disciplines in the synthesis that I am providing.

Contrary to the beliefs of some, critical analysis does not require an attitude of skepticism about the nature of the biblical text. Critical analysis should prevent us from being naive, but it does not intrinsically undermine belief. I am skeptical of superficial interpretations of the text and of flat readings that pervade popular culture, but I am not skeptical about the nature or truth of the text. I realize that the truth of the text may be more difficult than first imagined and may even be obscure if read without the critical tools or knowledge required to penetrate it. And I am committed to the face value of the text, as long as "face value" is defined by what the author intended to communicate. But I am also suspicious of the text's "face value" if it is defined by a flat, uninformed reading.

My commitment to critical analysis, therefore, is not contradictory to my evangelical beliefs about Scripture. I do not treat the Old Testament as another piece of ancient literature that should be analyzed impersonally and kept at arm's length. I am committed to the uniqueness of the Old Testament as Scripture, even *as* I treat it as an ancient piece of literature. This is not an either-or proposition but a both/and model.

Willing to depart from traditional exegesis without questioning traditional theology. It is true that our theology is built, in large part, on the foundation of Scripture. This means, among other things, that theology does not dictate what Scripture must say. Since our current theology has been shaped by a synthesis of many passages of Scripture (indeed, "the whole counsel of Scripture"), together with the logic applied to theological questions, we may find reason to depart from the traditional theological exegesis of a passage with no intent or consequence of undermining the larger theological issue for which that passage has been employed.

For example, the church has historically endorsed the theology of creation ex nihilo ("out of nothing"). This doctrine originally pertained to discussions concerning the creation of the human soul (i.e., whether it preexisted or came into being when the body did) and was eventually used during the Arian controversy, the debate about whether or not Christ had been created. Only in more modern times has this doctrine been applied to the material cosmos. Christian theology does not accept the eternality of matter; it insists that when God created the material cosmos, he created it out of that which did not previously exist. This doctrine is supported by logic (divine noncontingency) and by various scriptures from both the Old and New Testaments. Among the passages often used to support creation out of nothing is Genesis 1:1. However, a strong case can be made (both from context and from language) that Genesis 1:1 does not, in fact, describe creation out of nothing.[8] In this sense, I would argue that our traditional *exegesis*, insofar as it uses Genesis 1:1 to support creation ex nihilo, is flawed. At the same time, I continue to give full support to the doctrine of creation based on *theological* logic and other biblical passages. Readers will find such examples scattered throughout this book. Rethinking interpretation of a particular passage need not be viewed as undermining larger theological issues.

Willing to see the Old Testament text as authoritative in its own right (not only when Christ comes or in light of the New Testament). When we read the Old Testament christologically, we are at great risk of implying (or confirming in practice and results) that the authority of the Old Testament derives solely from whatever christological interpretations can be identified. If taken to an extreme, this methodology affirms the idea that the Old Testament (the Bible of Jesus and the apostles) had no authority in its own right or in its own literary context. As early as Origen these ideas are propounded, and they reach their pinnacle in the writings of Marcion. In modern times the idea is reflected more in neglect than in articulated theory. But the idea that we cannot get to the true meaning of the Old Testament until we read it in light of Christ demonstrates the extent to which this philosophy has been accepted into modern theology. This ideology tends to make us apathetic in finding the meaning of the text that may have been intended by the inspired authors in their Old Testament context.

In contrast, my approach will be to explore the authoritative message of the Old Testament in its own time and context in order to find the foundation of its meaning. When the New Testament picks up an Old Testament

---

[8]See, for example, John H. Walton, *The Lost World of Adam and Eve* (Downers Grove, IL: InterVarsity Press, 2015), 33-34.

text, those later authors are generally not interested in revealing the intention of the Old Testament human author. They are more often developing new meanings for their times, generally in light of Christ and related to the role they see Jesus as playing (e.g., recapitulating Israel's history). They have every right to do so, and those new levels of figural meaning are very important for the development of theology. The New Testament has its own basis of authority (inspiration connected to the New Testament authors), and that authority is not derived from its accountability to the intentions of the human authors of the Old Testament. The Gospel writers, rather, transform the meaning of the Old Testament (without dismissing it) and show how it is used to understand Jesus.[9]

But those new levels should not replace the meaning that the Old Testament author would have intended. The two levels of meaning can be held side by side. Since this project pertains to Old Testament theology, we will not be giving near as much attention to what the New Testament authors did with Old Testament texts. Instead, the focus will be on the Old Testament authors' intentions.

Belief that the Old Testament offers a sound theology (from a Christian's point of view), complete in its own right, even though it is not a fully developed theology in terms of modern systematics.[10] Pursuant to the points made above, I will give recognition to Old Testament theology as sound, even if it is incomplete. In the past, and often in popular culture, a person's individual salvation is the focus of the Christian faith to such an extent that the Old Testament is considered less important than the New Testament. But I contend that the Old Testament is God's revelation of his plans and purposes, and through them, of himself. If this is indeed so, then the revelation in the Old Testament is sound and needs to be considered seriously. God has not changed, and the revelation of himself in the Old Testament is therefore not obsolete. It continues to be valid and to require our attention. God did not *just* reveal himself in Christ, but, as Hebrews 1:1 says, "In the past God spoke to our ancestors through the prophets at many times and in

---

[9]Hays, *Echoes of Scripture in the Gospels.*

[10]We should likewise say that the New Testament is complete in its own right but not fully developed in terms of modern systematics. Constructive theology often has to turn to logic and philosophy to fill in some gaps left by the New Testament.

various ways." We can learn important things about God from the Old Testament that we do not encounter in the New Testament. The theology of the Old Testament is ultimately concerned with God's revelation of his plans and purposes, and through them, of himself; all other issues move us toward that larger goal. This stands in contrast to those who understand the mission of God in terms of establishing a community of redeemed people.[11] God's plans and purposes feature redemption prominently in the New Testament, but his larger plans and purposes focus on dwelling in the midst of his people, not just redeeming them. The concept of his presence takes center stage in the Old Testament.

Theology is to be understood within the framework of the ancient world, yet as the result of revelation that draws the people out of those ways of thinking. The Israelites were thoroughly immersed in the world and cultural framework of the ancient Near East, just as all of us are immersed in our own native cultures. However, God's revelation of himself, though grounded in a specific culture, is capable of transcending culture. As a result, we can be transformed by that revelation, regardless of the time and space that separate us from the original revelation.

The situation with ancient Israel was no different—God's revelation called them away from the ways in which their culture inclined them to think and to be transformed in their minds. We have, then, a revolutionary revelation in a cultural package. But it is important to note that the Old Testament's theology is situated against the backdrop of the ancient world's customary ways of thinking. We will often find that its theology has a foundation in ancient practices and ideas. For example, both circumcision and sacrifice existed in the ancient world long before they were formalized for theological use in the Old Testament. Therefore, in this book, we will be addressing the theology of Israel in its ancient context and then trying to understand the enduring theological concepts.

Tone and rhetoric. This book is not intended to be a polemical treatment. It is my intention to maintain an even tone and a balanced perspective. I do not intend to spend a lot of time criticizing those who have different opinions from mine. I do not find cynicism or polemics to be useful or productive

---

[11]E.g., Christopher J. H. Wright, *The Mission of God* (Downers Grove, IL: InterVarsity Press, 2006). For more discussion of this see below.

rhetorical tools. I would prefer to use rhetoric to strengthen faith, rather than to undermine it. Throughout the book, then, I will be proposing correctives to our Christian thinking, particularly in the exegesis of Old Testament passages. But I desire to do so in gentle ways that convey a respect for those who may think differently. In this way, it is my purpose to build up the faith of those who read what I have written.

Approach to Old Testament Theology

Biblical theology is often more descriptive than systematic theology, an area of study that tends to be synthetic. Typically, biblical theology pertains to the past, especially historical development, while systematic theology pertains to what is believed today. More specifically, biblical theology describes the beliefs conveyed in particular contexts, whether those contexts pertain to time periods (biblical theology during the postexilic period), a corpus of literature (the biblical theology of the Prophets), or even to a particular author (the biblical theology of Isaiah). But biblical theology can also focus on particular topics, such as the Old Testament theology of covenant or the afterlife. In other words, biblical theology is somewhat like historical theology conducted within the framework of the biblical canon; historical theology as a discipline picks up its descriptive task outside the canon. Systematic theology, on the other hand, endeavors to gather all the biblical information about a belief and to combine it with the history of the discussion since the close of Scripture in order to summarize (or to lay out in comprehensive detail) what it is that we believe today. At its best, it starts with Scripture, then employs tradition, reason, and experience to address its own cultural context.

Old Testament theology, then, is a subdiscipline of biblical theology focused on a particular section of the canon. The methods that will be used here will therefore glean information synthetically from across the Old Testament. In this way, we could talk about the shape of the sum of Israel's theological thinking, though they would not have been as concerned with systematization as we are, nor would they have used the same sorts of categories.

Such an approach, however, presents some serious challenges. Since the Old Testament covers a couple of millennia, it would be ideal if we could trace the development of theological thinking (the progress of revelation) through the centuries. Unfortunately, the nature of the preservation of the texts does not allow us to reconstruct dates and sequences with confidence. Yet at the same time, we would be remiss to engage in a flat reading that considers all of the Old Testament as a reflection of Israelite thinking in the postexilic period. Clearly, there are layers, and theological development is obvious.

In the approach that I use here, I will assume that there is older material embedded in texts that have been edited over time or that have been pulled together in a later period. So, for example, I will assume that Exodus preserves a view of the tabernacle that goes back to the time at Sinai, even if there is evidence of editing from the monarchic or the postexilic time periods. In other words, I will not simply assume that the understanding of the tabernacle has been filtered through the postexilic lens to the extent that it only preserves a postexilic perspective. I believe that the ancient perspectives were preserved, even as they were passed down and subjected to editing.

My treatment will also be organized according to topics of theology, rather than by corpora or particular biblical authors.[12] Where possible, in treating each topic, I will try to identify any development that might have taken place during the Old Testament period. I will furthermore discuss the ways in which common ancient Near Eastern thought is or is not represented, the distinctiveness of Israelite theology and the resulting enduring theology, and the ways in which such theology leads to the New Testament.

Using ancient Near Eastern literature in Old Testament theology. When scholars compile an approach to Old Testament theology, they tend to work within the confines of the canon. Theology is often extracted from the books of the Old Testament as literary-theological works, and it is not unusual that this is done with an eye toward the New Testament. This approach, however, does not typically make use of the ancient Near Eastern context of the Old Testament. And when the cognitive environment of the ancient Near East *is* factored into the discussion, the result is typically a descriptive history of Israelite religion.

---

[12]This is the approach listed as number four in the ten methodologies laid out in G. Hasel, *Old Testament Theology* (Grand Rapids: Eerdmans, 1975), and summarized in Paul House, *Old Testament Theology* (Downers Grove, IL: InterVarsity Press, 1998), 54-55.

In this book I am going to attempt to weave these two approaches together. The main reason for this approach is that I believe the theology of the Old Testament cannot properly be understood without taking the ancient Near Eastern cognitive environment into account. The Israelites were embedded in the ancient world, and they thought like ancient people. God communicated to them in that ancient world and used that which was familiar to them to communicate. Therefore, the theology revealed to them, true as it is, was clothed in ancient garb.

The underlying assumptions of this approach understand communication as either "high context" or "low context." In high-context communication, the author and audience share much in common and can communicate with minimal explanations; the author can assume a high level of basic understanding in his audience. In contrast, low-context communication describes a situation in which very little can be assumed about the base knowledge of the audience. When I talk about theology to graduate students, I am functioning within a high-context system. When I discuss theology with sixth graders, I have to switch to low-context.

The authors of Scripture operate in a high-context setting. They share a worldview, a history, and a set of experiences with their audience and can assume a lot of common ground. But when we come to the Old Testament as readers, we enter as a low-context audience, even as we are trying to interpret a high-context communication. Thus the theological substance of the Old Testament is not just embedded in literature; it is embedded in culture.

All aspects of a society and culture combine to construct what we might generally call a cosmology—a story of the world and a metanarrative that provides the basis for belief and action.[13] We tend to think of our own "cosmology"—perhaps we can refer to it as a "worldview" (despite the controversy and ambiguity that surround that term)—as universal and normal, even though other cultures may have very different worldviews. It is this "worldview" or "cosmology" to which I refer with the description "cognitive environment."

---

[13] Anathea Portier-Young, "Symbolic Resistance in the Book of the Watchers," in *The Watchers in Jewish and Christian Traditions*, ed. Angela Kim Hawkins, Kelley Coblentz Bautch, and John C. Endres, SJ (Minneapolis: Fortress, 2014), 39-49.

A cognitive environment encompasses how people think about the world, including the place of the gods and the role of humanity. Anathea Portier-Young appropriately observes that "cosmology demarcates inside from outside, center from periphery, normal from aberrant. Its logic legitimates claims about truth and morality."[14] Theology assumes such a cognitive environment. Consequently, if we are to understand the theology of the Old Testament, we must not neglect its cognitive environment. The only alternative is to impose our own Western or Christian cognitive environment on the Old Testament. If we do this, we are no longer describing Old Testament theology; we are describing our own theology. As a result, we will likely miss the intention of the Old Testament author entirely. And if we misunderstand the Old Testament author, we lose touch with the authority of the text.

Given the importance of what we might then call "cognitive environment criticism," we need to comment briefly on why such studies are hermeneutically and theologically sound. Some worry that if we read the Old Testament as an ancient text, we are admitting the existence of a pagan or mythological influence that has corrupted the Old Testament. Or some think that we are implying the Old Testament is just another piece of ancient Near Eastern literature. But such extremes are not the case. Ancient Near Eastern literature is valuable because it gives us essential insight into the cognitive environment of the ancient world (of which Israel was a part). Without the benefit of such a window, we would be blind, and our interpretation would be hampered. By using the literature from the ancient Near East, we are not marginalizing the uniqueness of the Old Testament. Rather, we are pursuing its trustworthy revelation from God.

Some might object that all throughout church history Christian writers did not have access to the literature from the ancient Near East. By engaging in cognitive environment criticism, are we therefore suggesting that their interpretations and resulting theology were flawed? To state the question in such a manner is misleading. The early Christian writers, for the most part, were addressing the theological concerns of their day as they interpreted and applied Scripture, defending its claims and answering heretics. They were not trying to recover the authorial intention, and they were certainly not

---

[14]Ibid., 40.

trying to compile an Old Testament theology. In that sense, our task is different from theirs, but it is nevertheless important.

For example, it is difficult for us to understand the problem of the golden calf or Isaiah's ridicule of those who make idols if we do not understand how idols functioned in the ancient world. We are also likely to miss the significance of Elijah's contest with the prophets of Baal on Mount Carmel if we do not understand how people thought about Baal in the ancient world. The hardening of Pharaoh's heart can be confusing, and even troubling, if we are thinking about our own issues with free will and salvation rather than reading the text against its Egyptian background. And we will inevitably misunderstand the tower of Babel if we have no knowledge of the great ziggurat towers of ancient Mesopotamia. All of these situations, and many more, testify to the need for modern interpreters to read the Old Testament against the cognitive environment of the ancient Near East. We must therefore also factor in this information as we construct an Old Testament theology.

We can identify three important kinds of questions to which comparative studies between the Bible and the ancient Near East can potentially contribute answers for Old Testament theology:

+ questions about whether cultural accommodation is providing a framework for packaging Scripture's teaching (Adam made from dust; solid sky; Garden of Eden; serpent symbolism; etc.)

+ questions about the Old Testament's dependence on ancient Near Eastern literature (Gilgamesh flood story; Ps 29; 104; Prov 23; etc.)

+ questions about the nature of objects, aspects, and ideas of the ancient world (temples, priests, rituals, images, divine council, etc.)

Regarding the first category, it would be desirable to have methodological guidelines in place to govern our interpretations. How should we navigate the complicated questions concerning which aspects of the text are culturally relative and which provide the normative theology of Scripture? We often approach the question backwards because we have traditionally assumed that universalization is the default understanding of Scripture. Everyone realizes, however, that some information is particularized and that we are inclined to label that information as accommodated and safe to set aside. Unfortunately, we then hold heated and often unresolvable discussions about which portions of Scripture are culturally relative (particularized or accommodated) and which are normative (universally applicable to all people everywhere).

In this approach we have failed to understand a very basic fact about communication: "accommodation" is essential to any successful act of communication. And since we consider Scripture to be successful communication from God through human intermediaries, the message is subject to accommodation at every level. It is not only the ideas we do not accept today that are accommodated and culturally relative; any communicative act is culturally relative. Communication can only address things for which there are words and ideas in the minds of the audience. The question, then, is not whether God or the authors accommodated the ancient audience; no other possibility exists.

The inherent truth, therefore, is that neither God nor the biblical authors accommodated us (or the New Testament, or the early Christian writers, etc.). All communication in Scripture occurs within the cognitive environment of the ancient target audience. This fact of accommodation does not mean that it has no significance for us, but finding significance is a separate endeavor from determining what is or is not accommodated. Many people assume that the Bible is intrinsically universalized, and they try to separate out anything that might be particularized as a result. They approach the text this way because they believe this is how the Bible speaks to them and how it can be considered authoritative. They desire Scripture to be relevant and to give them guidance in many aspects of life.

In contrast, I would propose that, since the Scriptures were communicated into a cognitive environment, we should consider everything in the Bible particularized and only then try to draw out specific elements that could carry a universal application. But our decisions about what should be considered universalized ought to be dependent on our understanding of the genre and speech-act associated with each text. In Scripture, whatever the particular speech-acts might be, the overriding and significant speech-act is the illocution of self-revelation. We believe that God has used the illocution of the human author and given it (all of it) the illocution of revelation.[15]

---

[15]This is not Nicholas Wolterstorff's theory of divine appropriation, because that is selective, suggesting God only appropriates some of what is in Scripture as his Word. Nicholas Wolterstorff, *Divine Discourse* (New York: Cambridge University Press, 1995).

Nevertheless, God's particularized speech-act to the original audience through the human author is culture locked. The universalized aspect of that contextualized speech-act stands as an invitation (illocution) to all to participate in (perlocution) God's Great Enterprise (more on this below). But we cannot participate until we understand, and this understanding (perlocution) comes as God reveals himself and his purposes (illocution). We know God's purposes only through his revelation in Scripture, and we can know him and truly participate in his purposes only to the extent that we understand those purposes. It would be a mistake to think that we can *infer* his purposes from a false confidence in our own knowledge of what he is or is not like. In fact, the more our conception of God is reduced to what we can know of him, the more our concept of God becomes a mirror of ourselves, rather than like his true image. In other words, potentially, the more we think we know God, the less what we know is actually like God.

Given this understanding of God's speech-acts, I would propose that the only aspect of Scripture that is universalized, despite its grounding in the ancient cognitive environment, is the illocution of God, the revelation of his purposes. The Bible is not a biography; it is a vision statement. We are given knowledge (of purpose) in order to participate (in purpose), and this knowledge and participation are what should be considered normative. The vision statement tells us what to believe rather than giving us rules to follow.[16] Yet we dare not neglect the responsibilities that rest on those who are identified with God and his purposes. Revelation brings accountability, and it calls us to be the kind of people God can use to great effect. So when we talk about the Bible's inerrancy in all that it affirms, the affirmations that are entailed in its divine illocution are much broader than is often thought.

It is typical to think that the Bible is by nature universalized and that we should look for things that for some reason or another might be particularized. But everything in the Bible is particularized; only the purposes of God and person of God are universalized. As unnatural as this approach feels, it brings resolution to the long-standing debates about accommodation and cultural relativity. It is not a "faith and practice only" reductionism and does not neglect the particulars; instead, the particulars find their significance in the big picture.

---

[16]Thanks to J. Harvey Walton for his formative thoughts in shaping this material.

We will have very few occasions in which we deal with literary dependence (category number two) because it is very difficult to demonstrate that literary borrowing has taken place. But, even if literary dependence were occasionally determinable, the Old Testament would recontextualize the ancient literature with which it was interacting.

The third category (the nature of objects, etc.) is the one of which we will make the most use. It goes without saying, for example, that we must understand the role of priests in the ancient world rather than assuming that the Israelite priests functioned as Roman Catholic priests do today. Likewise, we would be remiss if we somehow imagined that temples in the ancient world were like modern-day churches. In this regard, the literature from the ancient Near East not only will help us recover the way that the Israelites thought, but it will also alert us to the issues in which we subconsciously let our modern ideas affect our interpretations.

Old Testament theology and New Testament theology. Biblical theology is composed of Old Testament theology and New Testament theology. Together they exist on an external continuum. As such, they can be treated together, but there is also value in treating them separately. After all, a number of significant historical developments that left a deep imprint on the theology of the New Testament came after the Old Testament period (beginning with the influence of Persian thinking, but even that was extensively overshadowed by the influx of Hellenism). In recognition of the historical facts, we should be willing to look at Old Testament theology independent of New Testament theology. Much would be missed in the Old Testament text if we were to read it only through the lenses of Hellenism, the Greco-Roman world, and the concerns of Christianity. God's revelation came to the Israelites in ancient garb and came to the Jews of the first century in Hellenistic garb. We would be remiss to try to understand the ancient Israelite view of the afterlife through the viewpoints of the Pharisees and Sadducees, or even through the lens of Jesus' parable about the rich man and Lazarus. Likewise, we would not want to constrain the ancient Israelite views of cosmology by the hands of Aristotle's categories or perspectives. Just because people thought in particular ways during the first century CE does not mean that Israelites thought the same way. Consequently, Old Testament theology must be approached independently from New Testament theology, though New Testament theology cannot properly be done in isolation from Old Testament theology.

Driving Old Testament Theology

Above, we briefly addressed the questions surrounding the foundation of Old Testament theology. Here I want to press that discussion a bit further, particularly with regard to the label "redemptive history."[17] We should recognize that such a label is somewhat elastic and has been understood by different people in different ways. Does it pertain to the idea that God is a delivering God (whether from slavery in Egypt or from sins)? Does it reflect the idea that God is primarily concerned with redeeming the cosmos and everything in it from the devastating effects of sin? Salvation and redemption are commonly defined narrowly, as referring to the fact that Jesus has redeemed each one of us individually—paying our penalty, making us righteous in God's eyes, and forgiving our sins.

But when we consider Old Testament theology, it would be difficult to consider "redemption history" in the narrowly defined context described above. The Old Testament has little to say about God's eventual plan to save us from our sins through Christ (or even through the Messiah). Such a reading of the Old Testament can only be found if it is read through the lens of the New Testament. The contribution that the Old Testament makes to the trajectory of such theological developments can be adequately explored in the context of New Testament theology, but the Old Testament's own contributions are often overshadowed by this approach.

With regard to the first option—that Yahweh is a God who delivers—it is certainly appropriate to apply such a descriptor to God. Nevertheless, we have to ask whether this description captures the focus of the Old Testament. It would be difficult to see "deliverer" as the foundational attribute of God in the Old Testament story, though many significant examples of his deliverance are present. In fact, two major events that punctuate Israel's history (deliverance from slavery in Egypt and restoration from the exile) function as powerful testimonies of God's power to deliver his people. Furthermore, we find examples of God's deliverance on an individual level, such as in

---

[17]Also called "salvation history," or in more academic circles, *Heilsgeschichte*.

David's deliverance from Saul or Absalom. But none of these situations are remotely similar to Jesus' saving us from our sins. Those who prefer the "redemption history" model often want to use that model to draw together the Old and New Testaments, and the desire for such unity and continuity is indeed admirable. Yet if the metanarrative thread fails to do justice to the Old Testament, such efforts are counterproductive to the text's authority. We must be careful that our attempts to understand unity do not ultimately undermine authority.

The idea that God is concerned with the redemption of creation is preferable if "redemption history" is to be used to describe the Bible in general or the Old Testament in particular. It is true that God's plan is to restore all of creation and that he does so by redeeming it; redemption is his overall purpose. I continue to be reluctant to adopt this model, however, because I see little progress being made on this front in the study of the Old Testament. I am therefore not inclined to think of the Old Testament generally, or primarily, as "redemption history."

All of the efforts just described seem to be driven by a desire to see Christ as the center of the Bible, which is an understandable impulse. Christ is often viewed as the climax of God's plan and the instrument by which God redeems all creation, including humanity, to himself. Again, however, I would return to the distinction between "center" and "climax." Christ is the climax (though even that statement must be qualified by the recognition that new creation is still to come), but that does not justify centering the Old Testament on him. Again, we return to the idea that our interpretation should be christotelic rather than christocentric.

But what motivates so many to see Christ as the center of the Bible? Undoubtedly, there are good theological reasons for doing so, and we find many theologians throughout church history who have had such motivations. Each theologian likely had particular reasons for taking a christological approach, which sprang from, in many cases, the theological challenges of his or her specific time and situation. None of that important history need be lost for us also to insist that we must see the larger revelation of God's plan and purposes in the Old Testament in his covenant with Israel. We are trinitarian and therefore value the revelation of any of the persons of the Trinity.

Today, however, especially at the popular level, it is easy to be driven by a focus on one's own salvation. Salvation *is* important, but for some, it stands as a benefit that obliterates all other aspects of faith and relationship with God through Christ. As wonderful as the benefit of salvation is, we cannot allow it to be the center of our faith. People who are inclined to this perspective need to ask themselves, "If there were no promise of heaven, would I serve God anyway, just because he is worthy?" This challenge was the very one that God set before Abraham in Genesis 22, and it is this challenge that the Adversary introduces in the book of Job. We know, then, that unconditional service is not a modern or fabricated issue; it is a real and important aspect of our theology.

Perhaps the inherent necessity of a christological hermeneutic can be investigated by pondering whether a Jewish person today could do Old Testament theology without conceding that it points to Christ. Would a Jewish approach be any different from what I am suggesting? I would contend that such approaches could perceive quite a lot about God's plan and purposes as they are expressed in the Old Testament and that they would also be able to understand the idea of participating in God's plan. This point is significant; these concepts are the same ideas that we need to grasp from our own study of the Old Testament. The differences, however, are also significant. As Christian interpreters, we see God's plan and purposes as expanded in Christ. And when we participate in this New Testament expansion, the scope of the divine enterprise is not just extended, but it has taken a new form by virtue of the fact that the presence of God has been so radically transformed. God's purposes are clearer and more elaborate in the New Testament, and if we did not adjust our understanding to reflect this knowledge, we would be remiss. Nevertheless, if a Christian just looked at the Old Testament, he or she would not find anything there that a Jewish interpreter could not also find.

The history of Old Testament theology and where this book fits. The discipline of Old Testament theology is relatively young, having mostly begun early in the twentieth century, with a few scattered precursors as early as the late eighteenth century.[18] Here I will address only some of the

---

[18]The first published Old Testament theology was by Georg Lorenz Bauer in 1796.

trends and issues.[19] But from the beginning, Old Testament theology has been understood as a historical discipline in contrast to dogmatic theology. Early methodological controversies arose over how important the relationship between the Testaments ought to be and whether the study should operate within the realm of belief or be conducted objectively. And these are the issues that fostered debate between Otto Eissfeldt and Walther Eichrodt in the early twentieth century: Should the study be inherently historical or theological? And many now contend that Old Testament theology should be a strictly historical exercise, one that is absent of confessional ties or interference.

Another major debate, one that has perhaps been most commonly associated with Walter Brueggemann, concerns whether we should talk about a single theology or multiple theologies of the Old Testament. Rather than assuming that the books of the Old Testament are univocal, this approach contends that the Old Testament does not just represent development along a single theological vector but that there are contrasting and even conflicting voices. For example, proponents of this view may hold that Job and Ecclesiastes are in opposition to the retribution principle equations found in Proverbs, or that the putative P source of the Pentateuch is in conflict with the D source. Consequently, some are disposed not only to ask whether the discipline is historical or theological but whether even the texts themselves are characterized by unity or diversity.

Some even question whether or not a coherent Old Testament theology is possible or viable (J. Barr). But by the continuing activity in the discipline, it would appear that most have concluded that coherence is possible, even though there is a broad spectrum of opinions. From the discussions about method and presuppositions, we can move to the differences of opinions that have arisen concerning the subjects or themes of Old Testament theology. A sampling of supposed principal topics include: covenant (W. Eichrodt), communion (Th. C. Vriezen), God who acts (G. E. Wright), promise (W. C. Kaiser), credo (G. von Rad), kingdom (G. Fohrer, B. Waltke, E. Merrill, P. Gentry, and S. Wellum), (elusive) presence (S. Terrien), community (B. Childs, P. Hanson),

---

[19]More detailed treatment can be found in Ben C. Ollenburger, ed., *Old Testament Theology: Flowering and Future*, 2nd ed. (Winona Lake, IN: Eisenbrauns, 2004). See also the thorough treatment by House, *Old Testament Theology*, 11-52.

theodrama (K. Vanhoozer), salvation (G. Vos), image (R. Hubbard, R. Johnston, and R. Meye), name (M. Noth), *kabod* (T. Mettinger), knowledge of God (W. Zimmerli), sovereignty and holiness (B. Jacob), law/promise dialectic (R. Clements), blessing/deliverance dialectic (C. Westermann)—the list could go on. Other prominent themes include the land, sin, and wisdom. For some of these, the named topic is considered the "center" of Old Testament theology; for others, it is simply the most dominant theme or dialectic—perhaps even an organizing principle or metaphor. Opinions may vary, but most would admit that all of these topics at least have significance within the theology of Israel.

In this work, I will be attending to the historical place and setting of the Old Testament literature, but I will not be stopping at historical inquiry. I will instead seek to use historical inquiry to uncover the enduring theological revelation that remains God's Word to the church today.[20] That is, I will attempt to integrate the historical and the theological in a purposefully confessional context. This work will therefore be intentionally Christian and, more specifically, broadly evangelical. These statements define my confessional commitments, even though I will be attempting to read the Old Testament from an Israelite perspective. In other words, it is my intention for these commitments to define my target though not serving as a lens. I would like to set forth Israelite religion, insofar as it is based on God's revelation of himself to the Israelites, as a source for enduring theology, and so my interests are more than antiquarian or historical. I will also insist, however, that the elements must be understood in their Israelite context rather than through the eyes of the New Testament, the early Christian writers, or modern theology. As such, I am interested in addressing what Israelites believed as well as the theology that emerges from the pages of the Old Testament—preserving the theological voice of the Old Testament. I hope

---

[20]I will not be interacting much with the treatments of Old Testament theology mentioned in the previous paragraph—I am offering a different approach to the material from what I find in those approaches (worthwhile though they are). Perhaps the treatment of Old Testament theology that I resonate most with is Iain Provan, *Seriously Dangerous Religion: What the Old Testament Really Says and Why It Matters* (Waco, TX: Baylor University Press, 2014). I have learned much from Provan's work and recommend it highly to readers, especially those who want to begin to use the Old Testament in conversation with other religions and with the skeptics of our day. Nevertheless, I will not be interacting with his work because the two of us are treating the Old Testament with different objectives in mind.

in this way to be able to build a bridge between the academy and the church. I want to unlock the theology revealed in the Old Testament for Christians, reading it through an Israelite, rather than a Christian, lens.

PRESENCE OF GOD

When we turn our attention to the search for an idea whose progression spans the entirety of the Old Testament, a couple of possibilities come to mind, as evidenced by the historical survey above. "Covenant," of course, would be a prime candidate, and it would encompass a couple of others that have been suggested as possibilities such as "Torah" or "promise." But I am inclined to see even covenant as a part of something bigger.

Another suggestion is to focus on the "kingdom" theme in Scripture. Certainly divine kingship and the sponsored Davidic monarchy are central themes of the Old Testament. The reign of God is the theme of the Psalms, and his sovereign rule is developed in both the narratives of Scripture and in the Prophets. Furthermore, it is a theme that finds a home in messianic theology and plays a major role in the transition to the New Testament, particularly in the Gospels, with their emphasis on the kingdom of God. And notably, the book of Revelation focuses on the rule of Christ. Nevertheless, with no intention of minimizing the significance of the kingdom theme, I would again suggest that we should consider something even bigger.

I propose that the primary theme that progresses throughout the Old Testament, and indeed throughout the entire Bible, is the establishment of God's presence among his people ("I will put my dwelling place among you," e.g., Lev 26:11) with the explicit intention of being in relationship with them/ us ("I will . . . be your God, and you will be my people," e.g., Ex 6:7; Lev 26:12; Jer 11:4; Ezek 36:28). I do not consider this to be the "center" of Old Testament theology, but it is an overarching theme, arguably the most dominant and pervasive of themes, the trajectory along which the program of God moves. It is the *covenant* that gives formal articulation to the stages of the relationship between God and his people; it is the *promise* of God that he will make such a relationship possible; it is the *Torah* that governs how people may live in the presence of God and sustain relationship with him; and it is the *kingdom* of God that expresses his role in the cosmos and in which we participate as we live out our relationship with him.

A brief survey of the theme of God's presence and relationship with him as it progresses through Scripture. This theme is inaugurated in the opening chapter of Genesis, though we often are impeded in recognizing it because we are no longer aware of what is involved in divine rest, or we are distracted by science questions. In my interpretation (for details see chapter three as well as my prior publications), the seven days of creation are primarily concerned with God ordering the cosmos to serve as sacred space where he can be in relationship with his creatures. He rests when he takes up his rule in this sacred space, with its center in Eden. People forfeit access to God's presence and rupture relationship with him when they seek (through their disobedience) to supplant him and make themselves the center and source of order and wisdom.

After Genesis 1, Scripture tells the story of God's gradual restoration of his presence among his people and of his relationship with them, both of which culminate in new creation. We can see, then, that this theme permeates the entirety of the biblical text. People begin to call on the name of the Lord around the time of Seth (Gen 4:26), thereby invoking God's presence. The covenant is God's mechanism for establishing relationship, and it eventually (by the end of Exodus) leads to the reestablishment of his presence. The Torah is given so that God's people might learn how to live in the presence of God so as not to lose it again. The tabernacle provides a place for God's presence to dwell and is eventually replaced by the temple. And these sanctuaries serve as the palace of the Great King, from which God rules, but also as the place where his presence dwells among his people. Just in these few major stages, we can see that the Old Testament is tracking the themes of presence and relationship.

The Prophets speak of the future dwelling of God among the Israelites (Is 2; Mic 4) as well as of pending abandonment and punishment at the hands of the Babylonians (Ezek 10). The hope oracles of the Prophets, on the other hand, look forward to a time when God will restore his people and dwell among them again (Ezek 40–48). Just from these few examples, we can see that the Old Testament is tracking the themes of presence and relationship.

It is of some significance to note that this theme can be established as intrinsic to and dominant in the Old Testament on its own. But the theme of presence and relationship is also continued in the New Testament. In this way, this overarching theme is not dependent on the New Testament for its identification, but it is, at the same time, in continuity with the major trajectories in the Old Testament.

The New Testament picks up the theme with the incarnation: "the Word became flesh and made his dwelling among us" (John 1:14). The incarnation would have happened, even if there had been no sin for which to die, because the incarnation was an important step in the advancement of God's presence. Jesus would have ascended, and the Holy Spirit would have been sent (Acts 2) regardless of the state of humanity, because the indwelling Spirit is also an important step in the advancement of God's presence. Thereby the church becomes the temple of God (2 Cor 6:16) as God lives among (indwells) his people. The statement "And he will be their God, and they will be his people" is indicative of relationship.

The theme draws to a conclusion in the new creation detailed in Revelation 21 as God is dwelling in the midst of his people on the new earth. Relationship has been made possible through the work of Christ, and all of creation is restored to the state of God's original intention. The biblical story does not begin with kingship, covenant, promise, or law, and it does not end with them. It begins and ends with presence and relationship, which are at the heart of God's plan and which are the focus of Scripture, start to finish.

The plot line of presence is more important than the plot line of salvation (salvation history). Jesus did not just become human so that he could die for us; he became human to establish God's presence among us as one of us—so we would learn more about how we should live in God's presence. This perspective draws together the Old and New Testament themes of covenant, temple, and new creation. The Old Testament is about living in the presence of God so that it will not be lost again, as in the Garden of Eden. The New Testament is about participating in the kingdom of God, which is characterized by God's presence. From the opening chapters of Genesis to the closing chapters of Revelation, God's presence and relationship are the Bible's plot line and theological focus. This theme demonstrates what God has always wanted.

2

YAHWEH
and the
GODS

To begin, we need to reiterate a few ideas that were addressed in the introduction. If we are correct in thinking that the Old Testament is God's revelation of his plans and purposes, and that through that revelation we should be able to come to some basic understanding about God, it is then logical to conclude that the most important message of the Old Testament is found in what it teaches us about God. That teaching does not expire, grow obsolete, or change. It is not the sort of teaching from which we can pick and choose what parts we want to believe and what parts we want to set aside. Its truth about God should comprise our beliefs about God. Furthermore, there is much information about God revealed in the Old Testament that is never addressed in the New Testament. If we only read the Old Testament christologically or from the vantage point of the New Testament, we will miss some of what God has revealed about himself.

In important ways, then, this chapter has to be considered the most important of this book. What does the Old Testament teach us about God? What did it reveal, first to the Israelite audience of the ancient world and then to us through them? We will not find the complete revelation of God in the Old Testament, but we will find robust revelation that remains as vital today as it was when it was first revealed. It is revelation that calls the reader to respond by embracing this view of God, trusting its truth, and allowing it to transform our lives. As Richard Hays notes, God is not "a *concept* subject to general philosophical elucidation but a '*person*,' an agent known through the complex unfolding of his narrative identity—and only so."[1]

THE UNIQUENESS OF YAHWEH

How many gods are there? It is commonplace for modern readers to believe that the main difference between Israel and its neighbors was that Israel worshiped only one God, while the rest of the ancient world worshiped many gods. But this perception can be contested on several fronts. First and foremost, I contend that if we adopt such an unnuanced dichotomy, we will not recognize the most important difference of deity between Israel and its neighbors. The main issue was not the number(s) of god(s) but how God was understood. Nevertheless, before we address this issue, we have to explore the question of monotheism.

In order to discuss Israel's views about the existence of multiple gods, we should inquire what it means to say that a god exists (divine ontology). Obviously, the existence of a god is not defined by a physical or material presence, because gods are inherently spirit beings (i.e., nonmaterial). In modern philosophical terms, we might imagine that whether a god exists concerns whether or not a spirit being is present in the real world or is a real presence, person, or force. This approach would be less likely, however, in the ancient world. Ancient people recognized that humans were very limited in their ability to determine whether or not a spirit being existed in the real world unless the spirit being manifested its presence in some way. In other words, they would conclude that a spirit being existed when it manifested its reality in ways considered credible by their culture. In fact, they would consider manifestation the evidence necessary to affirm a spirit being's existence. Said another way, a god existed when it was perceived to function as a manifested god.

In the ancient Near East people believed that the gods were manifested in the forces of what we call the natural world, as well as in the celestial

---

[1]Richard B. Hays, *Echoes of Scripture in the Gospels* (Waco, TX: Baylor University Press, 2016), 280 (italics original). Of course, Hays is referring most particularly to Jesus as God incarnate, but we also engage God in the Old Testament as a character with a narrative identity.

phenomena. Abram came out of that cognitive environment, and Israel lived in that cognitive environment all throughout its history. Ancient people likely found it difficult to set aside those ways of thinking. Such was the experience of Israel, and it is well documented throughout the pages of the Old Testament.

The revelation of God was leading them to something different, but it is important for us to evaluate carefully what that process looked like. When Yahweh first approached Abram, he did not discuss how many gods there were or whether Abram needed to consider him the only God. But when we turn our attention to the Decalogue, the first saying indicates that no other gods should be worshiped before Yahweh. Yet it has long been noted that this phrase stops short of saying how many gods there are. As a result, the Decalogue easily functions as an entry point into a discussion of the differences between monotheism, henotheism, and monolatry.

As a starting point, *polytheism* reflects a way of thinking in which multiple gods function as a community and have multiple spheres of jurisdiction and authority. In such a belief system, worshipers interact with the god who is appropriate for a particular realm or territory and suitable to the occasion. In *monolatry*, people decide to focus all their attention on one particular deity whom they believe is able to function in whatever circumstance they might be facing. However, they also acknowledge that other deities function for other people and that those people can make whatever choices they want. *Henotheism* represents another type of theistic belief. This way of thinking still does not claim that only one god exists, but it insists that only one god is truly worthy of worship. Other gods are considered pretenders to deity, imposters, charlatans, incompetents, or simply inferior beings incapable of exercising divine authority. And henotheism is the view that permeates most of the Old Testament as it talks about the powerlessness of the other gods, prohibits their worship, and pronounces them frauds.

We might imagine that pure *philosophical monotheism* would countenance none of the concessions that such comparisons admit, but perhaps in the end, the distinction is only in semantics. Throughout the Old Testament, Yahweh consistently reveals that he is in a class by himself and brooks no competition. No other being is worthy of the designation "God," has the authority associated with the category, or is deserving of the worship that is

Functional Ontology

Functional ontology means that when the Israelites thought about what it meant for a thing to be, they thought in terms of what that thing did.[a] Similarly, if a thing were to be different from another thing, it would do different things (or different kinds of things, or the same things differently) from the other thing. If a thing were to be unique, it would do unique things, and so on.

This way of thinking is different from how we define *being* today. The Christian tradition followed the Greek philosophers in thinking of being in terms of irreducible definitional elements, called *substances*. A thing is different from another thing because it has a different substance. (Modern scientific material ontology takes this idea a step further and only acknowledges substances that it can link to matter and motion as described by physicists, but modern models of being are diverse and complex and beyond the scope of this work.) When the Council of Nicaea had to figure out how to say that Jesus was not a different thing from God, it did so using the language of substances (*homoousion*). It is worth noting in passing that function (i.e., what they do) is the primary differentiator of the persons of the Trinity (the Father does not suffer and die [patripassionism], the Son does not speak through the prophets, all things were not made through the Spirit, etc.), yet they are emphasized as the same in substance (*homoousion*), and this sameness makes them the same *being*.

This method of thinking also informs the definition we assign to the word *god*. For Israel, a god was defined in terms of what it did, such as establish and preserve cosmic order. For us, however, a god is an entity with a specific (and, in monotheism, a unique) ontology.

When we consider the biblical teaching about the being of God, then, we have a couple of decisions to make. We cannot simply avoid doing metaphysics, because anyone with a concept of being is automatically doing metaphysics, whether deliberately and systematically or not. On the one hand, we can decide that the Bible says nothing specific about the being of God. In such a case, it does demonstrably teach that God is unique (there is no one like our God, etc.), in the sense of being demonstrably different from anything else that is, but the actual concepts of being and god are undefined by the text. In this sense the Bible is teaching, "whatever you think a god is, Yahweh is one, and there is only one of them, however you define *is*." Such an approach would mean that our actual knowledge of God is reduced nearly to zero, since all of the key components used to describe what we think a god is are developed by us. At its extreme this approach is prone to syncretism and makes one wonder why we should bother at all—it is just how ancient people tended to think.

On the other hand, we can read the Bible's metaphysical method as a prescription for how to do it ourselves (it is not uncommon for a similar approach to be taken to hermeneutics in the New Testament approach to Old Testament prophecy, for example). This means that we would adopt Israel's definitions of *being* and *god* as our own. The biggest problem with this approach is, of course, that the text does not actually describe this method; we have to deduce it ourselves. And this ultimately means, again, that we are relying on something we are formulating, with the added difficulty that we then try to pass our constructs off as authoritative biblical teaching.

Further, it would be expected (and can be convincingly argued) that the Old Testament and New Testament use different models drawn from their respective cognitive environments and cultural influences. This difference, in turn, makes any concrete systemization of the method difficult or impossible. At its extreme, however, this approach makes the Bible completely time-bound and therefore irrelevant. For better or worse, our culture has its own way of doing metaphysics, which happens to be incompatible with the way ancient Israel (or even Hellenized Israel) happened to do it. But it is very difficult to fault us for developing our own method, since the text itself contains nothing explicit about how metaphysics ought to be done. Nevertheless, these two options can both lead to passable approaches as long as they are not taken to the extreme. Another possibility to consider is that ideas about God develop in cultural contexts, some of which God eventually affirms in revelation. In this way, concepts develop in time and culture but are not inherently culture-bound.

---

[a]Sidebar provided by J. Harvey Walton.

the natural response to such a being. If we resist modern philosophical classification (inevitably anachronistic), we can still see the message clearly. And
a proper understanding of Yahweh's revelation of himself will clear up any
confusion about numbers.

The next issue to consider is whether or not the perspectives about Yahweh's uniqueness developed increasing nuances and subtlety during the
period of the Old Testament. Interpreters are commonly inclined to
identify statements in a section of Isaiah heuristically referred to as
"Second Isaiah" as reaching new heights of theological expression.[2] These
verses contend that

✦ No god was formed before Yahweh (and none after).

✦ No other god saves or reveals.

✦ No other god can countermand what Yahweh has decreed or counteract
   what he has done.

✦ Apart from Yahweh there is no god like him, particularly in the ability to
   foretell what is to come.

The refrain of this particular section is "I am Yahweh, there is no other," and
the clarity of that message here can hardly be contested. However, the
question is whether this thinking is new to Isaiah in the Old Testament, or
whether it is simply a theme that has developed in an increasingly international context to which the prophet brings emphasis.

Statements that pursue the same line of thought are found in Deuteronomy 4:35-39 and in 1 Kings 8:60. This observation leads us into the murky
territory of determining the dates of the books or traditions of the Old Testament. Those who see new levels of theology in Second Isaiah are generally
inclined to see the passages in Deuteronomy and Kings as later additions,
which demonstrates a potential case of circular reasoning or begging the
question. Prior to considering the potential literary history, it would be significant to ask whether there are other passages that suggest a time when the
standard, ideal revelation of Yahweh did not show the level of sophistication
that is evident in these passages or that suggest a view not quite as stringent
as those of Second Isaiah.

---

[2]Primarily represented in Is 43:10-13; 44:6-7; 45:5-6, 21-22.

We cannot, unfortunately, ask whether there are *earlier* passages; the compositional histories of most of the books of the Old Testament are too complex. We can only ask whether there are expressions that communicate something *other* or *less* than what Isaiah proclaims here.[3] This method is not the same as asking whether there is evidence that the Israelites failed to understand this important distinction, rejected its truth, or were just incapable of reflecting it in their daily lives. In other words, a difference should be noted between the revelation and its corresponding expectation on the one hand, and Israelite practice with all of its shortcomings on the other. The motif in Isaiah may then be considered not as a new formulation but as evidence of an Israelite failure to shift paradigms. That is, this view of Yahweh's uniqueness should not necessarily be understood as progressively revealed, but only as persistently resisted, thereby calling for renewed emphasis with a more forthright rhetoric. No passage anywhere in the Old Testament conveys anything less than the uniqueness of Yahweh, notwithstanding the penchant for modern interpreters to impose a whole battery of "history of religions" presuppositions.

Even beyond the question of how this perspective is represented in the Old Testament, we can ask about the extent to which it is or is not distinguishable from what we find elsewhere in the ancient Near East. In this endeavor we will find mixed results

Pantheon, divine council, sons of god. The Old Testament tolerates no other gods qua gods; Yahweh stands alone. Therefore, one of the distinctions of standardized, ideal Israelite theology is that no pantheon is in operation. But in reality, the Israelites throughout most of the Old Testament period did not reflect that ideal in their practice. However, in this book, we desire to articulate the revealed theology of the Old Testament, not the failures, compromises, or syncretism of the Israelites.

In the pantheons of the ancient world, a high god usually occupied the leadership role over the other gods. At times this high god was the son of an even older god who was largely inactive (we might say retired with emeritus status). And sometimes there were changes in the leadership (e.g., when

---

[3]Of course, we would have to ask, if there were such passages, then why were these not expunged or at least modified by the same conscientious editors who purportedly were active in Deuteronomy and 1 Kings? Only unreasonably careless redactors could be accused of such oversights.

Šəmaʿ

The so-called šəmaʿ is appropriately considered the centerpiece of Israelite creed: "Hear, O Israel: The LORD our God, the LORD is one" (Deut 6:4). Much could be said about the šəmaʿ, but at this juncture, the affirmation it makes about Yahweh is most important.[a] More specifically, the way in which it differentiates Israel's belief from the beliefs of the ancient Near East needs to be carefully noted.

In the literature of the ancient Near East, there are, in fact, statements reminiscent of the šəmaʿ, even in contexts that are not at all monotheistic.[b] For example, in an Egyptian hymn to Amun Re, we find lines like "Praises to you, who created all this! Unique One, alone, the myriad-handed," and "Chief of the Great Ennead, exalted, alone, without likeness."[c] The Egyptian god Ptah, in one prayer from the time of Ramesses II, is referred to as "Unique God who is in the Ennead," which is a reference to his relationship to the high gods of the Egyptian pantheon.[d] These and other such epithets of deity in the ancient Near East show that references to a god being "unique" or "alone" are not characteristic of only Israel's theological ideas.

In light of this understanding, then, the šəmaʿ is not making a claim about Yahweh that others in polytheistic systems could not make as well. It certainly is insisting that Yahweh is "unique" or "alone," but it does not insist that "Yahweh is, but these others are not." It is not revealing a new

Marduk was elevated to the head of the pantheon, as recounted in the Babylonian creation epic, Enuma Elish). As a result, the pantheons were populated by unknown and uncounted numbers of deities, thousands of whom are identifiable through the available literature.

Not surprisingly, the hierarchy among the gods of the pantheon mirrored the sorts of bureaucratic structures that dominated the nations and cities of the ancient world. We can identify some of the categories, though we should strongly resist systematizing them, since that would inevitably impose our categories of thinking on them. Cosmic deities were associated with phenomena such as the lights of the celestial realm, the storms, the springs, the sea, the air, and so on. Each had his or her own jurisdiction, authority, and theological system; other gods were characterized in this same way, even in obviously polytheistic settings.[e] But the similarities do not suggest that Israelite theology tolerated polytheism, only that the *šəmaʿ* did not establish this particular distinction. Yahweh is *ʾeḥād* ("one"), and other gods make that same claim. The claim is no different from the declaration that Yahweh is powerful (as other gods are also portrayed). The main thrust of the passage is that Israel should "love Yahweh your God" because it addresses Israel's allegiance to Yahweh more than it functions as a philosophical declaration of his nature.

[a]Important contributions include the following: D. I. Block, "How Many Is God? An Investigation into the Meaning of Deuteronomy 6:4-5," in *How I Love Your Torah, O Lord*, ed. D. I. Block (Eugene, OR: Cascade, 2011), 73-97; R. W. L. Moberly, "'Yahweh Is One': The Translation of the Shema," in *Studies in the Pentateuch*, ed. J. A. Emerton, Vetus Testamentum Supplements 41 (Leiden: Brill, 1990), 209-15; J. Tigay, *Deuteronomy*, JPS Torah Commentary (Philadelphia: JPS, 1996), 438-41 (excursus 10); M. Smith, *The Origins of Biblical Monotheism* (Oxford: Oxford University Press, 2001), 151-94.

[b]This is different from the question about whether there are other examples of monotheistic belief and practice in the ancient world. I have commented on that briefly in *Ancient Near Eastern Thought and the Old Testament* (Grand Rapids: Baker, 2009), 93-94.

[c]J. Foster, *Hymns, Prayers, and Songs: An Anthology of Ancient Egyptian Lyric Poetry*, SBLWAW (Atlanta: SBL Press, 1995), 62-63.

[d]The prayer stele is a votive of Nefer-abu to Ptah; see M. Lichtheim, *Ancient Egyptian Literature* (Berkeley: University of California Press, 1976), 2:109-10.

[e]Note, for example, a hymn to Ishtar that declares that she, her incomparable greatness, is "unrivaled among the gods." See A. Lenzi, *Reading Akkadian Prayers and Hymns: An Introduction* (Atlanta: SBL Press, 2011), 126.

characteristics. National or city patron deities could also be one of the higher gods or celestial deities, but they could also be lesser-known gods with a lower status in the divine hierarchy. Clan deities, on the other hand, would not generally be gods from the other two categories and would occupy a lower, local level by definition.

However, the ancients did not maintain that all of this hierarchy was revealed to them by the gods. Instead, a number of rationales undergirded the development of their thinking. First, it is no surprise that the gods' interaction mimicked the way that governments were structured in the ancient world; the ancients concluded that the realm of the gods operated similarly to the human realm. Thus a hierarchical structure established rank and jurisdiction. Gods in more important positions were less likely to give attention to the needs of common people or be concerned about them, while other local deities were more attuned to those needs. In this way, the ancients created and organized the gods in their own image.

A second rationale was derived from some of the innate mindsets of those cultures. People in the ancient Near East found their most basic identity in the clan, rather than as autonomous individuals. Much could be said about this basic philosophy, but in this discussion, it is one of the keys to understanding the polytheistic pantheons of the region. Just as people functioned in community and found their identity in community, they were also inclined to believe that the gods functioned in community and found their identity therein. The pantheon, therefore, was the community of the gods.

With this brief discussion as a backdrop, we can understand the challenge of the theology revealed to the Israelites. How could one God do it all? *Why* would one God do it all? It would have been difficult for them to think of Yahweh as a cosmic deity, a phenomenon deity, a national deity, and a clan deity all at the same time. It just would not have made sense. It would be like people today thinking that they only need a general practitioner for a doctor rather than going to a variety of specialists.[4] Furthermore, where was Yahweh's community? Even if they could grasp the concept that he did not need anyone else, they would have had a sense that "it is not good for God to be alone." It was unreasonable and undesirable for people to function in such isolated, autonomous ways, and they would have thought that the divine realm would naturally be characterized by community and a complex web of interrelationships, not too different from their own experience.

In the Old Testament we do find, however, the provision of a functioning network and community for Yahweh in the divine council. He stands alone, but he does not work alone (i.e., no pantheon, but a functioning council). But before we turn to this concept in the Old Testament, we should look at the ancient Near Eastern backdrop. The divine council was the ruling body of the pantheon in the ancient world. The high gods met in session and made decisions about the administration of the cosmos (including the decreeing of destinies). Here the gods represented their constituencies and

---

[4]Analogy suggested by Josh Walton.

jurisdictions, protected their turf, jockeyed for power, negotiated their agendas, asserted their authority—in short, engaged in politics. The members of the council were sometimes designated as the sons of god, and they each had their own divine authority composed of the realm they represented and the constellation of attributes that they possessed.

In the Old Testament the divine council is portrayed as a structural reality of Yahweh's administration of the cosmos. It is Yahweh's community, but with some significant modifications to the picture we find in the ancient Near East. The council is composed of the "sons of God" (e.g., Job 1), and the sons of God are equated to the host of heaven in a manner just like the sons of god in the ancient Near East (the divine powers were associated with the celestial realm). In the Old Testament council, however, while the sons of God can be cantankerous or rebellious, they are always held in check with a tight rein (Ps 82). Yahweh gives them assignments (Deut 32:8, following the variant reading "sons of God," which is commonly recognized as the original reading, rather than "sons of Israel") and solicits them for their ideas (1 Kings 22:19-22). He engages with them and counsels with them (Gen 1:26; 3:22; 11:7; Is 6:8), though he does not need them (Is 40:12-14). But the major difference is that none of the sons of God in the council are on an equal par with Yahweh (Ps 89:6-8), nor do they carry their own divine authority. Whatever authority they have has been delegated to them (not distributed to them) by Yahweh.

I have proposed that the point above is therefore the main thrust of the first principle of the Decalogue.[5] When Yahweh indicates that the Israelites should have no other gods "before" him, we have traditionally been inclined to interpret the preposition as pertaining to priorities, i.e., that they should not consider anything else as more important than Yahweh. I maintain alternatively that this preposition *before*, when its grammatical object is personal, refers to a spatial location, i.e., being in the presence of someone. If this analysis (based on usage throughout the Old Testament) is correct, then the statement in the Decalogue should be understood to prohibit the Israelites from positing other deities in the presence

---

[5]John H. Walton, "Interpreting the Bible as an Ancient Near Eastern Document," in *Israel— Ancient Kingdom or Late Invention? Archaeology, Ancient Civilizations, and the Bible*, ed. D. Block (Nashville: Broadman & Holman, 2008), 298-327.

of Yahweh. This speaks directly to the *nature* of the divine council, though it does not eliminate the *idea* of such a council.

Yahweh's council, in other words, is not made up of gods that share his status or have their own, independent divine authority. The sons of God that make up Yahweh's council are lesser spirit beings who are delegated roles by the only God, Yahweh. If we adopt the reading of Deuteronomy 32:8 as a reference to the sons of God, we would then interpret the verse as suggesting that each of the sons of God had been assigned to a nation/people. From there, it is easy to identify those sons of God as the ones whom the nations have adopted as their gods and whom they have given a higher status than is justified. In this system, then, some of these beings were illegitimately elevated to divine status by peoples of the ancient Near East as the nations began to worship those who were "not gods" (Jer 5:7; 16:20; Gal 4:8). They are not "gods," and they are not demons (by our modern definitions at least). But they are not nothing, either; we should consider them misconstrued entities, not made-up beings.

When we observe a similarity between the Old Testament and the ancient Near East, we should sometimes conclude that it is the result of provisional accommodation. For example, the idea of a solid sky that is assumed by Israel and the ancient Near East alike can be understood not as God's revelation of ultimate truth but of his accommodation of an ancient worldview on an incidental issue.

At other times the observed similarities serve to help us focus on what are perhaps subtle differences, even though there are superficial similarities. An example can be observed in the sacrificial system. Even though significant overlap occurs between the sacrificial systems of Israel and the rest of the ancient Near East, we should not conclude that the sacrificial system is the result of provisional accommodation. The differences highlight something important about Yahweh and the way that he wants his people to relate to him.

With this methodological backdrop, we can now assess what we ought to think of the divine council. Is it the result of sound theological reality or of provisional accommodation? If it is the latter, then we can safely discard the divine council model as an example of God's use of the familiar for the purpose of communication. But even in the latter case, we would have to ask what it is that is being communicated. Since the divine council is a well-known idea in the ancient Near East, we would not conclude that God is revealing to the Israelites that there is indeed a divine council (whether there is or not); they already would be inclined to believe Yahweh works that way. Rather, using the motif of the well-known divine council, Yahweh is revealing distinctive characteristics about himself that set him apart from other gods.

What principles, then, do we learn about Yahweh from the passages that refer to the divine council?

✦ Yahweh uses servants to carry out his will, even though, theoretically, he does not need to do so.

✦ Yahweh holds his servants accountable and will judge them for their failings.

✦ Yahweh values community and consultation—even for himself.

✦ Even though he surrounds himself with servants to whom he delegates tasks, Yahweh retains his status as the sole being in his class. He is not simply a high god among others.

✦ Political wrangling does not take place in Yahweh's council, and his rule is supreme.[6]

In light of these principles, and others that could possibly be observed, we have good reason to believe that the portraits of Yahweh's council have theological value. Can that theological value be taken seriously if we do not believe that Yahweh actually works in a council? Is it an option to think that he used a council during the Old Testament but that he no longer uses one?

In the New Testament, reference is made to "authorities, . . . the powers of this dark world and . . . the spiritual forces of evil in the heavenly realms" (Eph 6:12), but this reference falls short of speaking specifically about a council. Indeed, Hellenistic Judaism had largely abandoned the idea and instead replaced it with a structured angelology. In the book of Revelation, however, a council scenario is envisioned, with twenty-four elders surrounding the throne (Rev 4:2-4), which could easily be an adaptation of the

---

[6]A long Christian tradition has seen an exception to this in the attempted overthrow by Satan. We will talk about this in chapter six and will discard it as unbiblical, to be considered fanciful, just as the tales in extrabiblical literature, such as the books of Enoch, should be considered.

council concept found in the Old Testament,[7] though the elders are only portrayed as worshiping, not deliberating or consulting.[8] A conclusion we can draw from this evidence is that nothing in any of the biblical texts suggests God does not work within a council, but neither does the use of a council undermine the full revelation that we get in Scripture.

Given these observations, it would be sensible to adopt the idea that God does operate in a council, and, furthermore, we cannot replace it with the idea that the council is really just the three persons of the Trinity in consultation. Such a conclusion runs contrary to all the information that we have about the council and posits an understanding of the Trinity that is not given anywhere in Scripture. Interestingly, this conclusion suggests that Genesis 1:26 not only would have been understood to refer to the council (not the Trinity) by the Israelite audience, but also that it is theologically unsubstantiated to impose a trinitarian interpretation on it based on later revelation (since no connection between the council and Trinity is set forth in Scripture). At the same time, an understanding of the beings who constitute the council of Yahweh remains elusive, especially concerning whether or not they correspond to beings who are adopted as gods by the nations.

Yet at the end of the day, if all of Scripture is culturally embedded, the authority of Scripture is not rooted in its metaphysics any more than it is rooted in its cosmic geography. All of it is filtered through the audience's perception. The council represents the factual idea that God considers the options and weighs them by his wisdom as he rules the cosmos. He is not an arbitrary despot. In this way, the council provides an imaginary and concrete model for speaking of divine will and agency. As a metaphor, it is like anthropomorphization in a cultural way. But that metaphorical projection into the heavens is the ancient Near Eastern language and grammar of divine sovereignty. The flexibility of the language is evident if you trace the throne-room scenes through the Old Testament, Jewish apocalyptic

---

[7]D. Aune, *Revelation 1–5*, Word Biblical Commentary (Nashville: Thomas Nelson, 1997), 288-92, especially option number six on 290-91; G. Osborne, *Revelation*, Baker Evangelical Commentary on the New Testament (Grand Rapids: Baker, 2002), 229; C. R. Koester, *Revelation*, Anchor Yale Bible (New Haven, CT: Yale University Press, 2014), 367-69 suggests that the vision builds from the pattern of the divine council but offers its own expansion of that idea, seen even in the designation of "elders."

[8]They may have a judicial function if they are the ones referred to in Rev 20:4.

literature, and Revelation. It is theological language, which is deeply contextual and adaptive. To reify it, to freeze it as concrete, is a mistake.[9]

We should not be deriving the authority of the text from the culturally relative perceptions of the audience. God is not revealing metaphysics; he is revealing his plans and purposes. The focus of the text is not to assert or affirm that there is or is not a divine council. All we learn from Scripture is that is how the Israelites thought. Through these passages, however, we learn that God is working in this world carrying out his plans and purposes. All beings, whatever their nature and whatever their organization, are created to be involved in this divine enterprise, and we, in his image, are part of that.

ATTRIBUTES

When discussing the attributes of Yahweh, we are generally interested in identifying the way that the Old Testament reveals Yahweh. This identification can be accomplished through static statements ("God is good") or through observations of his actions. At the same time, we should realize that God's actions do not always result in our ability to infer his attributes, especially when some of his actions can seem disturbing to some readers. Through static statements and observations of actions, we can come to some understanding of the identity of Yahweh, limited to the extent to which narratives and other texts are capable of revealing it.

In the ancient Near East the gods sometimes revealed the answers to oracular questions posed through divination and thereby gave verdicts or direction, but they never offered an account of their plans and attributes to the extent we find in the Old Testament (especially in the Prophets, though the ancient Near East also had prophets). In the ancient Near East it was more common for the gods to *manifest* themselves rather than to *reveal* themselves. Gods "manifested" themselves in objects, images, names, celestial bodies, or other things that comprised the divine constellation.[10] Examples of manifestation in Akkadian may go as far as statements such as, "Then you will see that I am Ishtar."[11] Akkadian terminology, nevertheless,

---

[9]Thanks to Dan Reid for these insights.

[10]Michael B. Hundley, *Gods in Dwellings* (Atlanta: SBL Press, 2013), 210-11, 234.

[11]S. Parpola, *Assyrian Prophecies*, State Archives of Assyria IX (Helsinki: Helsinki University Press, 1997), 27.

never features the divine name as the direct object of the verb *idu* (Akkadian "to know"). Hebrew, on the other hand, repeatedly and prominently talks about knowing Yahweh, which is the result of Yahweh revealing himself.[12] In contrast, manifestations in the ancient Near East relate to access, not to knowledge or relationship.

Despite these significant differences, we still have to ask what we can know about the being of God and how we can know what we know. Though Yahweh reveals himself in the Old Testament and also manifests himself in various ways to Israel, we should not make the mistake of thinking that the Israelites' metaphysical understanding is the same as ours (see discussion in this chapter). Everyone has a metaphysic, whether they are aware of it or not, just like everyone has a theology, whether they know it or not. Even today we would find variations in metaphysical thinking from one individual or group to another. It is sometimes difficult to unpack someone's metaphysical thinking, even when the same culture is shared, and the difficulty increases exponentially when we attempt the task crossculturally without a living informant.

Yet at the same time, we discern from the texts that Yahweh wants to be known, and he has communicated something of his identity in Scripture. It is appropriate, therefore, for us to believe that he has made knowledge of himself possible to some extent. Consequently, he *can* be known, but not *fully* known. By contrast, in Egypt, the nature of a particular god was considered hidden from people and even from the other gods:

> But One alone is the hidden God, who hides himself from them all,
> Who conceals himself from the gods, whose features cannot be known.
> He is farther above than heaven, deeper down than the world below,
> And no gods at all can know his true nature.
> No picture of him blossoms forth in the writings;
> There is no witness concerning him.
> He is mysterious to the depths of his majesty—great beyond any perception
>   of him,
> Mighty beyond comprehension.[13]

---

[12]Note something close when Shamash reveals a clay model of an image to Nabu-aplu-iddina so that he could make a replacement cult statue (Hundley, *Gods in Dwellings*, 230).

[13]Foster, *Hymns, Prayers, and Songs*, 77. Another hymn to the Egyptian sun god, Amun-Re, says: "There is no knowing you; there is no tongue to describe the likes of you" (ibid., 86). Akkadian prayers, at times, also express this idea: "The Lord [Marduk], he sees everything in the heart

Yahweh consistently acts in accordance with his nature, but we cannot know his nature. We can, however, deduce aspects of it from his actions and statements. He communicates himself anecdotally, mostly by story, but occasionally by more abstract statements (but don't we really only know anyone anecdotally?). The Old Testament certainly offers neither a formal systematic theology nor a theological metaphysics. Just as the Bible is not teaching physiology or cosmic geography, it is also not teaching an analogical or philosophical way of thinking about God. That is, it is not delivering systematics or metaphysics. It is packaging its content in conjunction with the way that the ancient Israelites thought. Any attempt to repackage that information into metaphysics or systematics would inevitably overspecify the text and end up making statements that are anachronistic or foreign to the text. In that way, such attempts are similar to concordism, which seeks to read scientific detail into the text. In the end these are eisegetical approaches.

Of course, we can know God enough to believe, trust, or love, and we can know him enough for relationship. We have enough information to participate in his plans and purposes. But even as we cannot know people completely, so all the more we cannot expect to know God completely. Yet we can know people well enough to be occasionally able to predict what they will do in a particular circumstance, what kinds of things they expect us to do, and how they will react. In the same way, God reveals what he does, so the most important part of the discussion of who God "is" is that he "is consistent." In this project we can learn from how the Old Testament differentiates Yahweh from the ancient Near Eastern gods. Beyond that, I am trying to discover the revelation the text offers about God, to synthesize the truth about God that we find there, and to embrace as truth that which informs our beliefs today.

We are now positioned to begin discussing what we can know about Yahweh as he is revealed in the Old Testament. We will find some areas of continuity with the ways that other ancient peoples thought about their gods and some areas in which there is total discontinuity. But even when there is a general aspect of continuity and commonality, we will often find important distinctions that need to be identified.

---

of the gods, (but) no one among the gods knows his way"; Lenzi, *Reading Akkadian Prayers and Hymns*, 499.

What we observe about God comes from his actions, and the actions that are mediated to us through the literature of Scripture serve as the primary way by which we can experience or perceive him. Some might believe that the nature of God can be deduced from the observation of such actions; others might believe that God's actions cannot be extrapolated to determine his nature, in which case nothing can be known about God's *nature*, per se. Ancient metaphysics[14] would likely have fallen into the latter category ("functional ontology"; see sidebar), whereas modern Western Christians would tend to fall into the former. If this is the case, Israel would not be distinguished from the rest of the ancient Near East by having a different metaphysics. However, it would differ from its neighbors in its perception of Yahweh's actions as consistent rather than ad hoc. One evidence that Israel did not conceive of its God as different from other gods on a deep metaphysical level is it did not feel compelled to use a different word. The Old Testament uses the default Semitic term, *'elōhîm,* to describe God, though admittedly the same words can take on diverse meanings in the cultures that use them. Due to the metaphysical inclinations of the Israelites, they would not have necessarily cared as much about who God *is* (that is, defining his nature) as about what God *does*—because his deeds were at the core of their ontology. Observing his deeds can lead to conclusions about God's revealed identity more successfully than to knowledge about his nature. In other words, his revealed deeds can only get us so far in reconstructing the mysteries and intricacies of the divine nature. Revelation through the literature of the Bible provides knowledge of some of God's deeds. This is sufficient for us to form an identity as it has been projected but only allows a superficial penetration of his nature.

We encounter problems when we try to make the transition from actions (expressed by verbs) to statements about God's nature. It is one thing to say that God acts justly or executes justice. But it is more problematic to say "God is just" on at least two counts. The first is that such an expression at least implies that there is something like a category of "justice" independent of God to which he conforms. The problem that we then face concerns what

---

[14]An unavoidably anachronistic label, since no such category in the ancient world would have been identified systematically, though, of course, everyone does metaphysics whether or not as a conscious category.

constitutes this category and what criteria establish its boundaries. It would be better to say that "justice flows from God."

A second problem is that as we observe God's acts, we often have questions about whether such acts are indeed just. We are not in a position to justify God, nor can we successfully explain how everything that he does is just. In this way, the statement "God is just" becomes meaningless, except as a conviction that is beyond our verification. Consequently, we may be able to say little with confidence about the nature of God, except that we trust that what he says about himself is true.

Furthermore, when we talk about the attributes of God, we want to be careful not to imply that he is constrained by those attributes. Concepts such as goodness or justice find their definitions in God, and so God is good because anything God does is good by definition. In the same way, God is just because anything God does is just by definition. But this system of definitions has the problem of not really being descriptive, because all the ideas reduce to tautologies. Nevertheless, aseity (self-sufficience, self-existentence) is important; transcendence is important; and uniqueness is important. The exact details are not important.

Despite the semantic problems from philosophical theology, it is not difficult to identify key ways in which Yahweh, as revealed in the Old Testament, is differentiated from the other gods in the ancient Near East. For example, Yahweh is, of course, never described in familial relationship to other gods (father, brother, or son). Sexual activity is never attributed to him. He is never compared with other gods as an equal or as a subordinate, and he never grants other gods jurisdictions. Since the Old Testament leaves no room for Yahweh to be in community with other gods in this manner, any familial terms are going to be applied to his community relationship with people (or with angels or sons of God). Despite that difference, many (not all) of the attributes associated with Yahweh are likewise associated (at least in some degree) with other gods of the ancient Near East.

Names and epithets. In the Old Testament and in the ancient Near East, gods were identified, praised, defined, and manifested by their names and epithets. Since the names were considered definitions of the various aspects of the deity, the more names a deity had, the better. For example, the well-known Babylonian creation epic, Enuma Elish, reaches its climax in the recitation of the fifty names of Marduk.[15] In other cases, the names of god are hidden to reflect the impenetrable nature of a god.[16]

Similarly, the names and epithets of God in the Old Testament number in the dozens, many of them combinations with either El/Elohim or Yahweh. Yahweh makes a point of personally revealing his name at the burning bush: "I AM" (Ex 3:14). He also distinguishes between his names and their significance (Ex 6:2-3). In particular, the designation of himself as I AM (Hebrew *ʾehyeh*) is interesting because he is never again called by this name in the Old Testament.[17] This lack of usage demonstrates that a name is not necessarily a moniker. In fact, in the very next verse, the form "Yahweh" is given as what he should be called (i.e., his moniker). However, it should not be inferred that this name encapsulates all that the God of Israel is. We have learned from the ancient Near East that no name, or even collection of names, is capable of circumscribing the whole of the deity to whom it is attached.

Unfortunately, because the scribes at an early date ceased vocalizing the name Yahweh, modern scholars can only guess at its pronunciation (which is the key to understanding its morphology and thence its meaning). The vocalization "Yahweh" is then an informed guess. It is the third-person masculine singular form of the verb "to be" (*hāyâ*), analyzed (arguably) as in the Hiphil stem, which would establish a sense of implied causation ("he causes [someone/something] to be").[18] Since we have no strong evidence of the reading, it would be incautious to draw conclusions about Yahweh from the

---

[15]For discussion of the concepts as well as the ancient interpretation of Marduk's names, see A. Livingstone, *Mystical and Mythological Explanatory Works of Assyrian and Babylonian Scholars* (Winona Lake, IN: Eisenbrauns, 2007); E. Frahm, *Babylonian and Assyrian Text Commentaries* (Münster: Ugarit-Verlag, 2011); M. Van De Mieroop, *Philosophy Before the Greeks: The Pursuit of Truth in Ancient Babylonia* (Princeton, NJ: Princeton University Press, 2016).

[16]Egyptian Coffin Texts, spell 1130; see *COS* 1.17.

[17]The form is used about fifty times in the Old Testament, usually when God assures people he will be with them or be Elohim to them. But in these instances, it is simply a verbal form, not a name or epithet. It may occur in Hos 1:9, though many consider this entry a scribal error.

[18]The first-person form (*ʾehyeh*) is clearly not in the causative stem. In fact, the verb never occurs in the Hiphil stem. The proposed pronunciation with the critical *a* vowel that suggests a Hiphil comes from nonbiblical texts and Greek renderings. For discussions, see D. Freedman, "יהוה," *TDOT* 5:501-11; K. van der Toorn, "Yahweh," in *DDD²*, 910-19. For argument against the Hiphil interpretation, see T. N. D. Mettinger, *In Search of God* (Philadelphia: Fortress, 1988), 24-36; J. C. De Moor, *The Rise of Yahwism: The Roots of Israelite Monotheism* (Leeuven: Peeters, 1997). Mettinger, along with others, considers Yahweh to be an epithet of El (i.e., the original name was YHWH-El).

grammatical form of the name. It is also interesting to note that an Egyptian god, Re, is recorded claiming "I am who I am."[19]

Individual qualities that pertain to Yahweh alone (not to humans and not to other gods in the ancient Near East). *Omni-X (that is, all the attributes beginning with "omni-").* Many of the terms that are mainstays in modern systematic theology have no equivalent in the Hebrew lexicon, though the ideas are not thereby absent from the Hebrew Bible. We conventionally derive evidence for God's omniscience and omnipresence from passages such as Psalm 139. His transcendence is seen in the statements of the middle section of Isaiah (Second Isaiah), and his immanence can be found expressed in many statements in the Psalms. However, we can also find statements in the hymnology of the ancient Near East that could support similar beliefs about particular gods that they worshiped. At the same time, we need to recognize that such beliefs could be held about several gods at the same time.

Even as we find support in passages that God can be characterized in terms such as those mentioned above, we should also affirm that, since the passages are not systematic treatises designed to give definition to God's qualities, they do not offer much metaphysical clarification (most are poetry!). From these passages we can, of course, draw conclusions that Israel would have affirmed: the related concepts of Yahweh's aseity (uncaused; existence derives from himself; he has no other source) and noncontingence (autonomous; depends on nothing and no one else). However, in the ancient world, Israel included, people were not inclined to circumscribe their beliefs about deity in such metaphysical or systematic garb. So if we are focusing on how they would have expressed their beliefs about God, we must largely abandon our familiar terminology. Instead, we should turn our attention to the terms that they were inclined to use.

Holy (qādôš). Yahweh is holy, not because he conforms to some outside standard defined as holiness, but because he is God. Describing something as holy means that it is situated in the divine realm. For everyone or everything so designated (other than God), this is a conferred status; it is not something that can be pursued and achieved. God is by definition holy. He

---

[19]De Moor, *Rise of Yahwism*, 268-69. He concludes, based on the context, that the meaning is "Re will remain constant" or "as he was in the past, he will be in the future."

conferred that holy status on Israel, and he intended to live among the Israelites. God's presence brought benefits and relationship, but Israel's failure to take its status into account in its behavior brought consequences. Its status could not be gained or lost, but Yahweh's presence could leave.

In the ancient Near East, gods were rarely designated as holy.[20] They were considered pure or clean, but there is no term comparable in semantic range to the Hebrew term (*qādôš*).[21] The closest concept we find in Akkadian is the concept of *dingir*.[22] This is a determinative noun used to designate the gods, the temples, objects associated with the gods (i.e., included in the divine realm), stars, etc.[23] It is not an indication of a quality but an indication of identity. In Akkadian literature it is very rare for a person's name to be categorized by use of a *dingir* (occasional kings), and never is a whole people group so designated (as Israel is designated as holy).[24]

For our understanding of the qualities of God, when we say that God is holy, we are affirming his defining category, but such a statement does not give us information about his acts. God does not act holy or do holy things; he is holy by definition. Anything brought into the circle of his being thereby shares that quality. When Yahweh declares Israel holy, Israel is made a part of Yahweh's identity. By means of this designation, Yahweh's identity also expands as he becomes the "God of Israel." But being designated holy does not mean that Israel is acting holy or doing holy things, even though it is called to live in a way that is appropriate to that status in order to remain in Yahweh's presence.

Jealous (qnʾ). This term communicates an expression of proprietary rights with exclusivistic implications. When someone belongs to someone else, it is expected that others will recognize it and respect those rights. The basis

---

[20]A few likely exceptions occur in Ugaritic, though they do not display the full semantic range observable in Hebrew.

[21]See "Syntactical/Semantic Analysis of *qds*," appendix to John H. Walton and J. Harvey Walton, *The Lost World of the Israelite Conquest* (Downers Grove, IL: InterVarsity Press, 2017), available at ivpress.com/the-lost-world-of-the-israelite-conquest.

[22]Reflected as a determinative before the word so categorized, e.g., ᵈMarduk, where the superscript d = *dingir*.

[23]M. Hundley, "Here a God, There a God: An Examination of the Divine in Ancient Mesopotamia," *Altorientalische Forschungen* 40 (2013): 68-107; B. N. Porter, "Blessings from a Crown, Offerings to a Drum: Were There Non-Anthropomorphic Deities in Ancient Mesopotamia?," in *What Is a God?*, ed. B. N. Porter (Winona Lake, IN: Eisenbrauns, 2009), 153-94.

[24]My colleague Adam Miglio reminds me also of the Akkadian *asakkum*, which is used of those things that enter into the presence of a god.

of "belonging" is not economic (e.g., a possession); it is relational. The term therefore pertains to the protection and preservation of something that derives from a relationship and has value (Ex 20:5; 34:14; Deut 4:24; 5:9; 6:15). It comes with a sense of entitlement based on a claim of either ownership or loyalty. Yahweh is not jealous of other gods but of the worship given to them (Ps 78:58). His entitlement, by virtue of the covenant, is to the loyalty of his people;[25] he is not afraid that others might receive gifts that he wants (i.e., not need-based). In the ancient Near East gods could be envious of the position of other gods and might even covet what people have, but they were not jealous of the worship and attention given to other gods that would lead to a posture of exclusivism.[26] In light of this analysis, we can see that applying this quality to God would carry none of the negative connotations that are often carried by the English word *jealous(y)*.

Ineffable plan. Among the most persistent claims made about Yahweh (particularly notable in Isaiah[27]) is that he makes plans and carries them out, here not only referring to ad hoc plans in the frame of the near future (also commonplace in the rhetoric of the ancient Near East) but to long term plans.[28] In this claim, he is both differentiating himself from other gods who cannot do these things and expressing his sovereignty, since none can subvert or challenge his plan.

Unchangeable. In a number of important passages Yahweh differentiates himself from humanity by virtue of the fact that he does not change (*nḥm*—

---

[25]When associated with God, eight occurrences are as adjectives (Ex 20; 34; Deut 4–6; Josh 24; Nah 1) followed by verbs such as "avenging" or "not forgiving." About twenty occurrences are as nouns (jealousy, zeal), more than half of which are in Isaiah and Ezekiel and are given as the basis for his action against his faithless people or their enemies. Nine occurrences are as verbs (English does not have a matching verb): two Hiphil (Israel's actions arousing God's jealous actions; Deut 32:16; Ps 78:58); seven Piel (God describing the state to which Israel's unfaithfulness had brought him). Israel also brings God into a state of jealousy (Deut 32:21; 1 Kings 14:22; Ezek 39:25; Joel 2:18; Zech 1:14; 8:2). For a helpful comparison of related terms, see John H. Elliot, "Envy, Jealousy, and Zeal in the Bible: Sorting Out the Social Differences and Theological Implications—No Envy for YHWH," in *To Break Every Yoke*, ed. R. Coote and N. Gottwald (Sheffield, UK: Sheffield Phoenix, 2007), 344-64.

[26]De Moor, *Rise of Yahwism*, 316. De Moor tries to minimize the uniqueness of the Hebrew designation, but he blurs important semantic distinctions. For cognates that pertain to "envy," see E. Reuter, "קנא," in *TDOT* 13:47-58.

[27]Is 41:4, 21-29; 42:9; 43:9-13; 45:21; 46:10; 48:3-7.

[28]I have oversimplified this long-standing debate, reflected decades ago in the debate between B. Albrektson, *History and the Gods* (Lund: Gleerup, 1967), and H. W. F. Saggs, *Encounter with the Divine in Mesopotamia and Israel* (London: Athlone, 1978).

Num 23:19; 1 Sam 15:29; Ps 110:4). Alongside of these passages, there are a number of other passages that seem to suggest Yahweh does indeed change (Gen 6:6-7; 22:2, 12; Ex 33:3, 14-17; 1 Sam 2:27-35; 15:11, 35; Jer 26:13; Joel 2:13-14; Jn 3:10; some translations in some passages render the word "relent," "regret," or "repent").[29] Nevertheless, the idea that God does not change offers a contrast to the gods known throughout the ancient Near East, who are inclined to be unpredictable, capricious, fickle, and inconsistent. But despite this important distinction, there are times when Yahweh changes his course of action under particular conditions or circumstances, such as when there is a change in human behavior that warrants reconsideration or when intercession leads to a concession on God's part. These reconsiderations or concessions do not suggest, however, that he had previously been mistaken or that he is admitting the intercessor is better informed or has superior logic. Like the previous characteristics discussed, this characteristic is one that differentiates Yahweh from the gods of the ancient Near East. For those gods, it may be affirmed that they make decrees that no one can alter, but that is a much more limited claim than Yahweh's claim.

Redeemer. This is the final characteristic that we will consider here, though other characteristics may be easily identified. Yahweh often redeems his people from their difficult circumstances, whether in the exodus, in the exile, or just in general times of trouble. The most frequently used terms used in this regard are *gʾl*[30] and *pd(h)*.[31] The former is used when someone or something is restored to a prior, inherent (normal) status. In human terms, the family or clan is most often the active party, but when Israel is the object, God can also function as the active party. Often, this verb identifies what someone or something is being restored *from*,[32] but the focus of the verb is more on the status that they are being restored *to*. It is typically an expression of duty. In contrast, the verb *pd(h)* often involves an exchange or transaction that focuses on freeing someone from a burden or obligation. Of course, it overlaps with *gʾl*, and either one can be applied to many situations.

The Akkadian cognate of *pd(h)*, however, is used with a god as the subject only very rarely (including with personal names).[33] It was not included as a

---

[29]See more extensive analysis in J. Walton, *Genesis*, NIVAC (Grand Rapids: Zondervan, 2001), 308-11.
[30]E.g., Ex 6:6; 15:13; Ps 19:14; Is 41:14; 43:1, 14; 44:6, 22-24; 47:4; 48:20; 49:7; 52:9.
[31]E.g., Deut 7:8; 13:5; 21:8; Ps 25:22; Is 35:10.
[32]In that way it is similar to verbs used for saving or delivering (*yṣl* or *yšʿ*).
[33]*CAD*, *padû*.

standard attribute of gods in the ancient Near East and never pertains to a people group (as in the case of Israel). Likewise, in the Old Testament, neither individuals nor groups were redeemed from their sins,[34] and so the Old Testament represents a different level of thinking from the New Testament. Given this information, it would be methodologically inconsistent to posit continuity between the Testaments by considering the concept of "God as Redeemer" in the Old Testament as in any way equivalent to the concept of "Christ as Redeemer" in the New Testament, even though the latter idea develops out of the former.[35]

Individual qualities that pertain to God and the gods of the ancient Near East (but not to humans). Before actually addressing a few selected qualities, it is important to discuss what the Israelites would have understood by the term *ʾelōhîm* (and its Semitic cognates, such as *ʾelim* and *ilu*). It was used generally to refer to any spiritual being not in the human realm and therefore applied to any of those considered divine by any of the people of the ancient Near East, as well as to the spirits who entered the realm of the dead (1 Sam 28:13). The "sons of God" are members of this class as well (e.g., Job 1–2; Ps 82; 89:6-7). In Babylonian thinking, furthermore, the stars or the images of the gods were *ilu*, because they were manifestations of the gods in metaphorical or mediatorial senses.[36] Those that were categorized as gods in the ancient Near East generally were so recognized by being venerated as objects of rituals. In the Old Testament, only Yahweh was the attention of legitimate ritual activity.

The gods as a class, however, could be more narrowly defined by the activities in which they engaged or the jurisdiction over which they had control. In the ancient Near East, only a god of a certain class could be viewed as a

---

[34]The possible exception is Ps 130:8, but it is inadmissible because there they are redeemed from their *ʿāwôn*, which likely refers to punishment (i.e., what God would do to them, rather than to what they have done against God).

[35]It should also be noted that Job's assertion in Job 19:25 that his *gōʾēl* lives cannot be applied to the anticipation of Christ. Job is not looking for someone who will redeem him from sins; he has been contending that he has no sins that need to be addressed. He is looking for someone who will restore him to his former status. Vindication is at the opposite end of the spectrum from justification; vindication assumes innocence, while justification assumes guilt.

[36]For important discussions, see Porter, *What Is a God?*, especially the articles by F. Rochberg, "'The Stars and Their Likeness': Perspectives on the Relation Between Celestial Bodies and Gods in Ancient Mesopotamia," 41-92; and B. N. Porter, "Blessings from a Crown, Offerings to a Drum: Were There Non-Anthropomorphic Deities in Ancient Mesopotamia?," 153-94.

creator or a warrior (and not every god was in this category). Gods, as a general category, could be identified primarily as those who participated in the Great Symbiosis, which meant that the gods were those cared for by humans (through rituals; see discussion in chapter four) and that they were involved in providing something of value to humans in return. Such gods would include cosmic deities, national or city deities, clan deities, and even ancestral deities. In Israel, Yahweh was originally encountered as a clan deity (Abram), but he was eventually understood as both a cosmic deity and a national deity. Such range is unknown in the rest of the ancient world.

Conversely, demons in the ancient Near East were nonhuman creatures, but they were not considered *ilu* because sacrificial rituals were not directed toward them and cults were not established for them. Rituals, instead, were focused on the gods who were invoked to control or withstand the demons. Interestingly, demons are virtually absent from the Old Testament.[37]

Creator/Maker. All cultures of the ancient world considered God(s) to be Creator. In the ancient Near East, different gods were considered creator gods in different traditions at various times. That one god (e.g., Marduk in Enuma Elish) could come to be considered the Creator, after succeeding an earlier god (e.g., Anu or Enlil) who was previously considered Creator, gives us an important insight into what was involved in being a Creator. It is not just that the Babylonians came to think that Marduk had been the Creator all along; in their minds, Marduk took up the reins. The creator god was the one who did all that was necessary to order the cosmos and to preserve that order. In Old Testament theology and Israel's understanding, then, Yahweh is this Creator-God (more on this in the next chapter).

Warrior. The role of divine warrior is well attested in the ancient world.[38] In fact, one of the major responsibilities of the gods was the maintenance of

---

[37]For further discussion of demons and their role, see chapter six on sin and evil. For a detailed treatment, see John Walton and J. Harvey Walton, *Demons and Spirits* (Eugene, OR: Wipf and Stock, forthcoming).

[38]S. W. Holloway, *Aššur Is King! Aššur Is King!* (Leiden: Brill, 2002); Sa-Moon Kang, *Divine War in the Old Testament and in the Ancient Near East* (Berlin: de Gruyter, 1989); Martin Klingbeil, *Yahweh Fighting from Heaven: God as Warrior and God of Heaven in the Hebrew Psalter and Ancient Near Eastern Iconography*, Orbis Biblicus et Orientalis 169 (Göttingen: Vandenhoeck & Ruprecht, 1999); Tremper Longman and Daniel Reid, *God Is a Warrior* (Grand Rapids: Zondervan, 1995); Patrick D. Miller, *The Divine Warrior in Early Israel* (Atlanta: SBL Press, 2006); C. Trimm, *YHWH Fights for Them! The Divine Warrior in the Exodus Narrative* (Piscataway, NJ: Gorgias, 2014).

order, a task that included dealing with disruptive parties who either came against or caused problems for a group of people valued by the deity. In this way of thinking, war conducted by the gods was not the opposite of peace but the response to encroaching disorder. The gods gave permission to fight and not only joined in the battle but were the ones who actually achieved victory. The Israelites similarly understood Yahweh as a divine warrior, just as the Canaanites, Assyrians, or Egyptians would have thought about some of their gods. Despite that general similarity, Yahweh engaged differently. For example, he could fight against his own people (even if that meant his own temple was destroyed), just as he could fight for them. The range of his martial activity is also much more limited than what we find in the ancient Near East. We can explore the similarities and differences under the category of "theomachy"—divine combat—which we will do in the next chapter.

Investigating the passages in the Hebrew Bible, we find that there are three fairly distinct and easily recognizable motifs involved with this characteristic. The "divine warrior" category includes all those passages in which victory over human enemies is recognized or requested. These enemies are occasionally the personal enemies of the psalmist, but more frequently they are the enemies of Israel.

When we consider the divine warrior's conflict with the forces of chaos (*Chaoskampf*) in poetical texts, we encounter the cosmogonic motif of the "Lord of the cosmos." The Hebrew Bible is consistently interested in divine kingship, an interest it holds in common with the rest of the ancient world. Cosmogony is, of course, one context in which divine kingship can be demonstrated, but it is only one of many. Yahweh's kingship is expressed over the operations of the cosmos, whether they pertain to precipitation or politics.[39] He is superior to other gods, and he rules nations and empires.

In contrast, theomachy is typically a motif in contexts in which Yahweh is harnessing those powers that would rebel against his rule. The passages in the Prophets and the Psalms nowhere indicate that the *formation* of the cosmos comes as a result of defeat of other powers,[40] only that Yahweh's

---

[39]See N. Forsyth, *The Old Enemy* (Princeton, NJ: Princeton University Press, 1987), 53-54, for Ninurta's rule as displayed by his harnessing of the Anzu bird, from whose mouth the rain waters flow.

[40]R. S. Watson, *Chaos Uncreated: The Reassessment of the Theme of "Chaos" in the Hebrew Bible* (Berlin: de Gruyter, 2005), 235.

rule of the cosmos is accomplished as he defeats rebels or harnesses powers. But even in most of these instances, the motif is more closely identifiable with divine warrior language than with theomachy language. It should not be surprising, however, that theomachy is difficult to identify in biblical passages, since most of the theomachy categories discussed in connection with the ancient Near East can only operate in a polytheistic system. Despite the fact that through much of Israel's history it had not succeeded in discarding polytheism, the biblical text does not adopt a polytheistic worldview for itself.

When we derive theology from the Old Testament, we should continue to maintain that God is a warrior. God fights on our behalf (as his people), just as he did for the Israelites. He also brings deliverance from enemies, whether spiritual, physical, or abstract. Nothing and no one can pose a threat to him or is beyond his control; the spiritual forces that threaten his people are no threat to him. He is the victor. This element is expanded when we view Christ as the victor who has brought deliverance from the power of sin as he overcame death, but we do not need this additional information from the New Testament (as important as it is) to understand this aspect of the nature of God. In fact, the Old Testament provides more detailed revelation on this matter, and we would be poorer without it.

I will reserve offering a summary and conclusion section for after we can deal with the idea of relationship in the next section.

RELATIONSHIP

I will be with you. One of the most commonly identified aspects of the God of the Old Testament is his relational nature. This nature is also often identified as a feature that sharply distinguishes him from the gods of the ancient Near East. However, in order for us to consider these common perceptions, we need to address what we mean when we inquire about a term as potentially elusive as *relationship*.

To begin, four major categories of relationships can be identified as follows:

✦ *de facto* (e.g., parents/children; metaphor: God as father)

✦ *formalized* (e.g., husband/wife; metaphor: God as husband)

✦ *imposed* by power or necessity (e.g., people/government; metaphor: God as king)

✦ *circumstantial* (e.g., student/teacher; employee/employer; metaphor: God as mentor)

In all of these cases, the relationship can potentially be healthy, neutral, or dysfunctional, but they are all also based on metaphors. We must, therefore, resist the temptation to describe the relationship(s) between people and God/gods in psychological terms (e.g., in light of the psychological nature of the relationship between parents and children). Psychological definitions do not clarify the nature of the divine/human relationship in the ancient world,[41] and even if there were psychological aspects involved, we would have great difficulty extracting them from literature.

We can, however, address the nature of the divine/human relationship by exploring the idea of "love" between God/gods and people in the ancient world and in Israel, since this is terminology that the texts actually use. The gods in general are considered to love (e.g., in Akkadian *râmu*) people, and people likewise love the gods, though it has been demonstrated that terms such as these in the ancient world are sometimes used to express the presence of political relationships rather than emotions. But such expressions from the gods are rare and are more often directed to the king than to the people at large. Even considering the myriads of royal inscriptions wherein the kings speak at length about the relationship between themselves and a god, clear expressions of *emotion* in either direction are little attested. When we turn our attention to Egypt, the love of the people for the gods is conveyed in phrases such as, "Praises come to him [Amun-Re] from every dwelling, each holy precinct endures in its love for him." Or, in a hymn to Thoth, "Love gushes out from his eyebrows as he opens his mouth to give life."[42] As in Mesopotamia, however, these types of phrases represent isolated instances, and as such, they do not represent fundamental or pervasive expressions of how the Egyptians perceived their relationship with the gods.

---

[41]Though sometimes even the psychological aspects are included in the development of the metaphor (e.g., a parent longing for children and weeping over them).

[42]Respectively, Foster, *Hymns, Prayers, and Songs*, 73 (Leiden Hymn 1 350) and 146.

The Old Testament, on the other hand, is replete with expressions of Yahweh's positive love and care for Israel, in a manner that far exceeds what is found in the literature of the ancient Near East. In fact, expressions of love are ubiquitous from both Yahweh and humans. We may also note that even though "love" ('ahāb) does not necessarily entail emotional feelings or attachment, it is nonetheless expressive of a positive relationship. In a few isolated contexts, we can find emotion expressed in raw terms, perhaps most notably in passages such as Jeremiah 31:3; Lamentations 3:22; and Hosea 11:1-11. These passages demonstrate that Yahweh may well be responding to his people emotively, yet this should not be understood as the primary level at which the relationship between Yahweh and Israel operates. In the Old Testament, Yahweh is also considered a friend of people and beloved by people—terminology used only sporadically in the ancient Near East. In other words, *the relationship between Yahweh and Israel is not driven by psychological need or by emotional feelings; it is defined by the partnership initiated by Yahweh as he enlists Israel to work beside him to carry out his plans and purposes.*

One example that has sometimes been considered a classic expression of emotional attachment is the identification of Israel as Yahweh's "treasured possession" (sĕgullâ). Admittedly, it is not frequent in the Old Testament, and it calls for closer attention. The term is used a total of eight times in the Old Testament, six of which refer to Israel (the other two pertain to the royal treasury). The nuance of the term can be further investigated by a look at its comparative Semitic usage, which reflects the same semantic footprint as Hebrew.[43] In Akkadian it refers to movable goods that are personal possessions. More importantly, it is used metaphorically in personal names to refer to someone's status with respect to a god. In these cases the term refers to an individual rather than to a whole people group, as it does in Hebrew. Perhaps even more importantly, the Ugaritic usage occurs in a letter in which the Hittite high king reminds the local ruler (ᶜAmmurapi) of his vassal status; the use of sglt in this letter reflects a personal bond that cements the vassal relationship.[44] It therefore suggests partnership in purpose, rather than emotional attachment.

---

[43] Akkadian sikiltu (with variants šigiltu, šagiltu, and šagālu) and Ugaritic sglt. E. Lipinski, TDOT 10:144-48.

[44] E. Lipinski, "סְגֻלָּה," in TDOT 10:146.

Regardless, as mentioned above, it is on the basis of partnership that we should judge whether the Old Testament relationship is healthy or dysfunctional. A healthy divine/human relationship is motivated by love and/or respect and is characterized by obedience or mutual submission (depending on the nature of the relationship). Conversely, a dysfunctional relationship is motivated by fear or need and is characterized by neglect or pedestrian performance at best. These categories and characteristics all pertain at some level to the relationship between people and the gods in the ancient Near East, as well as to Israel and Yahweh.

In ancient literature the use of de facto language is somewhat common. In Egyptian thinking, for example, a de facto relationship between the gods and people exists by virtue of creation. Parent/child metaphors are quite common in this literature, but they are limited mostly to use in relation to the king. During the New Kingdom period, at least, the god was viewed as father/mother to all.[45] Yet at the same time, the Instruction of Merikare describes the gods as tending the people as cattle. The familial metaphor of father/son also occurs in Mesopotamian literature, but again the metaphor is generally limited to the relationship between the god and king.[46] For example, though Marduk is considered compassionate, nowhere in all the vast collection of prayers to him is he ever referred to as "father." In Israelite thinking, however, the people of Israel (and eventually the king) are portrayed as children to Yahweh. Even though biological descriptions fill out the metaphor, in both Mesopotamia and Israel it is more a formalized relationship (more like adoption), since the relationship is established by election.[47] The gods of the ancient Near East chose to sponsor the king, and Yahweh chose Israel as his people. In other words, a de facto relationship exists between Yahweh and all people in that humanity as a whole is made in his image.

Formalized relationships, as already noted, occur across the ancient Near East between the gods and the king, though adoption language is more observable than husband/wife metaphors. But in Israel, this formalized

---

[45]J. Assmann, *The Mind of Egypt* (New York: Metropolitan, 2002), 234.

[46]Care should be exercised here, since most of the written sources that are available to us were composed under the sponsorship of kings and so address the king's relationship to the gods rather than any other.

[47]We could perhaps consider God's relationship to all humanity as de facto by virtue of his bestowal of the image of God.

relationship between Yahweh and Israel is supported by the husband/wife metaphor, and the covenant is the dominating element of the relationship. In contrast, the husband/wife metaphors in the ancient Near East are used for relationships between gods but not between gods and people.[48] Nothing compares to the identification of the Israelites as Yahweh's children (e.g., Deut 32:5, 19),[49] and neither is there a relational agreement (covenant) between any god and any group of people (see chapter four for more information). For example, in all the Babylonian prayers to Marduk,[50] he is occasionally referred to as the shepherd of the people, but not as the father to the people. Moreover, among all the hundreds of epithets of Marduk, some identify him as protecting, delivering, and watching over the people, but all of these fit neatly into the common model of the gods as protectors and providers.[51]

Imposed relationships between god(s) and people are perhaps the most common relationships by virtue of the gods being seen as kings and shepherds. For the ancient Near East, the patronage provided by the gods is an expression of what we can call the Great Symbiosis. In this view, gods had needs of food, housing, and clothing, and they created people to meet those needs. The people were expected to pamper the gods, who, in turn, would provide for the people and protect them so that they could continue to meet the gods' needs. Yahweh's kingship, in contrast, extends to all nations universally, but it also pertains more specifically to Israel and operates within the covenant framework. It is through his covenant that he provides and protects his people on the condition of their covenant faithfulness, rather than on the condition of their ritual provision for his needs, as in the Great Symbiosis.

Circumstantial relationships between gods and people in the ancient Near East also exist as the people are associated by their circumstances to the patron gods of their city, their guild, or their clan. In contrast, it is not circumstance from which Israel's relationship to Yahweh is derived.

---

[48]For extensive discussion, see M. C. A. Korpel, *A Rift in the Clouds: Ugaritic and Hebrew Descriptions of the Divine* (Münster: Ugarit-Verlag, 1990), 213-32. Note particularly the conclusion: "It appears that in Israel the imagery used to describe the love life and marriages of the Canaanite gods was deliberately and consistently transferred to the relation between YHWH and his chosen people" (231).

[49]Though see it attributed to Moabites in Num 21:29.

[50]Takayoshi Oshima, *Babylonian Prayers to Marduk* (Tübingen: Mohr Siebeck, 2011).

[51]Listed in ibid., 437-56.

Intentionality is evident throughout the literature to suggest that there is nothing ad hoc about it. When Yahweh initiates the covenant with Abram, the first step he takes is to eliminate all of the circumstances that may have attached him to other gods (he is instructed to leave his land and his family). By doing this he fashions a new identity as "people of Yahweh" (*'am Yahweh*, where *'am* is a kinship term).

As we can see, across these categories relationships between gods and people are understood in a variety of ways in the ancient world. Israel participates in this cognitive environment in numerous ways, but its relationship is most distinct in the formalized way in which it is represented in the covenant and in the general absence of circumstantial aspects of relationship. Although high levels of continuity can be observed in the types of relationships and the metaphors used to express those types, we will find greater discontinuity as we turn attention to the way that the divine/human relationship *works* in Israel and the ancient Near East.

As we noted earlier, the divine/human relationship was not generally understood in psychological terms, despite the metaphors used and their occasional extension. In Israel, relationship to Yahweh was defined by the idea that it was chosen by God to be partners with him in carrying forward his plan and purposes. In the ancient Near East there is little attestation to a similar relationship between gods and people.[52] Nothing in the ancient Near East parallels the oft-intoned status found in the Old Testament: "I am/will be your God, and you are/will be my people."

Communication. Communication between the gods and people in the ancient Near East is rare and ad hoc, mostly because the communication is provided in oracular contexts. The gods manifest themselves in a variety of ways, but they do not communicate their specific will or general instructions. The gods have ordered the cosmos, and the people are supposed to conform to the expectations of an ordered cosmos (including society) and to be in

---

[52]In the Ancient Near East the gods made covenants with kings, but covenants with a people group were rare. In fact, at this writing only one example is known. A seventh-century Aramaic amulet from Arslan Tash reads, "Ashur has made an eternal covenant with us. He has made (a covenant) with us, along with all the sons of El and the leaders of the council of all the Holy Ones, with a covenant of the Heavens and Eternal Earth, with an oath of Ba'l" (*COS* 2.86, p. 223). Nevertheless, the distinctiveness is not just in the covenant relationship but what that covenant relationship accomplished (coidentity) and what it entailed (Torah, divine presence, revelation).

harmony with those expectations. The gods, however, are not forthcoming with information pertaining to how such conformity or harmony ought to be accomplished.

Israel's distinctiveness on this count, however, is evident in the revelation represented in the Torah and through the Prophets; such communication is one of the primary ways that Israel is enabled to carry out God's purposes. Yahweh is a more communicative god than the others, though he does not usually communicate through personal conversation. Yet the Israelites were no different from those who lived around them (and all of us, for that matter) in wishing that they had more communication from God. Nevertheless, given the increased level of information from God in Israel, we can identify his communicative tendencies as representative of a higher relationality than the gods of the ancient Near East.

But when we turn attention to the communication from the people to their gods, no notable difference exists. Israelite prayers are not more frequent or more intimate, nor different in nature from what we would find among the people of the ancient Near East. Differences in content can be identified based on the Israelites' different perceptions about deity, but these differences do not indicate a difference in relationship.

Motivated by love and respect rather than fear and need. The most fundamental aspect of relationship can be discerned through an analysis of what motivates the relationship. In the ancient Near East, would the people have desired to be in relationship with the gods if they did not fear what would happen if the gods abandoned them? Would they even be inclined to pay attention to the gods if they did not need that which they believed only the gods could provide? Admittedly, it is difficult to assess the inner mind of a people so distantly removed from our time, place, and culture, but from every indication available from the literature, it was the Great Symbiosis that dominated the religious mind of the ancient Near East. The system was driven by need and fear.

Important distinctions also arise when we evaluate the reasons for which the ancients believed humanity was created. As will be developed in the next chapter, in the ancient Near East at large, people believed they were created to be the servants of the gods—to do the work necessary to provide for the needs of the gods. This mentality is central to what we have designated as the Great Symbiosis. In the Old Testament, by contrast, people were created by God to be in relationship with him (see development in chapter three). Mutual service (= Great Symbiosis) is one sort of relationship, but the Old Testament indicates that Yahweh has something more in mind for his people.

How can this advanced level of relationship be described? There can be no doubt that Israelite practice often reflected a Great Symbiosis mentality, but the testimony of the Old Testament decries the legitimacy of such a mindset. Yes, the Israelites were called on to "fear the Lord," and at times this command included fear of harsh reprisal should their ritual performance be flawed (Lev 10:1-3). But such a fear was not intended to dominate the relationship; it was, instead, to be based on love and respect. The fear of the Lord is only the *beginning* of wisdom. And, in turn, Yahweh's interaction with Israel was not based on the reciprocal exchange of benefits. Rather, the replacement for the Great Symbiosis in the Old Testament approach is the Great Enterprise. This enterprise is defined by Yahweh's plans and purposes in the cosmos in which Israel participates. Israel's role is, at least in part, founded on obedience—the observance of Torah—which brings us to our last point of consideration.

Performance and the role of obedience. In order to address the issue of obedience, we must consider what commandments or instructions were made known that the people were expected to obey. We have already noted the paucity of communication from the gods in the ancient Near East, which generates the question, What was there to obey in the ancient Near East? The heart of the Great Symbiosis is the performance of ritual, but such performance could be considered obedience only in the most general terms. Specific instructions were not given. Rituals were considered elements of obedience because the gods demanded such rituals in general, but which rituals, when, and how were all matters of traditions and priestly instructions and, perhaps more importantly, priestly performance.

In the ancient Near East no one could "obey the commands of the gods" except for those commands that were given through divination. In royal inscriptions, kings were said to obey the words of the gods (cf. Hammurabi, described as one who obeys [*šemû*] Shamash, presumably in the matters in which he believed that Shamash had given him instruction through oracles), but this type of circumstance is rare, even in royal inscriptions, and is unattested with regard to the general populace. In Amarna-period Egypt, obedience to the will of the god(s) is evident, though perhaps this type of obedience should be differentiated from obedience to the commands of a god. In Egypt, one of the most important expressions of relationship with the gods was found in the people's participation in the festivals in which the gods were perceived to walk among them.[53] Relationship, in this case, was expressed by service and loyalty: "Piety entailed remaining faithful to the town or city of one's god."[54] The values of Egyptian society (discipline, moderation, and subjection to the community) included silence as their central virtue, and in this manner piety was reflected as people submitted to the will of the gods.[55] In other words, doing good was an act of piety,[56] though not essentially an act of obedience. In the ancient Near East divine commands ordered the cosmos (both nature and society), but they did not dictate the specifics of human behavior. Humans were supposed to conform to the ordering of society, for such was the will of the gods, but this obligation is really a matter of conformity, not of obedience. Piety, in other words, is a matter of conforming to the order of the cosmos, and this conformity is how one exists in relationship with a deity or deities in the ancient mindset.

In Israel it is likely that the people also saw their ritual performance and behavior in society as upholding the order of the cosmos and conforming to the order established by God. But the explanation does not stop there. The testimony of the Old Testament is clear throughout each genre: obedience to the Torah is expected, is pursued (or tragically, not), and is the basis for Yahweh's blessing or judgment, though with some important caveats. Most importantly, we have to recognize that Yahweh does not need Israel's obedience; it adds nothing to him. God does not treat "good behavior" in the same way that the ancient Near Eastern gods treated rituals (even though the latter prophets do use that metaphor). Yahweh is not Santa Claus, and the "commandments" are not a revised symbiosis wherein we trade morality for blessing while a deity trades blessing for happiness.

Two aspects of this differentiation can be identified. First, we might note that the commands exist for our benefit—like a mother's command to her

---

[53] Assmann, *Mind of Egypt*, 231-32.
[54] Ibid., 233.
[55] Ibid., 235.
[56] Ibid., 239.

children not to play in the street. The motivation for the command is love, because the mother does not want her children to get hit by a truck. But her children do not want to get hit by a truck either, so this command is not part of any symbiosis. Second, since Israel is God's people, its behavior reflects on him, and the commands reflect the requirements for God's identity/honor as a result. If Israel does not represent him properly, he will have to represent himself by making an example of it. Again, there is no symbiosis here; it is simply a natural consequence of paired identity.[57]

The expectations given to Israel are detailed and specific (see discussion of the significance of those details in chapter five). Performance in Israel is an act of obedience, but obedience goes well beyond performance because it entails a response to the revelation of Yahweh and identifying with him in every way humanly possible.

SUMMARY

Many gods across the ancient world were considered incomparable, singular, unique in numerous ways, or as aggregating many gods in themselves. Similar statements about Yahweh are fundamental to Israelite theology and remain so in Christian theology today, but the concept of incomparability was not unique to Israel in the ancient world. What made Israelite theology stand out from the rest of the ancient world was the manner in which the divine community was understood. As we discussed, the polytheistic system of the ancient Near East framed the ways in which the gods lived and acted in community. Yahweh's community, on the other hand, was reframed both by the diminished status of the members of the divine council and, more importantly, by the formation of a community for himself by covenant relationship to his people Israel. This covenant proves to be the most distinguishing feature of Old Testament theology. Through it the people were brought into the divine community, made parties to a covenant with their God, and drawn into the identity of Yahweh as they were designated holy as he is holy.

The people of Israel were God's people. Other gods dwelled *among* people, but they were not prone to claim a people group as *their* own. However,

---

[57]Ideas provided by J. Harvey Walton.

Yahwism added a dynamic that went far beyond what was understood by "divine presence" in the rest of the ancient Near East. As party to this unique idea of community and identity, Israel was expected to be exclusivistic in its worship—an idea unmatched in its particularity in the rest of the ancient world. The thrust of Old Testament theology, then, flowed through this truth. In turn, Yahweh revealed his ways (to them and through them) and redeemed them, aspects that were also unmatched in particularity throughout the rest of the ancient world.

In the ancient Near East gods were considered creators and warriors, much as Yahweh was considered in Israel. Nevertheless, in both arenas, the emphasis that was part and parcel of the ancient cognitive environment differs significantly from our own. The ancient world, for example, emphasized order in creation, whereas we tend to focus on material origins in our discussions of creation. Moreover, we rarely give any thought to Yahweh as warrior, except in the vaguest, abstract, individual terms; we never think of him in national warfare contexts.

The expectations the gods had for human behavior were not very different in the ancient world from what we find in the pages of the Old Testament, but the basis for the behavior is distinct in numerous ways. Israel's behavior was connected to and derived from God's revelation of his purposes and identity. In the ancient Near East people refrained from killing one another because it disrupted order in society, and the gods required order. The same could be said of Israel, but we would have to add that, more importantly, Israelites were to refrain from killing one another less out of obedience to specific divine instructions and more because their perception of the nature of Yahweh would suggest that they, as his people, were required to hold a respect for life.

The ancient Near Eastern performance of ritual also demonstrates many similarities with the details of Israelite traditions (more to come in later chapters). Nevertheless, the underlying premise for the rituals of the ancient Near East illustrates how differently Yahweh was understood in relation to the other gods. This distinction is made obvious by the Great Symbiosis in the rest of the ancient world, as compared to the blood rituals for cleansing sacred space in Israel.

In conclusion, the Old Testament consistently and uniquely maintains that Yahweh has chosen Israel as his people and has made it holy. As a result, Israel's worship of Yahweh ought to be exclusive. He dwells among the people, is in relationship with them, and has revealed himself to them and through them. They are expected to obey his instructions both individually and corporately. We need no further explanation for Yahweh's choice than that it represents his strategy to restore his presence to the world—a boon for all.

What enduring theology do we, as Christians, bring from the Old Testament about God? We believe that God is singular and unique and that he requires and deserves our exclusive worship. We believe that God has revealed his identity through his purposes and plans and that he is the Creator. We can believe that God is a warrior who fights on behalf of his people, whether metaphorically or tangibly and whether in the spiritual or earthly realms. Nevertheless, since Yahweh is not in covenant relationship with a national identity today, it is problematic to claim that "God is on our side" in modern-day warfare.

Even though Christians are in a different covenant relationship through the new covenant, the revelation of God in the Old Testament (of a covenant-making God who chooses a group of humans as his community) remains not only valid for us today but essential to our status and identity as the people of God. This new covenant puts us in relationship with God, as it did Israel, but it does so with a value-added element that will be discussed further below in the Christian distinctives. The relationship between our God and us can still be healthy, neutral, or dysfunctional, and the characteristics of our formalized relationship fall into the same categories we discussed above.

The theology of divine presence also pervades the Old Testament, and this theology endures in the Christian understanding today. We believe that God's presence is now in us through the indwelling of the Holy Spirit, but many Christians fail to move beyond this blunt fact. The Old Testament, however, can help us understand the far-reaching implications of the reality of living in the presence of God (more about this in the chapter five).

When we consider the picture of God as one who redeems his people, the enduring theology of the Old Testament concept of redemption should not be lost in the bright glow of Christ's redemption through his blood. The Old Testament picture of Yahweh as redeemer involves two aspects: restoring a person or group to a prior, normal status (*gʾl*) or freeing a person or group from a burden or obligation in an exchange of some sort (*pdh*). These aspects continue to be characteristic of God in his interactions with his people, beyond the salvation that we receive through Christ.

Christian reflections. Perhaps one of the least understood, appreciated, or practiced aspects of Old Testament theology among Christians today is holiness. We know that holiness has been conferred on us because of numerous New Testament references (passages such as Rom 11:16; 12:1; 1 Cor 1:2; Eph 1:4; Col 3:12; 1 Thess 3:13; 4:4, 7; 2 Tim 1:9; Titus 1:8; Heb 10:10; 12:14; 1 Pet 1:15; 2:9; and 2 Pet 3:11). Yet we often make the mistake of equating holiness with a pious disposition. The Old Testament can help us correct this misperception. Holiness is in fact a conferred status, an identity we receive in our relationship with God. To "be holy" is not to achieve a status but to live a life worthy of that status. By identifying ourselves in accordance with the status of "holy," we can get a better idea about what constitutes "holiness."

The qualities that characterize God and that were expected of the Israelites (and even in the ancient Near East) have not changed. They are well represented in the New Testament, particularly in the convenient list of the fruits of the Spirit. These "fruits" are related to how God's people are to live lives worthy of a holy status and identity. Obedience still stands as an appropriate reflection of that relationship, even though the Torah is not the focus of our obedience (Mt 19:17; 1 Cor 7:19; 1 John).

In evangelical Christianity performance has often been undervalued and neglected. It has been perceived as the letter of the law or has been associated with the burden of the law, neither of which can save us. We need to remember that in our Christian faith we are in relationship with God through Christ *because* he saved us. Nevertheless, *relationship* is the goal; *salvation* is simply the means. This relationship is defined as the partnership that we have with God through Christ in the promotion of the kingdom of God, which stands as the core of God's purpose and plan. Performance has no role in salvation, of course, but it has a significant role in relationship. The sacrifices and rituals of the Old Testament played the role of relationship-building exercises. They provided culturally accommodated disciplines, routines, and focuses for an abstract idea that could otherwise be elusive, ethereal, and nebulous. But their performance was centered on the presence of God geographically located in sacred space. Now we can experience God's presence though his indwelling Spirit, through which we obtain the status of being "in Christ." Our performance, then, should be appropriately transformed, but not obviated. Elements of performance include all varieties of worship and prayer, as well as the observance of the Lord's Supper, baptism, sabbath (rightly understood; see chapter five), and recognized celebrations of the Christian calendar. *How* all of these performances are to take place is unstipulated, but *that* they should take place is simply sound theology. As in the Old Testament, we should be motivated by love and respect rather than by fear and need.

We should, however, exercise care and discretion before reading elements of New Testament theology into the Old Testament as if they belong there or are articulated there. For example, though in the New Testament Christians are encouraged to imitate Christ, the Old Testament has no comparable encouragement to imitate God. God's people are to follow the example of God by manifesting qualities that he values. Insofar as justice flows from God, we should be people who pursue justice. However, in the New Testament, we can be imitators of God as he is reflected in Christ (Eph 5:1-2; Phil 2:5-11).

As another example, we find nothing in the Old Testament about having a "personal relationship with God" in the way that it is often articulated in popular evangelical piety. Given that identity was found in the corporate community in the Old Testament, rather than in one's individualism, the relationship with Yahweh was through the *people* of Israel and reflected in the clan/family. We still see evidences of this mentality in the New Testament. The Philippian jailer, for example, makes a decision to follow Christ not only for himself but for his entire household as well (Acts 16:31-33).

How does the New Testament further develop the ideas in Old Testament theology? Just as the covenant is the basis of the distinction between the Old Testament and the ancient Near East, the new covenant is the basis for almost every distinction developed in the New Testament. Some of the highlights include:

✦ We are not redeemed from national crises; we are redeemed from *the* human crisis par excellence. We are redeemed from sin through the agency of Christ.

✦ Divine presence takes a quantum leap in the incarnation as the "Immanuel theology" brings God's presence among us in the flesh (Jn 1:14).

✦ Relationship, which had been provisionally available through the sacrificial system and Torah, is now established totally and permanently through Christ so that God's intention from the beginning for relationship is accomplished.

✦ The qualities that characterize God and that are desired by God are now available through the agency of the Spirit and are manifest as fruit of the Spirit.

✦ Added to the concept of God experiencing community with his people, we now learn of the community that exists ontologically in the triune Godhead.

These are developments based on new revelation and should not be sought or read into the Old Testament.

3

COSMOS
and
HUMANITY

Since Old Testament theology views the world in highly anthropocentric terms, it makes sense to consider the cosmos and humanity together in one chapter. According to the theology of the Old Testament, God created the world for humans. This theology, however, stands in contrast to the ancient Near Eastern idea that the gods created the cosmos for themselves. In this view, humans, as afterthoughts, were to function as slaves of the gods to ensure the cosmos would continue to serve the deities' needs.

Cosmos

Cosmic creation. We can unpack this significant distinction between the Old Testament and the ancient Near East by beginning with the way that we tend to think about a creator today. For modern, Western people, creation on the cosmic level is a material act. Matter that had not previously existed is brought into existence. It is also a one-time act; once the material object is created, it exists. In this way of thinking, existence is defined materially, and the Creator God's work is defined by the material objects he brings into existence, whether cells or stars. Yet even as we define our modern concept of existence, we must acknowledge the truth of the observation made by Ernst Käsemann that "Existence is always fundamentally conceived from the angle of the world to which one belongs."[1] Consequently, we need to ask what the ancients understood by existence. We should not be surprised to find that they think differently from how we do. For them the focus is not related to materiality but to order.

If we use the metaphor of a corporation, the modern view would compare the Creator to the founder of the corporation, who built the company and the physical plant that housed it. From the perspective of the ancient Near East, the corporate founder would certainly be considered Creator, but so would the CEOs who succeeded him or her, generation after generation, as each one reorganized the company and its structure under his or her control. The construction of the buildings, on the other hand, would have relatively little significance in the founding of the corporation.

Through this metaphor we discover that the role of Creator was not defined by a one-time material act in the ancient world. What *we* consider an initial material act in our worldview would certainly still be an act of creation. But in the ancient world, people were much more interested in the organization and ordering process—the founding of the cosmos.

In this ancient view of creation, any one-time material act was of little interest or significance because the ancients did not define existence materially. For them, something did not come into existence when it had materiality; it came into existence when it had been given a role, function, and purpose in an ordered system. Creation and existence found their significance in the spiritual dimension, not in the material one. Bringing order was the main job of the Creator, and it was something that was carried out continually, rather than as a one-time act. Divine agency was at work at every level every day as order was actively maintained. Thus the Egyptians viewed creation as taking place anew every day. However, this view of creation does not mean that they believed that all the material was destroyed every night when the sun went down. Rather, the sun was associated with order; darkness brought nonorder.

Within this view of creation, the levels of causation are also of less significance. Yes, only a Creator can call the material objects forth, but those

---

[1]E. Käsemann, *Perspectives on Paul* (Minneapolis: Fortress, 1971), 26. Admittedly, Käsemann is talking specifically about Paul's view of the "flesh" rather than the larger ontological issue I address here, but his observation pertains nonetheless.

material objects do not exist until they are integrated into an ordered system. The Creator's activity at every stage is part of being Creator. No distinction of significance would have been made between the initial creation of humankind and the creation of each individual human; the sun's first appearance would not have been more significant than its appearance each day. All are the acts of the Creator, and the level of his activity would be no less in one than in the other. Creating is not just an initial act; it is a full-time job. In the ancient world, people were much more interested in God/gods as agents than in the physical mechanisms of the cosmos themselves.

Today the category of "natural laws" pertains to the regularities of the modern world (e.g., laws of motion), and they are fixed, traceable, and relate to the material world. Though the ancients understood regularity, that regularity spoke of divine involvement. In fact, it was the very regularity of the cosmos that the gods were engaged in regulating. This mentality is true of the Israelites as well. The Old Testament does not speak of miracles (i.e., events to be characterized as "supernatural" as opposed to "natural"); it speaks of God's "signs and wonders." These signs and wonders, however, were manifestations of Yahweh's power, his care for his people, his superiority to other gods, and his ability to deliver. But they were no more to be distinguished as "supernatural" than the development of each child in the womb (Ps 139:13). Similarly, it is easy to see that in the biblical text, weather always reflects the activity of God. The winds do his bidding, and he sends the storm—always!

Of course, a modern explanation of natural causation does not preclude God's involvement, and the thinking about regularities in the ancient world included the relationships and behavior of material objects. However, ancient people were ultimately more interested in societal functions. In Mesopotamia, for example, the routine static aspects of the cosmos (their "natural laws") related mostly to the behavioral aspects of people—from larger institutions (e.g., kingship), to cultural phenomena (e.g., prostitution), to sporadic behavior (e.g., kissing), to abstractions (e.g., "dressing in black dress" or deceit), to technological capabilities (e.g., kindling fire), or to international relations (e.g., rebellious lands).[2] All of these situations, just like the

---

[2] All of these occur in a list of nearly one hundred such items in the Sumerian work *Enki and Inanna*, available through the ETCSL project, Faculty of Oriental Studies, University of Oxford,

workings of the human body, the movements of the stars in the sky, and the growth of crops, were regulated and administrated by the gods through the decrees that they made. These were considered the acts of creation.

We can therefore see that the creator god, according to the ancient world, does all that is necessary to order the cosmos and then preserve that order. The material cosmos is included, but its materiality is not the point. More attention is given to the way that the human world works, including the role the material cosmos has in ordering the human world. This ancient perspective on creation is not something that we would consider wrong (as we would the idea of a flat earth or solid sky); it is just different from how we think about creation.[3]

With this understanding of creator gods in the ancient Near East, we are now ready to turn attention to the Old Testament idea of Yahweh as Creator. Obviously, the Israelites thought Yahweh was the Creator, rather than Enlil, Marduk, Amun-Re, or Ptah. But did they have a different idea about what a Creator *did*? Were they more likely to think about the Creator in terms similar to our modern categories, with distinctions between natural and supernatural? Would they focus on the creation of material or on the bringing of order? Or would they configure the category of creation along the lines that were commonplace in the ancient world?

To address this issue, I use the metaphor of a cultural river. In our modern world we could easily describe the cultural river that is widely known. Among its currents we would identify ideas and ways of thinking such as human rights, freedom, capitalism, democracy, patriotism, individualism, globalism, postcolonialism, separation of church and state, postmodernism, and market economy, as well as elements associated with creation such as scientific naturalism, an expanding universe, empiricism, and natural laws, just to name a few. In more recent developments, social media has become a significant current in our cultural river. Though the United States may well be the primary source of the cultural river described here, it flows around the globe and affects many other cultures. Some may well wish to float in its currents,

---

http://etcsl.orinst.ox.ac.uk/cgi-bin/etcsl.cgi?text=t.1.3.1&charenc=j# (accessed April 1, 2017). See also Enki and World Order, also through the ETCSL project, http://etcsl.orinst.ox.ac.uk/cgi-bin/etcsl.cgi?text=t.1.1.3#.

[3]Of course, we still use this kind of thinking in other areas. A position in a company exists when its role is defined.

while others may struggle to swim upstream against them. However, all draw from the river's waters, though the shape the river takes in each culture shows a wide diversity. Nevertheless, we are all in the cultural river.

In the ancient world the cultural river flowed through all of the diverse cultures: Egyptians, Hittites, Phoenicians, Canaanites, Aramaeans, Assyrians, Babylonians—and the Israelites. Despite the variations from culture to culture and across the centuries, certain static elements remained. But those currents are not at all the currents found in our cultural river. In the ancient cultural river we would find currents such as identity within community, the comprehensive and ubiquitous control of the gods, the role of kingship, agro-pastoral economy, divination, the centrality of the temple, the mediatorial role of images, the reality of the spirit world and magic, mythological reality, and the movement of the celestial bodies as the communication of the gods, among others. The Israelites were also in that cultural river. They sometimes floated on its currents without resistance, while at other times the revelation of God encouraged them to step into the shallows or swim persistently upstream. Whatever their *interactions* with the cultural river, they were in *that* ancient cultural river, not in ours.

This metaphor can help us to formulate our approach to reading the Old Testament. God chose to communicate his revelation to Israelites through Israelite intermediaries. We often refer to those intermediaries as the "authors" of Scripture, though we recognize that much of the Old Testament was transmitted orally and that compilers at some point played an important role.[4] These intermediaries were fully immersed in the cultural river, as were their audiences. God communicated to them in the context of that cultural river, and they communicated to their audiences within that same framework. God's message, God's purposes, and God's authority were all vested in those communicators and took shape in their language and in their culture. We cannot be assured of authoritative communication through any other source, and we therefore find the message of God through the intermediaries who are situated in that ancient cultural river.

This means that if we are to interpret Scripture so as to receive the full impact of God's authoritative message, we have to leave our cultural river

---

[4]For detailed discussion, see John H. Walton and D. Brent Sandy, *The Lost World of Scripture* (Downers Grove, IL: InterVarsity Press, 2013).

behind and try to understand theirs. The communicators that we encounter in the Old Testament are not aware of our cultural river; they neither address it nor anticipate it. We cannot assume any of the constants or currents of our cultural river. The Bible is written for us (i.e., we are supposed to benefit from its divine message as we interact with our cultural river), but it is not written to us (not in our language or against our culture). The message transcends culture, but it is given in a form that is fully ensconced in the ancient cultural river of Israel. This message may well give us meaningful information as we think about our cultural river, but it does not address the specifics of our cultural river. The Bible does not address social media and its ills or benefits, but it does offer ideas about having wisdom when we speak to others and the power that words can have. It admonishes us to be cautious in what we say. It therefore helps us to think about our behavior as God's people without anticipation of the specifics of our cultural river.

As another example, the ancient cultural river had none of our modern science in it. Cosmic geography, physiology, meteorology, epidemiology, astronomy, and so on, as present in our cultural river, had their own unique shapes in their cultural river that show little resemblance to anything we would think. If we are going to interpret the Bible in a way that makes the power of God's authoritative message consistently and reliably accessible, we should be guided by methods that help us to understand the communication that God gave through the human intermediaries that he chose for the task. Since he communicated to them in terms of their own cultural river, we must read that communication within the context of that cultural river. That means that we cannot read it in light of our cultural river. The Bible does not make claims specific to our cultural river; it only makes claims with regard to its own cultural river.

As we have noted, in the ancient cultural river, of which we are informed though myriads of ancient Near Eastern texts, existence is less related to materiality and more to function with a role and purpose in an ordered system. The ordering of the cosmos is an act of creation (like we would speak of creating a corporation or a curriculum), and, in their river, it is the most important act of creation. This perspective is pervasive not only in cosmology texts but throughout the wide scope of literature, including, but not limited to, hymns, prayers, wisdom, incantations, and even historical

documents. Not only must we refrain from reading the Big Bang into ancient texts (including the Bible), but we must also refrain from reading a
material definition of existence and creation into the ancient texts. In that
cultural river, creation was always purposeful, and purpose is expressed in
ordering. Our interpretation of the authoritative message of Scripture must
derive from the biblical text on the basis of its own cultural river.

The profile of God as Creator in the Old Testament can now be constructed.
God does not create by defeating chaos; there is no battle to bring order.
Order is indeed the pivotal concept, but it is not achieved through conflict. It
is by his decree—no opposing forces, no enemies to overcome. Yet since
many of the traditions about creation in the ancient Near East also lack the
element of conflict, the Old Testament is not necessarily trying to argue
against the ancient Near Eastern viewpoint; it is simply giving its own account of creation and the Creator.[5] An analogy to this view of creation can
be found when we think about someone today moving into a new house. On
moving day, the house itself is ready to function according to its purpose
(roof, foundation, walls, electricity, plumbing, HVAC, etc.), but the furniture
has to be placed and the boxes unpacked. This is not a battle; it is just the task
of ordering with functionality and purpose in mind. The ordering is done
gradually and, in some sense, on a continuing basis. We can think of this as
creating the "home" rather than as creating (i.e., building) the "house."[6]

In the Old Testament, God certainly would have been considered the one
who built the house. But making the home is the more important job of the
Creator. People of the ancient Near East, including Israel, were more interested
in the home story, and Genesis 1 is that home story (as are all the other allusions to creation in the Old Testament and all the cosmology stories of the
ancient Near East). The "cultural river" of the ancient world features ordering
as the principal task of the Creator, and Israelites shared that perspective.

As Christians who take the Bible and faith seriously, the most important
distinction we need to draw is between agency and mechanism.[7] The Old
Testament teaching of God as Creator leads us to affirm the belief in divine

---

[5]For a more extensive discussion of the question of the Old Testament as polemical, see J. Walton,
"Polemics," in *Behind the Scenes of the Old Testament*, ed. J. Greer, J. Hilber, and J. Walton (Grand
Rapids: Baker, forthcoming).
[6]Notice that we even use the term *homemaker* for the continual job of maintaining the home.
[7]With thanks to April Maskiewicz.

Categories of Theomachy

✦ dissatisfied class revolt among the divine proletariat concerning roles

✦ order versus disorder in the macrocosmos (*Chaoskampf*)

   ◇ initial establishment of order (cosmogony)

   ◇ one-time threat from chaos monster

   ◇ renewal on a seasonal or daily basis

✦ struggle for rule among the gods between individual competing claimants

✦ generational coup seizing rule among the gods

✦ warfare against enemies of the people of the god

Dissatisfied class revolt among the divine proletariat concerning roles. Theomachy at this level occurs only in Mesopotamia in the ancient Near East, and it is most familiar from the major Akkadian epics, Atrahasis and Enuma Elish. In Atrahasis, insurrection among the gods results in the death of the ringleader. In Enuma Elish, the adversary must be defeated, which includes the ringleader, Kingu, and the champion, Tiamat (as well as her hordes). In these, the result is that humans are created to take over the work of the gods, and the role of the gods relative to labor is what is at stake. Nothing of this sort occurs in the Old Testament.

Order versus disorder in the macrocosmos (*Chaoskampf*). In the ancient cognitive environment, disorder loomed on numerous fronts. The joint task of gods and humans was to contain and combat the inclination toward disorder or the incursion of it into the ordered world. Order was first established at some point in the past, but that did not mean that the battle was over. Recurrent threats occurred both in the form of occasional attacks and in the seasonal and daily cycles. Though the legitimacy of applying the term *chaos* to these situations has been rightly contested, we can adopt it in the description of this category of theomachy with the important qualification that it pertains to elements representing macrocosmic disorder, whether they are personified or not. Given this qualification, we can now discuss three subcategories of *Chaoskampf.* All three of these subcategories have in common the feature that an adversary represents macrocosmic disorder, or at least nonorder. This type of adversary is what distinguishes the *Chaoskampf* category of theomachy from the others.

The first *Chaoskampf* subcategory is comprised of those texts in which macrocosmic order is being initially established (cosmogony). The classic piece of literature in this category is Enuma Elish, but it must be recognized that this is nearly the only piece of ancient literature with this feature.[a] Here Tiamat, the personified Sea, is the enemy, and cosmogony results. The only other example I have been able to locate in ancient literature is in a single line from the Egyptian Instruction of Merikare: "He [Re] made sky and earth for their sake; he subdued the water monster."[b] Again, the common ground in this category is that the adversary is the representative of the Sea, and macrocosmic order is established.

The difference in the second subcategory is that here an adversary arises who threatens an already established order among the gods and therefore, at least indirectly, in the macrocosmos.[c] Examples include a couple of little-known Akkadian tales (Nergal/Labbu;[d] Tishpak/Lion-Serpent[e]), as well as the more famous Akkadian tale of Ninurta and Anzu.[f] In the third subcategory the adversary threatens in regular cycles, usually associated with seasonal fertility, or in the daily appearance of the sun. The former is known from the Levant (Baal/Mot; Illuyanka) and the latter from Egypt (Apophis).

Struggle for rule among the gods between individual competing claimants. In this category of theomachy, the question to be resolved is which god is in charge. The adversary is an individual deity, and what is at stake is control of the divine realm. Enuma Elish fits into this category (the dispute between Kingu and Marduk), as well as other examples that can be identified throughout the ancient Near East: Seth and Horus in Egypt, Yamm and Baal in the Levant, and the Hittite Kumarbi Cycle. The adversary in these cases is positioned within the bureaucracy rather than within the cosmos per se. These accounts do not always involve actual combat, however, and the defeated adversary is not necessarily destroyed. These examples, moreover, do not represent cosmic conflict but political conflict.[g]

Generational coup seizing rule. In the Theogony of Dunnu the combat takes place as one generation of deity seeks to supplant the previous one. It is not the corporate younger generation pitted against the older ruling elites, but rather individual gods engaged in acts of conquest that include incest, patricide, and matricide.

Warfare against enemies of the people of the god. In this category we encounter many of the royal inscriptions of the Assyrians in which the god Aššur goes in the vanguard to fight the enemy. This category is represented in the Old Testament as Yahweh delivers his people from slavery in Egypt and as he fights on behalf of the kings of Israel.

---

[a]David Tsumura, *Creation and Destruction* (Winona Lake, IN: Eisenbrauns, 2005), 190.

[b]*COS* 1.35, line 131. This may also have to be discarded, however, if Lesko's translation has reason to be preferred: "He repelled the greed of the waters." See L. H. Lesko, "Ancient Egyptian Cosmogonies and Cosmology," in *Religion in Ancient Egypt*, ed. B. E. Shafer (Ithaca, NY: Cornell University Press, 1991), 103. The alternate reading offered by Lesko reflects the suggestion originally made by Posener that the word translated "monster" (*snk*, which occurs in all manuscripts of the work) is a metathesis for *skn* ("greed"). See J. Hoffmeier, "Some Thoughts on Genesis 1 & 2 and Egyptian Cosmology," *Journal of the Ancient Near Eastern Society* 15 (1983): 29-39, n90.

[c]It is certainly possible also to view the threat from Tiamat in Enuma Elish in this category. The difference is that, in the examples included here, cosmogony does not result.

[d]B. R. Foster, *Before the Muses*, 3rd ed. (Bethesda, MD: CDL, 2005), 495-97, 579-80. See discussion in T. Lewis, "CT 13.33-34 and Ezekiel 32: Lion-Dragon Myths," *Journal of the American Oriental Society* 116 (1996): 28-47.

[e]Foster, *Before the Muses*, 581-82.

[f]Ibid., 555-78. Other minor Ninurta battles may be included here, e.g., Ninurta and Azag.

[g]N. Wyatt, *Myths of Power: A Study of Royal Myth and Ideology in Ugaritic and Biblical Tradition*, Ugaritisch-biblische Literatur 13 (Münster: Ugarit-Verlag, 1996); N. Wyatt, "Arms and the King: The Earliest Allusions to the Chaoskampf Motif and Their Implications for the Interpretation of the Ugaritic and Biblical Traditions," in *'Und Mose schrieb dieses Lied auf. . . .' Studien zum Alten Testament und zum Alten Orient: Festschrift für O. Loretz*, Alter Orient und Altes Testament 250 (Münster: Ugarit-Verlag, 1998), 833-82. See the careful assessment of the *Chaoskampf* motif in Tsumura, *Creation and Destruction*, 143-97; and Rebecca S. Watson, *Chaos Uncreated: A Reassessment of the Theme of "Chaos" in the Hebrew Bible* (Berlin: de Gruyter, 2005).

---

agency that permeates the Old Testament. Whatever happened, God is the agent. Though our modern interests focus on mechanisms of creation, the Old Testament does not address mechanism. That question is not a constituent part of ancient people's understanding of creation or of God's role. Conversely, modern science can offer little information regarding agency one way or another, but it has a lot to say about mechanism. A wide range of explanations of mechanism are available to those of us who affirm God's agency. So, creation is about agency; evolution and other scientific explanations can only legitimately speak about mechanisms.[8]

Israel, then, would have identified the Creator differently, but it would not have had a different sort of "job description" for the Creator than was common in the cultural river of the ancient Near East. Since "creation" pertains to the act of bringing transition between existence and nonexistence, the Israelite view of the Creator and his work would also have included the view in the ancient cultural river of existence as it related to order and purpose rather than to material. Yahweh is the one who gave (and continues to give) shape, organization, order, and purpose to the cosmos, including people and the society in which they live. In this, Israelite creation theology was much closer to that of the rest of the ancient world than it is to ours. Besides the difference in the identification of the creator god, the only other major difference between Israel and the Babylonians (as an example) would have been that the Babylonians would have thought that the static elements of the cosmos, while regulated by the decrees of the gods, had not been initiated by the gods. Instead, those aspects were relegated to the realm of the metadivine. Israel would have considered Yahweh as the initiator of these static elements as well as the one who regulated them through his decrees.[9]

One aspect of creation that is occasionally found in ancient literature is connected to conflict, by which order is established in the face of opposing forces. To explore this facet of the ancient cultural river, we need to investigate the concept of divine combat. In the cognitive environment of the ancient Near East, the gods become involved in combat (referred to as theomachy) under a variety of circumstances and at various levels: among themselves, on an individual or corporate level, with entities or nonentities representing threat(s), or with humans.[10] The nature of the adversary and the stakes of the

---

[8]See R. Asher, *Evolution and Belief* (Cambridge: Cambridge University Press, 2012), 6.

[9]For discussion and many textual examples, see J. Walton, *Genesis 1 as Ancient Cosmology* (Winona Lake, IN: Eisenbrauns, 2011), 46-66.

[10]Major discussions include Bernhard W. Anderson, *Creation Versus Chaos* (New York: Association, 1967); Debra S. Ballentine, *The Conflict Myth and the Biblical Tradition* (Oxford: Oxford University Press, 2015); Bernard F. Batto, *Slaying the Dragon* (Louisville: Westminster John Knox, 1992); John Day, *God's Conflict with the Dragon and the Sea* (Cambridge: Cambridge University Press, 1985); Carola Kloos, *Yhwh's Combat with the Sea* (Leiden: Brill, 1986); Susan Niditch, *Chaos to Cosmos* (Atlanta: Scholars Press, 1985); David Tsumura, *Creation and Destruction* (Winona Lake, IN: Eisenbrauns, 2005); Mary K. Wakeman, *God's Battle with the Monster* (Leiden: Brill, 1973); Rebecca S. Watson, *Chaos Uncreated: A Reassessment of the Theme of*

conflict must be addressed, however, before decisions can be made about what role theomachy played in the cognitive environment.

The results of this analysis (as evidenced in the sidebar) are largely negative, which demonstrates the elements that should not be considered standard ingredients in the cognitive environment. For example, neither Canaan nor Egypt has a revolt of the gods; they only have occasional examples of one god challenging another god. Enuma Elish, as another example, merges three categories of theomachy: dissatisfied class struggle, which is resolved by the creation of humankind; macrocosmic chaos, which is represented in Tiamat's involvement and resolved in cosmogony; and struggle for rule, which is represented in Kingu's possession of the tablet of destinies and resolved in Marduk's ascension to the throne. In this way Enuma Elish should be viewed as an idiosyncratic conglomerate of theomachy categories (rather than as a foundational cosmogonic paradigm, as it is sometimes presented).

As noted in the earlier discussion of divine warrior (chapter two), in the rare instances in the Hebrew Bible in which Yahweh battles with the forces of nature that could be linked to nonorder, the better description is "Lord of the cosmos" rather than *Chaoskampf*. Divine kingship is the issue, not creation per se.

Having discussed the similarities (e.g., focus on order) and the differences (e.g., no creation through conflict) between Israelite thinking and that of the ancient world, we are now in a position to address briefly how we should think about the creation narratives—beginning with how we should think about the question of genre. Often this discussion turns immediately to the options of "history" or "mythology." But these options represent a false and misleading dichotomy that is deeply immersed in our modern cultural river. The discussion is further impeded by our modern categories and definitions. However, the ancient cultural river cannot so easily be manipulated into our categories of thought to address the distinctions we wish to make.

To begin, then, it is important to recognize that the ancient world evidences nothing quite like our modern history writing (with its methods, objectives, and literary forms).[11] Consequently, rather than identifying narratives in the

---

"Chaos" in the Hebrew Bible (Berlin: de Gruyter, 2005). This discussion is excerpted and abridged from my published article "Creation in Gen 1:1–2:3 and the Ancient Near East: Order Out of Disorder After Chaoskampf," *Calvin Theological Journal* 43 (2008): 48-63.

[11]For example, we might differentiate between "historiography as a science" and "historiography as a narrative."

Old Testament or the ancient Near East as "historical" or as "historiography," it is better to refer to them as narratives that use real events in the human world as their referents. Texts that we often label "mythological" are not very interested in events, but they nonetheless address what was considered reality by the people who crafted them. In the ancient world, cosmological texts fit into this latter category, and so we may describe them as narratives that use perceived cosmological reality as their referent. The realities conveyed in these texts transcend the events of history; their purpose is to convey metaphysical realities. To them, the events of history represent only a small slice of reality, and arguably not the most important slice. Reality, to the ancient mind, is a much larger category than that of "event."

In the Old Testament the cosmological texts operate in respect to that same sphere of reality.[12] They offer an understanding of the cosmos that transcends events. We often refer to them as "origins" accounts, but it would be more accurate to think of them as "identity" accounts. "Mythology" would be a misleading label, however, because it is a modern label and suffers from the baggage that relates it to our modern cultural river. But as in the ancient world, the cosmology of Israel transcends the confinement of events and portrays a larger reality. When the Israelites wrote about events, those events consistently found their meaning in the dimension of divine activity, and it is this belief and perspective that gave events intelligibility.[13] It is no surprise, then, that when the Israelites wrote about cosmology, even though their focus was not on events, they offered a view of reality that rendered the cosmos intelligible on a spiritual level. This spiritual level is what makes the account a more important reality.

The reality that the ancient authors sought to convey focuses on Yahweh's role as the one who has created by bringing order to the cosmos. That order is not different from the concepts found in the ancient world, but it could, perhaps, be identified as different in degree. Yahweh orders the cosmos, but not just at the mundane functional level, as in the ancient Near East. The other gods order the cosmos to function for themselves, and people merely

---

[12]For more extensive discussion, see John Walton and Tremper Longman III, *The Lost World of the Flood* (Downers Grove, IL: InterVarsity Press, forthcoming).

[13]J. Assmann, *The Mind of Egypt* (New York: Metropolitan, 2002), 242-43. This is the same as in the ancient Near East.

function as cogs in the machinery (see more below). But in the Old Testament, Yahweh orders the cosmos to serve people, not himself, and it is ordered to be sacred space (by virtue of his presence there). When he rests (Ex 20:8-11), he takes up his residence and his rule in terrestrial sacred space (Ps 132:13-14; more about this below).

HUMANITY

Human role and origins. *Image of God.*[14] If we want to derive the enduring theology from the Old Testament with regard to how we should think about ourselves and all of humanity, we must begin with an understanding of the information the Old Testament offers from its ancient Near Eastern perspective. In both the Old Testament and the ancient Near East, this task involves understanding the image of God. Here, as is almost always the case, we will find similarity between the Old Testament and the ancient Near East on the surface level but will find significant differences in the details.

In the ancient Near East the image of God can be explored using three different but related lenses:

✦ the image of the god that is manufactured to manifest his presence—the cult image

✦ the image of the god that is found in people (almost always the king)

✦ the image of the king that is represented in reliefs and statues and used in a variety of ways

Each of these lenses can offer us insight into how the image of God was conceived in the ancient world. The cult image of the gods was intended to function as a means by which the divine presence could be encountered on

---

[14]Most important resources: Z. Bahrani, *The Graven Image* (Philadelphia: University of Pennsylvania Press, 2003); Angelika Berlejung, "Washing the Mouth: The Consecration of Divine Images in Mesopotamia," in *The Image and the Book*, ed. K. van der Toorn (Leuven: Peeters, 1997), 45-72. E. Curtis, "Man as the Image of God in Genesis in the Light of Ancient Near Eastern Parallels" (PhD diss., University of Pennsylvania, 1984); W. R. Garr, *In His Own Image and Likeness: Humanity, Divinity, and Monotheism* (Leiden: Brill, 2003); S. L. Herring, *Divine Substitution: Humanity as the Manifestation of Deity in the Hebrew Bible and the Ancient Near East* (Münster: Vandenhoeck & Ruprecht, 2013); C. McDowell, *The Image of God in the Garden of Eden: The Creation of Mankind in Genesis 2:5–3:24 in Light of the* mis pi, pit pi *and* wpt-r *Rituals of Mesopotamia and Ancient Egypt* (Winona Lake, IN: Eisenbrauns, 2015); J. R. Middleton, *The Liberating Image* (Grand Rapids: Brazos, 2005); R. S. Peterson, *The Imago Dei as Human Identity: A Theological Interpretation* (Winona Lake, IN: Eisenbrauns, 2016).

earth. The image and the god were thereby coidentified. But it was understood that the image was not the god; it was a manifestation of the god. As such, it was thought that the image was born in heaven and made on earth to be a visible presence of the god (just as the stars were visible manifestations of the gods in the heavens). The image mediated the presence of the god to the people and mediated the worship given to the god from the people. The image was chosen by the god, commissioned by the god, and functioned on behalf of the god. It was not a separate entity functioning on behalf of the god, but it was one of the means by which the god functioned on earth. The image was furthermore given a status in the divine realm.

The image of the deity was also at times connected to people, but in almost every case it referred specifically to the king. In the Egyptian Instruction of Merikare, the only extant exception, all people are referred to as the images of the god. But when the king is referred to as the image of god, the title is applied to a particular king individually in an archetypal manner—that is, the identification is inherent in the office. Therefore, when a king ascends to the throne at coronation, a status is conferred on him by virtue of the office that he has attained. In this category, then, the image is seen as both representational and functional. The king is sponsored by the divine patron and therefore represents the god on earth. He also theoretically functions on behalf of the god; they are in a formal partnership. And this partnership is sometimes articulated through a written covenant and often formulated using filial language as the king is portrayed as the son of the god. By his patronage, then, the god has identified with the king, and the king, in turn, has identified with the god.

In the third category, when the king sets up an image in a temple, in a vassal town, or at the border of a territory, the idea is that the image stands there as a substitute for the king. It means that the king is to be considered present with his image, even when he is somewhere else.

From these briefly summarized examples, we can observe that the concept of image in the ancient world expressed ideas of function, substitution, representation, mediation, status, and identity. In no case was the ideology focused on a physical resemblance or on characteristic abilities, though its aesthetics were symbolic of the god's qualities. So, for example, the king was not identified as the image of god because he happened to have certain characteristics that the god also had or that he had been given by the god. The king "stepped in" to his identity when he ascended to the throne. In a similar way, the cult image of the god was transformed through rituals that enabled it to function in its mediatorial role, but it offered no information about the physical appearance of the god.

On the basis of these observations, we can now explore how the Old Testament develops the idea of the image of God and how its ideas are similar to and different from those of the ancient Near East. Based on the ancient Near Eastern background that has been referred to above, we can recognize that the idea of the image of God would not have been new to the Israelite audience—it is a prominent current in the ancient cultural river. They were well aware of such a category, and the text will likely express how they were supposed to think about this familiar concept.

The first time this concept appears in the text, we find that people (including male and female) have been conferred the status of "the image of God."[15] I have been using *status* to refer to something that is conferred on someone and about which they have no choice. In contrast, *identity* reflects how they choose to see themselves and what they want others to see in them. The image of God in the Old Testament is therefore seen as a status given by God. So in conferring the status, God identifies people with him. In doing so, he is revealing the identity that humans should adopt if they want to conceive of themselves in a way that will allow them to properly understand how they should live in order to serve the purpose for which God has created them. People can choose to identify as the image of God or not, but their choice does not change their status. The status is expressed as corporate (since all people by virtue of being people are included).[16] Consequently, we are not individually his images; we are corporately his image.

However, the categories that we developed in the ancient Near Eastern context also hold well here in the Old Testament. The idea that people corporately, as God's image, function alongside him to carry out his purpose is seen in Genesis 1:28, where humanity is granted the role of subduing and ruling the earth. These roles bring humanity into partnership with God as he

---

[15]Considerable scholarly debate has surrounded the use of the prepositions (*in* and *like*), which is not insignificant but which will not have an effect on this discussion.

[16]The corporate aspect is specified in Gen 1:27; 5:1-2; 9:6.

continues his creative work of bringing order. Aspects of substitution, representation, and the mediation of God's presence can all be generally discerned, though it would be difficult to cite texts that specifically identify those elements. At the same time, we can see that there is no cause in either the text or the ancient world for viewing the image of God in terms of psychological or neurological categories. The text does not address the issues that are distinctive to our cultural river. It is true that the Old Testament would see the image of God as differentiating us from animals (Gen 9 is clear on that), but any capability that we recognize as distinguishing ourselves from animals (e.g., self-awareness, conscience, awareness of mortality, and ability to think metaphysically) cannot thereby be considered the image of God. These characteristics may be thought of as capacities that God has given that enable us to function in our role, but the image is a status, not a set of capabilities.

The ancient Near Eastern context, alongside information from the Old Testament, also leads us to the conclusion that the image of God should not be defined by a list of things that we may have in common with God. We may talk about God being relational just as we are, but that similarity does not establish "relationality" as the image of God (though that does not preclude the image of God setting us in relationship to God). The same is true of a category such as "capable of emotions." These perspectives reflect more of our cultural river than that which is found in the ancient world or in the text of the Old Testament. Finally, we may also conclude, based on this evidence, that the image of God in the Old Testament does not refer to physical resemblance.

The main difference we find between the Old Testament and the ancient Near East lies in what has been referred to as the democratization of the image of God in the Old Testament. All humanity is conferred this status and therefore has this role. As we appropriate this theology for today, we can immediately set aside any consideration of whether certain individuals have the image of God or not. Whether someone is spiritually unregenerate, physically limited, mentally incapacitated, old or young, high functioning or low functioning, all who are human have the status "image of God." The image is not genetic or biological. We cannot lose it or fail to achieve it. As long as we are human, we are part of the corporate image of God.[17] It is

---

[17]At the same time, all of this does not help us to define what counts as "human."

humanity as a whole that functions to bring order, that represents the presence of God on earth, and that has the God-given status. In this way, the image of God can be compared to the New Testament concept of the body of Christ. None of us individually is the body of Christ, but we are all part of the body of Christ. Similarly, none of us individually is the image of God; we are all part of corporate humanity, which is the image of God.

This corporately conferred status also differentiates the Old Testament understanding of humanity from the ancient Near Eastern understanding of humanity. The status humanity is given in the ancient Near East is that of slaves (at best servants) created to meet the needs of the gods (more on this below). In Old Testament theology, however, humanity is given the role of vicegerent in carrying out God's purposes and is made steward of all that God has created. This was a paradigm shift for Israel, and it is taken up as a theological affirmation that continues to shape how we think about ourselves today in relationship to God.

Theological anthropology. It is common today for people to adopt the tripartite view that human personhood comprises body, soul, and spirit. This view is developed in conjunction with various Greek philosophical influences and is often seen as representing a position developed in the New Testament (1 Thess 5:23), though its technicalities (both metaphysical and semantic) are widely debated and were never universally adopted in Christian history (a bipartite view, body and soul, also enjoys popularity). But we cannot begin our conversation there. We have to examine ancient Near Eastern concepts and then compare Old Testament concepts without filtering them through later theology.

In the ancient Near East we find widely diverse views about personhood. Egyptians, like Israelites, at times portray the person as brought to life by the divine breath. But in Egyptian thinking, human nature is composed of the body (*djet*-body, as well as the *ha'u*-body), the *akh*, the *ka,* and the *ba,* and designations such as heart, belly, shadow, and name.[18] The terms *ka* and *ba* are impossible to translate adequately into English (or to Greek or Latin) because they do not have equivalent ideas in Western culture. In general, the internal *ka* expresses connectivity to the divine and to future generations. It is associated with one's personality and character. The external *ka* was like

---

[18]J. Assmann, "Dialogue Between Self and Soul: Papyrus Berlin 3024," in *Self, Soul and Body,* ed. A. Baumgarten, J. Assmann, and G. Stroumsa (Leiden: Brill, 1998), 384.

an invisible twin that was born when the person was born and that continued to exist in the afterlife. In contrast, the *ba* is associated with mental and cognitive capabilities. It is associated with a person's exterior self that is part of community, the persona projected to others. It is independent of the body and, in the form of one's reputation, remains behind after one dies. The gods also possess a *ba*, and that is what is considered present in the image of the deity. After death, a person's *ka* exists in the netherworld, their *ba* remains behind in the human realm, and their *akh* is represented in the form of the person's ghost (but more like their "spirit" than their "shade").

In Mesopotamia, the Epic of Atrahasis provides the most information about the composition of personhood.[19] Information from that piece of literature suggests that the various ingredients used to create humankind correspond to the various aspects of human nature. According to the interpretation of T. Abusch, the human ghost (*eṭemmu*) derives from the flesh of the god, while the blood (*dāmu*) of the god provides the human intellect (*ṭēmu*), self, or soul.[20] For example, "The blood is the dynamic quality of intelligence, and the flesh is the form of the body that is imposed on the clay."[21]

Nevertheless, to understand the Israelite view, we have to explore the usage of the two key terms: *nepeš* and *rûaḥ*. In general, a distinction has been proposed that the *nepeš* feels and senses, while the *rûaḥ* acts.[22] It is difficult to demonstrate that a person has his/her own *rûaḥ*. Rather, each person has God's *rûaḥ*,[23] which sustains human life (Job 34:14; Ps 104:29). The *rûaḥ* of all creatures returns to God because it is his.[24]

In contrast, the *nepeš* is given by God to all living creatures.[25] H. W. Wolff observes, "Man does not *have* [*nepeš*], he *is* [*nepeš*], he lives as [*nepeš*]."[26]

---

[19]T. Abusch, "Ghost and God: Some Observations on a Babylonian Understanding of Human Nature," in *Self, Soul and Body in Religious Experience*, ed. Baumgarten, Assmann, and Stroumsa, 363-83.

[20]Ibid.

[21]Ibid., 371-72.

[22]In general, see H. J. Fabry, "רוּחַ," in *TDOT* 13:365-402. Akkadian and Sumerian have no cognates for *rûaḥ*. The Ugaritic cognate is not as clearly or as essentially an anthropological term.

[23]Ibid., 386-87; note esp. Job 27:3-4. Most ambiguous on this point is Zech 12:1.

[24]Ibid., 387-88.

[25]For *nepeš*, see R. C. Steiner, *Disembodied Souls* (Atlanta: SBL Press, 2015), which also contains helpful information on ancient Near Eastern terms. See also H. Seebass, "נֶפֶשׁ," in *TDOT* 9:515-16, and the seminal work, H. W. Wolff, *Anthropology of the Old Testament* (Philadelphia: Fortress, 1974).

[26]Wolff, *Anthropology of the Old Testament*, 10. At the same time, we recognize that one's *nepeš* is described as being inside (Gen 1:30; 2 Sam 1:9).

This is supported by expressions such as the one found in Genesis 2:7, where Adam becomes a living *nepeš*. In rare and potentially contradictory occurrences in which the *nepeš* departs (Gen 35:18) or returns (1 Kings 17:22), it need not refer to a distinct soul or ghost; it could refer to a person's ceasing to be a "person."[27] The Israelites would likely think that a comatose person's *nepeš*, for example, had departed.[28] Nevertheless, God is the source of this "selfhood." Evidence that *nepeš* does not refer to anything like a soul distinct from the body can be deduced from the fact that God is also characterized as *nepeš* (e.g., Is 1:14; not as *rûaḥ* ["spirit"], though his *rûaḥ* is given to humans). In anatomical usage, the *nepeš* is the throat. In the metaphysical realm, the *nepeš* is that which experiences life and represents living (notice that the life, *nepeš*, is in the blood, Lev 17:11, and the blood is the *nepeš*, Deut 12:23). In the plural, it can refer to persons and is often related to the "self."[29] When a person stops breathing (dead, surprised, shocked, comatose, etc.), the *nepeš*, that vital force that makes one a person or self, is lost.

However, we have yet to determine whether the Israelites believed that the *nepeš* goes to the netherworld.[30] On the strength of the admittedly tenuous example of Psalm 16:10 and on the facts that (1) texts never suggest that the *nepeš* ceases to exist and (2) some remnant of the person is evidently considered to be present in the netherworld, I would be inclined to accept (tentatively) the idea that the *nepeš* makes its way to the netherworld. By adopting this conclusion, I am not thereby suggesting a return to the idea that a person *has* a *nepeš*. It is the body that is extraneous to personhood. During life, a person is a *nepeš* encased in a body. When the body dies, the *nepeš*, the person, makes its way to the netherworld through the tomb.

It is possible to lose *nepeš* without losing *rûaḥ*, but when you lose the latter, you also lose the former. When someone dies, their *rûaḥ* returns to God, and

---

[27]For the case that the *nepeš* is not the same as "life," see Steiner, *Disembodied Souls*, 69.

[28]Supported by Song 5:6, where the speaker describes herself metaphorically as virtually comatose, breathless, or fainting. See the helpful discussion in Steiner, *Disembodied Souls*, 70. Seebass prefers "vital force" (*TDOT* 9:515). At the same time, sometimes it is the *rûaḥ* that departs or returns (Judg 15:19; 1 Sam 30:12); see Steiner, *Disembodied Souls*, 81.

[29]In this semantic range, the Hebrew *nepeš* overlaps considerably with Akkadian *napištu* (*CAD* N/1: 296-304).

[30]Seebass thinks it does not. See *TDOT* 9:515-16, citing lack of evidence; Steiner thinks it does once the body has deteriorated in the tomb. See Steiner, *Disembodied Souls*, 106-9. But his most important information is Talmudic and supported by Second Temple period evidence that, he contends, may be extrapolated back to the Iron Age.

their *nepeš* (arguably) goes to the netherworld. In the netherworld, the problem is that the personality (*nepeš*) is retained but is not energized (*rûaḥ*).[31]

For our purposes, however, this conclusion will not carry a lot of weight. The Old Testament is not informing the Israelites about the proper structure of theological anthropology, particularly with regard to the authoritative biblical position about *nepeš* or *rûaḥ*; it is using those terms, which are well known to the audience, in appropriate contexts. It is not offering divine revelation concerning the proper, theological understanding of the terms or the true way to think about the metaphysical components of a human; it is only engaging the Israelite audience with the use of familiar terminology. In other words, by using these terms, the text is not affirming a particular theological anthropology for all readers to adopt. The terms simply represent the cognitive framework for communication, and characters use them to express their beliefs.

It has always been recognized that an important distinction must be made between the beliefs of the characters and the inspired message of the text. The Israelite terms do not find strong parallels with either Egyptian or Mesopotamian terminology. Yet the cognitive environment suggests that all of them tended to focus more on theological and functional categories than on psychological or philosophical ones (indeed, they do not have these latter categories). In all of this, we continue to be hampered by the likelihood that we have no English categories or words to adequately capture these ancient terms.

Even if we are right that the Old Testament offers no resolution to the component parts of humans and offers only an Israelite perspective (however distinct it may be from that of their neighbors), rather than a divine clarification, the metaphysical silence does not leave us empty of meaningful biblical ideas. The enduring theology that we can draw from the Old Testament is that regardless of how the metaphysical components are understood or identified, humans are given life, breath, personhood, identity, and being by God. We are given no insight about theological issues such as personal eschatology, metaphysical issues such as the location or nature of the self, or biological issues such as when the developing fetus becomes a person. All of these are questions rooted in our modern cultural river and are not addressed by the biblical text. Nevertheless, all that we are derives from God.

---

[31]Today represented in ideas of artificial intelligence, with its forerunner imitation of AI in Apple's Siri.

Origins. When we think about human origins today, we generally ask questions with regard to scientific issues: biology, genetics, anthropology, biochemistry, and so on. This is understandable in our world and is expressive of our cultural river. But in the ancient world, people had no such disciplines, no such knowledge, and no such interests. Throughout the ancient world, accounts of human origins demonstrate their keen interest in human identity, particularly as it relates to the divine world. Their focus is on how human *identity* is formed, rather than on how the human body or species came to exist materially. We can therefore conclude that these texts are more interested in what we classify as anthropology than in biology.

One interesting example can be seen in a Babylonian piece that concerns the creation of the king.[32]

> 31'   You are Belet-ili, mistress of the great gods,
>   You are the one who made the human-man:
>   Make a king, a counsellor-man,
>   Adorn his whole body with excellence.
> 35'   See to his features, make fair his body.

Then Belet-ili fulfills her commission, with the major gods contributing specific attributes:

> They gave the king warfare on behalf of the [great] gods.
>   Anu gave his crown, Enlil ga[ve his throne],
> 40'   Nergal gave his the weapons, Ninurta gave [his splendor],
>   Belet-ili gave [his] fea[tures].

In the previous lines, humans are created by Belet-ili, who pinches off a lump of clay, presumably mixes it with some other ingredients—the text is broken at this spot—and imposes the labor of the gods on them. Afterwards, attention is turned to the king. The verbs refer to creative acts (Akkadian *patāqu* in line 33' when referring to the king; *banû* in line 35' when referring to his features), and all of the features mentioned pertain to royal identity and function. A text such as this shows that creation in the ancient world is more interested in identity than materiality.

---

[32]Foster, *Before the Muses*, 495-97. See discussion in E. Jimenez, "'The Creation of the King': A Reappraisal," *Kaskal* 10 (2013): 235-54.

A similar point can be made from an Egyptian relief that shows a human being shaped on a potter's wheel by the craftsman god Khnum. The portrayal is sometimes doubled because both the king and his *ka* are being shaped—therefore again focusing on identity (*ka*) and function (context is the coronation of the king).[33] Biological origins are not in view; identity is what is considered important. "In the New Kingdom reigns of Hatshepsut and Thutmose III, [Khnum] is first portrayed as a fashioner of gods, men, and animals, enacting creation on a potter's wheel, a motif that becomes prevalent in texts and relief from the New Kingdom through Roman times and is associated with the divine birth of the pharaoh."[34]

A further indication that identity is more central to the ancients' thinking about human origins can be found by examining the way the texts talk about the ingredients used in human creation. Regarding the specific ingredients, no consensus exists, but a common thread can still be discerned in what is being conveyed by the identifying ingredients.

Table 3.1. Ingredients used in human creation in ANE texts

Literature	Language	Ingredients
Song of the Hoe	Sumerian	break from ground
Hymn to E-engura	Sumerian	break from ground
Enki and Ninmah	Sumerian	clay (potter's wheel)[a]
KAR 4	Sumerian & Akkadian	blood of slain rebel deity[b]
Atrahasis	Akkadian	flesh and blood of slain rebel deity
Enuma Elish	Akkadian	blood of slain rebel deity
Pyramid Texts	Egyptian	clay (potter's wheel)
Coffin Texts	Egyptian	tears[c]
Instruction of Merikare	Egyptian	God's body

[a]This may refer to special clay, since it is gotten from the "heart" of clay on the top of the Abzu—perhaps suggesting clay that has regenerative qualities. Jacobsen translates it "fathering clay" in *HTO* 156. Lambert ("The Relationship of Sumerian and Babylonian Myth as Seen in Accounts of Creation," in *La Circulation des biens, des personnes et des idées dans le Proche-Orient ancient*, ed. D. Charpin and F. Joannès [Paris: Recherche sur la Civilisations, 1992], 134), believes that blood may well be mentioned in the previous line, but not the blood of a slain deity—perhaps Enki's own blood. The text is very difficult. Note also that in the Atrahasis Epic, the Igigi and Anunna gods all spit on the clay before it is put to use (lines 233-34).
[b]There is no indication in KAR 4 that the two slain deities are rebels.
[c]In Egyptian the word for "tears" (*rmwt*) is very similar to the word for "people" (*rmtn*); see J. van Dijk, "Myth and Mythmaking in Ancient Egypt," *CANE* 3:1707. See Coffin Text spell 1130 in *COS* 1.17, p. 27.

[33]S. Morenz, *Egyptian Religion* (Ithaca, NY: Cornell University Press, 1973), 183-85.
[34]P. O'Rourke, "Khnum," in *The Oxford Encyclopedia of Ancient Egypt*, ed. D. B. Redford (Oxford: Oxford University Press, 2001), 231.

Only in Atrahasis is there a combination of common and divine materials.[35] Sometimes, however, the infusion of the divine takes place by means other than ingredients, such as by the mother goddess giving birth to humans (Enki and Ninmah) or by the divine breath (Coffin Texts, Instruction of Merikare). Thus in the Coffin Texts the deity states: "I will lead them and enliven them, through my mouth, which is life in their nostrils. I will lead my breath into their throats" (referring to all creatures, not just humans).[36]

Furthermore, in ancient Near Eastern texts *humanity* is created as a corporate population, not individual humans per se. No texts speak of an original couple through whom all others were born, because it is the *identity* of humanity that is being created.[37] They are not interested in how the first individuals arose but in the identity of the human race. Therefore the ingredients are used to encapsulate their understanding of this identity, not their understanding of biology.

In the account in the Old Testament, the ingredient is dust, and the divine infusion comes from the breath of God. We find, then, the same approach to the question of human origins, but with some differences in detail. In the ancient Near East, clay is used as a means to impose form for the body; Genesis uses dust. But dust and clay are not the same thing, since dust cannot be molded. Clay, on the other hand, has significance for the artistic process.[38] Though clay is not explicitly connected to death in these works, as dust is in Genesis, Erra and Ishum indicates that clay is what is left behind after the blood (life/intellect) is gone.[39] Dust is not fertile, nor is it able to be shaped; it represents a connection to the earth only in death. This perspective is unique to the Old Testament in the

---

[35]The bilingual version of Enki and Ninmah suggests that mixture may also occur there. See Lambert, "Relationship," 129-35.

[36]CT 80:106-8; James Allen, *Genesis in Egypt* (New Haven, CT: Yale University Press, 1995), 24.

[37]The only possible exception is in a bilingual creation text designated KAR4; see W. G. Lambert, *Babylonian Creation Myths* (Winona Lake, IN: Eisenbrauns, 2013), 330-45. For the interpretation that it may refer to two primordial individuals, see the discussion by R. Averbeck, *COS* 4.90, p. 338n31.

[38]T. Abusch, "Ghost and God: Some Observations on a Babylonian Understanding of Human Nature," in *Self, Soul and Body*, ed. Baumgarten, Assmann, and Stroumsa, 371: "[Clay] represents the material form of man and serves as a base."

[39]Cattle turn to clay at death in Erra and Ishum I.74 (*COS* 1.113). A. Kilmer suggests that the appearance of the placenta, since it bears some resemblance to clay, led the ancients to infer that clay was the stuff of creation. The placenta may have been viewed as the leftover stuff from the formation of the fetus in the uterus; A. D. Kilmer, "The Brick of Birth," *Journal of Near Eastern Studies* 46 (1987): 211-13.

ancient world. Furthermore, in the Old Testament, no physical divine element is provided (such as the tears of the god or the blood of a slain rebel god), but as in the ancient Near Eastern accounts, God is the source of life (infusion) and the one who forges human identity.

On the basis of the examination of both similarities and differences, we can conclude that Israel, like the ancient Near East, was more interested in the forming of the person, specifically their identity (*nepeš*, Gen 2:7, and *rûaḥ*, Zech 12:1), than in the forming of the body (*bāśār*).[40] In fact, a close reading of the Hebrew of Genesis 2 leads to the observation that the text does not say that God formed his *body from* the dust of the ground. It says that he formed "humanity" (*hāʾādām*—with definite article), dust of the ground (not "from dust").[41] Zechariah 12:1 also gives us another aspect of what it means to "form humanity" as it explains that God formed (same verb, *yāṣar*) the *rûaḥ* of humanity (this would not have been of dust because the human *rûaḥ* comes from God). As in the ancient Near East, Genesis 2 is conveying in conventional ways the divine creation of human identity—an identity that is true of all humans, not something uniquely, biologically true of only the first couple.[42]

This idea in turn leads to the conclusion that it is humanity as a whole that is the focus of Genesis, rather than two individuals. In Genesis 1 there is no mention of individuals; God creates *ʾādām*, which is humanity, including gender (male and female). Just as bird and fish populations were

---

[40]An alternative view can be found in 2 Enoch 30:89, where Adam's body is formed out of seven components: flesh from earth, blood from dew and the sun, eyes from the sea, bones from stone, reason from angels and clouds, veins and hair from grass, spirit from God's spirit and wind. See C. Böttrich, "The Figures of Adam and Eve in the Enoch Tradition," in *The Adam and Eve Story in the Hebrew Bible and in Ancient Jewish Writings Including the New Testament*, ed. A. Laato and L. Valve (Winona Lake, IN: Eisenbrauns, 2016), 226. This description remains focused on human identity.

[41]Grammarians (such as Bruce K. Waltke and Michael O'Connor, *An Introduction to Biblical Hebrew Syntax* [Winona Lake, IN: Eisenbrauns, 1990], 174) suggest that even though the preposition *min* (from) is missing, the syntactical arrangement can still at times be used to indicate materials (Song 3:10; Deut 27:6; 1 Sam 28:24). Others (P. Joüon and T. Muraoka, *A Grammar of Biblical Hebrew*, 2nd ed. [Rome: Gregorian and Biblical Press, 2011], §125v; C. H. J. van der Merwe, J. A. Naudé, and J. H. Kroeze, *A Biblical Hebrew Reference Grammar* [Sheffield, UK: Sheffield Academic, 1999], §29.3) point to other functions of appositional relationships that could also be considered. Appositional relationships exist when two elements in a clause have the same referent. Such appositional relationships can also express ideas such as a status, characteristic, or quality.

[42]I have discussed this in detail using the term *archetypal* in John H. Walton, *The Lost World of Adam and Eve* (Downers Grove, IL: InterVarsity Press, 2015).

created on day five, and animal populations on day six, a human population is created. In Genesis 2, the text turns its attention to the forming of personhood, but what it affirms is not biological information concerning human origins, such as we might think in our cultural river. Instead, it operates in the ancient cultural river to give information that conveys the identity of all of humanity. In this focus we will find the enduring theology of the biblical text, and it is a different identity than that which is offered in the ancient Near East, even though it uses the same approach to address the issue. In light of this it may be more accurate to refer to Genesis 2 as an account of human identity (anthropology, and specifically theological anthropology) rather than an account of human origins (biology).[43]

Human functions. Widespread interest in the purpose of humanity is evident in the ancient world. As with people everywhere, ancient people yearned to find meaning in life and wondered what purpose they served. For them, the obvious response was to look to the gods to discern the purposes the gods might have had for creating humans (often not the case in the modern world).

Across the ancient Near East, the prevalent view of human purpose is to serve the gods through the performance of rituals and through provision for the deities in the temples. This is the Great Symbiosis that we have already discussed. In this way, the favor of the gods is preserved. People can flourish, and the cosmos runs according to the design and desire of the gods. As discussed in chapter four, Israel also shares some of this profile. Rituals performed for Yahweh help to assure that the cosmos is running as it should. The difference is that Yahweh does not have needs, and though the Israelites desire the favor of Yahweh, the ritual system is not focused primarily on his favor, but on his presence, which is maintained by the preservation of its sanctity. The presence of Yahweh, therefore, is an expression of his favor, but the presence takes precedence over the favor. In contrast, people find their purpose and meaning in the ancient Near East by meeting the needs of the gods and thereby contributing to order in the cosmos. Israelites, on the other hand, find their purpose and meaning in their status as God's chosen covenant people and as the caretakers of God's presence on earth.

---

[43]In like manner, we may refer to the seven-day account as an account of cosmic identity (i.e., ordered as sacred space) rather than an account of cosmic origins.

People as Slaves of the Gods

In the ancient Near East, people thought they were created to provide for the needs of the gods. They were a remedy to a problem; an afterthought, rather than the planned focus of creation (as opposed to the perspective of the Old Testament). In the gardens that adjoined the temples in the ancient Near East, food was grown to offer to the gods. In contrast, God planted a garden in Eden (the same idea of a garden adjoining sacred space) to provide food for people. In the Old Testament, people serve God, but they do so as vicegerents, not as slave laborers. God had established sacred space because he intended to live among his creatures and to be in relationship with them as they pursued his purposes together. But in the ancient Near East, the gods lived among the people to be pampered by them.

A second function attested among humanity is service as the image of God. As we discovered, in the most common thinking observed throughout the ancient Near East, the king alone carries out this function. In contrast, the Old Testament attributes this status and function to all people. Consequently, in the ancient Near East, *human* functions were not defined by the image of God (since it is so narrowly characteristic), but in the Old Testament, the image of God provides the primary description of human purpose and meaning. Human dignity in the Old Testament is found in the status and function people have as God's image. In Israel, dignity, purpose, and meaning were extended beyond the image to their particular identity as God's chosen people, among whom he dwells. People in the ancient Near East, however, knew of no such status and therefore found dignity only in the confidence that the gods needed them (an idea inimical to Old Testament theology). Once the idea of meeting the needs of the gods is reduced to an equation that results in prosperity for the ritually conscientious humans, purpose and meaning become focused on one's own health, wealth, standing, and family. Unfortunately, such is the universal human tendency, regardless of theology or ideology.

In some ancient Near Eastern cultures, this idea of meeting the needs of the gods is built into the origins narratives. Particularly in Sumerian and

Akkadian texts, the gods tire of meeting their own needs and devise the idea of humanity to relieve them of their drudgery. This belief adds a certain poignancy to the idea of serving the gods, such as would not be present in Israelite thinking.

Conclusion on human role and origins. Armed with the results of our studies on the image of God, theological anthropology, human origins, and human function, we are now in a position to derive the enduring theology from the Old Testament, concerning humans, that should rightfully be part of our theology today. We can propose that the enduring theology connected to this topic in the Old Testament concerns human identity and function. These points differ significantly from what is found in the ancient Near East, but they are still far from the emphases so often found today pertaining to biology and material origins (see table 3.2).

Table 3.2. Views of human roles and origins compared

	Ancient Near East	**OT View of Humanity**	**OT View of Israel**	**Modern Secular**	**Modern Christian**[a]
Identity	byproduct of gods and mundane materials	dust; image of God	dust; image of God; elect as people of God	evolved primates	in Christ
Function	bringing order by serving the gods	bringing order by subduing and ruling	bringing order as priests maintain sacred space	propagate and survive	bringing kingdom order by means of Great Commission
Purpose	providing the needs of gods	relationship with God	keeping covenant to preserve presence of God	continuing and advancing species	participating in kingdom of God
Future Expectation	Egypt: status quo or exaltation Others: survival of person in netherworld	survival of person in the netherworld, joining community of ancestors		nothing survives	new creation; person survives; resurrection in new body

[a]As the New Testament would identify it, in contrast to the inclinations found in popular Christianity.

The Old Testament provides a basic understanding of human identity that remains true today. All humans are dust; they are mortal and frail. Just as all people were made to be more than dust by virtue of the conferred image of God, Israel was elevated to yet a higher status by virtue of the covenant. It continued to function as God's image, but God also intended it to function as priests, caretakers of the divine presence. Our Christian theology identifies us as all of the above and more. We continue to be identified as God's image, with the task of extending God's order (subdue and rule). Yet God has made us more by providing Christ to die for us and the Holy Spirit to indwell us. Our identity is not in what we are made from but in who God has made us in Christ. The groundwork is laid for this identity in the Old Testament, though the final elevation through Christ is not anticipated there.[44] We continue to extend order in the cosmos, but we are also those who bring kingdom order as we participate in and seek to promote the kingdom of God. For Israel, the covenant was the catalyst for order, with God's presence as its source, and though we have a different covenant, the task is not dissimilar.

The purpose of all humanity is to be in relationship with God—that is why he created us—and (as described above) is defined by the partnership between God and humanity, which is represented from the start in the image-of-God concept. Israel partnered with God through participation in the covenant, and today, Christians partner with God through participation in the kingdom. These ideas stand in stark contrast to Israel's ancient Near Eastern environment and to our own modern, secular environment. In the ancient Near East, people were merely slaves to the gods; in secular humanism, we are merely slaves to ourselves. Those in the covenant and in Christ are the people of God, members of the kingdom of God, conferred with holiness, and called by his name; we are slaves no longer. Therefore the ideas established in the Old Testament find continuity as they progress into New Testament theology.

The Fall

As we focus on the theology of sin in the Old Testament, we must observe that none of its literature ever refers to the event of Genesis 3 as "the fall" or talks about people or the world as "fallen."[45] The Prophets are more interested in how Israel has failed to carry out its divine human calling through the covenant than in how all of humanity has failed to carry out its calling to bear the image.[46] The terminology of *fall*, however, is logical enough,

---

[44]Idea contributed by J. Harvey Walton.

[45]For that matter, neither does the New Testament.

[46]As Ziony Zevit points out, the Prophets had ample opportunity to relate Israel's sin to the sin in

since biblical language does refer to "falling into temptation," and so on, but we should be cautious about giving the concept too large a role in our discussion of the biblical text. The Old Testament does not speak of Adam's sin as bringing sin on everyone, though the effects of sin are seen pervasively throughout the Old Testament. One of the earliest uses of "the fall" is found in the pseudepigraphal book of 4 Ezra (7:118): "O Adam, what have you done? For though it was you who sinned, the fall was not yours alone, But ours also who are your descendants."[47] With that disclaimer, I will continue to use the term throughout the chapter for convenience and because it has traditionally been used to encapsulate the problem of sin.

As we consider the Old Testament in its context, we should be clear that the fall is not just disobedience or the consumption of forbidden fruit. These actions could be considered crimes, but they were crimes that were simply expressions of the fall.[48] The fall was the decision to be like God (thus subverting the divine human calling), conveyed by the serpent's words (Gen 3:5), the woman's response (Gen 3:6), God's assessment (Gen 3:22), and the reason for the banishment (Gen 3:23). The way in which the man and woman have become like God is qualified in relation to what the tree represented. No suggestion is made that they have become omniscient or omnipotent.

I propose that, by disobediently taking the fruit, Adam and Eve were trying to be like God by positing themselves as the center and source of order—in sharp contrast to what the divine calling of humans entailed. God is, by definition, the source of wisdom, and his presence therefore establishes a center of wisdom. Furthermore, the fear of God is the beginning of wisdom. Wisdom in its biblical focus concerns seeking order in all categories of life (speech, family, government, interpersonal relations, relationship with God,

---

the garden, and they never do so (*What Really Happened in the Garden of Eden?* [New Haven, CT: Yale University Press, 2013], 19-22). When Is 43:27 makes reference to Israel's first father who sinned, it is talking about Jacob, not Adam.

[47]Translation from James H. Charlesworth, *The Old Testament Pseudepigrapha* (Garden City, NY: Doubleday, 1983), 1:541. The work is dated to about 100 CE. Note that this portion also affirms human participation in the sin. See also 2 Baruch 48:42-43. The expression "the fall" was popularized by early Christian writers but is little evidenced in the Greek writers. Even as late as the fourth century (Gregory of Nyssa) it is not being used as a technical noun representing a theological construct. Earlier in the Latin writers is where the concept took on more prominence. I am grateful to my colleague George Kalantzis for this historical information.

[48]I. Provan sees it as an inherent denial that God is good in *Seriously Dangerous Religion* (Waco, TX: Baylor University Press, 2014), 174.

decision making, etc.), and wisdom is the result when we perceive order, pursue it, preserve it, promote it, procure it, and practice it. True wisdom finds its source and center in God, not in oneself specifically or humankind generally. Fear of the Lord involves submitting to God's authority as the center of order.[49] In taking from the tree, Adam and Eve were trying to set themselves up as a satellite center of wisdom apart from God—an attempt to go off on their own rather than to remain in partnership with God. It is a childish sort of response, much like "I can do it myself!" or "I want to do it my way!" These responses are not a rejection of authority per se, but they represent an insistence on independence. The act is an assertion that "it's all about *me*," and this type of action is one that has characterized humanity (individually and corporately) since its first appearance in Genesis 3.

The result of this action (that of people as the source and center of wisdom) was not order centered on humanity but disorder. This disorder extended to all people of all time as well as to the cosmos. When we stepped out of harmony with God's purposes, we also stepped out of harmony with the rest of his creation. Now all creation groans, not because it suffered damage but because it is no longer in harmonious relationship with us. We changed; it did not. Worst of all, life in God's presence was forfeited. Wisdom is good, and we can therefore safely assume that God did not intend to withhold it from humanity. But true wisdom must be acquired through a process, generally from instruction by those who *are* wise. In other words, the fall is defined by the fact that Adam and Eve acquired wisdom illegitimately (Gen 3:22) and tried to take God's role for themselves, rather than eventually joining God in his role as they were taught wisdom, becoming the fully functional vice-regents of God involved in the process of bringing order.[50] If humans are to work alongside God in extending order ("subdue" and "rule" [Gen 1:28]), they need to attain wisdom, but they need to attain it as endowment from God, not as something to be seized for autonomous use. Examples of similar errors can be found in those who believed they knew what God's kingdom should look like and tried to bring it about on

---

[49]Insightful phrasing provided by Rhett Austin.

[50]This is similar to the idea expressed in Rom 8:17, that we are coheirs with Christ. It would not be appropriate for us to think of ourselves as autonomous heirs *instead of* Christ; we join him as heirs and are heirs through him. In the same way it was not appropriate for people to think of attaining wisdom apart from God. The only acceptable wisdom is found in participation with God.

their own. From Jewish zealots in the Second Temple period to Christian Crusaders, God's people have frequently looked to their own wisdom to understand and achieve the kingdom of God rather than actually working alongside God as participants in his plans and purposes.

Given this understanding, I would disagree with those who see the fall as disobedience to an arbitrarily chosen test case. I refer to the interpretation in which the trees were not associated with any inherent properties but rather served to provide an *opportunity* for obedience (knowledge of good) or disobedience (knowledge of evil). In this view, God could just as easily have said that Adam and Eve shouldn't walk on the beach. Instead, I maintain that *what* was taken (wisdom) is not arbitrary and that it is more important than *that it was* taken (failed a test). I would even go a step further: we did not *lose paradise* as much as we *forfeited sacred space* and the relationship it offered. We thereby damaged our ability to be partners with God and marred his creation with our own underdeveloped ability to bring order on our own in our own wisdom.

Thus far, the purpose of this chapter has been to try to recover an Old Testament perspective on these issues. However, we can now turn our attention briefly to the ancient world outside the biblical text. There is nothing like the fall in ancient Near Eastern literature because there is no idealized primeval scenario. In Mesopotamian thinking, civilization in the urban environment was the ideal, and the "world outside" was populated by "wild animals, primeval monsters, demons, drifting souls, and nomads."[51] That "world outside" picture was also the description of primeval times. There is no original pair, no sacred space, no disobedience of a command, no grasping for wisdom to become like God. Even the discussion of sin is problematic in an ancient Near Eastern context. They certainly understood the concept of offending a deity and suffering for it. But, as previously mentioned, the divine human calling was articulated in the Great Symbiosis, in which the responsibility of humans is to meet the needs of the gods. Their part in the Great Symbiosis mostly involved ritual performance, but it also included ethical behavior insofar as it was recognized that the gods desired sufficient justice in order to ensure a smoothly operating society. A lawless

---

[51]F. A. M. Wiggermann, "Agriculture as Civilization: Sages, Farmers, and Barbarians," in *The Oxford Handbook of Cuneiform Culture*, ed. Karen Radner and Eleanor Robson (Oxford: Oxford University Press, 2011), 674.

society would be a less productive society, and people would not be able to grow their crops, raise their herds, or make their gifts to the gods.

In both the ancient Near East and the Old Testament, sin was often objectified; that is, it was seen as something almost physical, something that could be carried by or lifted off a person. It was also realized in physical consequences (illness especially). For these reasons, we expect nothing like the fall in ancient Near Eastern thinking. The people of the ancient Near East saw themselves in partnership with the gods within the confines of the Great Symbiosis. What we find in the Old Testament is a reflection of the revelation of God that resulted in a uniquely Israelite theology. We will not be able to recover the Old Testament theology on this issue by learning more about the ancient Near East. Nevertheless, getting back to the Old Testament texts in their ancient context before taking into account the way the interpretation of those texts unfolded in the New Testament and in the articulation of theological understanding throughout church history can be instructive.[52] Of course, investigating the ancient context does not necessitate rejection of the later developments, but for the purposes of understanding the Old Testament text in its context, it is important to see the issues that frame the text in their ancient setting. In Old Testament theological thinking, Genesis 3 is more about the encroachment of disorder (brought about by sin) into a world that was in the process of being ordered than it is about the first sin. It is about how humanity lost access to the presence of God when its representatives tragically declared their independence from their Creator. It is more focused literarily and theologically on how corporate humanity is distanced from God—alienation—than on the sinful state of each human being (with no intention of diminishing the latter fact).

Summary of Enduring Theology

Throughout the chapter we have identified elements of the enduring theology of the Old Testament, so here we need only summarize them in conclusion.

---

[52]Much of the Protestant understanding of sin is more indebted to Augustine than to Paul. For more about Augustine and the fall, see Willemien Otten, "The Long Shadow of Human Sin: Augustine on Adam, Eve and the Fall," in *Out of Paradise: Eve and Adam and Their Interpreters*, ed. Bob Becking and Susan Hennecke (Sheffield, UK: Sheffield Phoenix, 2010), 29-49. Augustine was heavily influenced by Neoplatonism, asceticism, and the desire to refute Gnosticism, Pelagianism, and Donatism.

Importance of order. We benefit by extending our view of creation beyond the material to the establishment and maintenance of order—both activities of the Creator.

Importance of the cultural river. We can only derive limited enduring theology in some regards because the information that is communicated is characteristic of the cultural river of ancient Israel.

No opposing forces, no chaos to overcome. When the Creator God established the optimal order of our world, he did not have to win it through conflict with opponents. No competing personae or agencies exist.

God's agency. The enduring theology of creation places the emphasis squarely on God's agency, not on the mechanisms that he used. The latter are cultural reflections only.

Range of God's role as creator. Yahweh gave, and continues to give shape, organization, order, and purpose to the cosmos, including people and the society in which they live.

Image of God. Humanity has been given a status, and it is vitally important that we adopt the identity as part of this corporate image. All who are human have the status "image of God." The image is not genetic or biological. We cannot lose it or fail to achieve it.

Personhood. Regardless of how the metaphysical components are understood or identified, humans are given life, breath, personhood, identity, and being by God. We also noted that we are given no insight about theological issues such as personal eschatology, metaphysical issues such as the location or nature of the self, or biological issues such as when the developing fetus becomes a person. All of these are questions rooted in our modern cultural river and are not addressed by the biblical text. Nevertheless, all that we are derives from God.

Human identity. God is the source of life (infusion) and the one who forges human identity.

Our given status. Those in the covenant and in Christ are the people of God, members of the kingdom of God, conferred with holiness, and called by his name; we are slaves no longer.

4

COVENANT
and
KINGDOM

IDENTITY, STATUS, AND REVELATION

God's covenant with Abram allowed him the opportunity to participate in
the purposes of God, a privilege that was later bestowed on the nation of
Israel (Ex 6:7; 19:5-6). It served as a mechanism through which God revealed
himself to his people and prepared the way for God to dwell among his
people once again (which had not happened since Eden). The stipulations
given at Sinai also eventually provided the guidelines that would instruct the
Israelites in how they should live in order to maintain God's presence and
preserve his favor, given their holy status. In all of these ways, we can see
that the covenant has a pervasive impact on Old Testament theology and
permeated the thinking of the original authors and audience.

In the ancient Near East, the idea of a god who made a covenant with a
group of people was unique to Israel—a circumstance for which we have
little precedent.[1] Gods did, however, make covenants with kings, and we will

---

[1]One Phoenician (some say Aramaic) amulet from Arslan Tash dated to the seventh century BCE
is translated as referring to an "eternal covenant" between the god Ashur and "us." It further
elaborates that it was done "with a covenant of the Heavens and Eternal Earth." For the text, see
COS 2.86, pp. 222-23. For full discussion, see Z. Zevit, "A Phoenician Inscription and Biblical
Covenant Theology," IEJ 27 (1977): 110-18; David Sperling, *Ve-Eileh Divrei David: Essays in Se-
mitics, Hebrew Bible and History of Biblical Scholarship* (Leiden: Brill, 2017 [from a conference

explore that connection later in the chapter. Another point of comparison, which we will also later develop, is represented by the nature of the divine-human relationship—a contrast between the Great Symbiosis of the ancient Near East and the Great Enterprise of the covenant.

The covenant also serves as a foundation for developments that take place in the New Testament. Even though the new covenant takes an oblique turn, one of the numerous points of continuity is found in the central idea: God-in-partnership with humans to carry out his purposes. We will return to this connection various times throughout the chapter.

Identity and status. To begin this discussion, we must recognize that Yahweh is portrayed as a God who makes plans, who has purposes, and who includes humans in his plan as fellow workers. This type of portrayal is evident from the opening chapter of Genesis, where people are God's images who participate in bringing order (subdue and rule). Each phase of the covenant then continues with this idea. On his side of the agreement, God brings Abram, Israel, and David into his program to be participants and instruments. Even though the roles of Abram, Israel, and David differ slightly from one another, in each case they have a role to play as partners in God's plan and purposes.

With that established, we are now in a position to draw the important distinction between identity and status.[2] I am going to be using *identity* to refer to how you see yourself (e.g., member of an organization, profession, or demographic; people of God). It determines what you are willing, inclined, or could be persuaded to do. Identity involves choosing how to think of yourself, and it also extends to what you think other people think of you, or even to what you want them to think of you (e.g., "There goes a history professor"; "There goes a good wife and mother"; "There is a woman of integrity"; "There goes a guy who gets things done"). The persona that you create for yourself dictates the kinds of things you care about and the kinds

---

presentation in 1981]), 60-69. The problem is that the word translated "covenant" in this text is a word that typically refers to an "imprecation" sometimes associated with oaths and covenants. See the lengthy discussion in H. C. Brichto, *The Problem of "Curse" in the Hebrew Bible* (Philadelphia: SBL, 1963), 22-71. For the god Ashur to attach an imprecation to himself is not necessarily equivalent to entering a covenant. This issue needs more scholarly attention before it can be considered a parallel, especially since a few lines later the text refers to this imprecation in connection to an oath (presumably for protection, since this is an amulet).

[2]I am grateful to the insights of J. Harvey Walton for helping me develop these thoughts.

of things you want, which in turn dictate the kinds of things you do. After all, in the end, what you do is largely determinative of what and who you are.

In contrast, *status* is how others see you. It determines what is expected of you and is earned, acquired, or conferred. The Bible informs us about some of these statuses and applies them to either some or all people (e.g., holiness, sinfulness, image of God, creatures).[3] Status is defined by extrinsic markers, whereas identity is defined by behavior. So if your identity matches your status, all is well, though there are times when they line up well enough that no one notices. But if how you wish to identify yourself does not match your status, you might be able to behave in ways that do not match the expectations of your status (e.g., the prodigal son).

Through the covenant, Israel is given a status as the people of Yahweh, which they are supposed to adopt as their identity. And Yahweh, by entering into the covenant relationship, takes on the identity of the God of Israel. As the covenant unfolds, he chooses Abram (Gen 12; 15), Israel (Ex 6:7), and eventually David (2 Sam 7), and as will be developed later in this chapter, each of these covenant phases entails a new act of election and a new direction for revelation. Election, then, in the context of covenant, is an act of God that gives a new status to the person or group who is elected. Each of these acts of election then leads to a sequence of events through which we learn something of how God characteristically acts in accordance with the identity he adopted for himself through the covenant. Therefore, Yahweh should be understood not only as a God who elects but also as a God who confers a particular status and simultaneously adopts an identity in connection with the status that he has bestowed. And when people adopt the identity that accompanies their conferred status, it puts them in relationship with God.

However, "relationship with God" can be a vague term. For our purposes, we will define it as "the opportunity and privilege to participate in bringing about the purposes of God (eventually configured as the kingdom of God)."[4] Participation in a worthy cause far outweighs whatever benefits might accrue, and the opportunity to be part of something great can be a powerful motivator, even in the absence of benefits. Significantly, this

---

[3] One's role in family or community contains elements both of status and identity.
[4] For this helpful definition that I have adopted, I am grateful to J. Harvey Walton.

definition helps us to avoid aspects of emotion (relationship is not how we "feel" about God or how he "feels" about us) and reciprocity. It should also be noted that relationship with God in the Old Testament is on a scale beyond that of the individual.[5]

The covenant encapsulated this new status for Israel. This aspect of Old Testament theology, then, offers an important revelation of the nature of God, who gives a status and thereby adopts for himself an identity. All who are his people can find a new identity because of this status and can also find relationship with him. This new identity and relationship are what God has always wanted for his people; it is why he created us.

Revelation. The covenant is a complex of ideas, and it is important for us to unpack them. Many have seen the covenant from the vantage point of its final stage (Christ as the new covenant) looking backward, and consequently, with the advantage of hindsight, have seen the covenant as largely concerned with God's eventual redemption of his people though the death and blood of Jesus. This connection is by no means misguided, but it is myopic. Its built-in anachronistic perspective obscures some of the larger theological issues; the covenant has a much broader function than simply to begin the drive toward salvation from sins.

The purpose of the covenant is indicated in its earliest formulation in Genesis 12:1-3. God tells Abram that "all the peoples on earth will be blessed through you." We may well believe that there can be no greater blessing than in the death of Christ, but we need to enlarge our vision—not only to the Old Testament, but to the larger issues in theology.

We can reorient by asking the question, "How would the Israelite audience have understood God's blessing of the entire world through them?" Initially, we could identify specific passages and circumstances that would constitute such a blessing. Abram brought blessing to the whole region by defeating the kings of the east (Gen 14). Through Joseph, the whole world was saved from the famine (Gen 41). Solomon's wisdom had an impact that stretched well beyond the confines of Israel (1 Kings 10). Esther's courageous actions did not only spare the Jews, but they also removed a tyrant (Haman) from a position of influence.

---

[5]One could argue that this is also true of the New Testament, but that is not our focus here.

The Genealogies of Chronicles

To many modern readers, it would be difficult to find a more boring section of the Old Testament than the genealogies of 1 Chronicles 1–9. If we are going to address how these serve as the Word of God, we must first understand how they function in the book of Chronicles.

The placement of Chronicles in the Hebrew canon (last) and the estimated date (probably about 400 BCE) mark it as likely the last book in the Old Testament to be written. Even though we are familiar with most of its content from the books of Samuel and Kings, its perspective on Israel's history is distinct because of its historical vantage point. Both audiences desired to understand what God was doing in their present circumstances, but each was composed with slightly different questions in mind. For example, Samuel and Kings were likely finalized when Israel was in exile and asking questions about status and identity, essentially, "How did we get here?" Chronicles, on the other hand, was written perhaps a century and a half later, but it also addresses confusion about status and identity, particularly "Who are we?" The Israelites who composed the audience of the Chronicler had been "restored" to the land; for some of them it had been over a hundred years. Yet they still just plodded along as a small backwater province of the sprawling Persian Empire. The oracles given by the prophets had a hollow ring to them—their circumstances were hardly indicative of how they expected the glorious restoration to look. They likely wondered about their identity as a people. Were they still Yahweh's chosen? Where were those covenant blessings? They were in the land, but it could hardly have been considered theirs; they had been decimated as a people and felt stagnant; and only the grandest of imaginations could envision how the whole earth was being blessed by them.

So in light of this context, how do the genealogies fit into the Chronicler's purpose? Before the author can begin to develop his new vision for the centrality of the temple (God's residence in their midst), God's rule over the whole earth (regardless of the absence of a Davidic king), and the significance of the kingdom of God as presided over by the priests and Levites (all featured aspects of the Chronicler's view of history), he needs to inspire the Israelites with a sense of identity. And that is where the genealogies come in.

The genealogies help the Israelites to see the larger picture, to get a glimpse of where they fit in God's grand scheme. They have to look beyond themselves and their current situation to see that they are part of something big—a movement that has been afoot not just since David, or Moses, or Abraham, but that goes all the way back to Adam (this is in line with the definition of "relationship with God" offered above). What they need is to feel the solidarity that exists among those who have self-identified as the people of God throughout history. They need to recover this element of the foundation of their identity.

As the genealogies are recited, tribe by tribe, tracing from the earliest times, Israel is portrayed as a group of chosen people who stand as heirs of the kingdom of God. They are reminded of their continuing status as the people of God and are encouraged to adopt that status as the basis for their identity in the troublesome times in which they live. These genealogies serve as the same sort of call that the author of Hebrews issues to his audience as he encourages them to recognize that they are surrounded by "a great cloud of witnesses" (Heb 12:1).

This awareness is similar to what we should feel when we recite any of the creeds week by week. On any given Sunday, as congregation after congregation and parish after parish rise to recite the creed in commitment to the faith, their affirmations ripple across time zones and around the world (I picture it like "doing the wave" in a major sports stadium). As we recite, we affirm our status, assert our identity, and proclaim our solidarity with believers around the world. But the recitation extends so much further than a sports wave because the ripples are not only through space but through time as well. When we stand and proclaim the creeds, we stand shoulder to shoulder with those of centuries past and identify ourselves with them, all of us and each of us holding the torch as the people of God.

Though the genealogies constitute a different sort of solidarity statement than do the Christian creeds, they accomplish the same end. In Bilbo's birthday (and farewell) speech at the beginning of *The Fellowship of the Ring,* he recites a roster of the clans of the Hobbits. As each is named in turn, a cheer goes up from those belonging to the clan just mentioned. We need to picture the Israelites in a similar way as their genealogies (going back to the beginning of their history!) are recited. Cheers go up tribe by tribe as they feel a sense of continuity and solidarity as Yahweh's people. They recognize themselves as part of something really big. So when we read the genealogies of Chronicles, we should try to hold in our minds the same feeling that we have when we sing together in worship "We're the people of God, called by his name . . ."[a] Like the Israelites, God has given us a status that makes us more than what we came from, and that is the identity that we should adopt.

[a]Lyrics by Wayne Watson.

But this small selection of narratives does not suffice to provide the essential, larger perspective. The Prophets offer a greater agenda as they speak of the role of Israel as a "light for the nations" (pertaining to the Servant in Is 42; 49, and to Israel in Is 60). This description demonstrates the role that Israel was intended to play from the beginning of its election as a kingdom of priests and a holy nation (Ex 19:6).

As a kingdom of priests, Israel was to mediate both the revelation from God and access to the presence of God. Peoples were to stream to Jerusalem (come to its light) to gain access to God's presence (manifested in Jerusalem) and to learn of God's revelation of himself. As a result of their mediation, everyone would know Yahweh is God. Consequently, we can conclude that at least one of the reasons that God made a covenant with Israel was to reveal his plans and purposes to them, and through them, to the world. Indeed, all of the special revelation of God is mediated through Israel (their history, the law, prophecy, and yes, Jesus, born an Israelite of the tribe of Judah). God's revelation in the Old Testament is given through Israel, and through that revelation all the people of earth have been blessed.

Why should we think of revelation as a blessing? In the ancient world, the gods did not reveal much about themselves (with the exception of very specific and often cryptic responses to inquiries by means of divination). Babylonians or Egyptians were left to infer what their gods were like and what the gods wanted from them. The fundamental premise of the theology of the ancient world was that the gods had needs and that people had been created to meet those needs. Rituals were designed to provide food and drink for the gods, and temples were built as luxurious palaces for their dwelling. Images were made of the finest materials and were adorned in rich garments and accouterments. The gods enjoyed the performances of the finest musicians while they partook of their sumptuous feasts, and the wealth of offerings, tithes, taxes, and conquests filled the temple coffers. Conventional wisdom was that the gods wanted to be pampered, and if the people succeeded in meeting their every whim, the gods might just treat them well. After all, if the gods desired all of this pampering, they had to protect and provide for those who were diligent and conscientious in their ministrations. Experience, as the people interpreted it, had taught them that the gods were fickle, demanding, capricious, and disinterested in the cares of humans; the gods were interested only in their own comforts and were concerned primarily with their own needs.

This relationship between gods and people in the ancient world is one that I describe as the "Great Symbiosis" (introduced in chapter two). In this symbiotic relationship, the people took care of the gods (so that the gods did not bring ruin or destruction on them), and the gods took care of the people so that their needs continued to be met by those people. Given that this is the way people thought about deities in the ancient world, it was essential for Yahweh to offer revelation of himself in order to provide the basis for a newly forged relationship with the humans he created. And this revelation was especially important, because unlike the ancient Near Eastern gods, Yahweh did not have needs. As Yahweh revealed himself to Israel, this symbiosis of codependence, reciprocity, and mutual need was replaced by what we might call the Great Enterprise, which was established through the covenant. In the Great Enterprise, Yahweh protected Israel and provided for them just as the gods of the ancient Near East did for their worshipers. The difference was that instead of meeting the needs of the gods as their neighbors did, Israel was given a role in the plan and purposes of Yahweh.

Yahweh therefore revealed himself through the covenant as a different sort of God. His revelation included more than the idea that there was one God, as opposed to many; it had to do with God's purposes and identity. At the time of his appearance at Israel's side and on its behalf in the early chapters of Exodus, and reflected again prominently in the context of the exile, Yahweh's desire was always "Then you will know that I am Yahweh, and that Yahweh is God" (combining the elements of the frequently repeated refrain throughout the early chapters of Exodus). In this familiar formula we see God's agenda—that through the covenant he would reveal himself to Israel, and through Israel he would be revealed to the world. Israel was thus given the status of a participant in Yahweh's plan and purpose.

Revelation, however, is not an end in itself and was not the culminating rationale for Yahweh's covenant with Israel. In fact, we find that before revelation even began to unfold, God offered a relationship to Abram. Given the fact, however, that Abram had come out of a Great Symbiosis culture, a significant paradigm shift was necessary for a relationship to be formed. It is difficult to be in relationship with an unknown entity. *Therefore, the covenant should be viewed as a formal relationship that provides a mechanism for revelation; it is then itself the foundation for an ever-deepening understanding of what it means to have an identity-rooted relationship with Yahweh.*

The recurring formulae "Then you will know that I am Yahweh" and "I will be your God, and you will be my people" suggest that the Israelites would have seen the covenant in this way. Furthermore, these formulae occur across genres and throughout the time periods of the Old Testament. This common recurrence earmarks them as foundational to Israel's theology and positions them as enduring theological issues.

Given this perspective, we could conclude that the covenant represents more a history of revelation than a history of redemption. It remains a "sacred history"[6] in that it focuses on what God is doing more than on what humans are doing (the latter being the stuff of common history writing), and of course, the history of revelation culminates in salvation. Christ and the salvation he provides are revealed and accomplished in the grand finale of the cross and the empty tomb. And since revelation of the work of Christ represents a new aspect of God's revelation, we can see it as an important

---

[6]To translate *Heilsgeschichte* literally.

step in God's revelatory program. But during the time of the Old Testament, they did not know that this was the direction God's plan was heading.

Furthermore, as great a salvation as we have been given, we must recognize this salvation also as a means to an end—the end result of which is relationship with God (as previously defined). In that sense, revelation and salvation both stand as primary components of God's plan to dwell among his people and to be in relationship with them. By means of revelation, we come to know of God's plans and purposes. By means of the saving work of Christ, we are fully reconciled to him, and the relationship with us that God has always wanted is made possible. But Israel was aware only of the revelation component, not the reconciliation component. And the revelation component is essential for the Christian reader because knowledge of God is never irrelevant and is always necessary for a working relationship with him as we take our place in the kingdom of God and exercise faith in him. As we examine the Old Testament, then, we will be exploring the revelation that is taking place so that we, as Christian readers, might know God more deeply and coidentify with him as we participate in his kingdom.

On the basis of this perspective, we can agree that Abram and Israel were elected as the people of God. But how should their roles be defined? They are not the people of God because God elected them for salvation; salvation is not even in the picture here. They are the elect of God for a relationship with him (the sort of relationship that he envisions, on the terms that he established, and that is available in the Old Testament context); they are elect of God in order to be the instrument of his revelation to the world ("all peoples on earth will be blessed through you," Gen 12:3). They can, therefore, be referred to as the "revelatory people of God" because they have been chosen as the instrument of his revelation (not as those who have been saved from sin).

UNFOLDING PHASES

Now that we have laid the foundation for understanding the nature and purpose of the covenant, we focus our attention on the way that the covenant unfolded throughout the Old Testament and into the New Testament. From its inception in God's offer of a covenant to Abram (Gen 12:1-3), the covenant unfolds in phases, each of which has a new point of revelation and a new object of election.[7] The four steps follow this sequence:

Relationship—Dwelling—Reigning—Saving

Relationship: Abram and his family. The first step in the covenant comes when God offers and then establishes a covenant with Abram and the family that he will be given (ratified in Gen 15). It is of interest that God establishes a formal relationship before he offers the blessing of his presence. As the Old Testament unfolds, we come to realize that the covenant is intended to eventuate in the reestablishment of the presence of God on earth (the tabernacle, then temple), but no hint of that purpose is given at this early stage.

Abram invokes God's presence (presumably by means of the altars that he constructs in the land; Gen 12:7, 8), and God is *with* Abram and his descendants in any number of ways (e.g., Gen 21:22; 26:28; 28:15). However, there is no manifest dwelling of God in sacred space in the camp of Abram. Even though Jacob at one point recognizes sacred space (at Bethel, Gen 28:16-17; 35:6-7), God, at this point, is not dwelling in the midst of Abram's family.

It is also interesting that God begins with relationship rather than law. This order makes perfect sense once we recognize that the function of the law is to help Israel to know how to live in the presence of God (see chapter five). The law would not be relevant to Abram and his family at this stage because God's presence had not yet been established.

Likewise, God does not begin with doctrine—a set of beliefs to which one must agree in order to be in relationship. He does not ask Abram to believe in anything except in Yahweh's trustworthiness to deliver the benefits that he has offered. Initially, Abram needed to act (leave behind what God asked him to leave), and his action surely demonstrated belief. But specifically, Yahweh did not begin by demanding loyalty or worship of him alone. No mention is made about monotheism, or even monolatry or henotheism. No prohibition against images is front-loaded. Instead, we find that Yahweh has constructed a scenario that will create a vacuum that he can later fill.

We have already noted that the religions of the ancient Near East were formulated around the Great Symbiosis. If the main responsibility of the

---

[7]The covenant in the time of Noah is in a different category because it does not feature election or establish a new status. It is also not inherently associated with sacred space.

people was to provide for the needs of the gods, and if that provision, for the most part, took place in the context of temple rituals, then religious practice was generally local. That is, temple rituals could only be carried out on a regular basis by those who lived in proximity to the temple. Besides the temple rituals, another level of religious practice took place in the home, camp, or the clan compound as the locals cared for minor deities (such as family gods) or even their deceased ancestors. Consequently, when Abram was instructed to leave his land and his family, in all practicality he was being asked to cut off ties with the temple deities in his city and with his personal family gods. Thus the covenant begins with a formal relationship (stipulated in the covenant), and it is through these stipulations that Yahweh reveals himself as a God who is interested in relationship with people.

Religion of Abram and His "Personal God"

We do not know what gods Abram worshiped before he was called by Yahweh, but we do know that he did not come from a monotheistic, Yahweh-worshiping clan (Josh 24:2). He would, therefore, have thought in terms of the Great Symbiosis, would have acknowledged multiple gods, would have participated in Mesopotamian-style temple worship, and would have interacted with ancestral and personal family deities. And understandably, he would have done all these things through images designed to facilitate such worship.

The ancient concept of a personal god is one that is most interesting for understanding the way that Yahweh approaches Abram. In the time of Abram, this concept had only recently developed in the ancient world. The term "personal god" is a bit of a misnomer because we are not talking about a god worshiped by a single individual. Rather, the term pertains to a god who forms a more personal interrelationship with a family or clan. A personal deity was understood as one who, for reasons unknown, had taken particular interest in a family or clan. It was generally a minor deity, but the patronage offered could be of great mutual benefit (operating within the Great Symbiosis). Both deity and clan would receive much-desired care and protection.

When Yahweh came offering the relationship of the covenant to Abram, Abram would likely have perceived him as a personal (= family) god and would have acted toward him in that way. Since Abram's wife was barren (Gen 11:30), Yahweh's promise of a large family was significant. As a personal god, Yahweh would concomitantly become the focus of much of the family's religious and ritual attention (though not generally the exclusive focus). Yahweh did not, therefore, have to offer himself in some new guise that would have immediately required Abram to go through a paradigm shift. Instead, Yahweh proceeds with a strategy that becomes somewhat routine in his future actions: he begins with the familiar.

We find, then, that all the trappings of Abram's religion to which Genesis refers are common in the context in which Abram lives. Nothing new is introduced except that the dominant focus of his religious practice is now Yahweh. The use of altars and sacrifice are no different; teraphim (likely ancestral images) are in use by Jacob's household (Gen 31:34), as are other images (Gen 35:2). But at the same time, many gaps in the narrative lead to questions. Would Abram have used images of Yahweh? Was there a shrine of some sort established when he settled somewhere? The biblical text shows no interest in providing a detailed description of the shape of Abram's religious practice, so we don't know (and nothing is gained through speculation). Nevertheless, we would expect his practice to have a recognizably Mesopotamian shape to it, except where Yahweh has changed something. The covenant is an example of one such change.

Another change that we should note is found in Genesis 22. So far in Abram's experience, nothing has challenged his Great Symbiosis thinking. Abram would conceivably have been "taking care" of Yahweh through religious rituals (not specified, but no alternatives suggested), and Yahweh would have been acting as Abram's personal god. But with Genesis 22, the situation changes irreversibly. The reality of Abram's faith had previously been clarified (Gen 15:6), but now, another question arises, that of the motivation behind Abraham's fear of God.

When God asks Abram to sacrifice Isaac, the request would have likely been within the bounds of what could be asked of someone living within a Mesopotamian context (though admittedly, similar examples are difficult to document in the literature). But the covenant relationship makes this situation different from anything else that we find in the ancient Near East. It is not just his son that Abraham is asked to surrender; all of the covenant benefits would have been sacrificed on that altar with Isaac. With Isaac gone, the benefits of family, land, and blessing would all be forfeited. This request, then, constitutes a serious departure from the Great Symbiosis.

Until that time, everything that Abraham had done, though it required faith, came with a benefit (though not an immediate one; cf. Gen 15:13). The sacrifice of Isaac, on the other hand, would not bring a benefit, and it would mean the loss of all the benefits that Abraham had stood to gain within the covenant program previously. Consequently, this request by God tested whether or not Abraham had moved beyond the Great Symbiosis. Did Abraham still consider his relationship with God to be based on mutual benefit and reciprocity? Would he remain loyal to Yahweh if there were no benefit? Would he have faith if all benefits were lost?

Here Yahweh has raised the bar. Is Abraham's faith only driven by a perceived relationship of mutual gain? Or does he see the covenant as a relationship with God, regardless of the gain? Though Yahweh has much to offer, proper relationship must be founded in who he is, rather than on what he gives. This passage signals a shift in Abraham's thinking, from participation in the Great Symbiosis of the ancient world to participation in the Great Enterprise that is unique to Israel through the covenant. At the same time, it also reveals to us today the sort of God we serve as well as what he expects of us.

Dwelling: Torah for living in the presence of God. The next phase of the development of the covenant comes as Yahweh delivers his people from their slavery in Egypt and leads them back to the land of Abraham via Mount Sinai. There at Mount Sinai, the next step is taken. Here God elects the people of Israel, the descendants of Abraham, Isaac, and Jacob, to be his covenant people (Ex 6:6-8; 19:4-6). When Yahweh began his relationship with Abram, he was not stepping outside the bounds of what was known in the ancient Near East (except in the formalization of the relationship through a ratified covenant and the sign of circumcision). At this point in Israel's narrative, however, the covenant is extended to a whole people group—a concept that is, so far, little attested anywhere else in the ancient world (see sidebar).[8]

"Covenants" in the Ancient World

Sometimes the covenant (*bərît*) between God and Israel in the Old Testament is compared to international treaties of various sorts, loyalty oaths, or land grants from the ancient Near East. The discussion is complex, and even the translation of basic terms is cause for disagreement.

In Akkadian the term *adû* (generally considered a loanword from Aramaic) is used to describe formal, sworn agreements between parties that create an obligation, often of loyalty.[a] Some of these are rightfully termed "treaties," but the term *adû* cannot be limited to that usage. S. Parpola and K. Watanabe list other categories, such as bilateral and unilateral treaties, nonaggression pacts, peace and friendship treaties, mutual assistance pacts, alliance treaties, and treaties with exiled foreign royalty, among a number of others.[b] Another term, *mamītu*, pertains to the oath itself that is sworn in such agreements. These terms are also occasionally used in connection with the sponsorship into which a god enters with a king when he befriends him and supports his kingship.[c]

Most importantly, however, terminology that discusses a god's election of a particular people group, or the formulation of a formal relationship between a god and a people group, has been found in only one fragmentary text. Furthermore, there is little suggestion that the ancient Near Eastern gods desired to be in relationship with people in any way beyond the codependence of the Great Symbiosis or the sponsorship of kings.

---

[8]For discussion see Theodore J. Lewis, "Covenant and Blood Rituals: Understanding Exodus 24:3-8 in Its Ancient Near Eastern Context," in *Confronting the Past: Archaeological and Historical Essays on Ancient Israel in Honor of William C. Dever*, ed. S. Gitin, J. Wright, and J. P. Dessel (Winona Lake, IN: Eisenbrauns, 2006), 341-50.

These differences, however, provide some of the greatest glimpses into the theology of the Israelites, because it is where we are able to identify what differentiated the Israelites from their neighbors that we are apt to find the most important theological aspects of the Old Testament (for them and for us).

[a]For a technical discussion, including other terms used for agreements of various sorts, see J. Lauinger, "The Neo-Assyrian *adê*: Treaty, Oath, or Something Else?," *Journal for Ancient Near Eastern and Biblical Law* 19 (2013): 99-115. Most extensively, see S. Parpola and K. Watanabe, *Neo-Assyrian Treaties and Loyalty Oaths*, State Archives of Assyria 2 (Helsinki: Neo-Assyrian Text Corpus Project, 1988), xv-xxv. A good summary of the current state of the issue can be found in C. Crouch, *Israel and the Assyrians: Deuteronomy, the Succession Treaty of Esarhaddon, and the Nature of Subversion* (Atlanta: SBL Press, 2014), 106-24.

[b]Parpola and Watanabe, *Neo-Assyrian Treaties*, xv-xxiii.

[c]The best example is the covenant of Aššur made with Esarhaddon. See S. Parpola, *Assyrian Prophecies*, State Archives of Assyria 9 (Helsinki: Neo-Assyrian Text Corpus Project, 1997), 22-27; see 3.3, line 27. Other examples include the Marduk Prophecy and the Reform Text of Uru-inimgina.

The transition from an agreement with a family to an agreement with an ethnic group/nation is paralleled by the transition of Yahweh from a family God ("personal god") to a national God. No other examples exist in the ancient world of such a relational transition by a god. In this phase of the covenant, therefore, we see a couple of unique theological developments.

Here we not only find a new step of election (the people of Israel as God's elect people), but we also find a new step of revelation (indeed, one of the most substantial revelations in the Bible): the Torah. The Torah, of course, provides the basis for an orderly society, but it also does much more. What we call "laws" are the stipulations to the covenant that reveal to Israel how to conduct itself appropriately in the presence of a holy God (see chapter five) and how to adopt an identity that is appropriate to the people's status as the covenant people of God. God is holy, and he has designated them, his people, with a status that confers holiness on them. So as they become partners in this Great Enterprise, they adopt the identity that is conducive to the task. The Torah prepares them, even arms them, for the return of the manifest presence of God on earth. But the Torah is not the end; it is the means. In fact, the tabernacle (God's restored presence) is more important than the Torah.

The Stone Tablets

The stone tablets that Yahweh provides, written with his own hand (Ex 24:12; 31:18; 32:15), are today iconic representations of God's law and indeed, at times, of the whole Old Testament. We typically think of them as containing the Ten Commandments, and it is easy to arrive at such a conclusion (Deut 4:13; 10:4). It is significant to note, however, that in Exodus they are introduced and referred to in verses that frame the instructions for the tabernacle, not the Torah (Ten Commandments, book of the law).

In Exodus 31:18; 32:15, the tablets are referred to as the "tablets of the *ʿēdut*" (NIV "covenant law," although the phrase does not use the normal Hebrew word for covenant, *bərît*). The term *ʿēdut* refers to a formal agreement between parties (similar to the Akkadian cognate *adê*, which refers to a sworn agreement that carries with it an obligation and an expected response).[a] The term is also used in relation to the tabernacle (tent of the *ʿēdut*, tabernacle of the *ʿēdut*), as well as the tabernacle's constituent parts (e.g., the ark of the *ʿēdut*, the curtain of the *ʿēdut*). Generally, it is assumed that these designations indicate a copy of the Torah is kept in the ark, which is in the tabernacle, and the evidence could easily lead us to this conclusion.

Nevertheless, in light of where the references to these tablets are placed within the context of Exodus, the tablets may also have included the instructions for the tabernacle and perhaps even a diagram of its design. In the ancient Near East, the gods frequently gave instructions for the building of temples and also provided diagrams (such as the one pictured on the lap of Gudea in a well-known statue from about 2000 BCE). In fact, the biblical text refers to God's provision of such a diagram (*tabnît*; Ex 25:9, 40; 26:30; 27:8; Num 8:4),[b] and the Gudea Temple dedication cylinder suggests that tabernacle-building instructions and diagrams could represent sworn agreements. On this cylinder, Gudea refers to a "firm promise" of the gods, which is represented by the decision to build a temple for a dwelling place.[c] Furthermore, the connection between written instructions and the construction of sacred space is found in Esarhaddon's description of his work at the temple of Ešarra: "I made [it] beautiful as the heavenly writing."[d] The sworn agreement between Yahweh and Israel might then refer to Yahweh's promise to come to dwell among his people when they prepare an appropriate place for him.

All of this evidence then suggests that in Exodus the tablets were provided, first and foremost, for the building of the tabernacle, while the Torah serves contingently as instructions for living in proximity to sacred space.[e] This distinction does not mean that none of the Torah instructions were included on the tablets,[f] but it does suggest that we would be remiss to exclude the instructions for the tabernacle from among its contents.

[a] See Parpola and Watanabe, Neo-Assyrian Treaties, xv-xxv.

[b] V. Hurowitz, I Have Built You an Exalted House (Sheffield, UK: JSOT Press, 1992), 168-70.

[c] D. O. Edzard, Gudea and His Dynasty, RIME 3/1 (Toronto: University of Toronto Press, 1997), Cyl B: 24.11-14, p. 101.

[d] Hurowitz, I Have Built You an Exalted House, 245.

[e] See William Schniedewind, "Scripturalization in Ancient Judah," in Contextualizing Israel's Sacred Writings, ed. B. Schmidt (Atlanta: SBL Press, 2015), 313.

[f] Ex 34:1, 4, 27-29, when read together, seem to suggest that at least the "ten words" were included on the tablets and that they represent the covenant (bərît).

I maintain that the Torah is contingent on the tabernacle, rather than the other way around. Torah is designed to prevent a repeat of the fall, which was when access to God's presence was lost. It is also to provide a means for Israel to survive in such close proximity to the intrinsically dangerous presence of Yahweh. The Torah loses its primary significance if there is no abiding presence of God, which is the main reason the New Testament views the law as having lost its role after Pentecost. After all, once the Holy Spirit descended, God's presence dwelled in his people, who became the temple, rather than in a geographical location (1 Cor 3:16; 6:19; 2 Cor 6:16). Nevertheless, in this Sinaitic phase of the covenant, the Torah is revealed in preparation for the restoration of God's presence among his people. It is that abiding presence that provides the opportunity for a relationship that far exceeds the simple formal agreement that had existed with Abram. Indeed, Yahweh had formed that formal relationship with Abram precisely to begin movement toward the reestablished dwelling that is accomplished in the tabernacle (Ex 40:34).

Tent of Meeting

The term *tabernacle* (Hebrew *miškān*) describes the entire sacred installation, including the courtyard. The tent of meeting (Hebrew *'ōhel mô'ēd*), on the other hand, refers to the outer chamber (Ex 40:7, 22-26; Lev 4:4-7) that adjoins the holy of holies, which was the inner chamber where God dwelled.[a] In the courtyard, sacrifices were made, but in the tent of meeting the priests would meet with God (Ex 30:36). In other words, the *miškān* terminology focuses on God's dwelling; the *'ōhel mô'ēd* terminology pertains to the communicative interrelationship God intended with his people.

Prior to the construction of the tabernacle, a provisional tent of meeting was set up outside the camp where Moses met with Yahweh (Ex 33:7). In Numbers, once the tabernacle is constructed, it is placed in the center of the camp, along with the tent of meeting at its center. The tent of meeting is not mentioned in Judges and is only referred to once in Samuel and in Kings. The terminology is picked up more frequently in Chronicles, but it is likely that it is just there as a vestige from the tabernacle days and refers to the antechamber of the temple, not to an actual tent set up inside the temple (1 Chron 9:23).

As a final note, if we consider Genesis 1 to be an account of God's ordering of the cosmos to establish a sacred space in which he intends to dwell, and if we consider Genesis 2 to be an account of God's relation with his people from within sacred space (Eden), Genesis 1 could pertain to the cosmic *miškān* while Genesis 2 pertains to the role of the *miškān* as an *'ōhel mô'ēd*.[b] At the other end of the spectrum, we could argue that at his incarnation Jesus becomes a *miškān* (Jn 1:14) through whose work the dividing curtain in the *'ōhel mô'ēd* is torn (Mt 27:51), allowing unimpeded access to the presence of God (Heb 10:20) and removing the hazard posed to sinful people by the presence of God.

---

[a] For further discussion of the distinctions between these two, see L. M. Morales, *The Tabernacle Pre-Figured* (Leuven: Peeters, 2012), and Michael B. Hundley, *Gods in Dwellings* (Atlanta: SBL Press, 2013).

[b] For more discussion of these issues in Genesis, see chapter three.

Reigning: Our God reigns. For centuries the tabernacle served as the residence of Yahweh among his people Israel. A structural transition took place in the time of Solomon when the portable tent shrine was replaced by a permanent structure in the capital city of Jerusalem—a temple meant to be a luxurious palace for a holy God. But before that change took place, a more significant event marked the next phase in the development of the covenant: Yahweh chose David to be king.

In the ancient world, one of the greatest achievements that a king could undertake was the building (or at least the restoration) of a temple, which is understandable within the framework of the Great Symbiosis. The more glorious and luxuriant the temple, the more pleased the god would be and the more likely to bestow prosperity on the king and the people. It is therefore significant that Yahweh declined David's offer to build a temple (2 Sam 7:1-7). In the literature of the ancient world, a god occasionally would withhold permission for the construction of a temple, but the denial was due to the god's disfavor of the king.[9] It is clear, in contrast, that David *did* enjoy the favor of Yahweh, especially since the second half of 2 Samuel 7 entails Yahweh's offer of a covenant to David.

Yahweh offers this covenant, not incidentally, after David has restored the ark of the covenant to a central position in his newly established capital city, Jerusalem. The ark had remained in isolation ever since it had been briefly captured by the Philistines (1 Sam 4–6). And even though it had been returned to Israel, it remained in Kiriath Jearim throughout the reign of Saul (1 Sam 6:2–7:2). When David restores it (2 Sam 6), the presence of God is returned to prominence in Israel, and Yahweh's response is to offer a new level of relationship.

This new level of relationship is demonstrated by the new step of election in the Davidic covenant as David and his descendants are established as the dynasty of kings endorsed by Yahweh. In other words, it is through David and his line that Yahweh reigns, and this covenant is the new stage of revelation. God is not just present among his people; he is ruling the nations from his throne in the temple in Jerusalem. This element does not find much

---

[9]The king was Naram-Sin, and the details are given in a piece that was written during the next dynasty (Ur III) called "The Curse of Akkad," published in J. S. Cooper, *The Curse of Agade* (Baltimore: Johns Hopkins University Press, 1983).

expression in the narrative literature, but it is universally recognized as the major theme of the Psalms, most notably in the series in Psalms 93–100; the clear articulation of the relationship between dwelling place, resting place, temple, ark, and rule in Psalm 132; and the grand finale in Psalm 145, which is then concluded with the fivefold paean of praise in Psalms 146–150. God is the great king ruling over his kingdom, and David and his descendants serve as vice-regents whom Yahweh has placed on the throne and who serve at his pleasure and discretion.[10] Through these kings God not only rules, but he also reveals the nature of his kingship and kingdom. His dwelling is not only a palatial residence; it is a throne room. And from his throne room he not only rules Israel and the nations; he rules the cosmos.

Some of these elements can be understood from the context of the transition to monarchy that takes place in the first half of 1 Samuel. The books of Samuel, in which the Davidic covenant functions as a rhetorical center, begin by introducing Samuel as the prophet, priest, and judge who later plays a significant role as kingmaker. Of course, it was not unusual in the ancient world for any king to claim that a god supported his rise to the throne and deposed his predecessor. Every king wanted to legitimate his rule and often used divine appropriation as a source of legitimation. So why would David's rise to power be any different? The books of Samuel give the answer, and a big part of that answer is found in the character of Samuel. Samuel, the one who later anoints David as king, is established within the narrative in a couple of ways. For example, he was born under special circumstances to a previously barren, yet pious woman (1 Sam 1). He was then raised in the temple (1 Sam 2), where he was given a prophetic commission at a young age (1 Sam 3), and eventually, under God's authority, he led the Israelites to victory against their enemies (1 Sam 7). By establishing Samuel as Yahweh's chosen leader and instrument, Samuel's role in anointing David is justified as Yahweh's choice. Even the circumstances of David's anointing (1 Sam 16) give evidence of Yahweh's involvement, against Samuel's own better judgment.

Even so, it is not Samuel who initiates the transition to kingship. The move to transition comes from the people and is driven by less than

---

[10]Thanks to my colleague Adam Miglio, who reminded me of the shift between 2 Sam 7:16 ("Your house and your kingdom") and 1 Chron 17:14 ("my house and my kingdom").

commendable motivations. But it is important for us to examine this episode because it communicates much that will eventually influence our understanding of the Davidic covenant. Most significantly, we have to ask the questions "Why do the people want a king?" and "Why is Yahweh displeased by their request?" The people explain their request for a king by observing that Samuel is old and his sons incompetent. They express the desire to have a king "such as all the other nations have" (1 Sam 8:5) and to be like other nations by having a king "to go out before us and fight our battles" (1 Sam 8:20).

All of the reasons the Israelites give make sense within the context of the biblical text and the ancient Near East. Israel regularly suffered at the hands of its enemies during the centuries of the judges period, so it is logical for it to desire an alternative political structure. The people reasonably concluded that they needed to be unified under one leader in order to prevent the constant incursions of enemies. Of course, even the casual reader of the biblical text will notice that their subjugation at the hand of enemies was not due to their tribal structure but to their unfaithfulness toward Yahweh. Consequently, they were seeking a political solution to what was, in essence, a spiritual problem.

Kingship itself did not pose a theological problem; in fact, it had been anticipated since the earliest phases of the covenant (Gen 17:6; 35:11; 49:10; Num 24:17; Deut 17:14-20; 1 Sam 2:10). Nevertheless, Yahweh indicates to Samuel that in making their request, the Israelites have rejected him as king over them (1 Sam 8:7). *This* statement represents the part that is confusing. If the Israelites wanted a king like the nations, they were certainly *not* asking for a king who operated without the support of a deity. No nation in the ancient world would have wanted a king who had no divine sponsor. They would not have chosen between king and god; they would have specifically wanted a king who was closely allied with a god. Israel, then, would not have asked for a king to replace Yahweh—such a king would not be a "king such as all the other nations have." It would not have wanted a king who would lead them out to battle only in his own strength. So what is the problem here? How are they rejecting Yahweh?

The answer can be found by paying close attention to the flow of the context. In the recent context of 1 Samuel, the Israelites were struggling in a battle against the Philistines and decided that they could turn the battle in their favor if they brought the ark of the covenant to the battlefield (1 Sam 4:3-4). Though initially successful (1 Sam 4:5-9), the Philistines ultimately won the battle, killed the two sons of Eli, and took the ark as plunder. This narrative stands as an illustration of the misuse of the ark of the covenant. In the past, under instruction by Yahweh, the ark was indeed taken into battle as a symbol of his presence (Josh 6), but it could only serve in this manner if Yahweh so indicated. As it was, the sons of Eli were using the ark as a palladium that could coerce Yahweh to be at their beck and call.[11] Against this background we can understand that when the Israelites requested a king, they were on the rebound from an experience in which the ark "failed" them. Seeking an alternative palladium, they concluded that a king could serve in the role. And in the ancient world, they indeed viewed the interaction between the kings and gods in this way; the kings led the armies into battle under the banner of the gods from whom they enlisted support.

The bottom line is that the Israelites did not want the method or manner of their deliverance from oppressors to be subject to Yahweh's discretion; they wanted to control that process. Consequently, when Yahweh indicates that they rejected him as king over them, he reflects the fact that they have tried to seize control of their own destiny as a nation, thereby relegating him to a subservient status of compliance. This action, then, is certainly a subversion of his kingship.

Saul is given to Israel by Yahweh to fulfill the royal job description as they have imagined it, though their flawed reasoning does not bode well for success. When Saul fails, Yahweh is standing by to choose another king who will fulfill the job description as he intends it (1 Sam 13:14). And in the narrative of David's battle with Goliath, we discover what constitutes the main criterion that God had in mind.

When David comes to the battlefield to bring food to his brothers and hears the Yahweh-defying challenge of Goliath, he is filled with righteous indignation (1 Sam 17:26). Though Saul was the tallest, the most experienced, the one tasked with leading the armies of Israel, and the most obvious candidate to battle Goliath, he is eager to hear of David's interest (1 Sam 17:31).

---

[11]J. Harvey Walton, "A King like the Nations: 1 Samuel 8 in Its Cultural Context," *Biblica* 96 (2015): 179-200.

And in their conversation, we learn that David is jealous for Yahweh's reputation (1 Sam 17:32-36). He is willing to go out and fight a seemingly hopeless battle because he truly believes that Yahweh fights the battles and that Yahweh's name should be exalted (1 Sam 17:45-47). David's proclamation in his speech to Goliath, then, marks him as one who fights God's battles, rather than one who tries to get God to fight his battles for him. In short, David recognizes the full weight of God's kingship over Israel. This recognition is presumably why Yahweh has chosen David to be king and why he later makes a covenant with him.

In other words, this third phase of the covenant advances the nature of God's presence with Israel (through his direction of the nation and the choice of its king), establishes a new level of relationship with God (through kingship), and reveals Yahweh as the king of Israel, the nations, the world, and even the cosmos, as recognized throughout the Psalms.

Saving: New covenant in the blood of Christ. The final phase of the covenant is found in what is dubbed the new covenant in the Old Testament and is fulfilled as such in the New Testament. However, when the new covenant is introduced in Jeremiah and Ezekiel, it should be observed that this covenant is made with the house of Israel (Jer 31:31-33; Ezek 37:15-28). And in the formulation of this phase, we can also find all of the features that we have been tracing through the previous developmental phases. The children of Israel, under the new covenant, will live in the land given to Jacob (Ezek 37:25); they will observe Torah (Ezek 37:24); Yahweh will dwell in their midst (Ezek 37:26-27); David's line will rule over them (Ezek 37:24); and they will be in relationship with Yahweh as partners in his purposes and promoters of his kingdom ("I will be their God, and they will be my people," Ezek 37:27). They will also be a light to the nations because "the nations will know that I the LORD make Israel holy" by virtue of the sanctuary among them (Ezek 37:28). We also find elements that have not been featured, specifically the forgiveness of sins and the writing of Torah on the heart of God's people.

Even though it speaks of forgiveness, the Old Testament discussions of this covenantal phase say nothing about sacrifice, atonement, or salvation from sins. Forgiveness may be an innovation to this phase of the covenant, but it had long been a central feature in the ritual system by which Israel related to God at the temple. In this phase God intends to forgive the sins of

Torah on the Heart

It is common for modern readers, as well as theologians, to interpret "written on the heart" as a reflection of the internalization of the law, mostly based on references in Proverbs that use similar language in the same sort of context (Prov 3:3; 7:3).[a] A good reason to reconsider this conclusion, however, is that the idiom in Jeremiah 31, though referring both to writing and to the heart, is different from the idiom in Proverbs; in the latter, the person is writing on his or her own heart. When a person writes on the tablet of his or her own heart, the metaphor is that of a scribe with a wax-board practice tablet. These scribes would write their lessons over and over again and, by practice, perfect their skills. Writing on one's own heart refers to the repetition of living a certain way and may well refer to memorization or internalization. But when someone else writes on a person's heart (e.g., Yahweh), such an interpretation is less likely. Jeremiah can hardly be indicating that Yahweh is going to impose the law on his people by force. If someone else is writing on the tablet, the lessons are not being learned by experience.

A reasonable alternative can be discerned from the cognitive environment of the ancient Near East. In ancient literature we often find writing on the entrails (note that Jer 31:33 refers to "minds," which is actually the word for "entrails" [Hebrew *qrb*] and "heart") during the process of a divination procedure known as extispicy, a procedure instigated by someone who desires specific revelation from a deity on a particular matter. In the ritual, an animal is slaughtered before the deity, and a meal is offered to procure favor. The diviner priest then sets forth a request that the god write the answer to the question on the entrails. Afterwards, the entrails are examined to determine the god's communication. The entrails thus function as the writing pads of the gods.

In the new covenant it is Torah that is written on the heart (i.e., placed in the entrails). The Hebrew word *Torah* is cognate to the Akkadian term that refers to the oracles that the gods write on the entrails in extispicy (*têrtu*), and as students of Hebrew know well, *torah* in its most basic sense refers to instruction, which sometimes comes about by revelation.

By using the metaphors common to the practice of extispicy, Jeremiah is communicating to his audience how, in the new covenant, Yahweh will be revealing the Torah through his people. If we recall that the force of the Torah is to show the Israelites how to live in the presence of God and how to participate in his order and his purposes, then in this new covenant, the people will find that God has made himself (his ways and his expectations) known to each of them so that they will know how to live in his presence. Thus God is made known through the faithfulness of his people. People with the law written on their hearts become *mediums of communication*. It is of interest to note that Paul uses the metaphor with a similar understanding in 2 Corinthians 3:2-3: "You yourselves are our letter, written on our hearts, known and read by everyone. You show that you are a letter from Christ, the result of our ministry, written not with ink but with the Spirit of the living God, not on tablets of stone but on tablets of human hearts." In this interpretation of the metaphor, then, the heart is a medium, not a repository.[b] In this way the Torah in the new covenant is intended to draw status and identity together rather than serving (as could be inferred about the old covenant) as a collection of laws, rules, and moral norms.

---

[a]For variations that don't use the full metaphor see Deut 6:6; Ps 37:31; 40:8.

[b]J. Walton, *Ancient Near Eastern Thought and the Old Testament* (Grand Rapids: Baker, 2006), 258.

Israel that had resulted in its exile and to restore the people to the land, but he does not offer a new mechanism for forgiveness. Rather, it is left to the New Testament to elaborate the aspects of the new covenant that identify the new stages of election and revelation.

The Old Testament indicates that this last phase is coming, and it also delineates the result of the phase. It is silent, however, about the mechanism. Only in the New Testament do we learn how this result is achieved as we discover the way in which Jesus brings about the fulfillment of the covenant. Through his death and resurrection the aspects of the new covenant are realized. And the new step of election is that now, through the atonement and justification provided by the blood and death of Christ, election is extended to all who receive the work of Christ on their behalf. This election is no longer defined by natural or acquired ethnic identity but by a faith commitment. Furthermore, rather than being elected to be the people of God through whom Yahweh reveals himself to the world, the new group is elected to be the people of God whom he has redeemed from their sins. The new step of revelation is the mechanism by which God accomplishes these tasks—the salvation provided through the mechanism of the death and blood of Christ, which is revealed for the first time in the New Testament.

The People of God and the Kingdom of God

Whether in the Old or New Testament, the kingdom of God is populated by the people of God. But how should these designations be defined and understood? In the Old Testament, God chose Israel to be his people. As such, they had a specific status that came with both benefits and a role to play. The benefit was that they would become a nation living in the land God had given them and in which he dwelt. Their role was to be an instrument for God's revelation and to serve as a light to the nations. Since Yahweh dwelt in their midst, they were supposed to be the capital city of the kingdom of God. Indeed, they were given this citizenship, but they did not always behave in a manner befitting their holy status. In this we find a tension that has always existed, even until today: those who are the people of God living in the kingdom of God do not always act as the people of God, honor their place in the kingdom, or represent the kingdom well. The identity the people of God adopt does not always match the status that has been conferred on them. They are insiders by status, but too often outsiders by practice. Ethnic Israel was a manifestation of the kingdom of God, but only some (at times referred to as the righteous remnant) actually adopted an identity that was true to their status.

Through Christ, God has chosen the church to be his people, pulling down the dividing wall (Eph 2). Here we find the status from which our identity is derived (we are "in Christ"), and as a new creation (2 Cor 5:17), we have become partners in the Great Enterprise of God. In this relationship we experience benefits: our sins are not only forgiven but washed away, and we are given full access to God through Christ. Our role is encapsulated in the Great Commission. Since Christ dwells in us, we should live in a way that befits our status (righteous and holy), showing ourselves to be exemplary citizens of the kingdom of God. Nevertheless, while we are given this citizenship, we do not always live it out well. History is littered with the debris of Christians who failed in the worst ways to forge an identity that was in keeping with the status of the people of God. And so the same tension exists in the kingdom of God today that has always existed, and it testifies to the distance between status and identity. We are conferred a status that makes us insiders, but the resulting identity can still mark us as outsiders.

In these ways there is continuity between Israel and the church. Both are given a status through election, and both identify as the people of God, citizens of the kingdom of God who are committed to participating in the purposes of God as those who have the holy God dwelling in their midst. But discontinuity is found in the benefits that are made available based on the unfolding of God's plan. The concept of the kingdom of God is not first and foremost about salvation;[a] it is founded on the premise of faithful citizens who have pursued the relationship of partnership that God has made available. The most important common ground between the new covenant and the prior stages of the covenant is that God dwells among (and eventually in) his people. Whatever their role, the people of God are defined as those among whom God dwells.

---

[a]Here I use the term *salvation* as it is often thought of in individual terms. When extended to include the cosmos and corporate humanity in the cosmos, its process overlays with the kingdom of God nicely.

Now that we have laid out the framework of the covenant phases, it yet remains for us to fit some of the larger theological pieces of the Old Testament into this framework.

Land. One of the most visible aspects of the covenant is the land that was promised to Abram and given to Israel. To the tribes of Israel, it became their landholding (*'aḥuzzâ*) and their patrimony (*naḥalâ*) from generation to generation. It is one of the principal benefits of the covenant and one of the most controversial aspects of the covenant, as it continues to have a role in modern politics.

The first observation that needs to be made is that the Old Testament is consistent in its claim that ultimately the land does not belong to Israel; it belongs to Yahweh. His gift (a land grant, in ancient Near Eastern terms) is that he allows Israel to have possession of his land. This distinction affects every other discussion about the land. The Canaanites were driven from the land because it was being designated as ineligible for human use. Yahweh was going to use it as his dwelling place and to do with it as he desired. Israel did not do anything to deserve the land; Yahweh chose to settle it in this sacred land as a nation of his priests (Ezek 37:25-28).

Israel was also eventually driven out at the time of the exile (the people were guilty of specific covenant-related offenses). The covenant does not therefore establish a right to the land; instead, it requires one to seek to be worthy of the gift of the land. In other words, the Israelites of Joshua's time did not take the land. Rather, God took it from the Canaanites and gave it to Israel. Furthermore, Yahweh's gift of the land is often expressed by the common Hebrew verb *nātan*. Being a general term, this verb does not clarify whether the land is a gift or a grant, but clarification can be achieved by looking at texts and theology across the span of the Old Testament. If there is no presence of God, no priests are necessary, and there is no basis for tenancy (in modern-day terms). And if there is no faithfulness to the covenant by this appointed nation of priests, their role is forfeited, and again, any basis for tenancy is lost.[12]

We now return to clarifying the identity of the true and ultimate owner of the land. On this point, there is really no question. In a general but very real sense the land belongs to Yahweh (Lev 25:23-24; Josh 22:19; Jer 2:7; Ezek 36:5; Hos 9:3). This designation of ownership follows a pattern that is seen in the ancient world at large—that the gods were the ultimate owners of the land.[13] In the ancient world, it was common for elites (especially kings) to grant land possession to faithful or important associates or vassals. But the land, of course, remained the property of the overlord.

---

[12]This is not supercessionism because it does not involve the church replacing Israel or inheriting the benefits of Israel's covenant.
[13]See discussion in J. Milgrom, *Leviticus 23–27*, Anchor Yale Bible (New Haven, CT: Yale University Press, 2001), 2184-87.

Ḥerem

The theological aspect of Israel's conquest of the land is often miscon-strued because of a basic misunderstanding of the concept of "the ban" (*ḥerem*). The following points can reshape the conversation:[a]

1. The term *ḥerem* designates the land and its cities ineligible for mundane human use.

2. Priests are the exception as those who serve in the sacred precinct (Num 18:10; Ezek 45:1-5; 48:10-12). Otherwise, the land is off limits for hu-man use (Ezek 44:9).

3. The term likewise designates people as ineligible for being assimilated in any way. They must therefore be driven out or, if resistant, killed.

4. Current occupants need to be evicted, but not because they have done something wrong. It is their presence (not their deeds) that "defiles" and does not conform to the order that defines Yahweh's sacred space (*tô'ēbâ* = contrary to the criteria for order).[b] In Ezekiel's temple, Levites are banned from sacred space (the consequences of their *'āwôn*); they are not to come near because they committed *tô'ēbâ* (Ezek 44:12-13).

5. The main reason for driving out the people of the land is so that they will not lead Israel into syncretistic practices that would be contrary to the covenant.

6. The covenant means that Israel is a partner with God in the carrying out of his purposes. The Canaanites are not partners in the covenant and would distract Israel from fulfilling that role.[c] The land has been cordoned off, and those not involved in the project need to stay out of the way.

7. Passages that have appeared to suggest crimes of the Canaanites need to be reanalyzed:

   ✦ Genesis 15:16 should be understood as saying, "You (Abram) will die in peace, but the fourth generation (beyond your lifetime) will re-turn, because at this time (*'ad hēnnâ*), no eviction notices (*'āwôn*) are being processed (*lō'šālēm*)."[d]

✦ Leviticus 18:24-28 and Deuteronomy 9:4-6 portray the people of the land as outside of the confines of order as described by the covenant but nevertheless in proximity to Yahweh's sacred space. They are also portrayed in terms known from ancient Near Eastern literature as common designations for outsiders.

8. An interesting comparison can be drawn from Jesus' cleansing of the temple.[e] He "drives out" (*ekballein*, the same verb that the LXX uses in Ex 23:28-31) *both* the buyers and sellers (Mk 11:15) because they are violating the zoning laws (*tôrôt hābayit*, "law of the temple"; see Ezek 43:12) of sacred space (by conducting human activities). It is likely that some corrupt practices were involved (he does call them thieves), but they are being evicted because their occupancy (not their deeds) was defiling (*ṭāmēʾ*) and contrary to the order (*tôʿēbâ*) of the sacred precinct. They have made the temple a den of thieves. Notably, thieves do not thieve in their dens; the den is where they take refuge.

---

[a]For more details on each of these points, see John H. Walton and J. Harvey Walton, *The Lost World of the Israelite Conquest* (Downers Grove, IL: InterVarsity Press, 2017).

[b]Ezek 43:8: "When they placed their threshold next to my threshold and their doorposts beside my doorposts, with only a wall between me and them, they defiled (*ṭimmʾû*) my holy name by their detestable practices (*tôʿēbâ*). So I destroyed (*wāʾakal*) them in my anger."

[c]Participation would have been available to them (cf. Rahab), but they were not interested.

[d]Walton and Walton, *Lost World of the Israelite Conquest*, 50-63.

[e]Suggested to me by Bradley Cameron.

These grants were often broadly conditional but also of an enduring nature (that is, not for a specified term but in perpetuity, a lasting possession).[14] This arrangement is similar to the sort we find in the covenant. In the Old Testament, it is common for the covenant, or for the benefits of the covenant, to be designated as *ʿôlām*, which is often translated "eternal" or "everlasting"

---

[14]Weinfeld had built a case for the inherent unconditionality of the grants, but that has been thoroughly refuted by Knoppers. See M. Weinfeld, "The Covenant of Grant in the Old Testament and in the Ancient Near East," *Journal of the American Oriental Society* 90 (1970): 184-203; G. N. Knoppers, "Ancient Near Eastern Royal Grants and the Davidic Covenant: A Parallel?," *Journal of the American Oriental Society* 116 (1996): 670-97. See also Richard S. Hess, "The Book of Joshua as a Land Grant," *Bib* 83 (2002): 493-506.

(e.g., Gen 13:15; 17:8; 48:4). However, this translation is misleading because it suggests an abstraction that is not inherent in the word. In reality, the word ʿôlām designates the grant as open ended, or without a specified term. The grant, therefore, would have been of an enduring nature, granted in perpetuity. Possession comprises the full extent of the covenant benefit (i.e., no abstract right or permanent ownership). The word ʿôlām does not communicate that the possession of the land can never be withdrawn, as evidenced by the very fact that it *was* withdrawn at the exile.

So why did God offer land as part of the covenant, and what function does it have in the covenant? From the breadth of the biblical evidence, I suggest that the land is given not so that Israel will have a place to live but to serve Yahweh's purposes as he establishes his residence among his people. It does give them a place to live, but the point is that it is where they will live in the presence of God. Yahweh is going to dwell in their midst in geographical space made sacred by his presence. The land has to do with his intentions for his presence; he desires to establish a place where *he* lives among his people, not just to give his people a place to live (Ex 15:17). The land thereby finds it significance as the place where God's presence is reestablished and Israel serves as host to the presence of God.

Even when God's presence had not yet been established (from the patriarchs to the conquest), or when it had departed (during the exile), the importance of the land lies in its connection to what God intends to establish or restore. The offer of the land is therefore not essentially concerned with economics (land ownership) or with politics (land rights). These elements simply become issues for discussion in light of the fact that the land belongs to Yahweh and is the place of his presence. This explains, for instance, why land and temple at times are treated coextensively. In the end, the issue of land is related to the issue of sacred space. Yahweh claims the land as his own because he intends to reestablish his earthly presence there, and he grants it to Israel because he has chosen to dwell in the midst of his designated priests. Having the land is not an independent benefit; it is only meaningful if Yahweh is living among them.

All of these interconnections can be seen in Deuteronomy 6–12. His people are to remain faithful to Yahweh and to keep his laws, which were designed to show them how to live in his presence, as the Canaanites are being driven out of the land. And all of these chapters are leading inexorably to Deuteronomy 12, which indicates that Yahweh will place his name at a location of his choosing in the land—*his* land—of which he has given them possession so they may live in proximity to him.

But we do not have to wait until Deuteronomy to see the expression of these ideas. In Moses' song of the sea in Exodus 15 (generally considered one of the most ancient pieces in the Hebrew Bible), there are two interesting references to the land as God's holy land where he will dwell and reign. Exodus 15:13 refers to it as "your holy dwelling." Exodus 15:17 expands by indicating "You will bring them and plant them on the mountain of your inheritance." And then Exodus 15:18 draws the logical conclusion, "the LORD reigns." Through this we can see the manner in which the earliest Israelite traditions viewed the role of the land.

So when Abram was asked to leave his land in Genesis 12, the request included more than a mere change of location. Land in Mesopotamia was not understood to be real estate or the basis of a national identity. Land was the property of the gods, and the location of the land brought the people into the proximity of a temple whose gods they served. Everyone served the gods in their vicinity through the offerings that they brought to the temple and through various rituals and festivals. One's land was related to one's god. As we have previously noted, to leave one's land meant (perhaps among other things) to leave the gods who were connected to that land. Presumably, then, we could deduce that when Yahweh brings Abram to a new land, it is Yahweh's land where he will be served and, as we eventually learn, where he will take up residence in a temple. And in Genesis 12, when Abram first enters the land, very little detail is given except for the construction of altars at key sites in the land. This construction is not coincidental. Abram is invoking God's presence and establishing touch points for sacred space.

At the other end of the Old Testament, when the prophets speak of the future restoration of Israel and the return from exile, the return to the land is almost always associated with the restored presence of God in their midst (Is 2:2-5; 4:2-6; 14:1-2 [Yahweh's land!]; 57:13; 60:4-21; Jer 31:23-25; 33:10-11; Ezek 20; 39:25-29; 45:1; Hos 2:21-23; Zech 2:7-12). One of the strongest expressions of this sentiment occurs in Ezekiel 37:21-28:

> This is what the Sovereign LORD says: I will take the Israelites out of the nations where they have gone. I will gather them from all around and bring them back into their own land. I will make them one nation in the land, on the mountains

of Israel. There will be one king over all of them and they will never again be two nations or be divided into two kingdoms. They will no longer defile themselves with their idols and vile images or with any of their offenses, for I will save them from all their sinful backsliding, and I will cleanse them. They will be my people, and I will be their God. My servant David will be king over them, and they will all have one shepherd. They will follow my laws and be careful to keep my decrees. They will live in the land I gave to my servant Jacob, the land where your ancestors lived. They and their children and their children's children will live there forever, and David my servant will be their prince forever. I will make a covenant of peace with them; it will be an everlasting covenant. I will establish them and increase their numbers, and I will put my sanctuary among them forever. My dwelling place will be with them; I will be their God, and they will be my people. Then the nations will know that I the LORD make Israel holy, when my sanctuary is among them forever.

Land is not just property enfranchisement, and it is virtually meaningless in covenant terms if God is not dwelling in it. When Israel actually returns from exile, the neglect of the temple building project becomes a focus of the prophets. Haggai, for example, poignantly confronts his audience with the stark fact that their land is doing them no good since the temple has not been rebuilt (Hag 1:2-11). The land is nonproductive and desolate if God is not there in their midst. Therefore, the covenant promise of the land is fulfilled not just when Israel lives there but when Yahweh lives there as well.

In this way we can see that covenant, since the point of its inception with Abram, is an initiative by God to establish a relationship that he intends to be characterized by his presence among his people. Therefore, covenant and presence are closely related. The same concept is also true with the new covenant. When the new covenant is announced in Jeremiah and Ezekiel, Yahweh has left the temple that has been destroyed. A new covenant with Israel projects a reestablishment of the covenant relationship that has been interrupted by their unfaithfulness and his departure from the temple. In the new covenant, Yahweh is again going to take up his presence among his people. And this promise is fulfilled after the construction of the second temple and the renewal of the covenant and law at the end of the exile in the time of Zerubbabel. But Jesus also ushers in a further fulfillment of this new covenant ("in my blood") in the same context in which he announces the coming of the Holy Spirit at Pentecost (just seven weeks later). God's presence is about to be established on a whole new level.

Kingdom. The covenant formally establishes a kingdom in the stage when David and his line are chosen to serve as Yahweh's designated kings. But, as previously noted, the covenant had anticipated kings and a kingdom from the very beginning (Gen 17:6; 35:11; 49:10; Num 24:17; Deut 17:14-20; 1 Sam 2:10). Nevertheless, the covenant is not ultimately about David's kingdom; it is about the messianic kingdom, the kingdom of God. The covenant does not establish the kingdom of God; it gives it shape and direction. God's rule of the cosmos, of the earth, of Israel, over people, or in our lives is not subject to the covenant. The covenant actualizes the kingdom of God in a place and in a people. It communicates how God is manifesting his rule and his kingdom.

God's kingdom is always active regardless of whether the earthly kingdom in Israel is or is not a reality, and this concept is the very point of Chronicles. Postexilic Israel had no independent kingdom and had no king. Yet one of the important messages of the book is that God rules nonetheless. His presence in the temple (served by the priests and Levites) is a sufficient manifestation of God's kingdom and of the reality of the covenant. Thus covenant and presence are presented as more important than the manifestation of an earthly kingdom in a Davidic line, or even than their independence as a nation.

The revelation of the Torah in the covenant is to give the Israelites guidance as to how to live in the presence of God, which is the same guidance needed to live in the kingdom of God. The priests of Israel are the guardians of sacred space (see chapter five). The kings are to establish justice and security for the land as they serve as vice-regents of Yahweh, executing his kingship. The prophets are the champions of the covenant, calling Israel back to faithfulness through repentance and return to Yahweh. These offices and institutions have their ancient Near Eastern counterparts, but in Israel, all of them are designed to operate within the covenant and on its behalf.

Presence. To summarize the connection here, I submit that though the covenant establishes a relationship and serves as an instrument of revelation, its ultimate goal is to provide the foundation for the reestablishment of the presence of God on the earth (which had been lost at Eden and constitutes God's ultimate plan). As Yahweh formed a relationship with Israel through the covenant and became known to them through the revelation associated with the covenant, he intended to establish his presence on earth among them so that all the peoples of the earth would be blessed. Israel was not chosen because of its inherent worthiness; God simply decided to execute his plan in this manner. Nevertheless, it established Israel as a privileged people (compare Jesus' words to Zacchaeus in Lk 19:5, "I must stay at your house today").

Plan. The covenant embodies Yahweh's long-term plan for dwelling in relationship with people. Even given that there is a single fragmentary ancient Near Eastern text that speaks of a covenant relationship between a god and a group of people, this is far from comparable to the plan of Yahweh to establish his presence among the people of the earth. The shape and purpose of this covenant are intimately connected to the sort of God that Yahweh is, and there is no god who acts like him in the ancient world (see chapter two). Yahweh has a plan that he has been implementing over the full span of time, a plan that employs a group of people as instruments, even as he targets all humanity, and his goal is to dwell among his creatures in a relationship that he has intended but not needed from the beginning. All of these characteristics distinguish Yahweh as unique.

What does it all teach about God? Our approach throughout the book is to identify the enduring theology that emerges from the Old Testament, the theology revealed and understood by the original Israelite audience and still standing today as God's authoritative revelation of his plans and purposes for his people of all time and places. The first line of investigation of any portion of Scripture (since we believe it to be God's self-revelation) should be focused on what we learn about what God does. Such teaching derives from the Old Testament texts themselves, is contextually interpreted, and is not dependent on further developments in the New Testament (though any such developments would, themselves, also carry revelatory significance).

Some of the most important theology we learn from the covenant includes:

✦ Yahweh has a long-term plan to bring blessing to humanity through a relationship established with a particular person and, eventually, with his descendants.

✦ That plan is to dwell on earth among his people and to be in relationship with them.

✦ Yahweh offers to his people many of the same things that other gods offered (e.g., provision, protection), but his offer is not premised by the idea that he has needs.

✦ Yahweh is determined to reveal himself to humanity so that he may be known (at least in part), and this is the foundation of a healthy two-way relationship.

✦ Yahweh is faithful to his covenant promises.

✦ Yahweh expects his people to live out their holy callings guided by the Torah, dominated by the opportunity to be partners in the plan and purposes of God.

✦ Yahweh's actualized presence among his people is conditional.

Even as we make these observations, we need to take notice of what is not evident in the covenant:

✦ There is no indication that Yahweh has a plan to save people from their sins or that a permanent plan for atonement will be made available.[15] The covenant is not a plan of salvation in the Old Testament.

✦ There is no indication that the incarnation is planned as the next step or that Spirit indwelling will eventually serve as the way that Yahweh dwells among his people.[16]

✦ There is no indication that the expected Messiah will be the Son of God.

Extension of the covenant in the New Testament. We have already discussed the new covenant, so there is no need to reiterate that analysis here. We need only to be reminded that in the new covenant the covenant *does* take on a soteriological aspect. We can assume that salvation was always God's plan, and once it is articulated in the New Testament, we can look back and see hints of it in the Old Testament, even though it is not a feature that Israelites would have incorporated in their understanding. The three bullet points listed above all unfold in the New Testament as legitimate, albeit unanticipated, extensions of the covenant idea. They have

---

[15]The forgiveness referred to in the new covenant is not differentiated from the sacrificial system.

[16]The pouring out of the Spirit prophesied in Joel 2 is fulfilled in Acts 2, but the specific nature of the fulfillment in Acts includes information that Joel's Israelite audience would not have been given. The pouring out of the Spirit in Joel would have been seen in relation to the empowerment of the Spirit of Yahweh, which was well known and understood in the Old Testament context, but it is different from the indwelling that makes Christians the people and temple of God.

value for us, but at the same time, we should recognize that the covenant was a meaningful, authoritative revelation of God even without those particular pieces of revelation.

Perhaps the most important extension of the covenant into the New Testament is found in an understanding of Jesus' relationship to the covenant phases. Just as the covenant with Abram was intended to initiate a revelatory program, we find that Jesus is the culmination and climax of that revelatory program (Heb 1:1-2), the consummation of Israel's story. In this way Jesus fulfills the covenant as he brings its intentions to fruition. But his role in the fulfillment of the covenant is not limited to the larger concept of revelation.

In the second phase of the covenant, the revelation of the Torah focuses on the way that Israel should pursue living out its holy status as God's people living in his midst. The requirements given to the Israelites helped them to live in light of their coidentity with God (you will be holy for I, Yahweh your God, am holy; Lev 19:2). Jesus fulfills the law/Torah (Mt 5:17-18) as God incarnate, the physical manifestation of the divine identity, by living out holiness in its perfection and by giving us a path toward holiness that is found in imitation of him. In this sense he is the embodiment of the Torah's purpose; he guides us as we seek to take our place in the lingdom of God. By imitating him, we can be characterized by the fruit of the Spirit, which is evidence that we are living out the holy and righteous status that we have been given in Christ.

In the third phase of the covenant, the Davidic phase, it is obvious that Jesus fulfills the covenant in his role as Messiah. He is the ultimate ruler anticipated in the Davidic covenant and the ideal ruler for which the prophets hoped. He is Yahweh's king, perfectly demonstrating Yahweh's kingship and kingdom.

Finally, in the fourth phase, the new covenant, Jesus' blood is symbolic of the salvation that God is providing by virtue of the death and resurrection of Jesus. God reveals salvation from sin as he reveals the savior. We can therefore see that the four principal titles of Jesus (the Word, the Son of God, the Messiah, and Savior) each interrelate to respective stages of the covenant and proclaim his fulfillment of that covenant.

5

TEMPLE
and
TORAH

TEMPLE AND SACRED SPACE

Order was arguably the most fundamental aspect of the ancient cognitive environment.[1] God is the source of order. Order is established in and by creation, and it flows from God. In the ancient human experience, that order found its center in the temple, where God was present. Purity was also closely related to order, since it was one of the ways that order was upheld with regard to the temple. Furthermore, law was an expression of both order and purity and governed both cultic propriety and morality. Morality did not drive this whole system but was one of the end results of it. With this constellation of ideas in mind, we must begin our discussion with the temple.

An understanding of sacred space is one of the most underappreciated and neglected aspects of biblical theology. Though in recent decades it has received increased attention, historically it has been overshadowed by systematic concerns, such as Christology and soteriology, although it is central to both of those. While it does not represent one of the traditional categories

---

[1]P. Jenson, *Graded Holiness*, Journal for the Study of the Old Testament Supplement Series 106 (Sheffield, UK: JSOT Press, 1992), 215-16.

of systematic theology, I would contend that it is the most significant element in biblical theology and is essential to the metanarrative of Scripture.

Cosmic role of the temple. The temple was the central and fundamental component of the cosmos, the centerpiece of the function and identity of the community, and the principal mechanism for the interface between humans and the divine. As the god sat enthroned in the temple, the order established through creation was maintained, the forces threatening that order were held at bay, and the viability of the human community was maintained.

Temples were a place of divine residence, not just places where worship took place. Worship was only one part of a much larger enterprise represented in the idea that a deity had made his dwelling in the midst of a human community. As people engaged in various worship activities, they provided for the gods, provided for the stability of their lives and communities, and played their part in the functioning of the cosmos.

Hints regarding the cosmic role of the temple in the Old Testament are scattered throughout the corpus (Isaiah, Psalms, Solomon's dedicatory prayer), though no specific or extended treatments of the topic occur. Ancient Near Eastern literature, however, is replete with information, and much of it resonates with the biblical material. Temples were considered to be where the realms of the cosmos converged and cohered.[2] The central shrine in the sanctuary was therefore both in heaven and on earth. Furthermore, at the heart of the temple, the shrine in the sanctuary represented heaven itself. In addition to being the divine dwelling place, which brought heaven to earth, the shrine was a portal to heaven, the heavenly deity's entry point into the terrestrial realm.[3] Additionally, as the names of many temples indicate, they were considered the *axis mundi*, the linchpins of heaven and earth.[4] Mesopotamian ziggurats, for example, represented the stairways used to pass between the realms, and in Egypt the central holy space was built over what was represented as the first primordial mound.

Because of the deity's residence in the temple, it was the center of order in the cosmos. Different cultures had different ways of portraying the temple

---

[2]B. Shafer, "Temples, Priests, and Rituals: An Overview," in *Temples of Ancient Egypt*, ed. B. Shafer (Ithaca, NY: Cornell University Press, 1997), 1.

[3]Michael B. Hundley, *Gods in Dwellings* (Atlanta: SBL Press, 2013), 46.

[4]Temples were microcosms, that is, realizations in miniature of world order. There the visible met the invisible, the human touched the divine, and the earth joined sky and netherworld. L. Bell, "The New Kingdon 'Divine' Temple: The Example of Luxor," in *Temples of Egypt*, ed. Shafer, 132.

as cosmic nexus, but each believed that if the temple was not maintained and its god sustained, the cosmos would be in jeopardy and subject to collapse.[5] In this way the threat of temple dissolution had a similar impact to that which we would experience today with the threat of nuclear devastation, radical climate change, or the worst imaginable effects of pollution (i.e., the apocalypse). In the ancient world the same sort of logic was applied to the responsibilities that each person, each clan, and each city had in maintaining stability in the cosmos by being actively involved in maintaining the temple. Each one played their role in contributing to the continuing cosmic stability.

Relationship between order, wisdom, and sacred space. A space was made sacred, according to ancient Near Eastern belief, *for* and *by* the presence of the god. Because of this divine presence, the temple also became the operations hub of the cosmos. Moreover, because order and wisdom were believed to reside in deity, a god's presence in the temple made it the center of order, wisdom, and life in the cosmos. While order was threatened daily by chaos, from the temple nonorder was kept at bay and order was extended. Therefore the walls of the sacred precinct were seen as boundaries and fortifications against disorder and nonexistence.[6] Thus Michael Hundley observes: "In a dangerous and volatile world, where order was constantly under threat on a local and cosmic scale, the Egyptians constructed temples both to bring divine presence and favor to their world and to have some measure of agency in the divine world."[7]

Also:

> within the ideal world of the temple, the triumph of order was continually (re)enacted. This world functioned as intended, full and ordered, without lack. By both being carefully shut off from the chaos without and by overcoming the chaos within, the temple stood as the ultimate symbol of order. Thus, it is no wonder that when this small world functioned appropriately, the greater world around it would prosper.[8]

These ideas are not stated explicitly in the Old Testament, but scattered lines intimate the same ideology.

---

[5]Hundley, *Gods in Dwellings*, 48.
[6]There was a hall that represented liminal space between the disorder of the nonexistent and the order of creation; Shafer, "Temples, Priests, and Rituals," 6.
[7]Hundley, *Gods in Dwellings*, 41.
[8]Ibid., 48.

Sacred space and rest. In the ancient Near East, the rest of the gods was sometimes depicted as sleep or even sloth, but that was not the foundational concept of the ideology. The temple was the residence of the god, but it was also his palace and the center of his power. The god *ruled* from the temple. Rest in this context was not the opposite of activity; it was the opposite of unrest. Here the god did not disengage from the world but engaged in maintaining order as he reigned in the cosmos. From the temple the god provided stability and security for the people who worshiped him. Therefore people desired to have the god dwelling in their midst so that they could experience the stability that he/she was capable of establishing. The Bible similarly depicts Yahweh reigning from his temple (Ps 132) and bringing Israel rest (stability and security) from its enemies. Maintaining relationship with Yahweh, who dwelt in their midst, was a source of life for Israel (Deut 30).

Cosmos as sacred space. The concept of sacred space is introduced in the Genesis creation narratives. By making the cosmos the place of his residence, Yahweh establishes it as sacred space. But while ample evidence in ancient Near Eastern literature attests to the connections between cosmology and temples, it does not follow that Israel thought the same way. In both Egypt and Mesopotamia, as well as in the biblical text, one can find seven-day inaugurations of sacred space, but seven-day cycles certainly might have been used for other things as well. The conclusion that the seven-day account is about the inauguration of sacred space can, therefore, sound inferential. If Genesis 1 was written with this intention, the author could have said so much more clearly. Since the root *šbt* means only "to cease," it seems we have nothing in the seven-day account that overtly suggests sacred space, at least, not to our eyes. If it could be established, however, that the ancient Israelites thought about Genesis 1 in these terms, the similarity to the ideology of the ancient Near East (and the recognition that insider communication leaves unsaid what is transparent to the initial audience) would be sufficient to show that Genesis 1 is about the inauguration of sacred space.

That the Israelites interpreted Genesis 1 as the inauguration of sacred space can be established by the information provided in Exodus 20:8-11 and Psalm 132:7-15. When Exodus 20:8-11 reflects on the climax of the seven-day account and describes the observance of *šabbāt*, the text asserts that not only did God cease his ordering of creation (*šbt*), but he also took up his rest (*wayānaḥ*).

This second verb offers the sense that he rested in a place on the seventh day or attained a status, not just that he ceased his work. This point is further clarified in Psalm 132:8, 14, where we find that the temple is identified as the resting place (*mənûḥâ*) of God. This understanding of the word is confirmed by its use in Solomon's prayer of dedication of the temple in 2 Chronicles 6:41. In Psalm 132 we also learn that it is from God's resting place that he rules (the technical use of *yšb* in Ps 132:14; cf. Ezek 43:7).

If it is clear that the Israelites believed God rested (*nwḥ*) on the seventh day of the creation week (Ex 20), and if they connected God's rest to sacred space, as with the temple (Ps 132; 2 Chron 6), then it is also likely that they would have interpreted Genesis 1 as the establishment of the cosmos as sacred space. We then can circle back around to what was previously only circumstantial evidence (ancient Near Eastern connections and the significance of the seven-day structure) to strengthen the support for this interpretation. Further evidence for this reading is present at larger literary and canonical levels, which we will address later, but it is also provided in the role of the Garden of Eden, to which we now turn our attention.

Eden as sacred space. In the seven-day account in Genesis we learn that God ordered the cosmos to be sacred space, but it is not until Genesis 2 that we learn that the center of this sacred space is Eden, which features many of the characteristics of sacred space in the ancient world (e.g., adjoining garden, source of waters, cherub guardian, God walking about). Israelites would have known these typical motifs, so these connections would have been transparent to them, as later canonical interpretations indicate. Interpretations that link the Garden of Eden to the tabernacle/temple and therefore to sacred space have long been promoted in the history of interpretation.

Provisional sacred space (bush, Sinai). Once we move beyond the opening chapters of Genesis, we can catch glimpses of sacred space throughout the narrative, even as it moves toward the climax of the reestablishment of terrestrial sacred space through the tabernacle at the end of Exodus. One such glimpse occurs as Abram builds altars as he first passes through the land, presumably invoking God's presence and marking the land as Yahweh's. In a limited sense this is also a continuation of the comment in Genesis 4:26 that in the days of Seth people began to invoke God's name, presumably for some evidence of his presence. The strongest example of sacred space in the patriarchal period, however, is Jacob's encounter with El Shaddai at Bethel—a place of God's presence unrecognized by Jacob until it was confirmed in his vision.

As Exodus begins, not only is there no sacred space, but there are also serious doubts about God's presence among his covenant people, a group enslaved by cruel Egyptian taskmasters. They have no land and do not feel the blessing of God on them as a burgeoning nation. But God begins to make his presence known when Moses experiences it in the burning bush, and eventually the people of Israel encounter God at the sacred space of Mount Sinai. In both of these instances, sacred space is explicitly identified by the narrative and is demarcated by the presence of God.

Tent of meeting and tabernacle as sacred space. After the theophany on Mount Sinai, God's presence is transferred from the mountain to the tabernacle, which was constructed specifically to house that presence. During the transition God was present in the tent of meeting, and Moses met with him there. The tent of meeting was also considered sacred space, since God's presence was manifest there and access to it was limited. However, the tabernacle was carefully constructed to serve as sacred space, and it represented a return of God's presence to terrestrial space on a permanent basis, though this terrestrial space remained portable.

Attention to sacred space continues throughout the remainder of the Pentateuch. The rituals of Leviticus offer instructions for the protection of sacred space and for the people who regularly encounter it. Ritual does not just deal with fixing what is wrong, but it also provides ways for God to receive the honor he is due. The priests are not just ritual experts; they are skilled in all matters pertaining to the preservation and maintenance of sacred space. In the book of Numbers sacred space travels with the Israelites, but because it was in close proximity to Israel, it also endangered and made demands of them. For this reason, Deuteronomy organizes Torah: that the Israelites might understand their responsibilities in maintaining relationship with God and that they might preserve his presence among them. At the close of the Pentateuch, in Deuteronomy 30, Moses admonishes the Israelites to choose life—life found in relationship with God, gained by observing Torah, and accessed through the sustained presence of God. What Moses describes here is exactly the purpose of sacred space.

Connection between sacred space and God's presence. Throughout the ancient Near East and in Israel, sacred space was *sacred* because of the evident or inferred divine presence. Neither the temple itself nor the rituals performed there were more important than the presence of the deity. As Hundley observes, "Conceptually, the temple was integrally related to and dependent upon the divine presence and the interaction between that presence and humanity. . . . The temple was secondary to both divine presence and ritual action, serving as the setting for both."[9] Therefore, sacred space implies divine presence, and divine presence establishes sacred space.

Connection between sacred space and relationship. Though it was universally expected that the presence of deity in sacred space resulted in some sort of working relationship between the deity and the people, it is important to note that relationship with deity took a different form in Israel than in the rest of the ancient world. For example, Shafer observes that in Egypt, "To be in the temple was to experience the body of the god, to commune with the god physically and sacramentally."[10]

While we should not think that the Israelites lacked these more mystical ideas, they had something more concrete that derived from the revelation of Torah and their responsibility to be in relationship with God through the covenant. In contrast, the religious life of the Mesopotamians and the Hittites is understood through what we have called the Great Symbiosis that existed between the gods and the people. Again we turn to Hundley: "The ancient Near East temple was the primary point of intersection between human and divine. As the principle [*sic*] means of establishing security in an otherwise insecure world, it situated the deity in the midst of human habitation, so that humanity might offer service and gifts in exchange for divine protection and prosperity."[11] He further observes, "The temple was the site of a semi-permanent theophany, one that would remain as long as the deity remained content. It was the controlled and isolated environment that enabled divine presence on earth and mediated contact between the resident deity and its human servants."[12]

---

[9]Ibid., 3.
[10]Shafer, "Temples, Priests, and Rituals," 8.
[11]Hundley, *Gods in Dwellings*, 3.
[12]Ibid., 140.

Images of God

Israel is known for being aniconic—that is, no crafted cult image served as a receptacle for the divine essence or mediated divine presence. People are the only image that Yahweh tolerates. That means that all of the functions of the cult statue that were so central to temple ideology in the ancient Near East, if retained at all, had to be reassigned in Israel. In the ancient Near East, the temple lost its significance if the image was not installed. In Israel, the ark of the covenant stood in the center of sacred space and represented a part of God's throne, but it was not a receptacle for divine essence.[a] It represented God's presence, but it did not mediate it. Thus no parallel to the cult image is present in Israelite theology. Aniconism is observable in various ways in other times and places in the ancient Near East, but it is not programmatic, as it is in Israel.[b] Much controversy has centered on Israelite aniconism— when it began and how it was reflected. However, total aniconism in the ancient Near East outside Israel is unknown.[c] The significance of this is far-reaching and cannot be overstated. Having images of other deities would, of course, be a violation of the covenant arrangement between Yahweh and Israel.

The role of images in the religious practices of the ancient Near East can be best understood by investigating the way they were manufactured. The making of cult images to be used in the shrines and sanctuaries of the ancient world took place amid complex rituals that provided for the image to be approved by the god with the result that he/she would adopt the image into his/her identification. The material construction of the image (by the most skilled artisans, using the finest materials) was concluded by ritual processes that transformed (if not transubstantiated) the image so that it could take its rightful place in the sanctuary. Its ears, eyes, and nose were ritually opened so that it could function as the deity on earth. Much of its function entailed being able to receive the gifts of the people (food, drink, clothing, housing). In this way the image was central in the functioning of the Great Symbiosis. Through the images, the needs of the gods were met. Given this understanding, it is no surprise that images were forbidden in the worship of Yahweh. This was one of the ways that the Great Symbiosis was disrupted and rejected.

---

[a]Egyptian portable shrines, which sometimes housed divine statues, can be compared to the ark but cannot be used to determine characteristics of the ark not referred to in the biblical text.

[b]O. Keel and C. Uehlinger, *Gods, Goddesses, and Images of God in Ancient Israel* (Minneapolis: Fortress, 1998).

[c]Punic examples are ruled out due to their late date. In referring to "total aniconism," I am reflecting sensitivity to the distinction that Mettinger draws between "de facto aniconism" and "programmatic aniconism." For discussion, see the articles (including especially Mettinger's) in K. van der Toorn, ed., *The Image and the Book* (Leuven: Peeters, 1997), as well as the monograph by T. N. D. Mettinger, *No Graven Image?* (Stockholm: Almqvist & Wiksell, 1995); and B. Doak, *Phoenician Aniconism in Its Mediterranean and Ancient Near Eastern Contexts* (Atlanta: SBL Press, 2015).

In sum, sacred space is where humans encountered the divine, and whatever relationship was thought to exist between gods and humans was focused there. The relationship in Israel, however, was founded on the covenant, whereas the relationship in the ancient Near East was a utilitarian codependence.

It ought to be noted in passing that temples in Israel and the ancient world have little functional overlap with church buildings today. The church (defined as the people of God) is a better comparison than the church building because the presence of God no longer inhabits geographical sacred space. The building is not sacred space, and God is only present there as his people are there too. Though worship takes place in a church building, rituals comparable to sacrifices do not. The church (building), then, is simply a place where the church (people) gathers for worship. The temple was not a gathering place for regular worship services; people came to the temple to perform their rituals and then left. The priests were engaged in worship on behalf of the community, and while they might often have been watched by the people who came, corporate worship services would likely have been limited to special festivals. Of course, much of this is speculation because we are given little information about activities in the temple during the monarchy period.[13]

---

[13]Chronicles is the most informative.

Sacrifice

As far back as written records go, sacrifices were an integral part of life in the ancient Near East. The testimonies to the sacrificial system early in the Old Testament (e.g., Cain and Abel, Noah, Abraham) all show continuity with the practices in the ancient world. The forms of sacrifice were the same, and we do not get enough information in the Old Testament to distinguish them ideologically (a distinction that unfolds only gradually). When the Levitical system took shape at Sinai, we read of some offerings that were unknown in the rest of the ancient Near East (sin and guilt offerings), but much of the sacrificial system reflects offerings known in the ancient Near East.[a] We can therefore conclude that Yahweh built on existing sacrificial customs in the ancient Near East (since we never have a record of his institution of sacrifices prior to Sinai). It is interesting that at Sinai he does not explicitly address the fact that the sacrifices were not part of the Great Symbiosis; the sacrifices were not instituted to meet his needs, but that is not specifically articulated.

Because of our New Testament orientation, Christians often see sacrifices in connection to sin and salvation. They are not without connection to sin in the Old Testament, though that is not their main focus; in contradistinction, they have nothing to do with salvation. A couple of the sacrifices (the so-called sin offering and guilt offering—both widely recognized as inadequate translations) address the need to clear impurity (from sin as well as other things) from the sanctuary. Nevertheless, other sacrifices have nothing to do with sin (e.g., thank offerings, vow offerings, freewill offerings). In order to capture the full range of functions, we should consider them exercises for participation in the cosmic order that contribute to maintaining harmony between people and deity. With the exception of the Passover sacrifice, the sacrifices take place in sacred space and are related to sacred space. The theological significance of sacrifices is not to demonstrate that "God has made a way to himself" or to point us to Christ (though both of those have legitimacy). The enduring theology is in offering Israel a mechanism for partnership with him in the Great Enterprise as it participates in his plan and purpose.

This mechanism not only provides a way to deal with impurity that builds up in sacred space (remedial action necessary), but it also provides a tangible means for God's people to interact with him at a positive, constructive level. This is the aspect picked up in Romans 12:1, in which our lives are portrayed as sacrifices in a positive, constructive understanding of our participation in God's kingdom.

[a]D. Pardee, *Ritual and Cult at Ugarit*, SBLWAW (Atlanta: SBL Press, 2002); D. Clemens, *Sources for Ugaritic Ritual and Sacrifice* (Münster: Ugarit-Verlag, 2001); P. Merlo and P. Xella, "The Rituals," in *Handbook of Ugaritic Studies*, ed. W. G. E. Watson and N. Wyatt (Leiden: Brill, 1999), 287-304.

Limitation to a single, central location for sacred space (Deuteronomy 12). Another way in which Israel differed from the rest of the ancient Near East concerning sacred space was in the restriction in Deuteronomy 12 that there could be only one temple to Yahweh. In the polytheistic practice of the ancient world it not only was common in a large city to have numerous temples dedicated to various gods, but also for a god to have multiple temples dedicated to him/her in various cities. The result of this multiplicity is that the deity took on different qualities in the various places where he/she was worshiped (e.g., Ishtar of Arbela versus Ishtar of Nineveh). The same variance likely also occurred when, contrary to the Deuteronomic injunction, shrines to Yahweh were built in numerous locations in Israel. Yahweh of Teman would probably have been differentiated from Yahweh of Jerusalem. Presumably, then, the restriction in Deuteronomy was intended to give the priests a basis for maintaining the purity of the people's perception of Yahweh based on his revelation of himself. The idea of a central sanctuary may also be connected to the prohibition against the use of images in Israel. A temple loses its raison d'être if the divine presence is not there, and in the ancient Near East, the divine presence was represented in the image.

Role of ritual in sacred space. Neither sacred space in general nor the temple in particular was created for the sake of ritual—that is, sacred space is not designed to fill the need for an appropriate place to perform rituals. Sacred space is established by the presence of deity, a presence that, since it has distinct advantages, is a human desideratum. Once the boon of divine presence is granted, it is logical that people will want to sustain that benefit. Whether rituals accomplish the purpose of feeding the gods, presenting gifts to honor them, or dealing with offenses so that the god will not leave in anger, they all pertain to doing what is necessary in order to maintain a god's presence in the people's midst. They must be carried out diligently, conscientiously, constantly, and properly to avoid potentially deadly consequences due to the risks that divine presence poses. Therefore, as L. M. Morales and others have noted, liturgy and ritual play a role in sustaining order in the cosmos, a task that becomes the responsibility of both the gods and humans in symbiotic partnership.[14]

Sacred space is established precisely as the venue for the interrelationship between gods and people. In Israel this is infinitely more important than in the ancient Near East because Israelite religion held that God created people not to meet his own needs, but rather that they might be in a partnering relationship with him. Sacred space, therefore, from an Israelite worldview, is the mechanism by which God carries out this central purpose for humanity. It begins at creation. It finds its historical articulation in the tabernacle and temple, and it is for that particular historical phase that the rituals are designed and essential. Indeed, as already mentioned, Torah also relates specifically to that phase (see more below). Eventually (and without any foreknowledge given), its purpose is reified in the incarnation and enabled by the sacrificial work of Christ. It transitions from land to people at Pentecost and will find its final realization in new creation. Therefore sacred space is not just a major theme of the Old Testament, but it is significant through the whole canon of Scripture as an expression of the plan and purposes of God. Nevertheless, I would not consider this the "center" of Old Testament theology, because it is not a topic treated in every book. It is an overarching theme that stretches from beginning to end. Jesus, as God incarnate, is one of the major manifestations of this theme, but the other manifestations have a role in and of themselves, not only in light of Christ. In our interpretation of those other manifestations, our task is not to "find Christ" but to appreciate how God's

---

[14]"In a profound sense, then, life—the essence of being—is liturgical, so that worship not only fulfills the *telos* of human vocation but of creation itself. Liturgy sustains creation." L. M. Morales, *The Tabernacle Pre-Figured* (Leuven: Peeters, 2012), 114.

plans and purposes are carried out through each step and how they all integrate with what God does in Christ.

Significance of purity. Purity in the ancient Near East is associated with the elitist attitudes of the gods and the prerogatives to which they felt entitled. The attitude reflected is that they deserve the very best and could easily grow offended at any carelessness in performance or at any lapse in quality of what was provided for them.[15] They were persnickety and petty. Purity was designed to meet their exacting demands so that they would not express their inherently temperamental nature. In Israel, Yahweh is unarguably exacting, but a different rationale stands behind that understanding. Rather than reflecting divine pettiness and entitlements, the purity requirements in Israel are protection from the inherent hazards that can occur if the people misrepresent the identity of a holy God—a concept unparalleled in the ancient Near East. Such purity is required so that Yahweh will continue to dwell among them. Purity is also important as Israel seeks to represent well its identity as his covenant community.

Holiness. Even though *purity* was a concept well known in the ancient Near East and essential for participation in the rituals that were at the core of their religious practice, the *holiness* that is a staple of Old Testament theology has no immediate parallel. Holiness is not a quality to be achieved but a status that incorporates Israel into Yahweh's identity. Israel *is* holy as God is holy; that is, God has designated Israel as holy, as his holy people, coidentified with him. Holiness locates Israel in the divine realm, and the divine realm is the epitome of order since order emanates from God. God is holy (by definition), and he has conferred holiness on his people, who are then responsible for reflecting their holy identity in every way. Given this constellation of ideas, living out the holiness that has been conferred on them mandates that the Israelites maximize order, and Yahweh's instructions for maximizing order are embodied in the Torah (bound up in ethical, social, and ritual components[16]) and subject to cultural perceptions.

---

[15]For a good example see the instructions for the priests and temple personnel in Jared Miller, *Royal Hittite Instructions and Related Administrative Texts*, SBLWAW (Atlanta: SBL Press, 2013), 249.

[16]These cannot be distinguished by a classification system, but they do circumscribe the range of the Torah.

Priests

We often make the mistake of thinking that the priests' main jobs were performing sacrifices and teaching the people Torah (much like a pastor preaching today). From references to the priests as musicians in the temple festivals, we might even think of them as leading worship. All of these ideas suffer from anachronism at one level or another. Ultimately the priests were the guardians of sacred space. They were ritual specialists because they were trained to know what was necessary to maintain the sanctity of sacred space. They knew what would make something clean or unclean and could instruct the people in such knowledge. As we have come to understand the Torah as that which provided the means by which the Israelites could live in proximity to sacred space and coidentify with Yahweh, the priests' instruction in the Torah also focused on sacred space. Every kind of worship that took place in sacred space was subject to the oversight of the priests. They led in corporate worship from rituals (sacrifice and its rituals had to be performed with precision) to festivals. In the latter, sacred time was just as important as sacred space and needed to be managed appropriately. The role of the priests is therefore not comparable to clergy today. In Israel they mediated access to sacred space, mediated revelation given by Yahweh, and mediated worship that was given to Yahweh. Just as Torah was contingent on sacred space, so was their role.

It has been common in Christian thinking to approach the Torah through the filter of morality and therefore to attempt to discern which aspects have to do with morality (to be retained for Christian living) and which aspects could be classified as civil or ritual (and therefore discarded). This approach is misguided from the start because it assumes that morality is the overriding objective of the Torah. We will address this in detail in the next section, but for now it is sufficient to remark that morality is not the issue. Holiness is the issue, and holiness intermixes inextricably all of those categories.

Perhaps the closest parallel that exists to holiness in the ancient Near East is to be found in the way that Akkadian indicates the status of someone or something by attaching the *dingir* sign as a class determinative.[17] This determinative indicated that the object or person existed in the divine realm, with all the privileges and responsibilities associated with that status. Gods and temples were so designated, as well as celestial bodies, occasionally kings, and a wide assortment of sacred objects. In the ancient Near East, this classification designated prerogatives; in Israel, holy status identified Israel's relationship with its God. Holiness was a result of the covenant, was illustrated in the Torah, was an essential status for God to dwell among the people in the temple, and constituted the identity of Israel as partners in God's purposes to bring order to the cosmos.

LAW/TORAH

Now we are in a position to evaluate the nature and purpose of the Torah. In Israel, the Torah contained both ritual and societal responsibilities, all of which were designed to define cosmic order and to give shape to holiness. As such, the Torah gave direction concerning how to maintain access to God's presence and to the relationship that God's presence facilitates, in addition to how to preserve his favor so that God's identity would be well reflected by the people. Torah can therefore be seen as the foundation for Yahweh's presence because it gave Israel guidelines for living in the presence of a holy God. However, the Torah was contingent on the temple, not the other way around. It was designed for the temple venue and cannot be extrapolated to a universal context outside the temple. The Torah was incumbent on each Israelite because, in theory, any individual's neglect or violation of the Torah could potentially result in the removal of God's presence from his people.[18] In this sense, each person had a role in maintaining God's presence, and God's presence brought order to the cosmos and to Israel. Blood rituals such as those that were part of the sin and guilt offerings were designed to cleanse sacred space from impurity that, if left to build up, could result in Yahweh's departure or danger to the community.

---

[17]B. N. Porter, "Blessings from a Crown, Offerings to a Drum: Were There Non-Anthropomorphic Deities in Ancient Mesopotamia?," in *What Is a God?*, ed. B. N. Porter (Winona Lake, IN: Eisenbrauns, 2009), 153-94; M. B. Hundley, "Here a God, There a God: An Examination of the Divine in Ancient Mesopotamia," *Altorientalische Forschungen* 40 (2013): 68-107.

[18]This principle is illustrated in Josh 7 in the story of Achan, in which all of Israel suffers divine disfavor because of Achan's violation of the command.

Such blood rituals with this particular function are found rarely, if ever, anywhere else in the ancient Near East, but they play a major role in Israel's temple ideology.[19]

Law in the Old Testament and ancient Near East. We can achieve our clearest understanding of the function of the Torah by studying carefully the genre of legal collections in the ancient Near East. The legal collections of the ancient Near East fit into the category of "list compilation," a form of treatise on various categories of wisdom/knowledge.[20] This approach can be seen in collections of proverbs, lexical lists, medical symptoms and diagnoses, and divinatory observations. In these legal collections, the kings of the ancient Near East are not legislating; they are circumscribing the nature of cosmic order, particularly with regard to justice in society. These legal lists are not provided so that *people* will conform their behavior to them, but so that scholars, elders, judges, and magistrates might become informed in the wisdom/knowledge they are called to exercise. When justice is maintained in society, the resulting order brings legitimation to the kings and order in the cosmos (including society as well as nature), which the gods desire. In this way the king also enhances his reputation in the eyes of future kings and people; he forges an identity. The result of all of this is that society will conform to the decrees of the gods that are used to maintain order, which are perceived rather than recorded. This creates an ordered society that conforms to their perceptions of morality. However, the texts do not construct morality—they operate according to the moral sense the society already has.

Israel uses the same literary approach to the question—the Torah is composed of lists to circumscribe the nature of cosmic order. Furthermore, the content is quite similar because these texts are shaped according to some of

---

[19]Scattered blood rituals do exist in the rest of the ancient Near East, but not for the cleansing of sacred space, as in Israel. For Hittite blood rituals, particularly the *zurki* ritual, in which blood is used to cleanse a temple icon, see Y. Feder, *Blood Expiation in Hittite and Biblical Ritual* (Atlanta: SBL Press, 2011), 20-23. As early as Sumerian narratives, Lugalbanda pours the blood of a sacrificed bull into a pit for the gods to smell, but that does not pertain to the preservation of sacred space. See H. Vanstiphout, *Epics of Sumerian Kings*, SBLWAW (Atlanta: SBL Press, 2003), 123, lines 358-59.

[20]See M. Van De Mieroop, *Philosophy Before the Greeks* (Princeton, NJ: Princeton University Press, 2016), 143-81; J. Bottéro, "The 'Code' of Hammurabi," in *Mesopotamia* (Chicago: University of Chicago Press, 1992), 156-84.

the common elements that constitute moral order in the ancient world. These similarities in form and content notwithstanding, the legal texts in the Old Testament stand in contrast to the ancient Near East in many ways. Most obviously, Yahweh is seen as the source of this literature rather than the king. That eliminates the legitimation function evident in some of the ancient Near Eastern documents (Yahweh needs no legitimation), yet we can see that Yahweh, like the kings of the ancient Near East, is constructing his identity based on the reputation that he desires to have (honor being given to his name).

But Israel's understanding of the foundation, structure, and nature of cosmic order is vastly different. Their legal treatises (generally called Torah) are focused on maintaining order as it is founded on three related ideas— ideas that do not have a direct parallel in the ancient Near East. Israel[21] is expected to conform to the expectations of order (expressed by verbs such as *šāmar*, "keep," and *šāmaʿ*, "hear" or "obey") as established by the decrees of Yahweh in relation to their unique status:

✦ covenant people

✦ holy

✦ living in proximity to sacred space

Despite these significant differences, like the ancient Near Eastern collections, the Torah treatises are not legislation. They give guidance so that the people of Israel might corporately become wise and informed practitioners who can take their designated place as participants in Yahweh's plan and purposes. By living in conformity to these standards, Israel identifies as the people of Yahweh who are honoring the covenant relationship, properly reflecting its holy status, and maintaining the necessary sanctity of sacred space. These objectives are far different from those of the ancient Near East, but they similarly reflect what is required to maintain cosmic order and therefore utilize the treatise genre.

In both the Old Testament and ancient Near East, these legal lists, then, circumscribe how to avoid being out of order. In Hebrew, the term describing "out of order" is *tôʿēbâ* (often translated as "detestable"; see excursus

---

[21]Intentionally using corporate designation.

below), but for Israel, the covenant, holiness, and sacred space define order and therefore also what is out of order. Consequently, though what the ancient Near East would consider out of order may also be considered so by Israel (e.g., injustice in various forms), Israel's understanding of what constitutes order is in many ways far more extensive. Therefore being out of order takes on a new definition.

An example of "an idea that circumscribes the nature of something" can be illustrated by the way that students do math problems for homework. The idea is that by solving the posed problems, the students will begin to understand the concepts involved. The individual problem is of little significance in the grand scheme and may be quite artificial or even unrealistic. But the problems are providing ways to practice good math and to help students achieve an informed wisdom about math, thus enabling students to use math in life and to think mathematically. To advance the metaphor, the same approach and pedagogical principles are used whether one is doing algebra or calculus, and the same general goal of wisdom is in mind. Yet algebra and calculus are very different from one another. Using this illustration, we might suggest that we imagine the ancient Near Eastern system as algebra and the Israelite system as calculus.[22]

The series known as the Ten Commandments is often understood as the summary and most important part of the biblical law. The word *commandments* is itself misleading because everywhere the set is referred to in the Old Testament, it is called the "ten words" (five times: Ex 20:1; 34:28; Deut 4:13; 5:1; 10:4).[23] Attention is drawn to them in Exodus and Deuteronomy, the most familiar presentations, though the list in Exodus 34 differs from the others and is difficult to divide convincingly into ten sayings. Nevertheless, Exodus 34 is the only list that is actually identified as the "ten words" in the context. Regardless of which list we use, how we number them, or how we translate what they are, it is important for us to recognize that they cannot stand as the summary of the law and be singled out as more important than the rest. They function the same way that the rest of the Torah functions. As

---

[22]Illustration provided by J. Harvey Walton.

[23]There are even questions about how they should be divided. Daniel I. Block, "Reading the Decalogue Right to Left: The Ten Principles of Covenant Relationship in the Hebrew Bible," in *How I Love Your Torah, O Lord!* (Eugene, OR: Cascade, 2011), 21-55; Daniel I. Block, "How Shall We Number the Ten Commandments?," in *How I Love Your Torah, O Lord!*, 56-60.

we have been discussing, each of the collections of legal sayings in the Pentateuch stands as a list of illustrations that serve to circumscribe, in part, the realm of legal wisdom. When Jesus is asked to identify the most important parts of the law, he gives the two "great commandments" rather than citing the ten (Mt 22:37-40).

The Decalogue, then, is focused on directing Israel to construct an identity as the people of God. It provides information about the shape of the covenant community, both in terms of how the people interact with Yahweh and in terms of how they interact with one another. This focus on the covenant community is nowhere clearer than in the item about honoring parents: "so that you may live long in the land the LORD your God is giving you" (Ex 20:12). This pertains specifically to honoring parents by receiving instruction in the covenant so that the covenant benefit (life in the land) may continue. As stipulations to Israel's covenant with Yahweh, they are not intended to establish morality; they characterize the ways that Israel, Yahweh's covenant people, can reflect its coidentity with Yahweh and participate in the ordered world that he has created and in the covenant order that he has delineated for them.

In light of this information we can understand that the Torah was not intended to establish or reflect an ideal society. It is thoroughly situated as it focuses on how the community of Israel ought to conduct itself *given the structure of its society*. It is a community of people that is thereby transformed, not the shape or structure of society. They are given a new status, not shaped into a new society. They are given a mission statement, not a revised curriculum. The Old Testament Torah therefore does not give God's opinion of democracy versus monarchy, arranged marriages versus marriage for love, polygamy versus monogamy, patriarchalism versus gender equality, slavery versus no slavery, market economy versus agrarian economy, and so on. The law was not intended to give a universal moral/ethical system; it was designed to help Israel know that divine favor is extended as it maintains this sort of order as his covenant people living in the presence of a holy God. It was not so that the people could imitate God, or so that their society could achieve some utopian ideal, but so they could reflect the holy status that he had conferred on them in the world in which they lived.

Decalogue

Like the rest of the Torah, the Decalogue should also be understood against its ancient Near Eastern background. Such an investigation has some startling results. We learn that a few of the sayings stand in contrast to typical practice, while many of them coincide fully with what we can find in the ancient Near East. We will also notice that in some cases, cultural changes among Bible-reading audiences have pushed interpretation far from the original contextual understanding over time. Here we can only give a quick summary.[a]

1. Other gods. As discussed earlier (chapter two) the issue here is not metaphysics. Rather, it concerns the God who is the one making the covenant with them. No other gods are involved in this relationship—the covenant is not being made with a council of gods.[b] In treaties in the ancient Near East (remember that the covenant has adapted a treaty format), many gods are called as witnesses and are involved as sponsors of the agreement. Here it is only Yahweh. He is giving them their covenant status, and they are going to identify with him—no other. This is not dealing with metaphysics; it concerns the parties in the covenant relationship. Other nations could not stand in violation of this directive because he did not make a covenant with them.

2. Images.[c] Having images of other deities would of course be a violation of the covenant arrangement between Yahweh and Israel. In this case, however, even images of Yahweh are prohibited. Aniconism is observable in various ways in other times and places in the ancient Near East,[d] but it is nowhere as programmatic as it is in Israel.[e] Divine identities in the ancient world were extended into their images. Having different images of the deity fragmented the deity's identity into localized aspects: the aspect of Ishtar in Nineveh is distinct from the aspect of Ishtar in Arbela (enough so that they can even fight each other). In contrast, there is to be only one "aspect" of Yahweh, who holds one covenant over all Israel. There are to be no "local aspects" of Yahweh who serve only a portion of the community. This statement is not about sculpture or art. Images reify the divine presence, and through the image, divine revelation and care of the gods are mediated. That is not how Yahweh works.

3. Name. Someone's name is not just what they are called; name is connected to identity. Everyone in the ancient world thought this way, and this concept serves as one of the fundamental components of magic. This is true of the gods' names as well as those of humans. A name is powerful. Today when we think about honoring God's name, we often think of casual use of the name of God that fails to recognize its importance. That would certainly be a violation,[f] but a more significant violation would occur if someone recognized the power of the name and took steps to tap into that power for their own purposes.[g] Note that the Lord's Prayer begins by recognizing the sanctity of God's name. The prohibition does not concern pronouncing God's name; it involves invoking it for inappropriate purposes.

4. Sabbath.[h] The concept of sabbath is so far unique to Israel. Ancient Near Eastern texts can be cited for the significance of seven days, but not on a cyclical basis for theological observance. Likewise, most cultures had festival days that featured the absence of work, but not in anything like a seven-day cycle. In the sidebar on sabbath, we will discuss how the sabbath was interpreted as a recognition of Yahweh as the one who rules and brings order. Comparable at some level, festivals such as the Babylonian Akitu or the Zukru festival at Emar celebrated the reign of the patron god and his appointed king, but the Akitu was only an annual, or sometimes semiannual, celebration, while the main Zukru was a seven-day festival held in the autumn every seven years.

5. Parents. Respect for parents is characteristic in the ancient world, especially given the community identity that is characteristic of those cultures. One draws one's identity from family and clan, and values are preserved in that context. It would never occur to someone in ancient Israel to ask, "Would you still honor your parents if they tried to get you to abandon your faith or to engage in criminal activities?" Nor would any parent in Israel try to do this. The issue at stake here is the integrity of the community's identity and the individual's identity within the community.

6-9. Murder, adultery, theft, and false witness. These all prohibit behaviors that are disruptive to the community and destroy order within it. They are staples in any ancient literature that deals with order and justice in society.

10. Coveting. Discussion of coveting is not found in the legal collections of the ancient Near East, but it is addressed in Wisdom literature.[i] Both law and wisdom deal with order in society.

---

[a]For a more extensive discussion of the comparative issues and analysis of the first four, see John H. Walton, "Interpreting the Bible as an Ancient Near Eastern Document," in *Israel: Ancient Kingdom or Late Invention?*, ed. D. I. Block (Nashville: B&H, 2008), 298-327. For a discussion of the presence of items 5-9 in the ancient Near East, see K. van der Toorn, *Sin and Sanction in Israel and Mesopotamia* (Assen: Van Gorcum, 1985), 13-20. All ten are treated in some detail with citations in *ZIBBCOT*, in the comments by B. Wells on Ex 20 and those of E. Carpenter on Deut 5.

[b]It does not have to do with priorities in our lives.

[c]For more information, see the sidebar on images earlier in this chapter.

[d]See B. Doak, *Phoenician Aniconism in Its Mediterranean and Ancient Near Eastern Contexts* (Atlanta: SBL Press, 2015).

[e]Keel and Uehlinger, *Gods, Goddesses, and Images of God in Ancient Israel*, trace aniconism through the iconography known from the Levant.

[f]See *ZIBBCOT*, 1:232, 452.

[g]Today this would be like identity theft, when a thief uses a person's credit card number, bank accounts, or even Social Security number for their own benefit.

[h]For more information, see the sidebar on the sabbath later in this chapter.

[i]The best example is in the Ugaritic Instructions of Šūpê-amēli, from the middle of the second millennium. Line 27 simply reads: "Don't covet another man's wife." Y. Cohen, *Wisdom from the Late Bronze Age*, SBLWAW (Atlanta: SBL Press, 2013), 86-87. Half a millennium earlier, a treaty between Assyrians and some business partners in an area in Anatolia includes in their listing of expected business practices that the parties should not covet houses, slaves, fields, or orchards. V. Donbaz, "An Old Assyrian Treaty from Kültepe," *Journal of Cuneiform Studies* 57 (2005): 63-68; B. Wells, "Exodus," in *ZIBBCOT*, 1:236. Egyptian wisdom (Ptah-hotep) likewise identified coveting as a vice to be avoided. For discussion and citations of a number of sources, see E. Carpenter, "Deuteronomy," in *ZIBBCOT*, 1:454.

The conclusion that I would propose for understanding the law, then, is that the law was not intended to give a universal moral/ethical system; it was designed to help Israel know how to live in the presence of a holy God and as his covenant people. It was not so that the people could imitate God, but so they could reflect the holy status that he had conferred on them. To the extent that they were successful in reflecting the identity associated with the status that God gave them, they would bring honor to his name. Failing in that identity, they would bring shame to his name. Both theological and cultural elements comprise the idea of what would bring honor or shame to God in the context of the ancient world, Israel, and the covenant.

On *"communicable" attributes and imitating God.* Are God's people supposed to try to imitate him? For many years I would have answered with a resounding "yes!" But I have recently begun to question this point. It is not my intention to deal with each of the potential qualities individually, but the list of possibilities includes well-known items, such as faithfulness, love, goodness, compassion, mercy, justice (especially for the poor, vulnerable, and downtrodden), patience, graciousness, wisdom, and righteousness. These characteristics are clearly valued and commended in the Bible by God—of that there is no question. However, if we also investigate the prayers of the ancient Near East, we find that none of the qualities listed above are absent from among the hoped-for qualities that the ancient Near Eastern people sought in the actions of the gods toward them. Likewise, the gods of the ancient Near East looked for these qualities in people, if only as a way to preserve order in the cosmos and society. When people acted this way toward one another, society reflected good order, which in turn gave the people freedom to plant and harvest, to live their lives contentedly, and to fulfill their obligations to the gods. Yet these qualities that were expected by the gods and valued among the people were not seen as obligatory; the people were not required to imitate the gods in these ways. In the ancient Near East, people were never called on to imitate the good qualities of a god. The gods had established order and expected order to be maintained; people conformed to that expectation by living decent lives. The people hoped the gods responded to them in those same ways, but they had no guarantees, and the gods had no inherent nature that would bind them to act in those ways. But this would not be construed as imitation of the gods—it involved fitting into the ordered cosmos. The gods could not be known sufficiently to imitate them. It was not desirable to imitate the gods, and no one tried or thought they should do so.

Certainly the God of the Old Testament is different, and his revelation of himself is far more extensive. But that does not necessarily mean that imitation has now become desirable. Does the Old Testament make a point of calling people to imitate God? How would that work if it does? When we investigate the Old Testament, we find a situation similar to that in the ancient Near East. The Israelites look for the same qualities in Yahweh that the people of the ancient Near East sought in their gods, and Yahweh expects to see those qualities in the Israelites, both individually and as a people group. Based on revelation by Yahweh, however, this sort of response from Yahweh is more than a simple hope. Yahweh has revealed himself as predictably possessing these qualities. Even so, it is not generally clear just *how* God is doing something such as caring for the poor. We would not say that he is bound to these qualities, but they are enduring qualities that express his character (without defining it in constraining ways). He is believed to be consistent. When the qualities are not realized in Israel's experience with God, failure on Israel's part is responsible, not inconsistency or fickleness on Yahweh's part. In the ancient Near East, there are neither lawsuits against the gods nor by the gods against the people.

Similarly, these qualities are built into the covenant expectations of Israel. The Israelites maintain Yahweh's presence not just by ritual performance but by living according to these values. Yahweh has conferred a holy status on his people that brings them into the circle of his identity. In order to live in a way that reflects that holy status, these qualities should be evident in their lives. Even though the quality list is similar, then, that list pertains to both Yahweh and Israel in ways that are different from the ancient Near Eastern gods (who don't reveal themselves) and the other ancient Near Eastern people (who are not in covenant relationship with a holy status).

But can all of this be encapsulated by the idea that Israel was expected to imitate Yahweh? Imitation could never be straightforward, because the ways that people (ancient or modern) experience God may not, at times, be easily reconciled with the list of qualities given at the beginning of this section. Some of God's behavior may be appropriate for deity but not for people. Other times, we might find it difficult to imitate, for example, God's execution of justice when it is opaque to us how and when it is being applied. Israel is expected to reflect certain values and to trust that Yahweh is characterized by those values as well. However, we do not know enough to model God's exercise of those attributes precisely by watching him in action. But we are told, for example, that he is faithful, which we accept by faith even when we cannot detect it, and that God values our faithfulness. Consequently, we are not called to be "faithful as he is faithful" but to be as faithful as we can be. God values faithfulness. As a result, imitation would not be the most accurate way to describe our behavior, and the Old Testament never calls on Israel to do so. In the Old Testament the Israelites are never called to *act just as God acts*; they are called *to do just as the Lord commands*. In the New Testament, we are called to imitate Christ, but we have a clearer vision of what that entails because he lived among us as a human, though it was in a particular time and place. We can also understand that we should "follow God's example" in particular ways (Eph 5:1; see also Lk 6:36; Rom 15:7; 1 Pet 1:15; 1 Jn 3:3, 7), but it is through our vision of Christ that we are able to do so.

CONCLUSIONS

Enduring theology. Finally, we must explore the enduring theology we should draw from the Old Testament, the theology that continues to affect our thinking, our lives, and our beliefs today. How shall we then live? As is always the case, we need to live in a way that is consistent with what we know of God and his revelation.

God has a plan and purpose. Even if this were all that we had, it would be groundbreaking. Certainly no one else in the ancient world had reason to believe their gods had a plan and purpose focused on people, and in a similar manner, people without God today are left aimless and rudderless in a meaningless world. But the idea that God has a plan is great news that we embrace and that sustains us through difficult times. The temple and the Torah play a central role in conveying this plan and purpose as it moves toward Christ and beyond him to new creation.

He is willing to reveal it. At one level it is enough to know that God has a plan and purpose. The idea that he is willing to inform us about his plan and purpose is an act of grace that allows us to appreciate his plan, have some sense of it, and even participate in it. Moreover, as he reveals his plan, he reveals more about himself.

The Prophets

The prophets are those who proclaim the plan of God. They are not simple prognosticators, and much of what they have to say pertains to Israel's past and present even though they do have information to give about the future as well. No matter which time frame they are addressing, the point is that they are proclaiming the plan of God as they stand as champions of the covenant. An apt analogy can be found by considering a course syllabus. The syllabus talks about the future, but it does not exist to tell the future. It conveys the plan of the professor, and it is reliable because the professor is in control of what takes place class by class. A diligent student can tell a lot about the professor by attending carefully to the details of the syllabus. The syllabus, then, is more interested in revealing the plan of the professor (and, indirectly, the professor) than it is in revealing the future. The same is true of God and prophecy. The prophet would be like a student assistant coming into the class to distribute the professor's syllabus. It is not the assistant's plan; he or she is just delivering the message.

God's plan and purpose pertain to corporate humanity and intend human participation. Next we discover that the plan and purposes of God, though they are undoubtedly vast beyond our comprehension, actually include us. We learn that beyond all sensible expectation, the God of the universe has enlisted people, his creatures, to participate in his plan. This is an act of his grace, not a reflection of his need. In this role we have purpose, meaning, and dignity. In fact, his plan is the source of our purpose, meaning, and dignity. We are not just puppets or pawns; we are participants.

God has planned to dwell among people. We have learned that at the center of God's plan and purposes (even if not at the center of each book of the Old Testament), as revealed in the Bible, is his intent to be present with his people. It did not begin at the incarnation or with the Holy Spirit at Pentecost. It began at Eden, and when his presence was lost there, a second initiative was launched in the covenant that led to the reestablishment of his presence in the tabernacle, made possible for the people by the revelation of

"Vanity of Vanities"

The key term in Ecclesiastes (Hebrew *hebel*) is translated a variety of ways (meaningless, vanity, absurd). The variety of translations exists because there is not an English term suitable to capture the full impact of the word's sense. In such cases it is sometimes possible to get a better grasp of a word's meaning by recognizing its opposite, and that is the case here. English has a word that expresses well the opposite connotation: "self-fulfillment." Qoheleth looks at all of the pursuits and accomplishments that people consider capable of providing self-fulfillment or meaning in life. For most people life is a quest to achieve self-fulfillment, and in Ecclesiastes, Qoheleth does not offer an alternate quest. After he shows that every possible permutation of the quest is doomed to failure, he exhorts us to abandon the quest. Life is not about self-fulfillment. We receive both prosperity and adversity from the hand of God (Eccles 7:14), and we rejoice in the good things even as we are shaped by the adversity. Self-fulfillment should not be in the picture. His final advice, then, is to fear God and to attend to his commands (Eccles 12:13)—in these ways we become the participants that God has planned us to be.

the Torah. He established his rule among them, and in some senses, through them. He continues to carry out that purpose today as he indwells his people. The incarnation and the indwelling are only the most recent manifestations of this plan, a plan that will reach its culmination in new creation (Rev 21).

Interaction with him calls for purity (if only for our own sake). God cares about purity because he cares about how we identify ourselves as his people. Moreover, he cares about us doing damage to ourselves. If he did not care, he would not have bothered to reveal anything about it. In the Old Testament both repeated words and occasional events demonstrate that a lack of purity is inimical to covenant order and potentially holds danger for Israel. Impurity is not dangerous because God is petty or easily angered; it is dangerous because deviating from the standards of order brings risk. The purity that was mandated in the Old Testament included physical purity as a precondition for access to the geographical presence

Sabbath Today

Often in discussions of law in general, and the Ten Commandments in particular, the question arises concerning our responsibilities today. A criterion often applied concerns the appearance of the sabbath in the New Testament. Some contend that the absence of an affirmation for the sabbath in the New Testament implies that it is no longer applicable to us. The application of such a criterion presumes a complex hermeneutical understanding of the law, one that I have been arguing against. Rather, all of the law remains relevant to us as revelation and as understood within the context of the ancient world, and in this view, none of the law remains normative for us as rules that are carried across directly from Old Testament texts. As we have been suggesting, the Torah is situated in the ancient world, embedded in the covenant with Israel, and contingent on Israel's holy status in sacred space.

In light of this approach, we need to think about the sabbath the same way we think about all law in the Old Testament, and it has nothing to do with rules and nothing to do with its treatment in the New Testament. The sabbath reflects a way of thinking about creation (Ex 20:11) and about release from Egypt (Deut 5:15). The common denominator between these two associations, not surprisingly, is the concept of order. The former concerns order in the cosmos, and the latter concerns order for the Israelite community. Both concern God's rule over an ordered system. Note that another major passage in the Old Testament that concerns the sabbath, Isaiah 58:13-14, focuses on order within the Israelite community as well.

However, none of these passages indicates that the sabbath has to do with physical rest (leisure, downtime, naps, etc.). The premise instead is that God rules over this ordered system. We have been inclined in the past to think that God is taking a physical break and that because we are called to imitate him, we should also take a physical break (thus not doing our work on the sabbath, Ex 20:8-11). But in this we have misunderstood what God did on the sabbath, and we have made the mistake of thinking that we should imitate whatever it was he did.

When God ceased (*šbt*) his ordering (= creating) work on the seventh day, it was for the purpose of taking up his rest/residence (*nwḥ*) to rule over that ordered system. God's rest did not involve relaxation but rule (Ps 132:13-14; see discussion in chapter three). Obviously we are not called to imitate his rule; we are called to acknowledge it and participate in it. On the sabbath we are to set aside our own attempts to bring order to our world by our own efforts. God is the one who is the source and center of order. Therefore one day a week we are to focus on what should be undergirding our lives throughout the week: participation in the order of God's kingdom. The sabbath reminds us of this basic principle. We are the people of God, and as such, we are partners in the plan and purposes of God. We participate in God's rule rather than joining him in relaxation. It has nothing to do with law, and it has nothing to do with whether the New Testament affirms the sabbath or not. As Jesus asserts, the sabbath was made for man, not man for the sabbath—and the Son of Man is the Lord of the sabbath (God's rule, not God's rules; Mk 2:27-28). We should not approach the question of the sabbath through the paradigm of rules to which we are obliged; we should approach the sabbath as part of our participation in God's kingdom purposes and perspectives.

of God, and the ultimate goal was participation within the community of God's people as they observed covenant order. This was one of the ways that the community of Israel showed faithfulness to the covenant in their coidentity with God, and such participation prevented them from being destroyed (Deut 30:11-19).

Some of the elements that defined purity were simply a matter of perceived propriety. As an illustration, when I was a young kid growing up in church, it was not uncommon for adults to curb our exuberance by admonishing us, "No running in church!" Running is not inappropriate in other places, and it is not "sinful" or "immoral" even in church. But by the standards of that community, running was not an acceptable behavior in church.

Today the presence of God is still located in a community, though not in a geographical space that we need to approach for interaction. Furthermore, we are not in the same covenant relationship. Instead, God's presence is found in the abiding presence of the Holy Spirit in his people, who are referred to as the temple (1 Cor 3:16).[24] Physical purity remains important (e.g., in issues of sexuality), but the New Testament turns more concerted attention to purity of thought and deed (Mt 5:8; Phil 1:10; 4:8; 1 Tim 5:22). We have been prepared to be sacred space by the cleansing blood of Christ. Our sins are forgiven, and our justification is assured. But in another sense, Christ's blood continues to cleanse us from impurity as we become subject to it. Concomitantly, though our righteousness is as filthy rags, we seek in every way to be concerned about purity because it is appropriate to our holy status and essential for participation in the purposes of God and the community of God's people. At the same time, we recognize that we can only function in this manner through the sanctifying activity of the Holy Spirit. The similarity between Israel's situation and our own is found in the idea that both are related to what is an appropriate reflection of our community's coidentity with God. In both cases, when we fail, the jeopardy we face is to ourselves. The criteria concerning purity can change from culture to culture (cf. the dietary laws in the Old Testament). However, the criteria are based on (1) what could potentially damage us and (2) the perception of the people to whom we are conveying our identity as the people of God.

An analogy for the above concept can be found in the consideration of modesty. Modesty as a principle is important in all cultures, though its definition varies dramatically from one culture to another. The variability of definitions and even the difficulty in identifying specific standards in any given culture do not mitigate the importance of the concept. As a concept, however, it does not connect to the person of God or his standards. Nevertheless, it does affect how God's people are perceived in the surrounding culture, and if we fail to maintain culturally appropriate standards of modesty, we can do damage to our reputation or suffer from unwanted actions and attitudes toward us.

Order and sacred space remain significant theological issues. We learn about the concepts of order and sacred space from the Old Testament. They are

---

[24]Technically, Christ is the temple, and we are more like the land. However, the two are closely connected (synecdoche) and are therefore, to an extent, considered interchangeable as we consider our contemporary situation.

"Atonement" (Kipper) *and Blood Rituals*

Blood rituals in Israel are designed to purify something from ritual contamination. In the Old Testament they almost always focus on sacred space or on objects that represent sacred space (e.g., ark, altar).

The Hebrew verb *kipper* expresses this purifying action, the preparation of space to be suitable for God's use by the clearing away of contaminates. Understood in this light, we can see that it is very different from the theological concept of atonement. The Israelite annual practice of Yom Kippur is founded on the idea that everyday life in the community inevitably creates incidental or unaddressed impurity that the sanctuary absorbs. Yom Kippur figuratively loads that impurity on a goat and sends it away. This action serves as a reset button for the sanctuary, and it takes care of the buildup in the sanctuary. The blood is the regular designated mechanism for *kipper*, and it deals with both the uncleanness (*ṭāmē'*) and the sins (*ḥāṭā'â*, Lev 16:16). These terms refer to the community rather than to the individual, while in the New Testament, the blood ritual (blood of Christ) cleanses us (individually as well as corporately) from all sin because we are being made suitable for *use as* sacred space. The Old Testament system, on the other hand, was not even trying to do what the new covenant can accomplish in Christ. The old covenant is not a failure; it has a different purpose altogether.

topics addressed from the opening pages of the Old Testament, and they eventually find their focus in the context of the covenant community. Our understandings of creation and of wisdom are both inextricably related to these issues. Indeed, our understanding would be impoverished without the insight provided by the Old Testament. These are not just key theological concepts for the Old Testament; they remain central for our theological thinking.

Impact on behavior. Once we recognize that the Torah operates within the covenant context in connection to sacred space as the Israelites experienced it in their time and culture, we acknowledge that the specifics found in that covenant context are no longer intrinsically valid for people (such as us) who are not in that covenant relationship. That does not mean that these specifics carry no value for us. Rather, since they reflected order as perceived within the covenant and in the cultures of the ancient world, and since human society preserves across its breadth certain values, we find that some of what is required for order has not changed. More significantly, we learn from the Old Testament Torah that God is reflected in our community, not just in nebulous platitudes or clichés. Instead, attention should be given to every aspect of life. The Torah gives us a sampling of the areas that we need to consider as we seek order in our world and seek to reflect our identity in God.

We should desire to coidentify with him—holiness retains its significance for us in that coidentification. The Old Testament gives testimony to a people group (Israel) who has been given a holy status (through the covenant) and among whom Yahweh lives. They are given direction as to how to reflect this coidentity that God has given them (Torah) in ways that will be considered appropriate to their status, and they thereby will be active participants in the plan and purpose of God. This provides a pattern that offers sound theological thinking for us today. We as the community (body of Christ) have been given a holy status (through Christ, the new covenant), and the Holy Spirit indwells us. We likewise ought to reflect the coidentity that we have with Christ so as to participate effectively in the plan and purpose of God. God desires his people to participate with him in his plan and purposes as we coidentify with him. Therefore, holiness is central to both Old Testament and New Testament conceptions.[25]

We should note that this perspective stands in contrast to how Christians talk today about the mission of the Torah and the mission of God. Christopher J. H. Wright indicates that the law fits into the mission of God in that it was "given in order to 'shape' Israel into a community that would reflect the character of Yahweh, enabling them to be the public, visible exemplar of God's intention for a redeemed community of people. . . . The mission of Israel was to be a light and blessing to the nations. The 'mission' of the law was to shape Israel for that task."[26] I would agree that Torah is intended to

---

[25]The relationship between the Old Testament situation and our New Testament situation is a mixture of analogy and metaphor, but the similarity remains.

[26]Christopher J. H. Wright, "Mission and Old Testament Interpretation," in *Hearing the Old Testament*, ed. Craig G. Bartholomew and David J. H. Beldman (Grand Rapids: Eerdmans, 2012), 180-203, quote on 185.

shape Israel into a particular sort of community. The verb *reflect* is acceptable as long as it does not suggest imitation, and "character of Yahweh" works as long as it is understood to refer to his holy identity and reputation. God's people are supposed to reflect his identity. They are his visible exemplars insofar as they serve as a tableau of God's identity and those through whom he carries out his plans and purposes. So far, so good. The main dispute I have concerns the suggestion that Israel's identity is found in their being a "redeemed" community. It is true that they were delivered from slavery in Egypt, but that is not supposed to be their primary identity throughout history. The Torah is given to shape them as a community that serves as host to the presence of God. This is the sense in which they are a light and a blessing: God dwells among them. Through them there is access to the presence of God. Israel responds by living out its identity in the presence of a holy God. In turn, we today are also being shaped as a community to host the presence of God in terms of the Holy Spirit, who indwells us. We are redeemed, indeed, by the blood of Christ, but our identity is not just as a redeemed community. We are the people of God who, as we coidentify with him, serve as his instruments for participating with him as he carries out his plans and purposes in the world. God's mission goes beyond redemption; it is focused on dwelling among the people he has created. It is an Immanuel theology. Making disciples in the Great Commission does not pertain to converting people. As people come to Christ, they need to be instructed in how to be effective disciples of Christ—coidentifying with him and participating in his plans and purposes.

✣   ✣   ✣

EXCURSUS: HEBREW *TÔʿĒBÂ* (NIV "DETESTABLE THING")

Tôʿēbâ describes what is contrary to the inherent sense of order reflected in one's inclinations or conventions. No English word captures this meaning and its Hebrew nuances successfully.[27] Whether aspects of sexual ethics and identity are classified as nonorder (morally neutral) or disorder

---

[27] *Taboo* (in its colloquial use, rather than as an anthropological technical term) is an interesting option to consider since it also reflects the perspective of the person or society that classifies behavior in that way. Perhaps a more general term could be *uncouth*. The list of things that are *tôʿēbâ* in the Old Testament finds significant parallels in the list of practices that are *ikkibu* in Akkadian.

(morally defective) is not as relevant as the accepted fact in the ancient world that some aspects of cultic and sexual behavior were not conducive to order and were therefore *tôʿēbâ* (counterproductive to order; in Israel, contrary to holy status).

The Hebrew substantive *tôʿēbâ* is often translated as "despised" or "detested," but it covers an interesting range of activities whose common denominator is that something is contrary to the sense of order. It is not surprising then, that a large percentage of its uses occur in legal literature and Wisdom literature, which both pertain to order. It can be relative (the Israelite sacrifices and vocation as shepherds are both *tôʿēbâ* to the Egyptians, Gen 46:34; Ex 8:22). The term can describe inappropriate sacrifices (wrong attitude, Is 1:13; blemished animals, Deut 17:1) or animals deemed unclean (Deut 14:3, one of the few occurrences in which *tôʿēbâ* pertains to an object rather than a practice). It is often a label applied to the worship of foreign gods or to the use of images or other cult objects, and in this category it includes the practice of divination or human sacrifice (both in Deut 18:12). Violent or dishonest behavior (Ezek 22:2; Deut 25:16) are both considered *tôʿēbâ*, and the sinfulness of wicked enemies is characterized as *tôʿēbâ* (seven types of such behavior are listed in Prov 6:16-19). At the same time, someone who is suffering may be considered *tôʿēbâ* to their acquaintances (Ps 88:8), and the upright are considered *tôʿēbâ* by the wicked (Prov 29:27; cf. Amos 5:10; Mic 3:9). Since a fool's life is fraught with evil, it is *tôʿēbâ* (contrary to the pseudo-order in that way of thinking) for such a fool to turn away from evil (Prov 13:19). When used technically in the legal literature, *tôʿēbâ* is used to designate deviation from the conventions of sexual conduct. It is also used as a refrain in Leviticus 18 and is repeated in Leviticus 20:13 (cf. Ezek 22:11; 33:26). Though it is most frequently used in Deuteronomy to refer to unacceptable worship practices, twice it refers to practices associated with sexual identity (clothing, Deut 22:5; the proceeds of a prostitute brought into the temple, Deut 23:18).

These are all identifiable as practices that are contrary to order. Yahweh hates (*śnʾ*, Deut 12:31) at least some practices described as *tôʿēbâ*, and the opposite of the practices he considers *tôʿēbâ* are practices in which he delights (e.g., Prov 11:20; 12:22). But others reflect the particular perspectives of a group (Egyptian opinion of shepherds, the wicked person's view of the righteous). The key question, then, is whose perspective is being reflected. When God considers something *tôʿēbâ*, it is being characterized as contrary to order established by God for Israel. The next issue then, would be to determine whether something represents God's established order for Israel alone (unclean food and the use of images are prohibited for Israel but not for its neighbors) or whether a practice represents a deviation from universal order that applies to all humanity. The default would be the former; the latter would carry the burden of proof.

There can be no doubt that sin constitutes a violation of order and would therefore be labeled *tôʿēbâ*. But not all behaviors so labeled can be identified as sinful, even though they are consistently contrary to order. We find in Leviticus 18 that Israel is warned not to engage in a variety of sexual activities that are paradigmatically attributed to the inhabitants who preceded them in the land (Lev 18:26-30). Regardless of the extent to which the peoples of the land would have been engaged in each of those practices (some of the groups may have engaged in some of the practices) or would have considered those practices as *tôʿēbâ*, it would be *tôʿēbâ* for Israel to practice them because of the parameters of order to which it is accountable by virtue of its covenant status. The land is defiled by those practices, but the Canaanites were not responsible for purifying the land, and God had not been trying to reside there. Therefore, the text is not identifying universal standards that the Canaanites would have been expected to maintain. *Defilement* is a word that only has meaning relative to sacred space. Uncleanness is not inherently evil; it just does not belong in sacred space. The land cannot be defiled until it is sacred space. But once the land is purified for divine presence, any such defiling behavior (on the part of Israel) would be inimical to Yahweh's presence.

We have seen that *tôʿēbâ* is relative, and we therefore have seen that not everything that is *tôʿēbâ* is *tôʿēbâ* to Yahweh. Behavior that *is tôʿēbâ* to Yahweh is behavior that he hates or is contrary to that in which he takes delight. We might then inquire as to what practices are identified as *tôʿēbâ* to Yahweh in the context of the Israelite covenant. All of Leviticus 18 is included in that which is *tôʿēbâ* to Yahweh, and nearly all of the uses of *tôʿēbâ* in Deuteronomy specify behavior that is contrary to Yahweh's order (spanning the use of idols, worship in the manner of their predecessors, worship of other gods or celestial gods, the offering of flawed sacrifices, the sacrifice of children, divination, dressing as the opposite gender, bringing proceeds of prostitution to the sanctuary, and acts of injustice). In Proverbs behavior that is *tôʿēbâ* to Yahweh includes common wicked characteristics such as perversity (Prov 3:32), haughtiness, lying, shedding blood, devising schemes, rushing to evil, bearing false witness, and stirring up trouble (Prov 6:16-19). Other practices include using dishonest scales and other forms of injustice (Prov 17:15). In the Prophets, Ezekiel uses the designation far more than any other, but Isaiah condemns false sacrifices as *tôʿēbâ* to Yahweh (Is 1:13), as Proverbs also had done (Prov 15:8; 21:27). Ezekiel most frequently declares the false worship of Judah to be *tôʿēbâ*. He does not typically identify those practices specifically as *tôʿēbâ* to Yahweh, but it is nevertheless obvious from the contexts. In Ezekiel 16 the metaphor of sexual *tôʿēbâ* is used for the *tôʿēbâ* of deviant worship practices, but in Ezekiel 22:7-12, a list of sexual offenses mixed together with social offenses comes under the indictment of *tôʿēbâ* (cf. Ezek 23:36). From this list we can discern that anything that is *tôʿēbâ* to Yahweh deviates from the norms that are expected by Yahweh for his people as they observe Torah, live wisely, and manifest holiness. In this connection it is interesting that Yahweh even classifies his own people this way when they defile themselves (Ps 106:40). Although sinful behavior is *tôʿēbâ*, we cannot conclude that everything that is *tôʿēbâ* is sinful. The two categories overlap but are not mutually defining.

When we turn our attention to the question of how this material in the Old Testament contributes to our understanding of the issues that concern us today, we find ourselves faced with significant challenges. To begin with, we must recognize that Leviticus 18 does not deal with sexual *identity*; it deals with sexual *practice* as it pertains to *community identity*. It is therefore evident that the practices are not exonerated if some individual has a different sexual identity from which he or she perceives order.[28] In the ancient world, sexual identity and relationships were considered aspects of order (evident in the Old Testament by their role in law as well as in wisdom—both pursuits of order). Heterosexual relationships with those who were not immediate relatives defined order. Homosexuality, transsexual identity (as celebrated in the cult of Ishtar), incest, bestiality, and adultery were all viewed as nonconformity that

---

[28]In the same way, fools are not exonerated in their refusal to turn away from evil just because the behavior is natural to them (Prov 13:19).

was inherently disruptive of order. These are the facts of the ancient world, shared by the Old Testament and ancient Near East alike. At the same time, we must remember that these texts were not trying to define *morality*, but *order* within a particular frame of reference, both cultural and covenantal.

It is not sexual *identity* per se or sexual *inclinations* (either homo- or hetero-) that are deemed out of order (*tôʿēbâ*). Only sexual *practice* that deviates from Yahweh's order in his Old Testament covenant community is so considered. Those in the Old Testament who had same-sex inclinations may have been of the opinion that such behavior brought order to their lives, but it is evident through the Old Testament that it is *Yahweh's* order that is the standard, not someone else's. Furthermore, the covenant community seeks to uphold Yahweh's order. Anything that is sinful (i.e., morally flawed) is contrary to Yahweh's order and therefore to be avoided, but morality cannot be defined by listing those behaviors that are *tôʿēbâ* to Yahweh. If holiness is reflected by behavior that conforms to Yahweh's order, then everything *tôʿēbâ* to Yahweh in the Old Testament ought to be unacceptable to the community that seeks to be faithful to the status of "holy to Yahweh" by virtue of the covenant and proximity to sacred space.

This last characterization forms the bridge between Israel's situation (expressed in the Old Testament) and ours. It should not be our own intrinsic individual identity that forges the path for our behavior; it is the path that Yahweh has set for the community through the status that he has conferred on the community, a community he has designated as holy. We as individuals are called to participate in that community. None of us dare use our own natural individual inclinations to determine the definition of order, since we are not the center of order; we must bridle our own inclinations and yield to Yahweh's order as defined by the community of faith. Our understanding of these issues cannot be generalized to how we think about the Torah; they must be considered in light of what makes up the broad subset of that which is *tôʿēbâ* to Yahweh (without the derivation of proof texts). Our own sense of order may therefore change over time and from culture to culture.[29]

---

[29]Compare the definition offered by H. D. Preuss in "תּוֹעֵבָה," in *TDOT* 15:602: "Above all it is irreconcilable with Yahweh, contrary to his character and his will as an expression of that character, an ethical and cultic taboo. To call something *tôʿēbâ* is to characterize it as chaotic and alien, and therefore dangerous, within the cosmic and social order."

In the Old Testament, sexual orientation variations reflect an identity that is distinct from people who reflect covenant order. Immorality is out of order, but not everything that is out of order is immoral. Just because something is out of order does not make it immoral/sinful. The Old Testament does not construct a moral system. It indicates what is out of order in a "covenant-with-Israel" system. We cannot therefore use proof texting from the Old Testament to determine what general morality must look like. Some behavior can be designated out of order in Israel, but that does not mean it will be out of order in another context that is not covenantal. Order is relative to culture, and Yahweh demands a particular order in the culture of ancient Israel. Furthermore, if the Old Testament is not designed to define morality in general, and Israelite covenantal order cannot be equated with morality, we cannot depend on the Old Testament to offer a comprehensive exposition of morality, though it can help us to understand some behaviors that belong in our understanding of morality and others that do not.

Furthermore, we cannot approach the issues that we struggle with today simply by asking what will make Yahweh angry. Instead the fundamental question should be, "How does this help me participate in or contribute to the community through which the purposes of Yahweh are being carried out (previously Israel, now the church)?" God's revelation to Israel provides a guide for that purpose, but more importantly, it conveys how behavior and purpose are interrelated. We cannot extrapolate specific rules through proof texting. Rather, when we ask about how we can be contributing members to the community of which we are a part, we have to have some sense of how our community identity should look. Individuals usually cannot identify these principles on their own; it is a community activity that should take place at the largest level feasible within the structure.[30] This approach may differ considerably from society's sense of order, for Yahweh's order is not subject to society's discernment. At the same time, we should not think that we have the right or duty to impose our order on those outside the community, even if they do differ.

---

[30]In Catholicism, this would be at the top of the hierarchy of the church—the pope, advised by the cardinals. In Orthodoxy, this would be the seven patriarchs. In Protestantism, the denomination, or in some cases the individual congregation, when it does not align itself with a denomination. Both Catholicism and Orthodoxy tie strong connections to apostolic authority; Protestants consider themselves informed by Scripture above all else.

For example, we might ask whether heterosexuality is sufficiently intrinsic to community identity, so much so that homosexuality would be proscribed for any individuals who are part of the community. However, that would be the wrong approach to the question. The fact is that either homosexual identity *or* heterosexual identity can work against our community identity if we make it our principal identity and take pride in it. In such a case, our sexual identity becomes something that supersedes our identity in Christ. This is a problem with every sort of human identity: national, economic, ethnic, gender, or any other (see Gal 3:28). We are "in Christ," and every other identity must be subordinated to the extent that it ceases to be used as an identifying marker. Our old identities have been crucified with Christ. The old is past—we are new creation.

While the community can unanimously agree that a whole range of behaviors should not be tolerated, any subset of the community cannot be closed to all who sin in any way whatsoever; no one could qualify in that case. Nevertheless, the community can approve of or censure such behaviors in principle, realizing that some individuals continue to struggle with certain inclinations and occasionally capitulate to them. Such censure in principle also certainly results in a higher standard of behavior for the leaders of the community.

In today's world, we are all confused about identity, and our sense of identity drives how we live and the way we view ourselves and those around us. However, we can think about the issue of identity by first looking at how Israel should have viewed its identity.

Israel's identity was composed of the following:

1. covenant people

2. image of God

3. human

4. clan/family identity (including family status and marital status)

Now we can consider what our priority list should be:

1. in Christ

2. child of God

3. image of God

4. human

5. more specific elements

   a. based on inherent status

      i. family status (son, daughter, mother, father)

      ii. male/female

      iii. ethnic/racial

      iv. social status of family

      v. sexual orientation

   b. based on choices

      i. profession/vocation

      ii. accomplishments

      iii. political affiliation

      iv. church/denomination affiliation

In all of these we have an identity that we can choose to (1) live out, (2) virtually ignore (not to be confused with deny), or (3) live in contradistinction to. But when we elevate an aspect of our identity beyond its significance, our lives and society can become skewed. In our world today, we often elevate the least significant parts of identity, especially sexual identity (influentially promoted by the media), and become confused. All identities are not equally significant identities; some ought to be ignored. Paul suggests that we may need to set aside certain aspects of our identity: "For I resolved to know nothing while I was with you except Jesus Christ and him crucified" (1 Cor 2:2).

6

SIN
and
EVIL

DEFINING EVIL AND SIN

What is evil? The ancient world did not define evil in moral terms. That is not to say that they had no concept of moral evil—of course they did, as all people do. Their languages, like ours, use terms that describe the wicked (comparable to Hebrew *rāšāʿ*) and that consistently represent moral categories in their usage. Nevertheless, the ancient world likely did not partition the concept of moral evil as strongly as we do, and they certainly did not emphasize it as significantly, especially regarding the supposed opinion of the gods toward it. This may surprise us and raise questions from our own familiar theological and philosophical thinking about topics such as moral theology and theodicy.

Consequently, a few comments are necessary with regard to Old Testament perspectives on the issue of evil. The primary word for evil in the Old Testament (*rāʾâ*) only carries a moral nuance in certain contexts, and it is the other aspects of the context that provide evidence of a moral sense. In other words, *rāʾâ*, much like its opposite, *ṭôb* ("good"), pertains to how one experiences various people or situations. Something that functions negatively in one's life is labeled *rāʾâ*, even if it comes from God (e.g., Eccles 7:14); something that functions positively is labeled *ṭôb*. The meanings of these terms are not based on moral categories, and knowing this difference can be important when reading many passages in the Old Testament. Not only will this knowledge help us to refrain from imposing our moral categories on the text, but we can also get a better grasp of Old Testament categories if we use the classifications of order, nonorder, and disorder.

Order, nonorder, and disorder.[1] In Genesis 1:2, the state of the cosmos is not yet functioning as it should, and this nonordered state serves as the canvas for the creative acts that bring a semblance of order to the cosmos. Moreover, the Genesis account contains traditional descriptors of nonorder that were typical in ancient Near Eastern thinking: sea and darkness. It also features the spirit (or wind) of God as prepared to go into action;[2] in some Egyptian cosmologies, the wind, a manifestation of the god Amun, also plays a role in the initiation of creation.[3]

Then, into this nonordered state, God begins to establish order by decree. In the ancient Near East, one Egyptian text (the Memphite Theology on the Shabako stone) features creation by the spoken word. More importantly, however, throughout Sumerian and Babylonian sources, the gods bring order (both initially as well as year by year) by orally decreeing the destinies of members of the cosmos—to decree the destiny of something is to assign it a role and a function.[4] The decree is an act of creation as order is established. Consequently, the efficacy of the spoken word in creation is commonplace in the ancient world.

God's creative work is defined as bringing order into a nonordered cosmos. In Genesis this is carried out in stages through a process. Even as God brings order, aspects of nonorder remain. For example, there is still a sea (though its borders have been set), and there is still darkness. Boundaries and limits are imposed as the elements of nonorder are pushed aside

---

[1]This section is adapted from John H. Walton, *The Lost World of Adam and Eve* (Downers Grove, IL: InterVarsity Press, 2015), and J. Walton and T. Longman, *How to Read Job* (Downers Grove, IL: InterVarsity Press, 2015).

[2]For further discussion see John H. Walton, "The Ancient Near Eastern Background of the Spirit of the Lord in the Old Testament," in *Presence, Power and Promise: The Role of the Spirit of God in the Old Testament*, ed. David G. Firth and Paul D. Wegner (Downers Grove, IL: InterVarsity Press, 2011), 38-67, esp. 39-44.

[3]Mark Smith, *On the Primaeval Ocean: Carlsberg Papyri 5*, CNI Publications 26 (Copenhagen: Museum Tusculanum Press, University of Copenhagen, 2002), 53-63; see also 194. In earlier texts, the air god Shu uses a blast from his mouth in creation.

[4]See further discussion in John H. Walton, *Genesis 1 as Ancient Cosmology* (Winona Lake, IN: Eisenbrauns, 2011), 37-62.

to make way for order. This initial ordering, however, would not have eliminated natural disasters, pain, or death (elements that would be described as *rā'â* but are clearly not moral agents). We do not have to think of these as part of the ordered world (that which is *ṭôb*), even though they are not beyond God's control and often can be identified with positive results.[5] All nonorder is not perceived as being resolved until new creation. In Revelation 21, for example, we are told that there will be "no longer any sea" (Rev 21:1), no pain or death (Rev 21:4), and no darkness (Rev 21:23-25).

In this sort of thinking, pain and death do not have to be considered part of what is "good" (= ordered). Instead, these are aspects that have not yet been finally resolved into a fully ordered world. The world before the fall was a combination of order and nonorder combined with a strategy to continue bringing order. This progress toward order, however, was set back by the entrance of disorder. The serpent, as a chaos creature (see below), was part of the nonordered world. Its interference, however, launched disorder when humanity decided to make itself the source and center of wisdom and order. Furthermore, the consequence of humanity's role as the source and center of wisdom was not true order centered on them but disorder in which sin reigned because people are incapable of establishing order on their own with themselves as the center. The disorder that this introduced extended to all people of all time, as well as to the cosmos. Moreover, life in God's presence was forfeited.

Therefore, first of all, in the Old Testament people understood that they lived in a world characterized in part by *nonorder* because the world remained in the process of being ordered. This process, of course, was hampered by the fall because humans have not fulfilled the role for which they were created. This nonorder continues to be reflected in natural disasters, disease, and pain, among many other things. Sin is not the cause of all of the aspects of this situation, but these elements of nonorder demonstrate the human inability to enforce order within creation.[6]

---

[5]Mark Harris, *The Nature of Creation: Examining the Bible and Science* (Durham, NC: Acumen, 2013), 147. He contends that "suffering and death are not unmitigated evils; there are subtleties to account for"—note the praise to God for providing prey for carnivorous animals (Job 38:39-41; Ps 104:21; 147:9).

[6]Of course we acknowledge that sin can cause some of these effects. Someone can experience disease because of sin (e.g., STDs), and natural disasters can be indirectly linked to irresponsible behavior by humans (whether oil spills, defoliation, or greenhouse gases).

Second, the people of the Old Testament understood the world as characterized by *order* because creation established order. Humans have brought the benefits of order throughout history through discovery, invention, technology, and industry. These very same human advances that brought order, however, frequently also brought disorder. Too often, we follow the guide of our own selfish ends (ourselves as the center of order) rather than recognizing that we are stewards of sacred space.

Consequently, and third, the Israelites also recognized that they lived in a world characterized by *disorder*. This disorder is found in the ways that we harm one another and in the ways that we harm ourselves (and continuing today in the ways that we harm the environment). Disorder is the result of sin, and it continues to reflect our inability to be as good as we were designed to be. Among its many deleterious effects, sin has made us low-functioning creatures, and the paltry order that we manage to bring is a caricature of what God intended. All of creation groans (Rom 8:19-22) in this state of delayed order and rampant disorder, the latter being the result of sin, and this sin is most basically manifested in the idea that we thought we could do better than God, a delusion that still plagues all of us.

What is sin?[7] If we are going to try to understand the theology of sin in the Old Testament, we have to begin by removing whatever paradigm we have derived from our own systematic theologies or New Testament treatments. Adopting such a procedure is not meant to imply that those understandings are wrong; we are only recognizing that the ancient Near Eastern ways of thinking might not be the same as ours. We begin then by investigating a number of different models.

As Mark Biddle points out, one of the most common ways that people think about sin today is as a crime, a view that Biddle considers to be inadequate both biblically and theologically.[8] In a scholarly monograph, Gary Anderson considers the merits of the competing paradigms of sin as a "burden to be borne" and as a "debt to be repaid."[9] The former metaphor, burden, he contends, is the view supported by the idioms found in the Old

---

[7]This section is adapted from Walton, *Lost World of Adam and Eve*, proposition 15.

[8]Mark E. Biddle, *Missing the Mark: Sin and Its Consequences in Biblical Theology* (Nashville: Abingdon, 2005), vii-viii.

[9]Gary A. Anderson, *Sin: A History* (New Haven, CT: Yale University Press, 2009).

Testament ("bearing sin/guilt/punishment," as early as Cain's statement in Gen 4:13). The latter imagery, debt, becomes more prominent in the Second Temple period.[10] Both these paradigms speak eloquently to the consequences of sin (behavior that constitutes a burden or debt) and point the way to its resolution.

An alternate approach to analyzing the theology of sin in the Old Testament is to observe the various Hebrew words that are used to express it.[11] Here some caution is advisable. For example, it is not uncommon to encounter the statement that sin in the Old Testament means "missing the mark." This kind of statement, unfortunately, is an example of a potential misunderstanding about how semantics work. It is true that the verb *ḥṭʾ* can refer to the failure to achieve an objective (Prov 8:36; Is 65:20) and is even used once for slingers who do not miss their target (Judg 20:16).[12] It is reasonable, however, to ask why we should consider these uses as reflections of the "original" meaning of the word that is translated "sin." The meanings of words are derived from their use, not from their etymology,[13] and this verb simply means "to sin." Even if it were originally derived from a verb that referred to missing a mark or failing to achieve an objective (difficult to establish), we would have no reason to believe that it retains that idea.[14] The individual words for sin can help us to recognize its various guises (rebellion, transgression, iniquity, guilt), but such semantic analysis can only take us so far.

In a third approach, others might talk about what sin *does* rather than what sin *is*. In this sort of investigation, sin can be seen as a threat to relationship with God—it results in alienation.[15] This differs from the focus represented by the paradigms discussed above. The paradigms above address the consequences primarily regarding ourselves (burden, debt), whereas alienation

---

[10]Ibid., 27-28.

[11]See discussion in Alex Luc, "חטא (*ḥṭʾ*)," in *New International Dictionary of Old Testament Theology and Exegesis*, ed. Willem A. VanGemeren (Grand Rapids: Zondervan, 1997), 2:87-93.

[12]The latter, however, uses the Hiphil form of the verb, where other occurrences indicate misdirection. It is the Qal forms that mean "to sin."

[13]So in English, *awful* does not mean "inspiring," and *sinister* does not mean "left-handed."

[14]Similar observations could be made about the Greek terminology.

[15]See for example Mark J. Boda, *A Severe Mercy: Sin and Its Remedy in the Old Testament* (Winona Lake, IN: Eisenbrauns, 2009), 515; Luc, "חטא (*ḥṭʾ*)," 89. This concept is represented in the later development of the theological concept of "spiritual death," first introduced by Origen (though there is no textual reason to think that the punishment in Gen 3 was spiritual death rather than physical death).

addresses more particularly the consequences pertaining to our relationship with God. This concept of alienation is well recognized in the Old Testament, whether in the banishment of Adam and Eve from the garden or in the exile of Israel from the land. It is built into the ideas surrounding sacred space, in which holiness must be maintained for the presence of God, lest access to his presence be forfeited (evident in the covenant curses). Sin is therefore disruptive to the relationship with God, which is the deepest desire of humans. Relationship through partnership is cited as God's intention in the creation of human beings, and that partnership is what was lost in Genesis 3. The rest of Scripture documents the stages of its reestablishment (see chapter four).

Another way to express this is in terms of the disequilibrium caused by sin. The biblical model sees sin as the disequilibrium pervasive in a system in disarray. Authentic human existence aspires to realize its full potential of being in the image of God, while also consistently acknowledging its creatureliness and limitations. Sin is disequilibrium in this aspiration: humanity failing to reflect its divine calling and forgetting its limitations.[16] Notice that *sin*, then, takes its definition relative to an understanding of "divine human calling." Any creature who does not possess the image of God does not have the same divine calling (if they have one at all) and cannot therefore be guilty of sin (at least not in the way we think of "sin"). Furthermore, for other cultures in the ancient Near East that saw their divine calling as participation in the Great Symbiosis, their understanding of that which constitutes sin (still defined as divine human calling) would have been far different. It would refer to anything that disrupts the Great Symbiosis. This is why in most cases the category of sin in the ancient Near East is composed of ritual offenses or shortcomings.[17]

These approaches are not mutually exclusive, and though the first two have their validity and make a contribution to our understanding, it is the alienation/disequilibrium model that will serve as the focus for this chapter. This is a significant theological trajectory that is often neglected or not even recognized. If Genesis 1 is about order and sacred space, the disorder of sin takes on new importance.[18] Disequilibrium (disorder) has disturbed the

---

[16]Biddle, *Missing the Mark*, xii-xiii.

[17]Insight by J. Harvey Walton.

[18]Salvation is certainly an important trajectory, but that can be understood as what God has done to vouchsafe our access to his presence. Relationship in his presence is the objective; salvation is the instrument by which it is achieved.

equilibrium (order) that God has set in place. Systematic theology eventually develops other trajectories and gives them high priority, but in the Old Testament, this particular view accounts for how sin is introduced in the early chapters of Genesis, where order and its antitheses are so important.

DEMONS

The first problem we face concerns terminology.[19] No general term for *demons* exists in any of the major cultures of the ancient Near East or in the Old Testament. They are generally considered one of the categories of "spirit beings" (not gods, not ghosts). The term *demons* has had a checkered history; in today's theological usage the term denotes beings, often fallen angels,[20] who are intrinsically evil and do the bidding of their master, Satan. This definition, however, became commonplace only after the Old Testament canon was complete. The idea of evil spirits under the control of a chief demon cannot be identified in the ancient Near East or the Old Testament, and even its place within the New Testament requires careful assessment.

The Hellenistic period has creatures referred to by the Greek term *daimon* in the hierarchy of spirit beings. Even though the term *demon* is simply a Latinized spelling of this word, it cannot be used to label the Hellenistic category, because in its usage the Greek term *daimon* can refer to spirit beings who are either protagonists or antagonists, beneficial or harmful, benign or sinister. The term *daimon* could be applied to any being who was higher than a human and lower than a god.[21] In other words, these beings were morally neutral. Thus the English term *demon* is already a prejudicial label that undermines the investigation due to anachronism.

Some Hebrew terms refer to categories and others to individual entities. Many of the terms are debatable at one level or another. For example, a few

---

[19]Information in this section is excerpted from J. Walton, "Demons in Mesopotamia and Israel: Exploring the Category of Non-Divine but Supernatural Entities," in *Windows to the Ancient World of the Bible*, ed. B. T. Arnold, N. Erickson, and J. H. Walton (Winona Lake, IN: Eisenbrauns, 2014), 229-46. See this article for detailed discussion.

[20]Beginning especially with Origen, see J. B. Russell, *Satan* (Ithaca, NY: Cornell University Press, 1981), 132.

[21]Platonists defined them as intermediaries between gods and humans, as did Philo, who equated them with the Jewish category of angels. Eventually the ambiguous *daimon* was replaced by *daimonion*, "which had a more negative connotation, and the Christians connected the *daimonia* with evil angels" (Russell, *Satan*, 48-49).

terms, according to some interpreters, refer to animals that inhabit liminal areas; to other interpreters, the terms refer to theriomorphic (i.e., animal-shaped) demons. Most notable in this category are the ṣiyyîm (NIV "desert creatures")[22] and the ʾiyyîm (NIV "hyenas").[23] In Akkadian texts, spirits with theriomorphic characteristics are generally composites, though they can be described metaphorically as animals (e.g., "the owl which screeches in the city").[24] In ancient Near Eastern iconography, the "Lord/Lady of the Beasts" motif, which shows animals from liminal realms in its grasp, could potentially identify the animals with spirits.[25] Wildberger comments that "one cannot draw sharp distinctions between animals that are sinister, but still recognizable, over against demons."[26] Holladay, following the same line as Wildberger, concludes that "Given the association of wild animals and demons as expressions of the uncanny, there is no way to determine the meaning of these nouns with precision."[27] If the biblical text has no references in which words that could and do refer to animals from liminal areas can clearly be seen as spirits, the burden of proof rests on those who want to interpret them that way.

Collective abstractions associated with phenomena are also sometimes considered spirits (or are identified as "demons"). Most prominent among these are *deber* (NIV "plague"),[28] *qeṭeb* (NIV "destruction"),[29] and *rešep* (NIV "pestilence").[30]

---

[22]Is 34:14; Jer 50:39 (LXX Isaiah = *daimonion*, Vulgate Jeremiah = dragons). H. Wildberger, *Isaiah 28–39* (Minneapolis: Fortress, 2002), 315, "demons." Human enemies in Ps 72:9. Dwellers in liminal areas (deserts, ṣiyyâ).

[23]Is 13:22; 34:14; Jer 50:39. Wildberger, *Isaiah 28–39*, 315, "goblins." Human enemies in Ps 72:10. Dwellers in liminal areas (coastlands, islands).

[24]*UL* 5:9.

[25]See also the Egyptian palettes that show animals from liminal areas (dog palette, Narmer palette, goring bull).

[26]Wildberger, *Isaiah 28–39*, 335.

[27]W. Holladay, *Jeremiah* (Minneapolis: Fortress, 1989), 2:421; in Jer 50:39 he translates "goblins and ghouls."

[28]Hos 13:14; Hab 3:5; Ps 91:6 (F. I. Andersen and D. N. Freedman: "Association with demons is palpable in the context," but note that the plural form removes it from demon association; see *Hosea* [New York: Doubleday, 1980], 640). Note also *paḥad laylâ*—Ps 91:5. Malul in *DDD* considers Ps 91:5-6 to contain a series of demon names. John Goldingay: "Their terms correspond to Middle Eastern ways of describing the activity of hostile gods or demons, and the ancient versions refer explicitly to demons and spirits. But there is no explicit indication of this reference in the context, and it would be unique in the OT, which makes hardly any reference to demons." *Psalms* (Grand Rapids: Baker, 2008), 3:45.

[29]Deut 32:24; Is 28:2; Hos 13:14.

[30]Deut 32:24; Hab 3:5; Ps 76:4; 78:48. J. Tigay, *Deuteronomy*, JPS Torah Commentary (Philadelphia: JPS, 1996), considers the Deuteronomy passage not to be even literary personification. Andersen

One cannot use comparative data to argue that either these creatures or these phenomena must be spirits because of their similarity to spirits in Mesopotamia. Those in the theriomorphic class in Israel are neither benevolent nor malevolent. They are not composites. They exercise no power and show no aggression to humanity, and they are not associates of deity or instruments used for his work. The only point of similarity is that they dwell in liminal areas, but this is hardly sufficient for identification.

The collective abstractions associated with phenomena differ in that they are seen as instruments of Yahweh and are associated with him to bring a negative impact on humanity. But in biblical context, this is no different from a thunderbolt or rain. That a commonality of name can be demonstrated in some instances proves nothing because it is possible to have nominal commonality without conceptual similarity (e.g., Shemesh/Shamash). Even the literary personification of an element of the cosmos (when it can be demonstrated to exist) is not the same thing as viewing an element as a spirit being.

Setting these questionable examples aside, then, five terms remain to be considered more seriously—*šēdîm*, *śạ̄ʿîrîm*, *lîlît*, *ʿazʾazēl*, and *rûaḥ-rāʿâ*—the first two being groups and the other three individuals.

The terms *šēdîm*[31] and *śạ̄ʿîrîm* (goat gods)[32] are the ones most often translated or interpreted as "demons." The former has a possible Akkadian cognate, *šedu*, which refers to protective spirits. Alternatively, there is a possible Aramaic cognate, *šdyn*,[33] which refers to a group mentioned in the Balaam text from Deir Alla that is seated in the divine council. Since the *šēdîm* in the Old Testament are receiving sacrifices, they have more in common with the *šdyn* from the Transjordan than with the possible cognate from Akkadian literature.

---

considers Hab 3:5 a type scene of deity accompanied by four powerful attendants (though he sees only three, and one of those he provided). Personification here is questionable, and demonization more so. But if they are demons, they are in the Mesopotamian category of those that have been harnessed/commandeered by a deity to do his bidding (like those demons that become the associates of the gods). Of course, Resheph is a god in Ugarit and Ebla (Vulgate = *diabolos*).

[31]Deut 32:17 (LXX *daimonion*); Ps 106:37 (LXX 105:17 *daimonion*).

[32]Is 13:21 (LXX *daimonion*); Is 34:14; cf. Lev 17:7; 2 Chron 11:15.

[33]But if this is a cognate of Shaddai, as promoted by J. Hackett, *The Balaam Text from Deir ʿAlla*, Harvard Semitic Monographs 31 (Chico, CA: Scholars Press, 1984), 85-89, it cannot also be cognate with *šēdîm*. The connection with Aramaic is more likely, since rabbinic literature also uses the Aramaic *šdyn* as the equivalent to the Hebrew *šēdîm*.

The *śə'îrîm*, like the *šēdîm*, appear to be objects of worship. They receive sacrifices, which would make them unlike any similar spirits in Mesopotamia (which do not have any associated temples, cult, or priests and do *not* receive sacrifices). Though it is not uncommon to translate the term "goat gods" or "satyrs," there is no indication that they are composite creatures. The word occurs many other times as a simple reference to goats.[34] Therefore the case cannot be made that we must consider these *śə'îrîm* to be "demons" simply because they fit into what we see in the ancient Near East. They most definitively do not match up with anything we find in Mesopotamia, and the sacrifices they receive are illegitimate, which puts them in the same category as foreign gods.

One might argue, based on the New Testament, that the foreign gods *are* demons, but that equation is post-Hellenistic. Regardless, whether one accepts that equation ontologically or not, such a connection cannot be made from the Old Testament text or through a comparative analysis with the ancient Near East. In 1 Corinthians 10:20, Paul is referring to the beliefs of his time that *did* consider demons the recipients of sacrifices made to idols.[35] Paul's statement, then, may well have been descriptive rather than ontological. If one is governed by a contextual understanding of the Old Testament, there is no basis to consider *śə'îrîm* or *šēdîm* to be "demons" in Israelite thinking. With no clearly established demonology in the Old Testament, it is also questionable whether we can say that the Israelites believed the foreign gods to be demons.[36] If the textual variant in Deuteronomy 32, which reads "sons of God" rather than "sons of Israel," is to be preferred, as I think it is, the foreign gods would be associated with the divine council. Mesopotamian spirits, however, are never part of the divine council.

As for the other terms, *lîlît* occurs only in Isaiah 34:14. The support for considering this a reference to a demon is found in the Akkadian cognate, *lilû/lilitu*, which refers to an identifiable spirit. Nevertheless, as we know

---

[34]Of the domesticated variety—never clearly wild goats.

[35]Plutarch confirms that this is true: "Demons are the guardians of sacred rites of the gods and prompters of the mysteries." Plutarch, *De Defecto Oraculorum* 13 (thanks to J. Harvey Walton for the reference).

[36]Contrary to LXX treatment in Ps 96:5; 105:37; Deut 32:17; Is 65:11. For example, LXX Ps 96:5 renders the idols (*'elîlîm*) as demons (*daimonion*); cf. 1 Cor 10:20-21; Rev 9:20; and Origen; cf. Russell, *Satan*, 134.

with cognate terms, it cannot be assumed that these terms retain or carry the same meaning. However, it is interesting to note that in scholarly analysis the discussion moves from Akkadian to rabbinic and patristic literatures (where there is clear continuity).[37] It therefore remains possible that Isaiah refers to a spirit, but in the context, *lîlît* is not acting in any of the ways that spirits operate in Mesopotamia. Instead, *lîlît* is associated with creatures (who are not spirits) in liminal areas. So without further information, we must hold specific identification in abeyance.[38]

The second individual often classed as a demon is *ʿazʾazēl* from Leviticus 16. Here it is more likely, though still contested on many fronts, that a spirit is intended.[39] The demonic interpretation becomes prominent in Hellenistic Jewish literature (e.g., Enoch), but the context of Leviticus offers little elaboration or explanation. While it is designated as having a living area (wilderness), it does not have power, bring plague or illness, intimidate, or function as the object of incantation.[40] Furthermore, in elimination rituals in the ancient world, the animal that is used to carry the offense is not a sacrifice to the demon;[41] it is slaughtered so that the offense dies with it.[42] Rites of elimination do not view the killed animal as a sacrifice, because no part of the animal is given to a deity. It also cannot be a gift to a deity because

---

[37]Wildberger's two-page discussion contains no citation of any apocryphal or pseudepigraphal occurrences. Lowell Handy ("Lilith," in *Anchor Bible Dictionary*, ed. David Noel Freedman [New York: Doubleday, 1992], 4:324-25) indicates that the main sources of information are the Talmud (four references) and the Aramaic and Mandaean bowl inscriptions from a Jewish community in Nippur during the first millennium CE. Presumably native Mesopotamian ideas were picked up in Hellenistic Judaism (as numerous other ideas were) and through that medium transmitted into rabbinic and patristic literature.

[38]Tigay (*Deuteronomy*, 258) points out that both blessings and curses are treated almost as personified by virtue of the verbs that are used with them. Nevertheless, he concludes: "Actual personification is absent in Deuteronomy, which avoids any suggestion of independent supernatural powers in addition to God. . . . Instead, the blessings and curses are merely reified and treated as impersonal forces under God's absolute control." Similar statements could be made concerning Lilith in Isaiah.

[39]B. Janowski takes it as an entity different from a person and translates "for the elimination of divine anger" ("Azazel," *DDD*[2], 130).

[40]D. Wright, *The Disposal of Impurity* (Atlanta: Scholars Press, 1987), 22: "Caution must be exercised not to presume automatically that as a demon he functions like demons in similar rites outside biblical culture. Azazel's demonic nature must be sought primarily within the framework of the Priestly literature. Significantly, this corpus says little about demonic issues."

[41]Ibid., 24.

[42]*Ṭabaḫu*, in *UL* 12:80, *naqu*, 12.163; see G. Cunningham, *Deliver Me from Evil: Mesopotamian Incantations 2500–1500 BC* (Rome: Pontificio Instituto Biblico, 1997), 59.

it is tainted with the evil that has been transferred to it.[43] D. Wright therefore concludes that Azazel has been stripped of personality and that "He represents little more than the place or goal of disposal."[44] Furthermore, it is not just a harmless locale, but it is one that represents a place of disorder—where all offense belongs.

The final individual designation that I will discuss here is the antagonistic *rûaḥ*, particularly its occurrence in 1 Samuel 16. In these passages the spirit is an entity, but it is not portrayed as chthonic (in or under the earth), liminal (on the periphery of civilization), composite (numerous animal attributes), or theriomorphic (wholly or partially animal shaped). It exercises power against humans, thus differentiating itself from the other Old Testament spirits we have discussed. However, it is also subordinate to God and is employed by him (rather than acting independently). Finally, it is not controlled by magic, though David's harp playing is a response to its influence on Saul.

Synthesis of Old Testament data. None of the potential spirits in the Old Testament are portrayed as enemies of God.[45] They have no chief, and they are not fallen angels. Neither do any spirits have a relationship to *śāṭān*; he neither leads them nor works with them. They do not act as an organized, purposeful group, and whatever terrorizing they do, they do as instruments of God's activity, following his orders and working in subordination to him. Even the chaos creatures are created by God and are fully under his control (e.g., Gen 1:21; Ps 104:26).

Nevertheless, some of these Old Testament beings could be considered marginally volitional (e.g., the *rûaḥ* in 1 Kings 22 who takes initiative to offer a suggestion, or *śāṭān*), though most have no activities associated with them (*šēdîm, śaʿîrîm, lîlît, ʿazʾazēl, ṣiyyîm,* and *ʾiyyîm*). Regarding those who are active (*rûaḥ* or *śāṭān*), one cannot categorize their behavior as arbitrary or irrational. Most in the category can likewise not be considered independent moral agents. Almost all have no moral role, and those that become involved in God's moral agency (*rûaḥ* and, arguably, *śāṭān*) act only as agents of deity

---

[43]Cf., in contrast, *UL* 12:60-61, "make a sacrifice in the daytime, and call out the name of the victim's personal god," and note *UL* 12:151, "may his food-offering approach Shamash."

[44]Wright, *Disposal of Impurity*, 25.

[45]One possible exception to this is the reference to the princes of Persia and Greece in Dan 10:20.

and are morally neutral, intrinsically neither benevolent nor malevolent. The fact is that most supernatural beings in the ancient and classical world, including the high gods, are morally ambiguous.[46]

In other words, spirits in the Old Testament show no exercise of power, either malevolent or benevolent. They are not combatants and are not engaged in opportunism. They can occasionally terrify, but they do not possess (with the possible exception of 1 Sam 16), and they do not tempt. They are not connected to disease and are not controlled by practitioners through exorcism or incantations.[47] No magic is connected to them, and since the Great Symbiosis has been discredited and rejected in biblical theology, there is no relationship between these spirits and that system in the Old Testament.

Demonology, as it is represented by certain types of spirits in the ancient Near East, has no prominence in the Old Testament because these spirits in the ancient Near East cannot be separated from the world of magic and incantations. The conceptual continuum associated with them in Mesopotamia tracks with the magic conceptual continuum, and both would therefore be contrary to legitimate Israelite theology. Furthermore, legitimate Israelite theology contains no renegades or opponents that vie with Yahweh for control. The only form of opposition comes from those who promote the gods of the nations (e.g., Ahab and Jezebel). In biblical texts God might *send* disease, famine, or enemies as a punishment for evil or unfaithfulness, or he might protect a person from those attacks. However, all of these "punishments" are represented as operating entirely under the control of Yahweh.[48]

If there is no demonstrable Old Testament demonology spawned from an ancient Near Eastern cognitive environment, where does Hellenistic Judaism get the ideas that later flow (at least partially) into the New

---

[46]By this I am making reference to behavior that can be irrational or arbitrary, or lack integrity. As part of the Great Symbiosis they have no disinterested goodness or benevolence. Yahweh is not part of the Great Symbiosis and is characterized by a disinterested benevolence (J. Harvey Walton).

[47]In 1 Sam 28, Samuel's spirit (*ʾǝlōhîm*) is called up through the magical procedures connected with necromancy, but it is not subject to incantations or exorcism and does not act either benevolently or malevolently. Furthermore, it is a spirit who used to be alive and so should be considered in a different category.

[48]Even the divine abandonment motif in Ezekiel or Lamentations does not simply expose Israel to independent spirits. Yahweh is still in control of those nations (with their gods) that attack.

Testament and, much more strongly, into rabbinic and early Christian literature? Given the noticeable increase in dualistic tendencies during this time period, many have suggested that Zoroastrianism provided the matrix that transformed the traditional ancient monistic views of the spirits as morally ambiguous into the modified dualism evident at Qumran and in the Jewish literature of the Hellenistic period (in which the spirits are morally determined).[49] Zoroastrianism features *daevas*, "wicked, supernatural beings who demanded worship, but sought to lead men astray."[50] As Zoroastrianism developed, Ahriman (the chief evil spirit) is aided by these *daevas*, particularly the seven chief demons, with Aešma as their leader.[51] Aešma is a Persian spirit of wrath, and most believe that the (unattested) combination *Aešma Daeva* offers the best linguistic explanation of Asmodeus as the prince of the host of demons in the book of Tobit.[52] Thus these ideas that have no known root in the Old Testament or the ancient Near East made their way into Hellenistic Judaism.

SATAN

Satan and the devil.[53] Most English translations refer to the being who is introduced in Job 1:6 and other similar contexts as "Satan"—represented through capitalization as a personal name. Consequently, most readers draw the conclusion that this character is the devil, a figure well known to readers of the New Testament. However, that decision is premature, as will be discussed in this chapter. For the sake of delaying our decision, we will refer to

---

[49]Under the influence of Zoroastrian dualism, "The old gods of the nations and their servant divinities, the lesser spirits of nature and cosmos, were 'demonized,' demoted to the class of wicked spirits, tempting humans to sin and enticing them from the true faith by the false doctrines of other religions." C. J. Riley, "Demon," *DDD²*, 238.

[50]S. Shaked, "Iranian Influence on Judaism: First Century B.C.E. to Second Century C.E.," in *The Cambridge History of Judaism*, vol. 1, *The Persian Period*, ed. W. D. Davies and L. Finkelstein (Cambridge: Cambridge University Press, 1984), 285.

[51]J. B. Russell, *The Devil* (Ithaca, NY: Cornell University Press, 1977), 115.

[52]Ibid., 215. In the early Iranian and Avestan texts the word *daeva* referred to gods, but in Zoroastrian usage it referred to false gods and eventually to demons, especially evident in the Sasanian magical texts (see E. M. Yamauchi, *Persia and the Bible* [Grand Rapids: Baker, 1990], 237-38, 426-27).

[53]Part of this section is adapted from J. H. Walton, "Satan," in *Dictionary of the Old Testament: Wisdom, Poetry, and Writings*, ed. T. Longman III and Peter Enns (Downers Grove, IL: InterVarsity Press, 2010), 714-17.

him for now as "the challenger." We must not foreclose on the identity of this character by quickly jumping to the profile of the being we call Satan in the New Testament. We must begin by asking what an Old Testament author or audience would have thought. After all, an Old Testament author has adopted this character and given him a role. What do they know of Satan? Is this "the devil"? Is it a demon? Is it one of the "sons of God" (NIV translates this phrase as "angels" in Job 1:6)?

Though the Israelites undoubtedly believed in the reality of a demon world, demonology (as demonstrated above) is little attested in the Old Testament. In fact, there is no agreed-upon term for demons. We must begin, then, by investigating the terminology. In the Old Testament the Hebrew word *śāṭān* finds usage both as a verb and a noun. As a verb it means "to oppose as an adversary," "to challenge," or "to accuse" (Ps 38:20; 71:13; 109:4, 20, 29; Zech 3:1). As a noun it can be applied to a human being, thus designating him an adversary (1 Sam 29:4; 2 Sam 19:23; 1 Kings 5:4; 11:14, 23, 25; Ps 109:6). Finally, in the category of most interest to this study, the noun is applied to celestial beings (14x in Job 1–2; 3x in Zech 3:1-2; Num 22:22, 32; 1 Chron 21:1).

There are no cognates to the Hebrew term in Semitic languages, so they offer no help in unraveling the history of the term. If the technical usage (noun applied to supernatural being) is original, and the other usages developed from it, we have to conclude, judging from the nuances of those derived terms, that there is little of a sinister nature in the being (for these other usages evidence none of that element). In contrast, however, the broadly generic sense of the common noun and verb usage suggests that the technical usage is a secondary development.

If this is indeed the case, it would be logical to assume that a supernatural being would have been given this designation as a description of his function, i.e., serving as a heavenly adversary. This finds confirmation in the fact that, in most of the cases where the noun is applied to a supernatural being, the definite article is attached to it. In English, when we refer to someone by means of a proper name, we do not use a definite article (e.g., Sarah, not "the" Sarah). In this practice, Hebrew behaves identically. Therefore we must conclude that the individual in Job 1–2 and Zechariah 3:1-2 should be identified as "the challenger" (description of function) rather than as "Satan" (proper name).[54] Beyond the question of translation, however, we must also inquire as to whether this character is the devil—the character who goes by the name of Satan in the New Testament.

We have often carried blindly into the Old Testament the assumption that the technical term *śāṭān* always applies to the *same* supernatural being, a single *śāṭān*. This is easily refuted by the fact that Numbers 22:22, 32 refers to the angel of the Lord as being a *śāṭān*. Not only can we identify "satan" here as a functional designation, but we can now consider the possibility that, as a function, it is not intrinsically evil.[55] Furthermore, since we would not assume that the angel of the Lord is the challenger in every context where the term *śāṭān* occurs, we can thereby accept that the challenger is not necessarily always the same supernatural being.

Consequently, it is possible that the individual designated as the accuser in Job is not the same individual designated as the accuser in Zechariah or Chronicles. Though they may be the same being, we cannot simply assume that they must be or that the Israelites would have considered them to be the same individual. Pseudepigraphic literature refers to many *śāṭāns*.[56] We would likewise have no reason to identify the challenger of Job 1:6 with the devil.

Weiss concludes that nothing intrinsically evil emerges in the author's portrayal of the *śāṭān* in Job. Certainly what the adversary does has negative consequences for Job, who is a righteous man. But the text makes it clear that God is at least equally responsible for what happens to Job, thus freeing the actions of the *śāṭān* from being implicitly evil.[57] There is no tempting, corrupting, depraving, or possessing. The result of this profile is that we are not in a position to claim that the *śāṭān* in Job should be identified with the devil, Satan, as we know him in the New Testament, at least not on the premise that they act the same way. In fact, there is little if any overlap between their two

---

[54]For a discussion of whether 1 Chron 21:1 evidences the word as a proper name or an indefinite accuser, see S. Japhet, *1 & 2 Chronicles* (Louisville: Westminster John Knox, 1993), 374-75. P. L. Day, *An Adversary in Heaven*, HSM (Atlanta: Scholars Press, 1988), 128-29, suggests that the shift to using Satan as a proper name does not occur until the second century BCE. Whereas the deuterocanonical literature prior to 168 BCE speaks of specific names for evil demons and corrupt angels, no extant tradition employs the proper name Satan.

[55]M. Weiss, *The Story of Job's Beginning* (Jerusalem: Magnes, 1983), 35-41.

[56]There is a list of five *śāṭāns* in 1 Enoch 69:4-12, first century BCE at the earliest; see D. S. Russell, *The Method and Message of Jewish Apocalyptic* (Philadelphia: Westminster, 1964), 254-55.

[57]Weiss, *Story of Job's Beginning*, 37.

profiles. This does not prove that they are *not* the same individuals; it merely reduces (if not eliminates) the basis for claiming that they *must* be equated. The profile of the Hebrew *śāṭān* in the book of Job does not answer to the same description as the Christian view of Satan in the New Testament. While the pictures are not contradictory, and they may even be complementary, we cannot consider them homogeneous.

The profile of the *śāṭān* in Zechariah 3:1 shows a great deal of similarity to that which is in Job, so it is important to take a brief look at this passage to see what it contributes to the formulation of a larger profile. When Joshua the high priest stands before the presence of God, he is confronted by the *śāṭān* and opposed because he is covered with the stains of his and his people's guilt. Is the *śāṭān* wrong to oppose him on this count? Weiss says no:

> True, he "opposes," though not in a spirit of malice, but rather because he meticulously clings to justice, on the principle "Let justice be done though the heavens fall." After all, Joshua the high priest was in fact guilty: he was dressed in garments covered with excrement, and he himself donned them in his guilt. Satan did not garb him in foul clothes through an unjust accusation. The garments are removed when God forgives his sin: he is acquitted not through justice, but through mercy, through pardon.[58]

On the other hand, one significant difference between the scenarios in Job and Zechariah is that the *śāṭān* is rebuked in the latter, while in the former he is not.[59] Carol and Eric Meyers contend that this rebuke is not directed against the *śāṭān* performing his function, but it concerns the evidence he brings.[60] Here again, we find the *śāṭān* raising issues concerning God's policies. In Job, it was the policy of rewarding the righteous that was being questioned. In Zechariah, it is the policy of forgiveness and restoration.[61] Rather than a lengthy test to confirm the legitimacy of God's policy, as we had in Job, the *śāṭān* in Zechariah is rebuked on the grounds that punishment had been appropriately accomplished (Joshua is a smoldering brand drawn from the fire, Zech 3:2).

---

[58]Ibid., 36-37; see also C. Meyers and E. Meyers, *Zechariah 1–8* (Garden City, NY: Doubleday, 1987), 185-86.

[59]Weiss, *Story of Job's Beginning*, 37.

[60]Meyers and Meyers, *Zechariah 1–8*, 186.

[61]Day, *Adversary in Heaven*, 118-21.

A different profile emerges in other passages. In Numbers 22, 1 Kings 11, and 1 Chronicles 21, *śāṭān* is viewed as a quasi-independent agent by means of whom punishment is initiated. How does this compare to the profile of Job/Zechariah? In Job/Zechariah, his function is one directed *toward God* in the sense that he initiates challenges concerning God's policies. In these others, his function is directed *toward humans*. Does the Old Testament deal with two separate profiles or simply two aspects of a single profile? Only speculation could provide answers to these questions. Again, however, we must note how different the profile(s) is from that which is later provided by the New Testament, where Satan is linked directly to a principle of evil.[62]

The New Testament profile reflects the development of thought that took place throughout the intertestamental period, traceable through literature that evidences some of the progression in theological thinking that is later affirmed by the New Testament. By the time of the New Testament, much of this thinking has been accumulated into the profile of the one called Satan, the diabolical enemy leading the forces of evil. The New Testament devil is a tempter, a liar, a murderer, the cause of death, sorcery, and idolatry. He hurts people physically, and he blocks and obstructs the teaching of the kingdom of God wherever he can, assaulting us, possessing us spiritually, and tempting us to sin. In all this he is the enemy of the kingdom of God.[63]

This sinister being has been viewed in many different ways throughout history. In some Jewish writings, he is the personification of the evil impulse in all of us. The more dualistic offshoots of Christianity (e.g., Manichaeism) understood him as the hypostasis of the dark side of God. Another variation, perhaps the most popular view in contemporary Christianity, posits him as the apotheosis of evil from within the world of demons.[64] This latter profile portrays Satan as a fallen angel.

The role of the *śāṭān* in Job is as one who acts as a court functionary as-signed to investigate the execution of the policies of God. It is unclear whether he should be seen as legal opponent, litigant, or informant. In Job he is not an independent agent opportunistically fulfilling his nature. Whatever he does, he does through the power of God; all the events of the

---

[62]Russell, *Method and Message of Jewish Apocalyptic*, 189.
[63]Russell, *Devil*, 240.
[64]Ibid., 176-77.

book are understood as God's actions. He is a character used by the author in ways that correspond to what was known by an Israelite audience. Regardless of whether this is truly the being that the New Testament designates as Satan or the devil, the book of Job needs to be interpreted based on the profile that was available to the target audience. This makes the challenger of less theological significance in the book. He is not offered as one who can be blamed for Job's suffering, nor does his role provide an explanation for suffering or evil in our experiences or in the world. He is a minor character playing a minor part in the unfolding drama.

Fall of Satan. If *śāṭān* in the Old Testament is not to be equated with the devil, then he is not to be viewed as a fallen being, and we need to reconsider the Old Testament passages that have, at times, been interpreted as references to Satan's fall.[65]

Isaiah 14:12-15. From a contextual standpoint, this pericope concerns the king of Babylon and accordingly is placed among the oracles against the nations. It takes the form of a taunt (Is 14:5) anticipating the tyrant's imminent demise. His descent to the netherworld (Is 14:9-11) is described with relish, and Isaiah 14:12-15 refers to his downfall, despite his aspirations to divine grandeur.

Throughout most of church history, these verses have been applied to Satan. The earliest appearance of this association can be found in the writings of Origen.[66] Satan's fall had been discussed earlier by Tertullian and Justin Martyr but with no obvious references to Isaiah 14. This is not surprising, since Satan is mentioned nowhere in the passage. Jewish writings (cf. 2 Enoch 29:4-5) contained stories of the fall of Satan, but there is no evidence that Isaiah 14 was ever interpreted in relation to that fall.

The doctrine of his fall and its association with Isaiah 14 passed into the mainstream of Christian theology through *Moralia* 34 by Pope Gregory the Great in the seventh century. Once it was part of popular belief, it easily passed into the great pieces of literature, such as Milton's *Paradise Lost*, which sustained its place in theology. The doctrine was additionally solidified by the way Isaiah 14 was handled in translation. Jerome, interpreting the difficult Hebrew

---

[65]Discussion adapted from J. Walton, *Genesis*, NIVAC (Grand Rapids: Zondervan, 2001).

[66]Russell, *Satan*, 130. For a thorough discussion of the development of Origen's thought concerning Satan and his blending and use of the traditions available to him, see N. Forsyth, *The Old Enemy* (Princeton, NJ: Princeton University Press, 1987), 367-83.

term *hêlēl* in Isaiah 14:12 (NIV "morning star") as a reference to Venus, used a Latin term for Venus, *luciferos*, to translate it. As the interpretation of the passage as a reference to Satan became popularized in the centuries following, "Lucifer" was adopted as a variant name for Satan—but only because that was what Satan was called in this passage. Tertullian, other early Christian writers, Gregory the Great, and the scholastic commentators, regarding Luke 10:18 as an explanation of this verse, applied it also to the fall of Satan, from which has arisen the popular perversion of the beautiful name Lucifer as another name for the devil.[67] By the sixteenth and seventeenth centuries, when the major English translations were being produced, the interpretation was so ingrained that "Lucifer" was retained, even in the King James Version, thus reinforcing to the lay English reader the belief that the passage explicitly concerned Satan.[68]

Despite the popular support of this interpretation, there was no lack of opposition. Neither John Calvin nor Martin Luther supported the idea that Isaiah 14 refers to the fall of Satan. Calvin was particularly undiplomatic as he heaped his scorn on those who would adopt such a noncontextual intrusion.

> The exposition of this passage, which some have given, as if it should refer to Satan, has arisen from ignorance; for the context plainly shows that these state-ments must be understood in reference to the king of the Babylonians. But when passages of Scripture are taken up at random, and no attention is paid to the context, we need not wonder that mistakes of this kind frequently arise. Yet it was an instance of very gross ignorance to imagine that Lucifer was the king of the devils, and that the prophet gave him this name. But as these inventions have no probability whatever, let us pass by them as useless fables.[69]

From a hermeneutical standpoint, one can hardly claim that Isaiah was intentionally addressing the issue of Satan's fall. Aside from not mentioning

---

[67]J. A. Alexander, *The Prophecies of Isaiah* (repr., Grand Rapids: Zondervan, 1953), 295. Modern conservative commentaries also commonly reject any association between this passage and Satan. Cf. J. Oswalt, *The Book of Isaiah: Chapters 1–39* (Grand Rapids: Eerdmans, 1986), 320; E. J. Young, *The Book of Isaiah*, 2nd ed. (Grand Rapids: Eerdmans, 1972), 1:441; G. V. Smith, *Isaiah 1–39* (Nashville: B&H, 2007), 314-19 (he only mentions the Lucifer interpretation in a brief footnote, 314n94); J. A. Motyer, *The Prophecy of Isaiah* (Downers Grove, IL: InterVarsity Press, 1993), 144. Motyer does not even mention the possibility of the passage referring to Satan.

[68]For a summary of the use of the name Lucifer in medieval literature, see J. B. Russell, *Lucifer* (Ithaca, NY: Cornell University Press, 1984), 247.

[69]John Calvin, *Commentary on the Book of Isaiah 1–32*, trans. William Pringle (repr., Grand Rapids: Baker, 1979), 442.

Satan, we have already seen how little the Israelite view of Satan would have accommodated such an understanding. Given our knowledge about what the Israelite audience knew (or did not know) about Satan, we have no reason to assume that Isaiah would consider his audience automatically able to relate the information about the king of Babylon to Satan or his fall.

Nevertheless, those who continue to interpret Isaiah 14 as a reference to the fall of Satan base their beliefs on the statements made in Isaiah 14:13-14. They typically maintain that no human being could make such statements or seriously entertain such possibilities. Such assessments sadly underestimate the inclinations of the rulers of the ancient world to make grandiose statements that would mock the label "hyperbole" as a vast understatement. One need not even read the inscriptional literature (though that would be instructive[70]), for ample evidence of royal hubris is even provided in biblical records such as Isaiah 47:8, where Babylon claims for itself, "I am, and there is none besides me" (cf. Zeph 2:15).

Finally, we do not need to view Isaiah 14:13-14 as statements the king would actually make, for here the prophet is drawing a caricature, perhaps even referencing well-known mythical material. This king, who takes his own mythology too seriously and supposes himself capable of grandiose accomplishments like those sometimes enshrined in myth, will find himself in a similar situation to that which is portrayed in other mythology instead: the outcast or would-be usurper.

Ezekiel 28:12-19.[71] In contrast to Isaiah 14, this passage has more obvious references to a primeval situation. Although it refers contextually to the king of Tyre, reference to the Garden of Eden (Ezek 28:13) and the cherub (Ezek 28:14) has given interpreters sufficient basis to move beyond the stated context. Admittedly, it is within the function of metaphor to point to something outside itself, yet the interpreter must still ask to what the author intends the metaphor to relate in this particular context.

---

[70]See, for instance, the royal inscriptions of Esarhaddon and Ashurbanipal (*ANET* 289-301), especially the account of Nabonidus's rise to power (*ANET* 308-11) and the Verse Account of Nabonidus (*ANET* 312-15).

[71]For extensive treatment of the issues and interpretations, see D. Block, *The Book of Ezekiel: Chapters 25–48*, New International Commentary on the Old Testament (Grand Rapids: Eerdmans, 1998), 99-121. He stands with nearly all contemporary commentators in rejecting any connection to the fall of Satan.

Commentators have traditionally stated three reasons to support their claim that the king of Tyre should be understood as Satan: (1) the king is in the garden, (2) the king is identified as the cherub, and (3) the passage alludes to a fall from a blameless condition. As we examine each of these in light of Old Testament theology, however, the interpretation becomes increasingly difficult to maintain.

With regard to the first point, we must recognize that there is no indication in the Old Testament that the Israelites believed Satan was in the Garden of Eden. No Old Testament passage either equates or relates the serpent and Satan, whether in Genesis or elsewhere (see below for further discussion). If Ezekiel 28 were phrased as an instruction that suggested such an equation should be made, it would be another matter. But those who interpret the passage as a reference to Satan only claim that this passage refers to the fall of Satan metaphorically. For such a metaphor to work, it must make reference to well-known information. There is no evidence that Israel would have known that the serpent was a tool or representation of Satan. That being the case, they would not have placed Satan in the garden.

As to the second point, we must ask where any scripture suggests that Satan was a cherub.[72] The cherubim are a specialized class of supernatural beings with very specific functions. There is no basis for the speculation that Satan was once among their number, and there is certainly no reason to suggest that the Israelite audience would have recognized such a metaphorical allusion.

Finally, as previously noted, the Old Testament nowhere portrays Satan as a fallen being.[73] Therefore, that Ezekiel 28 refers to a fall would not have suggested to the Israelite reader that the author was metaphorically invoking the fall of Satan for comparison to the fate of the king of Tyre.

---

[72]Origen initiated the idea that Satan originally sang among the cherubs, but this only reflects his conclusion that Ezek 28 was talking about Satan (*Beginnings* 1.5.4, 1.8.3; see Russell, *Satan*, 129). Subsequent to Dionysius's description of the celestial hierarchy (ca. 500 CE), in which seraphs were considered the highest beings, Western writers generally assumed Satan had been a seraph prior to his fall; see Russell, *Lucifer*, 32. Gregory also adopted the "cherub" view. See ibid., 94. For the discussion among the scholastics, see ibid., 173n36.

[73]In Tertullian's context (and to a lesser extent, Origen's also) the existence of a "fallen being" is contrived as an anti-Gnostic cosmological argument. Not only are they reading a metaphorical passage literally, but they are reading external assumptions into the account; the evil of Satan is Tertullian's premise, not his conclusion. I am grateful to J. Harvey Walton for this observation.

Is there, then, any single datum in Ezekiel 28 that parallels information known about Satan in the Old Testament? I see none. So how can we possibly suggest that Ezekiel is making use of the account of the fall of Satan as a metaphor to describe the impending fall of the king of Tyre?

But, the objection would arise, to whom else could the passage refer? What would we make of a story of a cherub in the garden who was created blameless but then rebelled? It must be some sort of metaphor, because no one suggests that Ezekiel thought the king of Tyre actually was a cherub in the garden.

One popular suggestion has been that Ezek 28:14 should be read as noting that this individual was with the cherub but was not a cherub himself.[74] Such a reading opens up the possibility that the king of Tyre is being compared to the primeval man, Adam.[75] This suggestion is problematic, however, because in the Genesis account, Adam is never with the cherub in the garden. The cherub is only stationed in the garden after Adam and Eve are expelled. Those who maintain this identification are therefore obliged to posit a variant form of the Eden tradition in Ezekiel.

While the passage presents difficulties to all interpreters, scholars have made important progress in recent years. H. J. van Dijk and I. Goldberg have both noticed that Ezekiel 28:12-15 features very close parallelism, as shown in table 6.1.[76]

Table 6.1. Parallelism in Ezekiel 28

	Ezekiel 28:12b-13	Ezekiel 28:14-15a
Identification	you are a seal	you are a cherub
Description	perfect, full of wisdom, resplendent	guardian, ordained, spread winged/anointed
Residence	you were in Eden, the garden of God	you were on the holy mountain of God
Position	all the precious stones	among the stones of fire
Intrinsic Quality	your settings and mountings were made of gold; on the day you were created they were prepared	you were blameless in your ways from the day that you were created

---

[74]This requires changing the pointing of the first word in Ezek 28:14 from ʾat (personal pronoun, "you") to ʾet (preposition, "with"); see NRSV.

[75]See, e.g., W. Zimmerli, *Ezekiel* (Philadelphia: Fortress, 1983), 2:90; and among conservative commentators, J. Taylor, *Ezekiel* (Downers Grove, IL: InterVarsity Press, 1969), 196-97; and Douglas Stuart, *Ezekiel* (Dallas: Word, 1989), 273-74.

[76]H. J. van Dijk, *Ezekiel's Prophecy on Tyre* (Rome: Pontifical Biblical Institute, 1968), 114; I. Goldberg, "The Artistic Structure of the Dirge over the King of Tyre," *Tarbis* 58 (1988–1989): 277-81 (Hebrew).

Given these parallels, two suggestions can be made: (1) there are two parallel metaphors in the passage rather than one single metaphor, as the other interpretations assumed; (2) the metaphors do not extend to the fall but only refer to the high station of the individual. The king of Tyre enjoyed a lofty status because of all that was entrusted to him; he was the guardian of extensive natural resources, just as the individuals in the two metaphors were guardians.[77] Unfortunately, he was corrupted by them and was found to be treacherous and irresponsible. The metaphor ends where the parallelism ends, and from Ezekiel 28:15-19, the king's conduct and punishment are addressed (though the end of Ezek 28:16 refers back to the metaphor). Thus there is no reason to reach beyond the context and its metaphors for a sensible interpretation of the passage.

If neither Isaiah nor Ezekiel (nor any other passage in the Old Testament) offers any information about the fall of Satan, what do we know about it? Any putative information in the New Testament concerning the fall is arguable and vague at best. In Luke 10:18 Christ remarks, "I saw Satan fall like lightning from heaven." It must be noted, however, that this is his response to the disciples' successful ministry, of which they observe, "Even the demons submit to us in your name." It is therefore a possibility, if not a probability, that Christ is referring not to the primeval past but to their recent triumphs (cf. Jn 12:31), though he may be doing so through allusion to the distant past.

Revelation 12:9 is also often invoked on the matter of Satan's fall, but here the reference is to the events of John's vision, which were still to take place in the future (whether our future or only his). Therefore they can offer no insight into the occurrences of the past, though it is not improbable that parallels were seen to exist between a primeval fall (which would have been known through other contemporary literature, as noted above) and the future total defeat portrayed here.

In 2 Corinthians 11:14 Paul observes that Satan masquerades as an angel of light, but he makes no suggestion that he once *was* an angel of light or any other sort of angel. It is true that the New Testament authors

---

[77]This fits well with the understanding of the cherub as the guardian of the tree of life. The first metaphor concerns a "seal" if the text is taken as it stands, which may refer to king as a "signet ring" (cf. Hag 2:23). The metaphor is not drawn from myths but from known literary motifs.

show awareness of the existence of fallen angels (e.g., 2 Pet 2:4), but they nowhere suggest that Satan was once among them, much less the leader of the rebellion.

Finally, 1 Timothy 3:6 indicates that "the devil" has fallen under judgment because of his conceit. This is the most information that any passage offers, and we can see that it is quite scant. In addition to conceit, John 8:44 acknowledges Satan as the father of lies, but neither of these offenses is specifically identified as the sin that led to his fall.

In conclusion, the New Testament offers few details about the circumstances of Satan's fall or about his status prior to the fall.[78] Most of the details brought to bear on our theological discussion of the fall find their source in the pseudepigraphic literature of the intertestamental period or in the allegorical interpretations of the early Christian writers, especially the theories of Justin, Tatian, Irenaeus, and Origen.[79]

Satan and the serpent.[80] The Old Testament offers not the slightest hint that the serpent of Genesis 2–3 was either identified as or inspired by Satan.[81] The earliest extant reference to any association is found in the Wisdom of Solomon 2:23-24 (first century BCE):

> For God formed us to be imperishable;
> the image of his own nature he made us.
> But by the envy of the devil, death entered the world,
> and they who are allied with him experience it. (NAB)

Even here, the devil is not given the name "Satan" and was, in fact, variously named in early literature. This figure normally became Sammael

---

[78]Origen was largely responsible for the concept that Satan fell as a result of pride prior to the creation of Adam and Eve; see Russell, *Satan*, 130. For a summary of the elaboration by Augustine, see ibid., 214, and Forsyth, *Old Enemy*, 428-34.

[79]For a summary of some of the early theories concerning the cause of Satan's fall, see Russell, *Devil*, 241-42. For an exhaustive summary of the thinking of the early church fathers, see Russell, *Satan*.

[80]Discussion adapted from Walton, *Lost World of Adam and Eve*; Walton, *Genesis*; and J. Walton, *Job*, NIVAC (Grand Rapids: Zondervan, 2012), 24-27.

[81]Cf. G. J. Wenham: "Early Jewish and Christian commentators identified the snake with Satan or the devil, but since there is no other trace of a personal devil in early parts of the OT, modern writers doubt whether this is the view of our narrator." *Genesis 1-15* (Waco, TX: Word, 1987), 72; see also I. Provan, *Discovering Genesis: Content, Interpretation, Reception* (London: SPCK, 2015), 79-80.

in the Targum and in rabbinic tradition. However, in a text known as the Apocalypse of Abraham, preserved only in the Slavonic translation but datable to the same period that inspired the Syriac Baruch and the Apocalypse of Ezra, the seductive angel is called Azazel.[82]

Nevertheless, throughout the ancient world the serpent was endowed with divine or semidivine qualities; it was venerated as an emblem of health, fertility, immortality, occult wisdom, and chaotic evil and was often worshiped. The serpent played a significant role in the mythology, the religious symbolism, and the cults of the ancient Near East.[83] In the Gilgamesh Epic, for example, a serpent steals the plant of life from Gilgamesh, and in the tale of Adapa, one of the guardians of Anu's palace is Gizzida (= Ningishzida, "Lord of the Productive Tree"), who has the shape of a serpent and is accompanied by horned serpents (*bašmu*). He is known as the guardian of the demons who live in the netherworld.[84]

In Egypt we find serpents everywhere from the crown of Pharaoh to pictures on painted sarcophagi, as well as in the Book of the Dead (as deadly enemies along the path to the afterlife). These creatures are associated with both wisdom and death. As an example, Apophis was a serpent of chaos who tried to swallow the sun as it rose every morning.[85] Other elements can also be found in the Egyptian Book of the Dead that connect to ideas that are evident in the

---

[82]Forsyth, *Old Enemy*, 224. Perhaps the earliest reference to Satan as the tempter (through the serpent) is in the Apocalypse of Moses 16–19 (properly titled Life of Adam and Eve), which is contemporary to the New Testament. This text also links Is 14 to Satan's fall; see Forsyth, *Old Enemy*, 232-38. In the writings of the church fathers, one of the earliest to associate the serpent with Satan was Justin, *First Apology* 28.1. See Forsyth, *Old Enemy*, 351.

[83]Walton, *Genesis*, 203; N. Sarna, *Genesis* (Philadelphia: Jewish Publication Society, 1989), 24. For a brief summary of some of the supporting archaeological finds, see J. Scullion, *Genesis* (Collegeville, MN: Michael Glazier, 1992), 47. For more detail, see K. R. Joines, *Serpent Symbolism in the Old Testament* (Haddonfield, NJ: Haddonfield House, 1974), 19-29; J. Charlesworth, *The Good and Evil Serpent: How a Universal Symbol Became Christianized* (New Haven, CT: Tale, 2010).

[84]Thorkild Jacobsen, "Mesopotamian Gods and Pantheons," in *Toward the Image of Tammuz and Other Essays on Mesopotamian History and Culture*, ed. William L. Moran (Cambridge, MA: Harvard University Press, 1971), 24; Jeremy Black and Anthony Green, *Gods, Demons and Symbols of Ancient Mesopotamia* (Austin: University of Texas Press, 1992), 139. See also W. G. Lambert, "Trees, Snakes and Gods in Ancient Syria and Anatolia," *Bulletin of the School of Oriental and African Studies* 48 (1985): 435-51.

[85]Nicole B. Hansen, "Snakes," in *Oxford Encyclopedia of Ancient Egypt*, ed. Donald B. Redford (New York: Oxford University Press, 2001), 3:297.

Genesis account, including crawling on the belly,[86] eating dust,[87] a crushed head,[88] and striking a heel.

For an example of several of these items, see the Pyramid Texts, utterance 378:

> O Snake in the sky! O Centipede on earth! The Sandal of Horus is what
> tramples the nhi-snake underfoot. . . . It is dangerous for me so I have
> trodden on you; be wise about me (?) and I will not tread on you, for you are
> the mysterious and invisible one of whom the gods speak; because you are
> the one who has no legs, because you are the one who has no arms, with
> which you could walk after your brethren the gods . . . beware of me and I
> will beware of you.[89]

All of these examples show us that serpent symbolism has been connected to fertility, sexuality, protection, life, death, and numerous other important attributes throughout the ancient Near East.[90] The serpent is therefore a meaningful character in the text without having to have any connections to Satan.

In the context of Genesis, the serpent is merely one of the creatures that God created. It is shrewd but not sinister. Unlike in Christian theology, in Israel there was no inclination to embody all evil in a central figure or to trace its cause to a single historical event.[91] Therefore the Israelites were quite willing to recognize the serpent as the representation of an evil influence without attempting to associate it with a being who was the ultimate source or cause of evil. In fact, it would appear that the author of Genesis intentionally underplays the role or identification of the serpent; this would correlate with the other polemical elements of the early chapters of Genesis. It is important to remember that, in the ancient world, most cosmological models were built around a god taming or defeating the

---

[86]PT 226, 233, 234, 288, 298, 386. All Pyramid Text citations refer to utterance numbers and are taken from Raymond O. Faulkner, *The Ancient Egyptian Pyramid Texts* (Oxford: Oxford University Press, 1969). There are occasional depictions of serpent creatures with legs. *Bašmu* is sometimes portrayed as having two front legs (Joan Goodnick Westenholz, *Dragons, Monsters and Fabulous Beasts* [Jerusalem: Bible Lands Museum, 2004], 190). For a picture of the seal of Gudea showing Ningishzida introducing him to Enki, see Black and Green, *Gods, Demons and Symbols*, 139.

[87]"May your poison fangs be in the earth, your ribs in the hole" (PT 230); "spittle in the dust" (PT 237).

[88]PT 299, 378, 388.

[89]Faulkner, *Ancient Egyptian Pyramid Texts*.

[90]Full discussion in Charlesworth, *Good and Evil Serpent*.

[91]Sarna, *Genesis*, 24.

chaotic forces, often represented in the sea.[92] In Canaanite literature, this role of chaos was played by the serpentine Leviathan/Lotan. In contrast, the biblical narrative asserts that the great sea creature was simply another of the beasts God created (Gen 1:21). This tendency may explain why the author avoids associating the existence of evil with any conspiratorial uprisings theory.

If the Israelites would not have thought of the serpent as Satan, then what would they have thought? We can begin with the description that is given in Genesis 3. The main adjective used there identifies the serpent as ʿārûm, variously translated as "subtle," "wily," "cunning," "shrewd," "prudent," or "clever." It is an adjective that operates primarily in reference to wisdom and is inherently neutral (that is, it is a quality that can be used well—Prov 1:4; 8:5—or in questionable ways—Ex 21:14; Josh 9:4).[93] Ziony Zevit offers a helpful profile of someone who is ʿārûm:

> [They] conceal what they feel and what they know (Prov 12:16; 23). They esteem knowledge and plan how to use it in achieving their objectives (Prov 13:16; 14:8, 18); they do not believe everything that they hear (Prov 14:15); and they know how to avoid trouble and punishment (Prov 22:3; 27:12). In sum they are shrewd and calculating, willing to bend and torture the limits of acceptable behavior but not to cross the line into illegalities. They may be unpleasant and purposely misleading in speech but are not out-and-out liars (Josh 9:4; 1 Sam 23:22). They know how to read people and situations and how to turn their readings to advantage. A keen wit and a rapier tongue are their tools.[94]

Ultimately, such a descriptor does not aid us in determining the creature's nature. Other than that, we can only identify the serpent as one of "the wild animals the LORD God had made" (Gen 3:1). At the same time, we should notice that the serpent is not described as "evil." This significant creature does not become associated with evil until much later.[95]

---

[92]Cf. J. Day, *God's Conflict with the Dragon and the Sea: Echoes of a Canaanite Myth in the Old Testament* (Cambridge: Cambridge University Press, 1985). See discussion above.

[93]Michael V. Fox, *Proverbs 1–9*, Anchor Bible (New Haven, CT: Yale University Press, 2000), 35-36. Note that the Septuagint uses a Greek term that means "most intelligent" (*phronimōtatos*).

[94]Ziony Zevit, *What Really Happened in the Garden of Eden?* (New Haven, CT: Yale University Press, 2013), 163.

[95]Ibid.

Recent study has focused attention on the serpent as a chaos creature. Chaos creatures in the ancient world were typically composite creatures that belonged to the sphere of the divine yet were not deified.[96] Their composite features gave them a combination of attributes. For example, in the ancient world the chaos creatures were not thought of as evil. They were amoral but could also be mischievous or destructive. They caused problems if left unchecked, but they could also be domesticated and become associates of the gods. Demons could function much like chaos creatures as well, as did liminal creatures (e.g., coyote, screech owl).[97]

It is true that the Hebrew word for the serpent, *nāḥāš*, is one of the normal ways to designate a common snake. Furthermore, the snake in Genesis 3 is identified as among the creatures of the field that God created, and nothing in the text suggests it is a composite creature. Nevertheless, all creatures in the Hebrew Bible, including chaos creatures, were created by God (Gen 1:21; Job 40:15-19; Ps 104:26). That *nāḥāš* can also designate a chaos creature is evident from its usage in Isaiah 27:1, where it describes Leviathan.[98] Such an understanding is confirmed finally in the Apocalypse of John, in which the serpent, now Satan, is described as a great dragon (Rev 12:9)—the chaos creature par excellence.[99] We could therefore conclude that the serpent in Genesis 3 is a chaos creature based on its role in the story and other supporting contexts.[100]

R. Averbeck is then correct to observe that this is not just a snake story: "The Israelites would have seen a great deal more in Genesis 3 than a simple tale about snakes and mankind. . . . From their point of view, this would

---

[96]In the Bible such composite creatures are identified as cherubim and seraphim, though they are not chaos creatures per se. Chaos creatures would be ones such as Leviathan and Rahab. For an extensive treatment of such creatures, see Westenholz, *Dragons, Monsters and Fabulous Beasts*.

[97]For discussion of these, see Walton, "Demons in Mesopotamia," 229-46.

[98]Charlesworth, *Good and Evil Serpent*, 438. Note, however, that on 294 he rejects the idea that the serpent in Gen 3 should be considered a chaos creature.

[99]It is interesting that many interpreters insist that since Revelation identifies the serpent as Satan we have to accept the identification as biblical truth (not just an associative picture). Yet I have encountered few who view the serpent as a dragon based on the information from the same verses in Revelation (though Augustine did view the serpent that way in his Sermon 36; Augustine, *Sermons*, trans. Edmund Hill, The Works of Saint Augustine: A Translation for the 21st Century III/2 [(Brooklyn, NY: New City Press, 1990], 281).

[100]This would also offer a ready explanation of the serpent speaking without the necessary anatomical analysis of the larynxes of serpent species.

have been the very beginning of a cosmic battle that they were feeling the effects of in their own personal experience and their national history."[101] Though I am not ready to go as far as he does and conclude that this account also represents the fall of Satan, I believe that viewing the text from the ancient Israelite viewpoint should lead us to think of the serpent in terms of a chaos creature.

What is the result of such an approach?[102]

✦ An Israelite reader would not identify the serpent as Satan. The consequences were far more significant in the account than the agent. The serpent was the catalyst more than the cause.

✦ An Israelite reader would recognize the deleterious effects of the temptation but would not necessarily consider the serpent morally evil or bent on the destruction of humankind. An Israelite also would not give any unique status to this serpent—he would be considered just one of any number of chaos creatures rather than as a spiritual, cosmic power of some sort.

✦ The Israelite reader would have thought of the serpent as a sort of disruptive free agent with less of a thought-out agenda; the Old Testament does not give the serpent an ongoing role. Like the serpent in the Gilgamesh Epic (who did what its nature led it to do and then disappeared from the scene), no continuing role or place is recognized for the Old Testament serpent, though the consequences of the human act remain in place (as in Gilgamesh).

✦ The serpent's insertion of doubt and his nuanced denial of the woman's understanding of the consequences stated by God would not be interpreted any differently from our traditional understanding. Deception, misdirection, and troublemaking are all within the purview of chaos creatures.

---

[101]Richard E. Averbeck, "Ancient Near Eastern Mythography as It Relates to Historiography in the Hebrew Bible: Genesis 3 and the Cosmic Battle," in *The Future of Biblical Archaeology: Reassessing Methodologies and Assumptions*, ed. James Karl Hoffmeier and Alan R. Millard (Grand Rapids: Eerdmans, 2004), 328-56, esp. 352-53.

[102]Part of this section is adapted from Walton, *Lost World of Adam and Eve*, 133-36.

✦ The Israelite reader would understand that the result of the serpent's role was evil's establishment among humanity. This is clear from Genesis 3:15, where an ongoing battle is portrayed between humans (generation to generation) on one side, and the "seed" or "offspring" of the serpent (the "offspring" here does not refer to future generations of serpents but to the resulting evil) on the other side. The reality that the two verbs in the verse that describe the antagonist actions are from the same root (despite the fact that many translations render them differently) shows that the verse does not indicate who the victor will be. Instead it indicates that there will be an ongoing exchange of potentially mortal blows.

✦ As a chaos creature, the serpent would be more closely associated with nonorder than with disorder. Nonorder has a certain neutrality to it, whereas disorder is evil in nature and intent. We might describe an earthquake or a cancer as a force of nonorder with evil consequences, but neither is inherently evil. We do not control them, and they therefore can have disastrous effects. If the serpent truly is in the category of chaos creature, neither his contradiction of God's statement nor his deception about the consequences is part of an evil agenda. They are simply the disruptive, ad hoc behavior in which chaos creatures engage. A more complete understanding is offered in intertestamental literature and New Testament theology, but if we limit our analysis to the ancient context of the Old Testament, things look very different.

In conclusion, the established occurrences of *śāṭān* in the Old Testament do not show the profile that we find developed in the intertestamental period or that reach full expression in the New Testament. None of these Old Testament passages attest to the fall of a being known as Satan; when we see a being who exercises the function of *śaṭan*, the text gives no indication that the *śāṭān* is intrinsically evil. The Old Testament theology surrounding the challenger must be developed using only those passages in the Old Testament that make reference to this role. If we do this, we will find a far different profile from the one the New Testament or the early Christian writers would have brought.

God and the Serpent: Who Told the Truth?

It is important to note the syntactical subtlety that is evident in the serpent's words. He does not say "You will not die." Instead the placement of the negation results in something more like "Don't think that death is such an immediate threat."[a] The woman had not been careful in her wording, and the serpent, picking up on the discrepancy, told the truth and contradicted her (not God) by saying that death was not an immediate threat. In this way the serpent's deception came as the exploitation of a misrepresentation by the woman; he told her of a benefit of eating the fruit without likewise including the harmful effects. Notice that the serpent does not suggest outright that Eve should eat the fruit or disobey.[b] At the same time, there is no room for the suggestion that it was the serpent who told the truth (you will not die; you shall be like gods) and God who was wrong (in the day that you eat from it you will surely die).[c] God's statement did not indicate immediate death ("in the day" is the Hebrew way of saying "when"). The penalty was carried out by removing Adam and Eve's access to the tree of life. Furthermore, the construction often translated "surely die" expresses only that they would at that time be *doomed* to die, which is exactly what happened when the way to the tree of life was barred.[d] God told the truth: when they ate from the tree, they were doomed to die.

[a]See the grammatical-syntactical discussion in Walton, *Genesis*, 204-5.

[b]Zevit, *What Really Happened in the Garden of Eden?*, 202-3.

[c]See this suggestion in Ronald Veenker, "Do Deities Deceive?," in *Windows to the Ancient World of the Hebrew Bible*, 201-14.

[d]Walton, *Genesis*, 174-75; Zevit, *What Really Happened in the Garden of Eden?*, 124-26.

CONCLUSIONS: ENDURING THEOLOGY

As demonstrated in this chapter, the Old Testament contains very little of our Christian theology about evil, sin, Satan, and demons. In the Old Testament, evil includes moral failure, but it is not itself defined in moral terms. The ancient Israelites had no concept of original sin (though they did recognize a universal sinful inclination) or of the fall (as articulated with all its ramifications in contemporary Christian theology). Sin was recognized as imposing a burden, but it was more commonly considered in terms of its disruption to God's order. It was a source of disorder primarily related to the covenant. The satan character in the Old Testament is not the devil, not the chief of the demons, and was not considered a fallen angel. Demons were virtually nonexistent in the literature, operate primarily by instinct rather than by volition, and are morally neutral (though capable of destructive behaviors). Neither satan nor demons tempted, possessed, or took any active role in human events (except on rare occasions when God directed the event). Only the vaguest hints would indicate that the Israelites would have adopted the ancient Near Eastern view that many illnesses were caused by demons. At the same time, no polemic or disagreement of that perspective can be found in the Old Testament either.

What should our response be to such discrepancies? Several possibilities can be identified, including the following:

1. Consider Old Testament theology uninformed and obsolete and therefore to be largely disregarded.

2. Consider some of the elements in the New Testament to be the cultural products of the Greco-Roman, post-Hellenistic cognitive environment rather than new revelation.

3. Recognize that most of the discrepancies perceived between the Old Testament and New Testament derive not from the New Testament itself but from Second Temple Judaism and the interpretation of the New Testament by Christian theologians who assumed that the two Testaments revealed the same metaphysics.

Table 6.2 can help (in simplified ways) to show some of the differences between these views.

The descriptions in the table are unavoidably simplistic and are arguable in every line. Their purpose, however, is to provide a rough comparison that can be used for analyzing the similarities and differences. What is particularly interesting is that when we are able to compare the Old Testament to the New Testament, rather than to the formulations provided by the theologians after the New Testament period, we find fewer differences, and some of the ones we find occur as the New Testament reflects its Greco-Roman cultural environment. To the extent that this is true, we may find that Old

Table 6.2. Comparison of issues related to sin across cultures

Elements	Ancient Near East	OT	Greco-Roman[a]	NT	Historical/ Systematic Theology
Evil	defined circumstantially by results rather than ontologically	defined circumstantially by results rather than ontologically	opposite to order, goodness, and sound reason; regardless of who/ what sets the standards	underlying cause of disorder and difficulties; opposite of holiness; may also be defined by circumstantial results	behavior contrary to the revealed will of God
Sin	contrary to order as defined by the Great Symbiosis	contrary to order, particularly covenant order	actions opposite to the well-being of the community and contrary to the virtues of dignity, justice, and respect for the gods, land, and family	behavior that violates God's character and purposes; results in death and separation	failure to give God proper honor and respect (Anselm)
Fall	idyllic but uncivilized primordial history; no fall; people inherently prone to sin	event, yes; original sin, no; inclination to sin	memory of an idyllic primordial history lost due to human misdeeds	limited articulation of fall or original sin; sin nature accepted but unformulated	made all humans guilty before God and incapable of not sinning (West); original sin and sin nature formulated
Satan	no identifiable parallel	challenger operating within council	source of cosmic or supernatural phenomena that cannot be attributed to the gods, often including the material world, no single adversary	devil, enemy of God's people; antagonistic but not autonomous; little information about his fall	the first sinner and perpetrator of all evil; fights a war with God in which humans participate on one side or the other
Demons	• liminal • composite • instinctive more than volitional • benevolent or malevolent	• liminal • amoral • nonintrusive • instinctive more than volitional	• servants of the gods • occupy the cosmic realm between the earth and the moon • higher in the hierarchy of beings than humans, lower than gods • could act with good or bad intentions	• obnoxious agents of disease and distress • propagate suffering rather than sin	• Satan's henchmen • counterparts to God's angels • soldiers in cosmic war • encourage or force humans to do evil

[a]Many of these issues were not very well formulated in the Greco-Roman world. For example, "sin" is not something that was pondered very deeply. I am grateful to my colleague Brent Sandy for his help in putting together the Greco-Roman and New Testament segments of this chart.

Testament theology can help us to make some important adjustments to our contemporary theology. Let us consider the possibilities row by row.

Evil. In the ancient Near East evil had been defined according to a human perspective, with the gods above and apart from moral association. Although the gods battle chaos, they do not do so out of anger or wrath and do not seek to destroy chaos, only to hold it back to preserve order. On this count, the Old Testament does not show a significant distinction. The New Testament, following the lead of Greco-Roman philosophical developments, has a new emphasis on the theological aspects of evil, specifically regarding the idea that the gods are exemplars of the good that should be aspired to and imitated. Evil, in Greco-Roman philosophy, is generally considered the opposite of "good," and since the New Testament redefines "good" in relationship to God, some virtual redefinition also takes place. In the Second Temple period, however, humans and gods share a common perspective, and evil is defined according to this joint perspective. The New Testament therefore adds significant reformulation to the nature of evil.

Nonetheless, this reformulation does not invalidate what the Old Testament has to offer. Moreover, the Old Testament has perspectives that are not as clearly addressed in the New Testament. In the Old Testament we can understand some passages better, especially the ones that present God as doing "evil," by applying the Old Testament definition. We can also understand sin in relation to creation and God's purposes in the world. The New Testament offers more specificity theologically by factoring Christ into those purposes, but the Old Testament provides the basis on which this specificity is built.

Sin. Sin is commonly understood through the use of metaphors, and a variety of metaphors can be useful in trying to gain a fuller understanding. We have found that the Old Testament and New Testament use different metaphors. But each metaphor contributes to our understanding, and we would not want to eliminate either one. The Old Testament certainly saw life and death as hanging in the balance in connection to covenant order. In fact, the account of the fall in Genesis 3 would have been understood as an action against God's order. The Old Testament pays little attention to this universal perspective, however, since once the covenant is in place, covenant order is the only level that matters to the Israelites (see Deut 30:11-19). Therefore remedies for covenant disorder of various sorts are articulated in the Torah. Nevertheless, the Old Testament has no remedy for cosmic disorder, nor does it feature any anticipation or hope for one. That universal remedy is provided by Christ.

Fall. In this category the difference between the Old Testament and the New Testament is slight. The key theological developments come *after* the

New Testament. Nevertheless, when we pay attention to Old Testament theology, it can help us to get a biblical focus and to distinguish the perspectives
that are central in both Testaments. This is not intended to suggest that
postcanonical theological interpretations should therefore be discarded. It
may be important, however, to remind ourselves that we may find reason on
occasion to revisit those theological formulations and to evaluate whether
they still serve well.

Neither the Old Testament nor New Testament focuses on the moment
of the fall, though they both recognize it as a pivotal occasion. The Old
Testament is more interested in the discussion of the covenant as God's reestablishment of his presence, which had been lost at Eden. The focus, then,
is on God's plans and purposes to dwell among people rather than on the
desperate plight of humanity in light of the fall. The New Testament carries
this along in the sense that it presents God's solution to the establishment of
his presence in perpetuity (in Christ, the church as indwelt by the Holy
Spirit, and new creation), though it certainly does more than that. Our plight
needs to be addressed, and Christ addresses it. But this solution for sin is
about the remedy to our situation and pays little attention to the moment
when sin first entered creation.

Satan/demons/chaos creatures. We can understand this issue better if we
begin with an analogy to cosmic geography. When we consider what the
Bible (Old Testament and New Testament) has to say about cosmic geography, we recognize that the two Testaments are using descriptive terminology that is fully embedded in their respective cognitive environments.
We have long recognized that the Bible is not offering God's authoritative
perspective on cosmic geography. Instead, he is providing a larger theological understanding of his role and rule in the cosmos, even while the
descriptions of the cosmos are couched in the terminology and worldview
of the writers and audience. We have therefore made a necessary and proper
distinction between descriptions embedded in the cognitive environment
and the normative theological teaching of Scripture.

We have to bring that same hermeneutical nuancing to our understanding
of Satan and demons. Neither the Old Testament nor the New Testament
actually teaches anything about Satan or demons, yet the idea that spiritual
beings affect the human world is undeniable, even when varying explanations

could be given for the observed results. The passing references to these beings are descriptive and based on the contemporary thinking in the native culture. In this regard, then, we should approach the metaphysics of these elements in much the same way that we approach the scattered comments about cosmic geography referred to above. We cannot derive specific metaphysical knowledge about Satan and demons from the Bible—but we can discover something about how the antagonistic elements that we fear and that can hurt us relate to the workings of God's kingdom. This is therefore not what we thought and leaves much of our curiosity unfulfilled. Yet, it is not without significance.

Whatever reasons we may or may not have for believing that there are created beings that bring disruption to our human attempts to participate in God's plan and purposes, the Bible does not step far enough away from its cognitive environment to give us any insight into the metaphysical reality. Nevertheless, we do know that God can use elements that we perceive as hostile and that these elements cannot do anything they are not permitted to do. Both the Old Testament and New Testament agree that God is above all principalities and powers, "spiritual" or otherwise. This is the enduring theology. We cannot use the descriptive information in either the Old Testament or New Testament to arrive at metaphysical specifics. Nevertheless, we would be remiss to classify them as enemies of God, because God is not threatened by anything and does not have to struggle against enemy forces. Various things may threaten God's people, but God is above the fray and strengthens his people to stand firm. The point is that these forces have no power against God and no power beyond what God allows to them to wield.

EXCURSUS: RETRIBUTION PRINCIPLE

Given (1) that the world is characterized by continuing nonorder and disorder, both of which are capable of bringing *rāʾâ*, and (2) that people believe that the gods/God are active among humans to bring benefits or punishment, people inevitably try to figure out how the system works.[103] The system derived by people in the ancient world can be called the retribution principle.

---

[103]This section adapted from Walton and Longman, *How to Read Job*.

The retribution principle articulates one of the basic beliefs of human beings from most cultures in most periods of time—at least those who believe in gods of some sort. Simply stated, the retribution principle (RP) is: *the righteous will prosper, and the wicked will suffer.* The oft-appended corollary is that if someone suffers, they are wicked, and if someone prospers, they are righteous. In this formulation all the major words are being used to point to larger categories:

✦ *Righteous* refers to behavior that pleases God and brings his favor. In some cultures, righteousness is found in moral behavior; in others, it is found in ritually meticulous performance. In some cultures (such as ancient Israel), it is found in both. However, it is not an absolute quality (comparable to the righteousness of God); it is a relative standard.

✦ *Prosper* refers to anything perceived as a blessing or benefit in one's experiences. It includes material prosperity, many children and grandchildren, good health, and success in one's endeavors (for Israel, think of humanity's state in the Garden of Eden, or in a postfall situation, think the blessings of the covenant [see, for instance, Deut 27–28]). The presence of prosperity often also results in high social standing and respect from others.

✦ *Wicked* is used in this formula to identify behavior that is displeasing to God and/or unacceptable in society. It can describe failure to behave in certain ways or failure to participate in necessary rituals.

✦ *Suffer* covers the general category of negative experiences, from crop failure and ill health (oneself or one's family) to any negative set of circumstances (bad luck, nothing working out right, people taking advantage, or threats). Many of the laments in Psalms identify these sorts of situations, as do the curses of the covenant as enumerated in Deuteronomy 27–28.

It is common for people to believe that their circumstances somehow reflect that they are in or out of favor with God/the gods, or that they have done something to bring certain circumstances on themselves. The Israelites in the Old Testament were no different, and we find similar expectations among the people of the ancient Near East. This belief is at the core of the wisdom literature from the ancient Near East, a corpus that explores cases of ostensibly righteous, innocent, or upright people who experience difficulties. It is also at the core of the book of Job: it represents the basic belief of both Job and his friends. This worldview frames their expectations and stands, from their perspectives, as the foundation of how the world operates.

The RP, in other words, was an attempt to understand, articulate, justify, and systematize the logic of God's interaction in the world. That human experience often seemed to deny the tenets of the RP required that the RP be qualified or nuanced in order to be employed realistically in philosophical/theological discussion. For example, how can God be just if he does not punish the wicked? In order to answer this question, the RP was frequently under discussion in Israelite theodicy, driven particularly by the context of ethical monotheism.[104] The RP does not, of necessity, operate in the context of theodicy, but because of Israel's theological commitments, this tendency can be observed in the Old Testament. We will return to the consideration of the relationship between the RP and theodicy after examining the status of the RP in the ancient Near East.

The retribution principle in the ancient Near East. The literature of the ancient Near East consistently attests to the belief that the administration of justice in the human world was a concern and responsibility of the gods. It was, for example, considered the duty of the Babylonian god Shamash to administer justice (thus he is the god to whom Hammurabi reports in his legal collection). Nevertheless, the questions that swirl around the RP lose their philosophical urgency in the ancient world due to the fact that injustice in the world is often blamed not on the gods, but on demons and humans. In Mesopotamian thinking, evil is built into the cosmos by means of the "control attributes" (Sumerian ME) that are woven into the fabric of the cosmos. But even the control attributes were not established by the gods, and since evil therefore existed outside the jurisdiction of the gods, the divine administration of justice did not necessarily eliminate suffering.

To the ancient Near Eastern mind, some misfortune came about simply because of the nature of the world. In both Egyptian and Mesopotamian thinking, the gods were not considered responsible for evil in the world, and the presence or experience of evil did not have to be reconciled with the justice of the gods (this is in contrast to Israel, where nothing existed outside

---

[104]Theodicy is defined as the defense of God's justice in a world where suffering exists (though the conversation has grown into a philosophical discussion of the origin of evil).

the jurisdiction of God's sovereignty). In the Sumerian Lament over the Destruction of Ur, the city is destroyed not as an act of justice or injustice, but because it is time for kingship to be transferred. Likewise, with regard to individuals, suffering can sometimes be one's lot in life for the present. It is also clear that personal misfortune can be considered to be the result of offending the gods, even if the offense is committed innocently. In such cases, it is not that the gods are unjust, but that they simply are not very forthcoming with their expectations.

Though Mesopotamians did not seek to defend the justice of the gods, they still believed in the RP.[105] Since they lacked revelation of what the deities required, the people believed offense against the gods was unavoidable, and thus "sin" (as they defined it in reference to the Great Symbiosis) was pervasive. Consequently, no one could claim to be innocent.[106] But if worshipers had been ritually conscientious, the expectation was that the god they worshiped would protect them. This expectation was not based on the belief that the god was just, only on the idea that he or she was sensible. The gods needed what humans provided, and they in return were capable, in most circumstances, of providing protection. The system did not work in this manner because the gods were just but because they were needy. Thus the RP remained intact.

In this sense, though the people of Mesopotamia might have believed that the gods punished those who earned their wrath, that belief could not explain all suffering. The explanation "those who suffer must be wicked" could not work; in the ancient Near Eastern worldview, much of the suffering that people experienced was not orchestrated by the gods but was due to their inattention, a course of circumstances, or the nature of the world. Even if the gods abandoned a person because of some offense, they were not responsible for the ensuing evil—they merely did nothing to prevent it. They withdrew their favor and protection.

In Egyptian thinking, the RP represents one aspect involved in the establishment of *ma'at*, which is the ultimate goal of the gods and therefore of those who exercise authority on behalf of the gods in the human realm. This

---

[105]D. Bodi, "The Retribution Principle in the Amorite View of History: Yasmaḫ-Addu's Letter to Nergal (ARM I 3) and Adad's Message to Zimrī-Līm (A. 1968)," *ARAM* 26, nos. 1-2 (2014): 285-300.

[106]K. van der Toorn, "Theodicy in Akkadian Literature," in *Theodicy in the World of the Bible*, ed. A. Laato and J. C. de Moor (Leiden: Brill, 2003), 62.

connection between the RP and *maʿat* is inherent in J. Assmann's definition of *maʿat*: "the principle that forms individuals into communities and that gives their actions meaning and direction by ensuring that good is rewarded and evil punished."[107] So defined, Assmann considers *maʿat* to represent the totality of all social norms. If *maʿat* is to be preserved and attained, positive behavior should be recognized and recompensed, while negative behavior should be punished. This is not rooted in divine attributes (e.g., justice) but in divine goals (the pursuit of *maʿat*). Nevertheless, as Assmann also indicates, the Egyptians did not believe that it was the gods who brought misfortune for offenses. "Misfortune was not the manifestation of an incensed deity but of the power of evil, of chaos, of non-being."[108] We have referred to these concepts as nonorder and disorder. For the Egyptians, these forces had to be met with magic if one hoped to fend them off.

The Egyptian way of thinking about this issue was closer to the Israelite way of thinking than that which we find in Mesopotamia. For the Israelites, order was not established by *maʿat* but by the covenant. This affirms in Israel what was stated about Egypt in the last paragraph: conformity was not rooted in divine attributes but in divine goals. Israel was to conform to the order represented in the covenant.

In conclusion, in the ancient Near East the gods had a level of responsibility to see that good and right prevailed, not because they were compelled by their character or attributes but because they had the power to exercise such influence. It also worked to their advantage to do so. The RP is understood as a logical syllogism in a context where gods expected their needs to be met and had the power to punish or recompense accordingly. In Mesopotamia, the most natural matrix for RP thinking was in the realm of ritual, whereas in Egypt, it was one of the primary mechanisms in the establishment of *maʿat* and the employment of magic. Orienting the comparison to the realm of order, we can differentiate the three cultures by observing that in Mesopotamia the basis of order was the Great Symbiosis associated with the mechanism of ritual. In Egypt, the basis of order was *maʿat* associated with the mechanism of magic. In Israel, the basis of order was covenant associated with the mechanism of Torah.

---

[107]J. Assmann, *The Mind of Egypt* (New York: Metropolitan Books, 2002), 128.
[108]Ibid., 239.

7

SALVATION
and
AFTERLIFE

SALVATION

Death reigns as the great inevitability. In previous chapters we discussed theological anthropology and which aspects of a person survive death. In this chapter we will address more specifically the question of salvation: how one achieves a felicitous afterlife experience, as well as various perspectives on the afterlife and resurrection.

Salvation, the exodus, and the exile. The first clarification that must be made concerns what we mean when we talk about salvation. Use of the term *salvation* presumes that there is a transition. Someone is being saved from situation (A) by means of some mechanism or intervention (B) and thereby transitions into a very different situation (C). Furthermore, to engage in a meaningful comparison between scenarios, there must be some equivalency in the identification of situations A and C and the mechanism, B, from each scenario.

In the Old Testament theology scenario, the nation of Israel experiences God's salvation on two major occasions. First, it is delivered from slavery in Egypt (A) to the Promised Land (C) by the mechanism of God's signs and wonders, his gracious provision for the people in the wilderness, and his acts as divine warrior in the conquest (B). Second, it is delivered from exile in

Babylon (A) to restoration in the land (C) by means of God's providence through the decree of Cyrus (B). These both refer to specific circumstances at a particular time in history.

These salvific experiences are not really in the same category as the scenario of the Christian theological idea that refers to salvation from sins (A) to a relationship with God that will stretch through eternity (C) by means of the work of Christ on our behalf (atonement, justification, forgiveness, reconciliation, (B). Logic could support a typological association of what Christians experience with what the Israelites experienced, but we would do justice to neither by drawing them too closely together. To identify the entire Bible as the "history of salvation" suggests that somehow what the Israelites experienced was a foreshadowing of what we as Christians experience. Without denying the relevance of the most basic of comparisons, they are very different experiences in the end, and we ought to exercise some care lest we overstretch the association to the detriment of one or the other. They are analogous phenomena, but the analogy breaks down quickly and can only accomplish so much. As stunning as the deliverances of Israel are, they are of an entirely different nature from what Christ provides. We will therefore set these great deliverances from the history of Israel aside, significant as they are in their own right, to discuss more particularly the issue of salvation as it pertains to soteriological and eschatological ideas. In the remainder of the chapter, *salvation* should be understood to refer to this technical theological sense.

Salvation in the ancient Near East. The Mesopotamian concept of "sin" was defined primarily in cultic terms and pertained to what was contrary to the order established in the Great Symbiosis (see chapter two). Situation A for Mesopotamian people consisted of the disorder that they were experiencing in their life or community. They desired transition to situation C, which included stability and equilibrium, and the way this transition was accomplished was through ritual performance. However, this system could only be considered soteriological in the broadest terms, and it was temporal, not eschatological.

Egyptians, on the other hand, recognized a continuum between *ma'at* in the world of the living (temporal) and *ma'at* in the world beyond (eschatological). The accumulation of offenses, as is evident in the Book of the Dead judgment scene, could hardly be identified as a soteriology. But in either

Table 7.1. Salvation in the Old and New Testaments

	Ancient Near East	Israelites: Historical	Old Testament: Covenantal	New Testament: Theological
A Initial condition needing resolution (disorder)	*Mesopotamia:* disorder experienced in life or community	slavery in Egypt (community disorder)	disorder in covenant relationship	sinful condition (disorder in relationship with God)
	Egypt: absence of ma'at	exile in Babylon (community disorder)		
B Mechanism for transition	*Mesopotamia:* ritual performance	God's signs and wonders, his gracious provision for them in the wilderness, and his acts as divine warrior in the conquest	Torah and its rituals	work of Christ on our behalf (atonement, justification, forgiveness, reconciliation)
	Egypt: magic (amulets and spells)	decree of Cyrus and leadership of the returning remnant		
C New situation (order)	*Mesopotamia:* stability and equilibrium	land promised to Abraham in the covenant	reestablishment of covenant order	relationship with God that will stretch through eternity
	Egypt: restored ma'at	restoration to the land		
Focus	*Mesopotamia:* temporal	temporal	temporal	eschatological
	Egypt: temporal and eschatological			

Salvation is defined broadly for comparison as a transition from an undesirable situation of disrupted order (A) to a desirable new situation of order (C) by means of a particular mechanism (B).

temporal or eschatological thinking, there was a situation A to be saved from, which was the absence of *ma'at*. They also recognized a state of *ma'at* that they desired to achieve, so there was a contrasting situation C. Their mechanism (B), in both the temporal and eschatological contexts, was magic, and only through the proper use of amulets and spells could they hope to transition from A to C.

Salvation in Israel. When we turn our attention to Israel, we find points of both continuity and discontinuity. As was the case in Egyptian and Mesopotamian thinking, situation A pertains to a lack of order, but in Mesopotamia order was defined through the Great Symbiosis, in Egypt by *maʾat*, and in Israel by the covenant. When we consider the mechanism (B), Mesopotamia used ritual, and Egypt used magic. Israel, on the other hand, was prohibited from using magic, and its rituals functioned very differently from those in Mesopotamia. But in all three cases the revised situation C was seen as a reestablishment of order. We can see, therefore, that Israel compared only generally to the equations in the ancient world. However, this general comparison should not lead us to conclude that what we find in Israel has continuity with the New Testament or Christian ways of thinking.

We can thus proceed best by examining each part of the equation in turn. Situation A has already been examined at length in the previous chapter. There we identified the major strands as alienation, disequilibrium, and anything contrary to order, particularly covenant order. The concept of a situation "contrary to order" was conceptually similar to what was found in Mesopotamia and Egypt, with the proviso that order was perceived differently in each culture. Furthermore, in distinction from the Christian equation, Israelites did not think about fixing the disorder that existed in the world at large. Old Testament theology instead provided a way to redress covenant disorder.

Mechanism B in Old Testament theology is well known—it consisted of the complex of rituals that made up the sacrificial system (discussed in chapter five). However, this mechanism only restored equilibrium to the covenant relationship. In this instance we find easy agreement with Hebrews 10:4: that the blood of bulls and goats could never take away sins. Israel's mechanism, therefore, was not designed to resolve the same situation A that Christianity is most interested in (human sin as a whole), and its mechanism B would not be able to do so. None of the operations provided by the death of Christ (atonement, justification, forgiveness, reconciliation) were provided by the sacrificial system.[1] Israelites were not looking for salvation from sins; they were expecting resolution of covenant disorder, and their mechanism B provided exactly that. God said it would, and it did.

Situation C in Israelite thinking, then, had none of the aspects that are characteristic of situation C in Christianity (a relationship with God that

---

[1] Even though not provided by the sacrificial system, some analogues exist: e.g., atonement, as it is, is provided by the death of the animal (penalty is thereby paid), and justification is approximated by the act of cleansing away all evidence of offense by the *kpr* of the blood rituals.

stretches through eternity). Their equation was only loosely soteriological and was not eschatological at all. As we will discuss in the next section, Israel had no mechanism to provide for the Christian situation C and therefore had no expectation or hope of such a situation. In this way their thinking was much more like their Mesopotamian counterparts; they looked for a restoration of order in their temporal circumstances.

If the Old Testament is dealing with a different situation A (disorder within the covenant community), a different mechanism B (rituals), and a different situation C (temporal, not eschatological), then it would be misguided to talk about salvation from sins in the Old Testament. This means that even as the people developed a messianic expectation, they were not thinking about the Messiah as providing mechanism B with relation to a Christian understanding of situations A and C. Without situations A and C, they would not imagine a role for the Messiah in a Christian understanding of mechanism B. The Messiah in the Old Testament is a king, not a savior. This ideal king is associated with a time of restoration and has a role to play in the regular Israelite situation C—the restoration of covenant order.

We can therefore understand that in Old Testament theology there are two variations for understanding the equation for salvation:

Equation 1, repeated circumstances:
  A: sin leading to covenant disorder resulting from impurity in sacred space
  B: sacrificial system
  C: equilibrium restored to sacred space

Equation 2, one-time circumstance:
  A: accumulation of offenses leading to covenant disorder and activating covenant curses, leading to exile
  B: historical circumstances leading to return
  C: equilibrium of covenant stability in restored covenant community with an ideal king

Here we can see that the Messiah is not the *mechanism* for the new situation but part of the *description* of the new situation C.[2] This observation leads to

---

[2]Granted that Cyrus, the anointed one in Isaiah, brings about deliverance. But his is a passing role, however significant. His actions resolve the Israelite displacement, and in doing so, he brings an end of sorts to the exile. But he does nothing to resolve the problems that led to the exile.

the need for a reanalysis of the Christian interpretation of a few significant Old Testament passages that traditionally posit the Messiah as mechanism B in the person of Christ who, in Christian interpretation, is indeed mechanism B.

For example, Genesis 3:15 is often labeled the "proto-evangelium"—the first proclamation of the gospel. Such an interpretation asserts that situation A has taken shape (the presence of sin) and that situation C (resolution of the sin problem) has thereby become a desideratum. The interpretation then suggests that the mechanism B is already in the works (the seed of woman who will bring victory over sin and death). As we have already discussed, no Old Testament evidence suggests that any connection was made between the serpent and Satan, thus mitigating any suggestion that Genesis 3:15 would have been understood as pertaining to a victory over sin in that context. The serpent is simply not that important of a figure in the Old Testament context.

More importantly, we should recognize that such an interpretation does not find support in the Hebrew text. The above interpretation is based on the idea that the verse focuses on one descendant, and that assumption is itself arguable. On the basis of grammatical fact, the Hebrew word for "seed" is collective, and as such, it will typically take singular grammatical associations (pronouns, verbal forms). That issue has been debated at length,[3] but it is not the most significant issue in the interpretation. Our focus instead should be on the verbs that describe the interaction of the two parties.

The verbs that the NIV translates "crush" and "strike" are now properly identified as belonging to the same root, šûp.[4] We must therefore conclude that the actions expressed by these verbs are comparable. Furthermore, if

---

[3]Jack Collins, "A Syntactical Note (Genesis 3:15): Is the Woman's Seed Singular or Plural?," *Tyndale Bulletin* 48 (1997): 139-48, collects a database to demonstrate that when *zeraʾ* ("seed") refers to posterity, it invariably takes plural pronouns. Unfortunately, (1) most of his examples are in situations where the text is speaking of several people's posterities, thus demanding a plural (cf. Gen 9:9; this is similar to English where the collective "people" can be pluralized when referring to several people groups), and (2) there are examples in which singular pronouns are used even though "seed" = posterity (Gen 22:17; 24:60, discounting as special pleading T. D. Alexander's attempt to argue that they do not refer to posterity, "Further Observations on the Term 'Seed' in Genesis," *TB* 48 [1997]: 363-67).

[4]This has not always been the case. Even the venerable lexicon by Brown, Driver, and Briggs attempted to draw the second one from the root *šʾp*. Claus Westermann, *Genesis 1-11* (Minneapolis: Fortress, 1984), 259-60, attempts to hold on to both. V. P. Hamilton, *Genesis 1-17* (Grand Rapids: Eerdmans, 1990), 197-98 has the best discussion. The LXX translates them as the same, while the Vulgate differentiates them.

the verbs are the same, we must next ask whether the potential damage is the same. While it is true that a strike to the head appears more devastating than a strike to the heel, a *serpent's* strike to the heel is another matter altogether. It would have been observable that not all snakes are poisonous, but the threat provided by some snakes would, in the haste to protect oneself, lead a person to consider any attacking snake potentially poisonous. Of the thirty-six species of snake known to the area, the viper (*vipera palaestinae*) is the only poisonous snake in northern and central Israel. However, poisonous snakes are the most aggressive, so an attack by a snake could always result in a potentially mortal blow.[5] Given the repetition of the verb, and the potentially mortal nature of both attacks, it becomes difficult to understand the verse as suggesting an eventual outcome to the struggle. Instead, both sides may exchange potentially mortal blows of equal threat to the part of the body most vulnerable to attack.[6] Consequently, in the context of the Old Testament, no victory is forecast here, and by extension, no mechanism B is indicated for the resolution of situation A. Likewise, then, there is no identification of a desired situation C.

Of final significance for the interpretation of this verse, we should recognize that the New Testament never indicates that Genesis 3:15 has the special status given to it in later Christian interpretation, or that it should be understood as projecting a mechanism for dealing with sin. In fact, the only reference to Genesis 3:15 in the New Testament is in Romans 16:20, where Paul identifies the church as the one whose heel is doing the damage to the serpent's head, in which case we must totally revise our view of the situations and mechanisms involved.

The second example is the Servant Song in Isaiah 52:13–53:12. However, our treatment here must be distinguished from what was said about Genesis 3:15, because in this case, the New Testament clearly identifies Christ as the fulfillment of various aspects of this passage (Mt 8:17; Lk 22:37; Jn 12:38; Acts 8:32-33; 1 Pet 2:22). The New Testament authors demonstrably viewed the passage as fulfilled in Christ in his role as mechanism B in the equation.

---

[5]Part of this paragraph is adapted from John H. Walton, Victor H. Matthews, and Mark W. Chavalas, *The IVP Bible Background Commentary: Old Testament* (Downers Grove, IL: InterVarsity Press, 2012), 21.

[6]This paragraph has been adapted from J. Walton, *Genesis*, NIVAC (Grand Rapids: Zondervan, 2001), 226.

Divine Sonship

In the rhetoric of the ancient Near East, kings regularly identified themselves as the sons of one god or another. Various elaborations allude to being conceived by a god, birthed by a god, nurtured at the breast of a god, sponsored by a father god, and protected by a mother god. Consequently, the divine sonship of the king was a staple of royal ideology. The Old Testament likewise reflects this sort of thinking, though it is not elaborated in the same ways. In the Davidic covenant, Yahweh indicates that he will be a father to David's successor, who in turn will be like a son to him. The Psalms also feature this sort of relationship between God and king. When Jesus begins to be identified as the Son of God, then, the audience would have likely understood the reference as a royal motif that correlated with the other royal title, Messiah. This title, then, remains far removed from the idea of God incarnate. An identity as God's son is not the equivalent of a claim to full deity—there are other ways that Jesus makes his claim to deity (e.g., "before Abraham was, I AM").[a] Consequently, the use of the divine sonship rhetoric in the Old Testament should not be interpreted as prophetic allusion to the deity of the anointed one of God. No one in the Old Testament would have thought of those references in those terms.[b]

---

[a] Jn 1 also presses this case.

[b] Ps 2:7; see the discussion by J. Hilber, *Cultic Prophecy in the Psalms* (Berlin: de Gruyter, 2005).

That being said, however, we recognize that in many cases, New Testament identification of fulfillment represents an extension of meaning beyond that which would have been understood by the author and audience of the Old Testament. In such cases, the Old Testament and New Testament need not be thrown into contention over the truth, nor does either one need to correlate to the other. The model that I propose recognizes that the New Testament authors are offering a second illocution (illocution being that which the communicator is intending to accomplish with the words being used; here the illocution is identifying fulfillment) that can come and stand alongside the Old Testament prophet's illocution (proclaiming restoration, see below) as a full partner in the production of a canonical interpretation. Neither one has to be subordinate to the other.[7] We can therefore come to the Old Testament passage independent of how it is treated in the New Testament to ask what sort of equation this Servant Song would have projected into the minds of Isaiah and his audience. Whatever it is, it would carry the authority that is accorded to all of Scripture.

The most striking aspects of Isaiah 53 that are considered suggestive of the New Testament equation are in Isaiah 53:4-6, 12. These verses describe the Servant as the one who bears the punishment for the sins of the people, which results in their healing. These elements identify an initial situation A—transgressions; a mechanism B—crushed, punishment, wounds, death; and situation C—peace, healing, intercession. The Servant, then, bore the transgressions and served as a sin offering. It is quite easy to see the similarities between this equation and that of the New Testament.

But would this New Testament equation be understood by the prophet and original audience of Isaiah 53, or would it be read in alignment with one of the standard Old Testament equations? When it is read as a text in the context of the Old Testament, I propose that the situation A that it envisions is, as it regularly is in the Prophets, the corporate sin of the Israelite community, which has, by extension, brought disorder to the covenant (note: not addressing individual sins). It is also evident that situation C entails the restoration of the community from that disordered state. The unusual feature, then, is mechanism B. In Isaiah 53 that mechanism is the death of the Servant on behalf of the sins of the people (rather than the familiar rituals of the sacrificial system). Even given this radical departure from the mechanisms previously encountered, we should recognize that the mechanism is still operating within the covenant community (i.e., not directed toward the individual's sins), and the anticipated situation C is not equivalent to the Christian situation C (thus explaining why no one at the time of Jesus was prepared for or understood Christ's actions).

---

[7]For fuller discussion, see J. Walton and D. Brent Sandy, *The Lost World of Scripture* (Downers Grove, IL: InterVarsity Press, 2013), 224-32. This way of thinking is also in line with the "figural" interpretation of the Old Testament by the New Testament authors worked out by Richard B. Hays, *Echoes of Scripture in the Gospels* (Waco, TX: Baylor University Press, 2016).

We can identify a similar mechanism from the Assyrian background of the Iron Age in the well-documented substitute king ritual.[8] In this scenario, situation A is that the king is under threat from the gods (determined from celestial oracles, usually an eclipse). Since the king is the embodiment of order in Mesopotamia, his possible annihilation threatens order in the community. All the people stand under this threat, and the community, embodied by the king, stands guilty of some unknown offense. The situation (C) that they desire is that the threat be withdrawn and stability restored. It is interesting that in this case the disorder has come about not by something that has already happened but by something that could potentially happen. Nonetheless, destabilization can take place just as easily by fear of what might happen as by an actual occurrence. The mechanism (B) in this case is that the king steps down from his throne, divests himself of his regalia and symbols of authority, and relocates to the countryside. In his place a lackey is set on the throne to be the foil who experiences the anger of the gods. He is given a consort, and he performs all the rituals that the king regularly conducts. He does not actually rule (that is still being done by the court and by the king in absentia), but he becomes the representative of the community identity. In reality, of course, this action has mitigated the threat to the community because this substitute king does not actually embody the community identity. Order in society does not depend on him. After one hundred days, if the gods have not struck the substitute down, he is put to death, along with his consort, and buried in a royal tomb. He dies for the offenses of the community in order to restore order, stability, and equilibrium. In other words, a substitute is the mechanism.

Now we return to Isaiah 53, armed with information about how the Servant is presented as a mechanism from an Old Testament perspective. Once we take account of the differences in how Israelites and Assyrians perceived the nature of order, we see that situations A and C are comparable between the Israelite and Assyrian scenarios. However, differences ought to be noted: the prophet identifies the offense, as opposed to a diviner's identification of an offense, and the offense is specified in Isaiah, rather than

---

[8]J. Walton, "The Imagery of the Substitute King Ritual in Isaiah's Fourth Servant Song," *Journal of Biblical Literature* 122 (2003): 734-43.

unknown, as in Assyria. Nonetheless, in the light of the similarities, we can now understand that the mechanism B in Isaiah, as in the substitute king ritual in Assyria, alleviates the disorder threatening the community by channeling the punishment through an individual (the Servant in Isaiah, the substitute in Assyria). In the Assyrian context, the substitute is one who is not identified with the community, an outcast or an outlaw, and the same is observable in the description of the Servant. As such, just as the substitute in Assyria is the flip side of a king (the king is embodiment of the community identity and personifies order—the ultimate insider; the substitute is outside of the community identity—the ultimate outsider), the Servant in Isaiah is the flip side of Messiah (instead of the one who represents order in the restored community, he is an outsider who has been rejected by the community).

Nevertheless, I would suggest that Isaiah is already implying that the messianic ideal entails both, and that is exactly what Jesus and the New Testament authors noticed. Importantly, however, although this innovation by Isaiah entails the double identity of the Messiah (ultimate insider/ultimate outsider), it is left to the New Testament to develop a revised eschatological situation A and C for which the Messiah eventually serves as mechanism B. The main evidence of this is that situation C in Isaiah is a temporal restoration, not a transformed eschatological hope.

Based on the analysis of these two passages (Gen 3:15; Is 53) in their Old Testament context, we can see that they do not anticipate the role of Christ as a mechanism who dies for the individual's sins to provide reconciliation, atonement, justification, forgiveness, and eternal life. Jesus does all of that, but his actions represent a new development that was not anticipated or addressed in the Old Testament. The only salvation in Old Testament theology was temporal, communal, and related to covenant order. The Israelites experienced this throughout their history as their community identity and stability were maintained through the sacrificial system. The remnant also experienced this in the exile and restoration, as the equation expresses.

In conclusion, then, lack of evidence to the contrary should persuade us that salvation in the soteriological, eschatological sense was not part of the Old Testament equation. The Israelites' theology did not even consider that level of salvation. They did not know that it was possible, and in their minds no means was available to provide for it. After all, if Jesus is the only means of salvation, and he had not yet come and died, then they could not be saved in the Christian sense. Even so, however, our recognition of this fact may allow us to see everything more clearly because salvation operates on a larger scale than we imagined. We will address this further below, after a discussion on the afterlife.

The Exile and the Remnant

The exile can be equated with death, since it brought disruption to Israel's community identity with Yahweh. Their status as covenant people was not lost, but they were no longer living in proximity to sacred space and could not observe the Torah that was designed for that context. However, the returning remnant began to experience the restoration, and the full scope of their community identity was reestablished as a result. In this they were delivered from their exile and experienced a temporal salvation, but this deliverance can in no way be considered "salvation from sins." Paul identifies a remnant by analogy (Rom 11:5), but even this reference says nothing about salvation in the Old Testament. The remnant that returned from exile should not be understood in soteriological or eschatological terms.

As a final note, we should recognize that the ancient Israelites in the Old Testament did not think that they were saved from their sins through the works of the law. They did not even think in terms of personal salvation from sins. The New Testament conversation pertained to the issues as they had taken shape during the Second Temple period. Therefore, we should not project whatever misconceptions the Pharisees might have had back onto the Old Testament or judge the Old Testament on that basis.

We should also recognize that research over the last several decades has provided some important nuancing about Judaism in the first century. Rather than imagining that Jews believed they could work their way to heaven, Jews in the late Second Temple period thought of salvation in light of their identity in the covenant community. Those in good standing in the covenant would be saved, and good standing was achieved through good deeds and obedience to the Torah. It is easy, then, to see how it could be said that they were depending on works for their salvation.

AFTERLIFE AND RESURRECTION

Afterlife.[9] In the ancient world, as famously attested in the Gilgamesh Epic, everyone desired immortality—in that, they were little different from people today. Our main question here, however, concerns whether Israelites in the Old Testament had a hope of heaven and a means to have that hope fulfilled. Related to this we will discuss heaven and hell (reward and punishment) as well as the concept of resurrection. As usual, to address these issues in the Old Testament, we should first take a look around the ancient Near East to see what was in the cultural river.

In Christian theology we tend to think of the afterlife in theological terms. This emphasis is traditionally expressed in terms of reward and punishment; we are either going to be with God (heaven) or separated from God (hell). Furthermore, the criteria that distinguish what sort of afterlife one might experience are based on theological elements. In Christian thinking, our belief about the afterlife is that those in Christ will experience the apotheosis of relationship with God. It is deeply theological, as it is viewed as the culmination of our Christian experience. We do not therefore expect, and often don't see, that in Mesopotamia it is exactly the opposite, where nothing is less theological than

---

[9]The most important sources for this study are T. Abusch, "Ghost and God: Some Observations on a Babylonian Understanding of Human Nature," in *Self, Soul and Body in Religious Experience*, ed. A. I. Baumgarten, J. Assmann, and G. G. Stroumsa (Leiden: Brill, 1998), 363-83; J. Assmann, "A Dialogue Between Self and Soul: Papyrus Berlin 3024," in *Self, Soul and Body*, 384-403; J. Bottéro, *Religion in Ancient Mesopotamia* (Chicago: University of Chicago Press, 2001); H. C. Brichto, "Kin, Cult, Land and Afterlife—A Biblical Complex," *Hebrew Union College Annual* 44 (1973): 1-54; E. Hornung, *The Ancient Egyptian Books of the Afterlife* (Ithaca, NY: Cornell University Press, 1999); P. Johnston, *Shades of Sheol* (Downers Grove, IL: InterVarsity Press, 2002); D. Katz, *The Image of the Netherworld in Sumerian Sources* (Bethesda, MD: CDL, 2003); K. Spronk, *Beatific Afterlife in Ancient Israel*, Alter Orient und Altes Testament 219 (Kevelaer: Neukirchener Verlag, 1986); N. Tromp, *Primitive Conceptions of Death and the Nether World in the Old Testament*, Biblica et Orientalia 21 (Rome: Pontifical Biblical Institute, 1969). See also the helpful summaries on death and afterlife in *CANE* 3: in Egypt (L. Lesko, "Death and Afterlife in Ancient Egyptian Thought," 1763-74), in Mesopotamia (J. Scurlock, "Death and Afterlife in Ancient Mesopotamian Thought," 1883-93), in Hittite thought (V. Haas, "Death and Afterlife in Hittite Thought," 2021-30), and in Canaanite and Hebrew thought (P. Xella, "Death and Afterlife in Canaanite and Hebrew Thought," 2059-70), and numerous articles in *Death in Mesopotamia*, ed. B. Alster, Mesopotamia 8, Rencontre assyriologique internationale 26 (Copenhagen: Akademisk Forlag, 1980). An accessible, wide-ranging comparative study can be found in the unit "Death, the Afterlife, and Other Last Things," in *Religions of the Ancient World* (Cambridge, MA: Belknap, 2004), 470-95.

the afterlife experience. In Christian thinking, the anticipated new creation is the height of order—indeed, it is absolute order (Rev 21). In Mesopotamia the netherworld is a place outside the ordered cosmos—it is ultimate disorder.[10]

This perception of the netherworld makes good sense when we remember that the theological thinking in Mesopotamia revolved around the Great Symbiosis. If humans existed to care for the gods, the gods would have no interest in the dead, because the dead could not care for them (no rituals). It is interesting that priests are mentioned by status in the netherworld,[11] but there is no discussion of what they do, only passing references to rituals.[12] Overbalancing those passing references are the many passages that indicate that food is not produced in the netherworld. For example, note Ningish-zida's Journey to the Netherworld:

> The field of the netherworld grows no grain, flour is not milled from it, would you sail then?

> The sheep of the netherworld carries no wool, cloth is not woven from him, would you sail then?[13]

Indeed, the offerings listed in the Death of Urnammu are funerary offerings provided to the gods of the netherworld by the living on behalf of the dead. If there is no food to offer the gods and no cult or temple in operation, there are no rites being performed.

Furthermore, the dead did not care about the presence of deity (living eternally in God's presence), because they were no longer dependent on the gods for care. The dead also had no means of caring for the gods. No temples or images were present in the netherworld, and they could not grow food to feed the gods, sew garments, or build glorious temples to meet their needs. The dead were "off the grid."

---

[10]It is likely that this idea is behind Job 10:22, though *lōʾ ṣədārîm* (NIV "disorder") is difficult, because it occurs only there in the Old Testament. The word occurs most commonly in the Dead Sea Scrolls in the War Scroll (1QM) in reference to battle formations or battle array. See listing in *Dictionary of Classical Hebrew*, ed. David J. A. Clines (Sheffield, UK: Sheffield Phoenix, 1993–2014), 6:122. A similar semantic range for this root is also attested in Aramaic, Syriac, and Akkadian. In the latter, the verb *sadaru* also refers to lining up in battle formation as well as to doing anything with regularity or consistency (*CAD* S:11-14).

[11]Katz, *Image of the Netherworld*, 195.

[12]For example, the Death of Urnammu mentions "sacrificing the offerings of the *kur* (= netherworld)" (lines 85-86). See Katz, *Image of the Netherworld*, 215, though Katz indicates that this probably refers to the rituals performed at the funeral of the king on his behalf (216).

[13]Ibid., 219.

Likewise, the motivation to care for the gods while people lived was to assure that the gods protected them. In the netherworld such a concern was no longer relevant. The people there were already dead. No invaders threatened, and death was not a fear but a reality. The denizens of the netherworld could not even meet their own needs, let alone try to take care of the gods, nor were the gods interested in taking care of them any longer. Consequently, the symbiosis that framed the land of the living was shattered in death. People were not going somewhere to be with the gods or to serve the gods; the dead were dependent on living descendants to care for them. Their sense of community identity remained, and so they existed in *sociological* continuum.[14] But their continuum was one without *theological* significance. Such was the situation among the Assyrians and Babylonians as well as in the Levant.

In other words, the prospects of the afterlife are glum. Enkidu's description of the netherworld to Gilgamesh related a dreary existence where the denizens ate dust or excrement. At the same time, it was not without structures: "The netherworld was visualized as being parallel to the world of the living and subject to the same principles of government and norms of behavior."[15] In these cultures we find veneration (and fear) of the ancestors and a system of caring for the dead that began with proper burial and generally included periodic rites to provide for the dead and to remember them. The ultimate death came when one was remembered no more (thus the importance of having descendants and "making a name" in other ways). There was neither reward nor punishment in the land of the dead, but everyone was assigned their appropriate social station.[16] There was no judgment of the dead to determine their station, and the gods who were the judges in the netherworld maintained social structures there. They did not decide whether a person entered one type of afterlife or another.[17] As early as the Ur III period, the understanding of the netherworld was

---

[14]See M. Malul, *Knowledge, Control and Sex* (Tel-Aviv: Archaeological Center, 2002), 438, 453.

[15]Katz, *Image of the Netherworld*, 190.

[16]Ibid., 191.

[17]Ibid., 190-91. Some elaboration can be found in the Sumerian Elegy on the Death of Nannaya, available through The ETCSL project, Faculty of Oriental Studies, University of Oxford, http://etcsl.orinst.ox.ac.uk/cgi-bin/etcsl.cgi?text=t.5.5.2# (accessed April 3, 2017), lines 99-103. "May your god say "Enough!," may he . . . . . . your fate. May the god of your city . . . . . . compassion on you. May he release you from wrath and sin. May he erase the reckoning of the guilt of your house. . . . . . . the evil planned against you."

based on the sociopolitical realities of the organized urban community that was the people's historical reality.[18]

Egypt, however, had quite a different way of thinking about the afterlife. In contrast to what was just described for Mesopotamia and the Levant, in Egyptian belief an extensive system was in operation, with the intention of ensuring that the afterlife would be pleasant. Even social status and lifestyle could be retained if all went well, and much more attention was given to the desired status than to the threat of punishment, though references to the latter occasionally appeared: "Amun-Re judges the earth with his finger, and his words shall rest in the heart; He judges the unjust and sends him on to the Place of Fire; the just man goes to the West."[19] The judgment of the dead was dominated by magic (e.g., the spells of the Book of the Dead) as one sought to procure a felicitous situation. One of the ways that this could be achieved was to be reintegrated into community. This reintegration first involved the body, the *ka*, and the *ba* coming back together—personal reintegration. Second, the reintegration involved the dead taking their "rightful place" (however that was defined) in the community of the netherworld. Survivors, as in Mesopotamia, continued to provide meals for the dead as attempt was made to retain the place of the dead in the community of the living. In letters to the dead from the First Intermediate Period, the living ask for the dead to intercede on their behalf in difficulties they are facing— punishing enemies, fighting on their behalf. In return the living provide "invocation offerings" or "deposit offerings" and "outfit the offering slab" for the dead.[20] In these and other ways, community relationships were preserved between the living and the dead.

In Egypt one might also easily find passages that suggest a more theological aspect to the afterlife when the continuing relationship to deities is considered. For example, one can find statements about being in a place with a god or joining the sun god on his cyclical journey.[21] Additionally, judgment

---

[18]Katz, *Image of the Netherworld*, 192. Note that kings receive control of armies (215).

[19]J. Foster, *Hymns, Prayers, and Songs: An Anthology of Ancient Egyptian Lyric Poetry*, SBLWAW (Atlanta: SBL Press, 1995), 150.

[20]*CANE* 3:1765. See full listings on 1773.

[21]Assmann states: "We must realize that 'to go forth' and 'to see the sun' is the very center of Egyptian hopes and ideas about life after death" ("Dialogue Between Self and Soul," 392). This is expressed as the main objective of kings in the pyramid age. Other options included becoming a star in the sky with the moon god or remaining in the fields of Osiris (*CANE*

after death is ostensibly based on a code of ethics (cf. the negative confession and the judgment scene in the Book of the Dead), but the code of ethics itself was sociological more than religious. Furthermore, one's circumstances in the afterlife were achieved through the knowledge of the spells. More importantly, the Egyptians did not anticipate any relationship with the god or a resumption of the earthly symbiosis.

The Egyptians evidently never experienced a longing for union with the deity. They kept their distance from the gods, whom no one could approach too closely without being punished; but their hopes for the next world were based on becoming "like a god," on assuming the role of one of the great gods, and thus themselves affecting the course of the world.[22]

The language of these texts often indicates that the king will *become* Re or Osiris, a far different thing from living in the presence of those deities. This is exaltation, not relationship. For nonroyals the unhappy prospect of compulsory labor (serving the god of the netherworld, Osiris) loomed, and attempts were made to avoid it through the burial of *ushabti* images in the tomb (to do labor on behalf of the dead). Those serving in the fields of Osiris were not providing the needs of Osiris; rather, their work was to provide for fertility in the land of the living.[23] But even the nonroyals eventually developed the hope that they too would become gods.

However, as different as the afterlife systems in Egypt and Mesopotamia were, we must notice some important similarities that distinguish all of these ancient views from the ways that we think today. As we consider the spectrum of ways to think about the afterlife, we can identify four prominent categories, with options in each.

1. Society: The afterlife may be described as a certain type of society, in which either the earthly status quo is retained or utopian features are expected.

3:1767): "Truly, he who is yonder will become a living god, punishing the evildoer's crime. Truly, he who is yonder will stand in the sun-barque, making its bounty flow to the temples. Truly, he who is yonder will be a wise man, not barred from appealing to Re when he speaks" (399).

[22]E. Hornung, *Conceptions of God in Ancient Egypt* (Ithaca, NY: Cornell University Press, 1982), 207.

[23]The deceased official is not a god but rather an *akh*-spirit who has generative powers: he causes the work in fields and workshops to bring blessed prosperity. He keeps in motion the same segment of the world that was assigned to him in life. Donald B. Redford, ed., *Oxford Encyclopedia of Ancient Egypt* (Oxford: Oxford University Press, 2001), 1:34.

2. Judicial: One's situation in the afterlife may or may not be determined by judgment. If there is judgment, it could be on the basis of human action (deeds, spells) or on the basis of divine action (Christian grace).

3. Communal: Expectations are often formulated in terms of a continuing sense of belonging in a community, whether with those who yet live or with those ancestors who have already died.

4. Deity: Afterlife that was focused on deity could involve a continued or strengthened relationship with deity or an exaltation of the deceased, either to become one with deity or to become deity. In contrast, it could be an existence absent of deity.

The Cult of the Dead

Death in the ancient world can be said to refer to a state of nonbeing (out of the ordered world) that usually (but not necessarily) corresponded to the absence of biological life.[a] Some describe it as anything that puts one out of Yahweh's sphere of influence.[b] Malul suggests that many who are in the category of the living (e.g., lepers) would nonetheless be classified in this general category along with the dead.[c] This same sort of classification system can be seen in comparing the "living God" (not a biological classification) to the idols (who are ineffectual—deaf, mute, or impotent in other ways).

Lacking the modern instruments and precision for distinguishing between life and death, death in in the ancient world was more like a liminal frontier than a solid barrier. People could be considered part of the world of the dead when modern medicine might judge them still living or be able to revive them. In other words, the criteria that determined death were not clear cut and not necessarily medical in nature. This has ramifications not only for our understanding of the physical aspects of death but also for the communal relationships between the dead and the living. As in the physical sense, the community preserved a graduated continuity between the living and the dead. This was probably represented in their understanding of the flesh and bones in the tomb as related to the person's journey to the netherworld.[d]

But while the funerary rituals of ancient Egypt are well known, the cult of the dead in the Levant is less so. In recent decades this cult has been the subject of intense study, specifically the identity of the Rephaim (a class of shades), the celebration of the *marzēaḥ* (a communal banquet that sometimes took place in funerary contexts with the ancestors who had already died),[e] and the role of the *kispu* (a ritual that provided offerings for the dead).[f] The spirits of the dead could be benevolent and invoked for the help they could provide to the living, or they could be malevolent. In the latter case, interaction with these spirits would be of a preventative nature, attempting to avoid the damage the spirits might wield for one reason or another. In either case, experts in necromancy facilitated communication between the living and the dead. If the dead had not been buried, their spirits continued to roam the earth and trouble the living. But when they were buried, they were often buried with grave goods that were intended to be useful to them. In the netherworld, the spirits needed provisions, and the key to their contentment there was in being remembered.

Regardless, the cult of the dead, to whatever extent it was practiced, took place within the realm of the family rather than in a temple venue. In other words, all of this shows the persistent belief across the ancient world that the dead continued to exist beyond the grave.

---

[a]Notice, for example, that in Ludlul bel Nemeqi the sufferer is being treated as dead, including by the mourners who are already chanting their lamentations, even while he is still alive (1:100-108). This may well be similar to the situation in which Job considers himself (Job 19).

[b]H. W. Wolff speaks of the stages of dying in *Anthropology of the Old Testament* (Philadelphia: Fortress, 1974), 106-13.

[c]See the nuanced discussion in Malul, *Knowledge, Control, and Sex*, 274-78.

[d]R. Steiner, *Disembodied Souls* (Atlanta: SBL Press, 2015). For other discussions about death see E. Bloch-Smith, *Judahite Burial Practices and Beliefs About the Dead* (Sheffield, UK: JSOT Press, 1992); R. S. Hallote, *Death, Burial, and Afterlife in the Biblical World* (Chicago: Ivan R. Dee, 2001); C. B. Hays, *A Covenant with Death: Death in the Iron Age II and Its Rhetorical Uses in Proto-Isaiah* (Grand Rapids: Eerdmans, 2015); P. Johnston, *Shades of Sheol* (Downers Grove, IL: InterVarsity Press, 2002); T. J. Lewis, *Cults of the Dead in Ancient Israel and Ugarit*, Harvard Semitic Monographs 39 (Atlanta: Scholars Press, 1989); B. Schmidt, *Israel's Beneficent Dead* (Winona Lake, IN: Eisenbrauns, 1996).

[e]For a thorough discussion of the Rephaim and the *marzēaḥ*, see W. D. Barker, *Israel's Kingship Polemic* (Tübingen: Mohr Siebeck, 2014). For more on *marzēaḥ*, see Lewis, *Cults of the Dead*, 80-94.

[f]Often the focus is dead kings. For extensive discussion, see Schmidt, *Israel's Beneficent Dead*.

Despite the many differences between Mesopotamia and Egypt, the dominant ideas about the afterlife in both are framed sociologically. The goal in each is to form community. If someone does not receive a proper burial, they cannot enter the netherworld, and they become social outcasts, part of neither world and without a community identity. Once they are buried, they are "gathered to their fathers"—the communal family tomb being the picture of the community of the ancestors.

Furthermore, the rites for the dead that were carried out by the living were devised to help the dead continue to feel like members of the family community. Once dead, people were no longer dependent on the gods; they were dependent on their living descendants to care for them.[24] This sociological value and emphasis are also seen in the Egyptian interest in reintegration. In the earlier periods of the Old Kingdom, when only the king could hope to enjoy the afterlife, all that was done was intended to help the king achieve a higher status in the netherworld. Once the afterlife became democratized, in the latter part of the Old Kingdom (seen in the Coffin Texts), a reunion with loved ones became one of the highest desiderata. Assmann labels these socially significant faculties "connective virtues," and he names love and memory as the most important of these virtues.[25] In summary, then, we can see that community and society were the main focus of the connective issues in the ancient Near Eastern views of the afterlife.

What are the results of bringing this cognitive environment to bear on our understanding of Israelite concepts? When we peruse the Old Testament looking for revelation that the Israelites received concerning the afterlife, there is little from which to build a theology. What we get, instead, is a description of their default thinking that is, on many counts, indistinguishable from what is found in Mesopotamia or the Levant. The netherworld is called Sheol (a Hebrew term without a Semitic cognate), where there is neither reward nor punishment. God could redeem someone from Sheol by sparing them from death, but there was no expression of a hope to be with God in heaven and no means offered by which such a hope could be achieved. The psalmists express that there is no praise of God in Sheol (Ps 6:5; 115:17), and

---

[24]This point is specifically made in Egyptian letters to the dead; the living describe themselves as "the one who cares for you" (*CANE* 3:1765).

[25]Assmann, "Dialogue Between Self and Soul," 397.

though God has access to Sheol (Ps 139), it is not a place where his presence dwells in any significant way. Sheol is a place where one is cut off from God's hand and remembrance (Ps 88:5, 10-12; cf. Is 38:18, where the dead cannot experience the faithfulness of God). Proper burial, remembrance of the dead, and "being gathered to one's fathers" all continue to be important (e.g., Gen 49:33; 50:13). However, these concepts are not limited to burial contexts; they also refer to joining the ancestors in the afterlife.[26]

Nevertheless, all of this information does not help us to figure out exactly what the Israelites thought about the netherworld. There is much less evidence of a social understanding in Israel, but there is even less evidence of a theological understanding. Their ideas were much more like Mesopotamia than like Egypt, but they were far distant from our own theological understanding. Though the biblical texts indicate that there may well have been an ancestor cult operating in Israel, biblical theology certainly does not endorse it. But neither do the biblical texts put any alternative way of thinking in its place. We are under no compunction to conform our understanding of Israel to that of the ancient Near East, but we can now be more cautious about what we assume about Israelite beliefs. The cognitive environment of the ancient world provided a concept of the afterlife that was inherently social. Therefore, a social understanding of death is more likely to be the default thinking of Israel than the concept of an afterlife that is rooted in theology.

When considering the differences between Israel and its neighbors to the north and east, we return to the fundamental distinction between the Great Symbiosis in Mesopotamia and what we have termed the Great Enterprise in Israel (founded on the covenant). In Mesopotamia the absence of the Great Symbiosis determined the shape of the people's understanding of the afterlife, as discussed above. In Israel the dead also lost their role and status in the Great Enterprise. Even though they continued to be considered a part of the community of their clan and family, they no longer had a covenant identity. They could not participate in the covenant or in the rituals associated with sacred space. Those who were dead were cut off from the worship of Yahweh and could not observe Torah. As

---

[26]Johnston, *Shades of Sheol*, 33-34.

in Mesopotamia, death carried with it theological negation, not theological apotheosis. Therefore, with the categories and concepts before us, we can now use table 7.2 to compare details.

Table 7.2. Aspects of afterlife belief

Categories	Christian Theology	Ancient Near East: Egypt	Ancient Near East: Mesopotamia and Levant	Ancient Israel
Society	utopian	status quo	status quo (diminished)	no indication
Judicial	divine action	human action: spells and deeds	none	none
Communal	with the dead	living and dead	living and dead	living and dead
Deity	relationship	exaltation	none	none

Even though the ancient Israelites believed in some level of continuity with the social community, we receive no information in the Old Testament about how they viewed the existence of society in the netherworld. Descriptions of Sheol and the desire to avoid it suggest a diminished existence. Nothing suggests an upgrade to a utopian position or a theological apotheosis, and no suggestion is found that the afterlife held either judgment or reward (with the possible exception of Dan 12, for which see below). The living and the dead were part of an extended family community, but no possibility of relationship with Yahweh is admitted (Ps 6:6; 88:3, 10-12; Is 38:8). Comparing the columns above, it is easy to see that Israel tracks well with what would be standard thinking in Mesopotamia and the Levant.

It is therefore advisable for us to turn our attention to the questions of heaven and hell. We previously suggested that the Israelites had no hope of heaven, and we can now add that they also had no fear of hell. I maintain, along with many other interpreters of the Old Testament, that there was only one possible destiny after death: Sheol, which was clearly not a place of reward, but neither was it a place of punishment (Eccles 6:6). It was a place of negation outside the ordered world. One way to check this conclusion is to investigate whether another option existed in the minds of the Israelites. Did they believe that they could go to be with God at death?

Perhaps the evidence that has convinced readers of the Bible that the Israelites believed in an alternative is the interpretation of Psalm 16:9-11 offered in Acts 2:25-28, 31; 13:35. As Peter preaches to the Pentecost crowd about the resurrection of Christ, he invokes Psalm 16 as the words of David spoken "about" Jesus: "Fellow Israelites, I can tell you confidently that the patriarch David died and was buried, and his tomb is here to this day. But he was a prophet and knew that God had promised him on oath that he would place one of his descendants on his throne" (Acts 2:29-30). But here we can see that Peter does not use this psalm to suggest that David went anywhere else; he uses it to indicate that Christ rose from the dead (Acts 2:31; the same is true of Acts 13:35). We are therefore left to the Old Testament contexts to determine what Israelites believed to be their fate.

Three expressions that occur in the Psalms are commonly believed by Christian readers to suggest alternative destinations. The first is the psalmist's expression of hope that he will "see his face" (e.g., Ps 11:7). This is expressed as the hope of the upright. Psalm 17:15 also associates this hope with righteousness and believes it will take place "when I awake." The conclusion traditionally drawn is that the psalmist expects to awake from death, find himself in the presence of God by virtue of his righteousness, and be allowed to see God's face/likeness, which could not be experienced in life.

We could easily question this interpretation based solely on the theology. Such a reading posits a salvation by works-righteousness (not only because of the terms used by the psalmist but because the atoning work of Christ was not yet available). Furthermore, however, an analysis of the Hebrew terminology offers a very different understanding of the verse. In both psalms, the word for "seeing" is *ḥzh*. This is also the verb used in Exodus 24:11, where the elders, having ascended Mount Sinai, see God. Therefore, we can conclude that "seeing" can be experienced by those who still live. The experience of the elders in Exodus 24 is that of a theophany, so it is recognizably a unique experience. But we find in the Psalms that it is in the temple that one gazes on Yahweh (Ps 27:4; 63:2). This leads to the conclusion that the psalmist expects to see the face of God when he is granted access to the temple.

Although a few passages can be identified that use the verb "awake" to refer to awakening from death (Is 26:19; Dan 12:2, see discussion of both below), in the Psalms it refers to awakening in the morning from a troubled night with renewed hope for God's deliverance from enemies (Ps 3:3; 63:3; 139:18). We will recall that when David confronts Saul, he complains that

Saul's pursuit of him has prevented him from worshiping in the temple (1 Sam 26:19). Jonah also looks forward to being received in the temple favorably (Jon 2:4, 7). Therefore it is vindication from one's enemies that will allow someone to "see the face of God." If someone were already dead, no one left living would consider the action to be vindication.

A second concept that has led Christian readers to think that the Israelites had a concept of eternity in heaven is found in the statements that the psalmist will not be abandoned to Sheol. In Psalm 16 we have already encountered this language. First, we must recognize that the text does not refer to abandoning him *in* Sheol, but abandoning him *to* Sheol—that is, God will not consign him to Sheol. This phrase does not mean that he will send him somewhere else after death; it means that he will remain alive (at this time) rather than dying. The same is true of the phrase "redeemed from Sheol" (Ps 49:15). Readers of English translations are easily led astray by some of these translation decisions. For example, the Hebrew term *nṣḥ* in Psalm 16:11 ("eternal") pertains to a temporal condition in its other uses, not to eternity. Furthermore, as already discussed in chapter three, the word *nepeš*, sometimes still translated "soul," should be understood as "life" (NIV renders it correctly). Strong evidence is provided by the same phrase also used in Psalm 30:2-3, where the context makes it clear that being brought up from Sheol means having been spared from death at the hands of one's enemies. Moreover, Job 33:28 (NIV) sets up this concept very clearly: "God has delivered [redeemed] me from going down to the pit, and I shall live to enjoy the light of life."

The third phrase that draws attention is in the passages where God "takes" someone (Ps 49:14-15; 73:23-24; and narrative occurrences in Gen 5:24; 2 Kings 2:11). Again, the translator's decisions hamper us. In Psalm 49:15 the NIV translates "he will surely take me to himself." But "to himself" has been supplied by the translator. In contrast, the ESV has "he will receive me," which retains the ambiguity of the Hebrew well. In Psalm 73:24 the NIV has "you will take me into glory," which gives English readers the impression that "into glory" refers to heaven (for we use the word *glory* that way in English idiom). Nevertheless, the word *into* is not in the Hebrew text. The NRSV follows Hebrew idiom more closely with the translation "you will receive me with honor." Consequently, neither of these psalms suggests that the psalmist is being taken *somewhere*. Through the translations that favor "receiving" rather than "taking," which corresponds more to the Hebrew text, we can eliminate the question of "where?"

This direction is strongly affirmed by the use of the verb *lqh* in a psalm that clearly demonstrates how we should understand it. In Psalm 18:16-19 the text reads:

> He reached down from on high and took hold [*lqh*] of me;
>> he drew me out of deep waters.
>
> He rescued me from my powerful enemy,
>> from my foes, who were too strong for me.
>
> They confronted me in the day of my disaster,
>> but the LORD was my support.
>
> He brought me out into a spacious place;
>> he rescued me because he delighted in me.

This context makes it clear that the verb *lqh* is used in these passages in Psalms to convey deliverance from enemies.

Nevertheless, the problem persists when interpreters consider some of the pertinent narrative uses of *lqh*. Of Enoch it is stated, "Enoch walked faithfully with God; then he was no more, because God took (*lqh*) him away" (Gen 5:24). In more detail, the text tells us that Elisha was separated from Elijah by a chariot of fire while a whirlwind took Elijah up to heaven (2 Kings 2:11). Earlier, in 2 Kings 2:9, Elijah had spoken of being *taken* from Elisha (using *lqh* as used with Enoch).

Though Elijah is said to have gone up (*ʿlh*) "to heaven," it must be kept in mind that the word translated "heaven" here (*šāmāyîm*) can also refer to the sky and therefore does not clearly suggest that Elijah was taken into God's presence. One should note that the sons of the prophets did not have that understanding at all, for they wondered where Elijah may have been put down (2 Kings 2:16).[27]

---

[27]Spronk observes this response and concludes that the terminology here must be understood in the same terms as Ezek 3:14; 8:3, where it concerns "being transported by YHWH within and not from this world" (*Beatific Afterlife in Ancient Israel*, 259). This is also what happens to the flood hero in the Gilgamesh Epic, whom the gods take (Akkadian *lequ*) and deposit in a faraway place where he will enjoy unending life (but not heaven and not in the presence of the gods).

Where did Enoch and Elijah go, then? Or, perhaps a better question, where did the Israelite audience think that Enoch and Elijah went? It would not make much sense for God to take them from life if he was only going to take them to Sheol. It was never thought that Sheol was better than life, yet the "taking" of these godly individuals was seen as a direct result of their close relationship with God.[28] It is notable that neither text reveals anything about an understanding of the eternal destiny of the individual. The most logical conclusion, then, is that the author did not know where they went.[29] It would be an argument from silence to suggest anything else, unless we can demonstrate that the Israelites knew of another alternative besides Sheol.

The material we have covered so far appears to leave no room for any hope of heaven. P. Johnston is a good example of a serious Old Testament scholar who has evaluated the same evidence that we have just surveyed and has yet concluded that Israel *did* have an alternate hope. He dismisses the examples of Enoch and Elijah with the agnostic statement, "These two may have escaped death, but this had no obvious relevance to Israelite beliefs or aspirations."[30] When he gets to Psalms 16; 49; 73, he allows for only the slightest hint of vague hope for communion with God beyond death: "These Psalms give no elaboration of how, when or where this communion will take place. They simply affirm it in faith. For most Israelites, hope remained firmly anchored in the present life. But a few seem to glimpse some form of continued communion with God beyond it."[31] This does not say much, and even so, in my opinion, it says more than the evidence can bear. Even if Johnston is right, those vague glimpses do not help us define an Old Testament doctrine of afterlife. The Israelites had no hope of heaven. The text offers none, implies none, and there would be no theological basis on which to posit such a belief, given the lack of an efficacious mechanism.

---

[28] Enoch's "walking with God" is a positive assessment (cf. the only other occurrence of the phrase describing Noah, Gen 6:9).

[29] Spronk considers an intriguing suggestion that Elijah has joined Yahweh's chariotry and become part of the heavenly host, but the textual evidence he garners remains vague. Spronk, *Beatific Afterlife in Ancient Israel*, 260-61. Spronk also attempts to relate to the Israelite doctrine the Canaanite belief that the spirits of the royal dead accompanied Baal each year when he returned to the land of the living (cf. his conclusions, 195-96). He sees this as an element in Israelite folk religion from the preexilic period and also sees it reflected in the tomb inscription of Uriyahu from Khirbet el-Kom (307-10).

[30] Johnston, *Shades of Sheol*, 216.

[31] Ibid., 217.

HELL

The reason why biblical passages so often refer to the wicked's descent to Sheol is that they are referring to the punishment of an early death, not because Sheol is a place where only the wicked go. Everyone goes there. Neither Sheol nor the pit (*bō'r, šāḥat*) should be thought of as hell. The former is the Hebrew word for the netherworld, and the latter likely describe the pile of bones at the back of the rock-carved tombs that were used for family burials. *'Abaddôn* is used only five times in the Old Testament[32] and occurs in parallel with Sheol and death. Its root connects it as an abstraction to the verb "destroy" and refers to the place of the dead. If hell is a place of punishment, the Old Testament has no such concept and no words that convey it.

The passage most commonly associated with punishment in hell is Isaiah 66:24, the last verse in the book, because it discusses the new heavens and new earth: "And they will go out and look on the dead bodies of those who rebelled against me; the worms that eat them will not die, the fire that burns them will not be quenched, and they will be loathsome to all mankind." Nevertheless, the focus here remains on the corporate level rather than on individual destinies, as can be seen even in the first extant use in Judith 16:17 (NABRE):

> Woe to the nations that rise against my people!
>> the Lord Almighty will requite them;
>
> in the day of judgment he will punish them:
>> He will send fire and worms into their flesh,
>> and they will weep and suffer forever.

Here it is nations that are subject to judgment, not individuals. In sum, no theological instruction concerning the nature of hell as a place of judgment for individuals can be extracted from any Old Testament passage.

Resurrection.[33] Texts from the ancient Near East nowhere offer evidence of any substantial belief in resurrection, so we can only evaluate Hebrew texts that could be or have been so interpreted. To begin the investigation of resurrection in the Old Testament, we must phrase the question a little more carefully. Resurrection may be viewed in three different categories. First, there is

---

[32]Job 26:6; 28:22; 31:12; Ps 88:11; Prov 15:11.
[33]Johnston, *Shades of Sheol*, 218-39.

Divine Abandonment

The notion of divine abandonment was understandably feared in the ancient world. When people were abandoned by their god, they were vulnerable to demons, disease, and death, and when a city was abandoned, destruction was inevitable. People generally had typical ways of explaining divine abandonment. One standard explanation was that something had been done to anger the god to such an extent that s/he left. But in the Sumerian laments over the fall of cities, an alternative explanation is given—that the gods had simply made a decree that it was time for destruction.

In Israel, individuals often felt abandoned by deity when they suffered illness or tragedy in some way (cf. Job, the psalmists). The ultimate abandonment was to death and Sheol. Corporately, the covenant curses did not stop at abandonment but indicated Yahweh's aggressive hostility toward them (Lev 26:14-39; Deut 28:15-68). Yet in Ezekiel 10, the abandonment motif is clear.[a] Consistently, however, Yahweh's abandonment of the people is motivated by their abandonment of him, and therefore these situations differ from both the city laments in Mesopotamia and from the individual's plight in the afterlife.

[a]See expression of it in Deut 31:17; 2 Chron 12:5; 15:2; 24:20; Is 49:14 (clarified that yet he cannot forget them; see also the book of Lamentations). A few narratives also feature the threat of divine abandonment of the people (e.g., Ex 33:3; Josh 7:12) or of an individual (e.g., Saul in 1 Sam 16:14).

the resurrection that represents an individual's return to life. Several Old Testament passages refer to such an occurrence (1 Kings 17:22; 2 Kings 4:35; 13:21). Second, there is the doctrine of the individual resurrection of the body in the afterlife, what we might call the "eschatological" resurrection. Third, we could speak of a corporate resurrection: a people brought back into existence from apparent extinction. This last category is represented in Ezekiel's vision of the valley of the dry bones, where Israel is brought back to life as a nation (Ezek 37; see also Hos 6:1-2). Of course, we are not surprised to find exile paralleled with death. Both death and exile bring a loss of identity: exile for the community and death for the individual (who loses their community identity). It is therefore logical that the concept of resurrection should occur in conjunction with talk of the restoration of community identity.

The first and third types of resurrection listed above demonstrably occur within the beliefs of ancient Israel, but what about the second category? Passages such as Isaiah 26:19 and Daniel 12:1-2 offer the statements most easily connected to eschatological resurrection. Additionally it is claimed that certain Hebrew terms carry a technical meaning connected to the concept of resurrection (cf. the discussion of the verb "awake" above).

Isaiah 26:19.

But your dead will live, LORD;
> their bodies will rise—

let those who dwell in the dust
> wake up and shout for joy—

your dew is like the dew of the morning;
> the earth will give birth to her dead.[34]

One important observation is that Isaiah 26:19 must be understood in contrast to Isaiah 26:14, where much of the same terminology is used. There the dead among the powerful who used to exercise power over Israel are not expected to rise. Rather, they have been punished and brought to ruin. Isaiah 26:14, then, has a corporate sense to it that concerns the restoration of a group to life in this world as they regain their community identity. In Isaiah 26:15 the author begins to contrast the prosperity brought to the nation Israel. This would lead to the conclusion that the passage is concerned with a national resurrection (type three above), much like Ezekiel 37.[35] Though the grammar and text of Isaiah 26:19 remain enigmatic, the parallels to Isaiah 26:14 provide the context.[36]

---

[34]This passage is replete with textual difficulties. The second line of the text, contrary to the NIV, reads, "my corpse will arise." Not only is the switch from "your" to "my" a problem, the fact that the noun *corpse* is singular while the verb *will arise* is plural presents added confusion. The antecedents to all the pronouns are in question, and to crown the whole passage, the controversial Rephaim (the shades?; NIV "the dead") are brought into it at the very end of the verse. For an analysis of Is 24–27 in relationship to Canaanite ideas, see W. D. Barker, *Isaiah's Kingship Polemic* (Tübingen: Mohr Siebeck, 2014).

[35]John J. Collins, *Daniel* (Minneapolis: Fortress, 1993), 395.

[36]"The context is one of national revival and restoration. The nation is already portrayed in personal imagery, as a woman in labour but unable to give birth. So the imagery of resurrection also applies to the nation." Johnston, *Shades of Sheol*, 225. He does go on to say that he also believes that the imagery "presupposes a concept of individual resurrection."

Daniel 12:1-2.

> At that time Michael, the great prince who protects your people, will arise. There
> will be a time of distress such as has not happened from the beginning of nations
> until then. But at that time your people—everyone whose name is found written
> in the book—will be delivered. Multitudes who sleep in the dust of the earth will
> awake: some to everlasting life, others to shame and everlasting contempt.

This is the only passage that speaks forthrightly about differing destinies,
though no explicit indication is given that righteousness and wickedness are
the criteria that determine those destinies.[37] Nevertheless, we must not jump
too quickly to a standard Christian doctrine of the resurrection. A few observations are in order.

First, the text says "many" (NIV "multitudes") will awake, not "all"; this
is not a general resurrection. Second, the text speaks of those who sleep in
"the land of dust" (NIV "dust of the earth"). This is the only occurrence of
this phrase in the Old Testament, but since it refers specifically to a "land,"
and since Sheol is often connected with dust (e.g., Job 17:16), one could
deduce that it is a reference to Sheol, the netherworld. If this is the case, both
classes of individuals are to be found in Sheol. Third, the phrase translated
"everlasting life" (*ḥayyê ʿōlām*) occurs only here in the Old Testament, but
similar phrases occur (in Greek) in pseudepigraphic literature such as
1 Enoch and the Sibylline Oracles.[38] In these contexts it is equated to specific
periods of time, such as five hundred years (1 Enoch 10:10).[39]

Finally, we must observe that the text conveys nothing concerning the place
of resurrection; that is, it does not speak of lasting life *in heaven*, in the new Jerusalem, or on the new earth, nor does it speak of lasting contempt in any particular locale. In fact, it does not clarify whether the resurrection to which it
refers is an afterlife condition or a restoration to life on earth. Additionally, it
does not indicate what criteria qualify an individual for one category or the other.

---

[37]The "book of life" is precisely that—a record of who is destined for life.

[38]R. H. Charles, *Eschatology* (New York: Schocken, 1963), 212-13n3.

[39]The Hebrew term *ʿōlām* ("everlasting") has been recognized as less abstract than the philo-
sophical concept of eternity. Similar cautions can be found in J. Barr, *Biblical Words for Time*
(London: SCM Press, 1969), 73-74, 93, 123-24; D. Howard, "The Case for Kingship in the Old
Testament Narrative Books and the Psalms," *Trinity Journal* 9 (1988): 29n38; Allan MacRae,
"ʿōlām," in *Theological Wordbook of the Old Testament*, ed. R. L. Harris, Gleason Archer, and
Bruce Waltke (Chicago: Moody, 1980), 2:672n1631.

What is it, then, that this passage is saying, and what ideas does it reflect? The author anticipates that numerous individuals will be brought back to life, but he does not indicate whether they will be brought back to life in this world. However, it is important to note that the Old Testament does not speak clearly of any bodily existence in a world to come in any passage. Nevertheless, the passage does make clear that in this resurrected life they will either enjoy an extension to their life (as a reward for their faithfulness?) or will suffer ongoing humiliation (as punishment for their treachery?).

Interpreters such as G. Nickelsburg see this passage, like the other Old Testament passages, as most concerned about the reconstitution of the nation:

> For Daniel, judgment is the prelude to the reconstitution of the nation. Verse 1 mentions the register of the citizens of new Israel. The resurrected righteous of verse 2 are not isolated individuals; they are raised to participate in this new nation. . . . The dead apostates are raised so that their bodies can be exposed in the Valley of Hinnom.[40]

While this relatively late passage exceeds any other statements in the Old Testament, it remains quite basic and does not approach the fully developed doctrine of the New Testament. Johnston, though willing to grant more than I am, nevertheless concludes, "Resurrection remained marginal to Old Testament belief, whether chronologically or theologically."[41] In the Hellenistic period, Jewish literature shows much more interest in resurrection and develops it as a doctrine (e.g., 1 Enoch, Psalms of Solomon, Testaments of the Twelve Patriarchs).[42] It is well known that in the New Testament period the topic was still under discussion among Jewish groups, and the disagreements about it between the Pharisees and Sadducees are cited (Mk 12:18; Acts 23:8).

While the precise shape of Israel's doctrine is difficult to define, and various interpreters have arrived at vastly different conclusions, most would agree that the Israelite doctrine should not be equated with the doctrine eventually formulated in New Testament theology and church history.

---

[40]G. W. E. Nickelsburg, *Resurrection, Immortality and Eternal Life in Intertestamental Judaism* (Cambridge, MA: Harvard University Press, 1972), 23.

[41]Johnston, *Shades of Sheol*, 227.

[42]For more information see Johnston, *Shades of Sheol*, 229-30. Much attention has been given to the extent that Persian Zoroastrianism or the Greek thinking of the Hellenistic period influenced Jewish thinking, but (without denying the possibility) it is difficult to trace such lines of influence convincingly. See Johnston, *Shades of Sheol*, 234-37.

Holy Spirit/Spirit of the Lord

In Christian theology, when we talk about salvation, we discuss not only the role of Jesus as the one who secured our salvation, but we also discuss the Holy Spirit as the one who seals our salvation. The indwelling of the Holy Spirit assures our identity in Christ and that establishes us as sacred space by virtue of God's presence in us. We have proposed above that the Old Testament has no soteriology of which to speak, and here we would also contend that the Old Testament has no pneumatology. This is easy to understand, since Israel had no concept of a Trinity. Furthermore, since Israel had no concept of salvation, the Spirit could have had no role in salvation in the Old Testament, and since the Old Testament has no means of preparing a person for God's presence, the Spirit, in the Old Testament, is not providing the presence of God through indwelling. Finally, since the Old Testament has no space for trinitarian thinking, the Spirit cannot be considered the third person of the Trinity in the ancient Israelite context of the Old Testament.

In the Old Testament, the party of interest in this discussion is termed the Spirit of the Lord/God.[a] The Spirit of the Lord functions as an extension of God's power and authority, and it comes upon people or "clothes" them when Yahweh is ready to use them in particular ways to advance his purposes. This extension of God's spirit is classified in the same category as the "hand of God" (e.g., Ezek 37:1) and is not viewed as a person.

The spirit comes upon prophets to energize their gift. It also comes upon army commanders as they muster troops and go into battle (Gideon, Jephthah, Saul). It even empowers Samson in a number of his exploits. It is not, however, a permanent endowment and does not engage in sanctification. It comes upon kings (Saul, David) in a more sustained way, but it can also leave (1 Sam 16:14). It also is active in creation (Gen 1:2), where it can be associated with the effective word of God throughout Genesis 1 (Ps 33:6, NIV "breath").

Based on hindsight and the development of trinitarian theology in the New Testament and the church, we can retrofit the work of the third person of the Trinity into some of these events (especially the inspiration of the prophets). But in the Old Testament, the Israelites did not interpret these phenomena in that way. Nevertheless, even though we would have a basis for the claim that the Holy Spirit was indeed active in some of those ways, we must also recognize that many of the most significant roles of the Holy Spirit in our theology are totally lacking in the profile of the Spirit of the Lord in the Old Testament.

---

[a] J. Walton, "The Ancient Near Eastern Background of the Spirit of the Lord in the Old Testament," in *Presence, Power and Promise: The Role of the Spirit of God in the Old Testament* (Downers Grove, IL: InterVarsity Press, 2011), 38-67.

CONCLUSIONS AND ENDURING THEOLOGY

In this chapter, we have learned that Israel had no ideas about salvation, afterlife, or resurrection that could produce a theology on which we could build. We have seen that Israelites had no hope of heaven, no mechanism that could possibly have achieved an eternal, heavenly existence for them, no sense of reward or judgment in the afterlife, no thought that they would spend eternity with God, and no concept of personal resurrection. They also had no thought of salvation from sins. They thought in terms of corporate, community identity, rather than of their individual plights or destinies. Given all these lacunae, we are burdened with questions that leave us reeling. How could any Israelite end up with God after death? Christians today generally believe that they will encounter the Old Testament saints in heaven. But beyond that, what theology can we possibly derive on this topic?

Salvation. One of the most important contributions of this discussion is the clarification of the focus of our faith. As Christians it is easy for our attention to focus on salvation and eternal life. Consequently, we may define our faith, and even our identity, in those terms ("saved and heaven bound"). When this becomes the case, it is no wonder that we cannot understand how the Israelites could have had faith if they were not "saved and heaven bound." Then, considering what we just have discovered about Old Testament theology, we learn that they were not, in fact, "saved and heaven bound." But we can't imagine that Abraham or Moses would not be in heaven, and so our confusion becomes complete. The problem is that we have mistaken the benefits of our faith for the substance of our faith. The Old Testament can help us sort out the important distinctions that we should be making, because by looking at the Israelites, we can reorient ourselves to a proper understanding of our faith and Christianity.

Our faith is in God. We can easily dismiss such a commonplace statement as a self-evident cliché. But we must start there and follow the logic through its proper steps. Our faith is in God, and he has made provision for us. The means he has provided is the death and resurrection of Jesus, which has afforded numerous benefits to us; forgiveness, salvation, and eternal life are usually at the top of the list. Because we value these benefits so highly, the equation of our Christianity can easily be reduced to the idea that we have faith in God to bring us benefits. In our modern individualistic, narcissistic culture, it is easy for us to think first about ourselves and what we stand to gain. Without any intention to diminish the incredible benefits Christ bought at a great price, it is important for us to realize that our Christianity is not about the benefits that we gain, and these benefits must not shape our faith.

We can see this point made clearly in two narratives in the Old Testament. On the first occasion, God asks Abraham to sacrifice his son Isaac (Gen 22).[43] We often wonder about this passage because it is difficult to imagine why God would ask for such a thing. At this point, Abraham has already proven his faith on numerous occasions (leaving his land and family, and note the accolade in Gen 15:6). We can sort this out, however, when we recognize that what Abraham is asked to put on that altar is more than just his beloved son. This is not a story about whether God condones human sacrifice or about whether any of us would give our children to the Lord. Instead we understand that, at that point in time, all the benefits of the covenant reside in Isaac. If Isaac is killed, there will be no large family—in fact no family at all. Prospects of land and blessing would all collapse in the aftermath of his death.

Abraham, then, was asked to forfeit all the benefits of the covenant. When he obeys, Yahweh indicates that he now knows that Abraham fears God (Gen 22:12). This does not suggest that God is gaining new cognitive knowledge. In Hebrew, what one "knows" is often established on the basis of what one experiences. Abraham, rather, demonstrates that his faith in

---

[43]See discussion in J. Walton, *Genesis*, NIVAC (Grand Rapids: Zondervan, 2001), 513-15, 519-20.

God is not dependent on covenant benefits. He is willing to give them all up. His faith is in the covenant identity found in the God who has forged a relationship with him. In other words, Abraham demonstrates that benefits are not the focus of his faith.

The second example is Job.[44] When Yahweh praises Job's faith, he is challenged with regard to the motivation for Job's faith: "Does Job fear God for nothing?" (Job 1:9). This is the very same question that was posed (though not explicitly) in Genesis 22. Job has enjoyed extensive benefits—health, wealth, family, respect, and standing in society. It is therefore sensible to question whether he is motivated by what he stands to gain or by his fear of God. The only way to tell in this thought experiment[45] would be to take it all away. Through the book of Job, we learn the importance of recognizing that our faith cannot be focused on our benefits (even when some of those benefits can never be lost!). The question that all of us should ask is, "Do we fear God for nothing?" Would we be Christians if none of our benefits remained? For Abraham, that meant no covenant; for Job it meant no prosperity. For us, the question might include whether we would have become Christians without the prospect of eternal life and salvation. We have come to realize that the Israelites were asked to do precisely that (though they had a separate set of benefits).

Salvation is more importantly about what we are saved *to* (renewed access to the presence of God and relationship with him) than what we are saved *from*. We have been given a new identity in Christ. This point is significant because too many Christians find it too easy to think only that they are saved, forgiven, and on their way to heaven, instead of taking seriously the idea that we are in partnership with God day by day, here and now, as we participate in the kingdom and in his plan and purposes for the cosmos and for us.

So we need to revisit our initial question about faith. Our faith is in God to provide a mechanism—that part stands. But we should not imagine that the mechanism of Jesus' death and resurrection is focused on benefits. The

---

[44]These ideas are developed at length in J. Walton and T. Longman, *How to Read Job* (Downers Grove, IL: InterVarsity Press, 2015).

[45]J. Walton, *Job*, NIVAC (Grand Rapids: Zondervan, 2012), 24-27; Walton and Longman, *How to Read Job*, 34-36.

benefits are real and valuable, but they are not the main idea. We have faith in God to provide a mechanism for identity and relationship. That is what our Christianity is all about: a new identity in Christ; becoming, with God through Christ, partners in the kingdom of God; working with him to carry out his plan and purposes. Our Christian banner should not be "saved and heaven bound," but "in Christ, members of the kingdom of God." This identity, like any relationship, comes with responsibilities. We have a role in forging our identity daily to correspond to the status we have in Christ as we eliminate other competing identities. We are not saved by those efforts, but they are essential to the relationship.

If we think back to the equation we used at the beginning of this chapter when we talked about situation A, mechanism B, and new situation C, we would thus formulate our Christian theology in this way:

✦ Situation A—We are sinners who are apart from God and are participating in the disorder that comes from making ourselves the source and center of order. We find our identity in ourselves and are subject to death.

✦ Provision (operative means) B—Christ died for our sins (and our old self/identity died with him, Gal 2:20).

✦ Situation C—We have been given a new identity and are in relationship with God as partners in the kingdom.

Armed with this information, we are now ready to return to Old Testament theology and the situation of the Israelites. Their faith, like ours, was in God and specifically in the means that he provided. The provision for them was the covenant (including rituals and Torah), and it had certain valuable benefits (the covenant benefits: family, land, and blessing). Yet as with us, and as demonstrated by Abraham, their faith could not focus on the benefits package. What God had provided in the covenant was a means by which they could have a new identity and a relationship with him, a partnership in his plan and purposes. The provision for them was different from the provision that we have (Christ had not yet come or died), and therefore their benefit package was different from ours. But the point of it all, and the focus of their faith, is the same: a new identity with a relationship forged as partners with God in his plan and purposes. We do not have their benefits, and they were not offered the ones that we have received.

Typology and the Sacrificial System

We have considered the sacrificial system in Israel. We now turn attention to the relationship between Christ and the sacrificial system. Has the sacrificial system been devised in anticipation of the sacrifice of Christ? Should we consider the work of Christ as recapitulating the sacrificial system? Does the sacrificial system serve as a type of Christ?

We have discussed how the Old Testament sacrificial system reflects common ancient Near Eastern thinking, which makes it difficult to contend that it was designed in anticipation of Christ. In its inclusion of vow offerings and thank offerings, for example, its range stretches beyond what Christ did. Even some of the offerings that accomplished *kipper* (NIV "atonement") have no connection to the work of Christ. For example, the *'āšām* (NIV "guilt offering") remediated the offense caused by the profane use of something that was sacred.[a] It is more productive to see the sacrificial system as a bridge of continuity linking Christ to the Old Testament.

As one point of continuity, the Gospels relate the inauguration of the new covenant through the blood of Christ to the inauguration of the covenant in Exodus 24:8. In the Old Testament, however, that is a one-time event rather than an aspect of the sacrificial system. As a second point of continuity, the Gospel of John gives ample evidence to associate the death of Jesus with the Passover lamb, which, like the covenant inauguration ritual, plays a role in the establishment of the covenant people, though, likewise, the Passover is not part of the sacrificial system. The timing of Jesus' death at Passover and the description of the "Lamb of God that takes away the sin of the world" are the most obvious connections (and it is stated explicitly in 1 Cor 5:7),[b] with attention given to substitution.

The third explicit connection made in the New Testament is with Yom Kippur (Heb 9–10). The author of Hebrews, however, is not interested in the actual function of Yom Kippur (removing built-up impurities from the temple; see chapter five) and does not equate Jesus to either of the goats. Instead, he compares Christ to the high priest, focusing on the idea of limited access to the most holy place, only possible by means of blood.

This comparison then leads to the conclusion that Christ is the mediator of a new covenant (Heb 9:15, returning to the issue in the Gospels), a role that he builds in Hebrews 9:16-22 by analogy. Besides the three main connections just enumerated, other New Testament passages also carry brief allusions to the sacrificial system. Romans 8:3, for example, is generally considered a reference to Christ as a "sin offering" (so NIV),[c] though it does not address any aspect of what the sin offering does in the Old Testament[d] compared to what was accomplished by Christ.

Beyond these explicit comparisons between Christ and the sacrificial system, the author of Hebrews uses various terms to indicate the nature of the relationship. He uses vocabulary such as "illustration" (parabolē, Heb 9:9); "imitation," "example" (hypodeigma, Heb 9:23; NIV "copies");[e] "copy" (antitypa, Heb 9:24),[f] and "shadow" (skian, "foreshadowing," Heb 10:1). The author is offering these insights to his audience for their understanding in their contemporary setting rather than suggesting that these ideas were inherent in the implementation of the sacrificial system or that they were embedded in the message of the Old Testament. This is analogy by typology, not an elaboration of the contextual theology of the Old Testament.[g]

Based on this analysis, we can read the work of Christ as parallel and analogous to the sacrificial system, but we have no reason to think that he is the fulfillment of the sacrificial system or that the sacrificial system was implemented with him in mind. We would therefore not be justified in using a christocentric approach, especially one that allowed any interpreter to go beyond the New Testament to find other parallels between Christ and the sacrificial system. We can agree that the Old Testament sacrifices provide categories that are used and transcended by the sacrifice of Christ but need not conclude that the Old Testament sacrifices were "merely" shadows of the sacrifice of Christ, which fulfilled them.[h] The insertion of "merely" unnecessarily undermines the significance of the Old Testament sacrificial system in its context. Christ fulfills the *law*, but the New Testament writers never suggest that he *fulfills* any part of the sacrificial system. The Old Testament sacrificial system does not find its *only* or even it *primary* meaning in Christ, though Christ does give additional meaning to some of the Old Testament sacrifices. Even though the sacrifice of Christ transcends the Old Testament system, the theological significance of the Old Testament system in its own right also transcends the ways in which it finds additional meaning in Christ.

---

[a]J. Milgrom, *Cult and Conscience* (Leiden: Brill, 1976).

[b]P. Head, "The Self-Offering and Death of Christ as a Sacrifice in the Gospels and Acts of the Apostles," in *Sacrifice in the Bible*, ed. R. T. Beckwith and M. J. Selman (Grand Rapids: Baker, 1995), 119-23.

[c]Paul uses *hamartias*, which is a general word in Greek, but it is the word the LXX uses for sin offering in Lev 4–5 (for other hints at sin offering, cf. Heb 10:4, 11-12).

[d]N. Kiuchi, *The Purification Offering in the Priestly Literature: Its Meaning and Function* (Sheffield, UK: JSOT Press, 1987).

[e]The same Greek term in Heb 8:5 is parallel to both *typos* and *skian*. The LXX uses the term only in Ezek 42:15, but there is no equivalent in the Hebrew text. For comparison to Philo's allegories based on Platonic metaphysics see the excursus "The Heavenly Temple and Its Significance," in H. Attridge, *Hebrews*, Hermeneia (Minneapolis: Fortress, 1989), 222-24.

[f]Hebrew *tabnît*, Ex 25:40, is translated in the LXX by *typos*, which refers to what God showed Moses on Sinai regarding the construction of the tabernacle.

[g]This is typical of the figural reading of the Old Testament that is common for New Testament authors.

[h]R. Beckwith, "The Death of Christ as a Sacrifice in the Teaching of Paul and Hebrews," in *Sacrifice in the Bible*, 135.

Faith is something that we share with the Israelites of old, and we can learn much from the Old Testament to help us hone the sharp edge of our own faith, lest we give in to our ready narcissism and become obsessed with our benefits instead of attending to the fine points of our identity. Everyone has faith; the question is, "In what?" When we focus on benefits, the object of our faith is our own happiness and, by extension, ourselves. Even if we "trust in God," we only "trust that God will make us happy." The Israelites struggled with that all-too-human tendency in ancient times, and we continue to struggle today.

This finally brings us to the question of whether any Israelites were ever able to receive the benefits that we as Christians enjoy: salvation and eternal life. In the end, that is God's business, not ours, and it is not our main concern. The Bible has little to offer by way of explanation that would suggest an answer. It is possible that Romans 3:25 indicates that God had a plan in mind, and, given one possible interpretation of Ephesians 4:8-10, we may

have a hint concerning what Christ provided for the Old Testament saints
(see also 1 Pet 3:19).[46] But neither the Old Testament nor New Testament
offer sufficient clarity of revelation to provide us with confident knowledge.
Regardless, our careful study can result in a better understanding of our
faith, and we can see that this same faith was shared by the faithful Israelites
of the Old Testament (faith in a mechanism for new identity and relationship
with God). But having discussed the focus of our faith, we should turn our
attention briefly to the nature of faith, for that will also help us to distinguish
faith from the benefits that we receive.

Heaven and hell. Now, as little more than an afterthought, we can offer a
few comments on what we know of these benefits (to be accurate, eternal
life is the benefit, paired with the benefit of avoiding hell). We have learned
that the Old Testament has no concept of hell, no words for hell, no place
for hell in the ideology, and it therefore has no teaching to offer about it.
One's perceptions about hell are typically shaped by one's beliefs about other
doctrines—primarily sin and salvation. We should also note that even the
New Testament is indeterminate about hell.[47] A survey of New Testament
passages reveals a mix between those that seem to suggest eternal torment[48]
and those that are used to support annihilation.[49] This is not the place to
engage this discussion, but our interaction with the Old Testament may
suggest that in our own theological formulations we should be willing to

---

[46]This is at the root of the disputed line in the Apostles' Creed: "He descended to the world of
the dead."

[47]The variety of "view of hell" books demonstrate that evangelicalism is unresolved on the issue:
Preston Sprinkle and Stanley N. Gundry, eds., *Four Views on Hell*, 2nd ed. (Grand Rapids:
Zondervan, 2016); Steve Gregg, ed., *All You Want to Know About Hell: Three Christian Views of
God's Final Solution to the Problem of Sin* (Nashville: Thomas Nelson, 2013); E. W. Fudge and
R. A. Peterson, *Two Views of Hell: A Biblical & Theological Dialogue* (Downers Grove, IL: Inter-
Varsity Press, 2000).

[48]Mt 8:12—outer darkness, weeping, gnashing of teeth (subjects of kingdom thrown out); Mt
13:42-43—blazing furnace, weeping, gnashing of teeth; Mt 22:13—darkness, weeping, gnashing
of teeth (wedding crasher parable); Mt 24:51—weeping, gnashing of teeth (unfaithful steward
parable); Mt 25:31-46—eternal punishment (for those who did not help); Jude 13—blackest
darkness reserved forever (ungodly people); Rev 14:9-11—suffer God's wrath, tormented with
burning sulfur, smoke of torment will arise forever (those who worship the beast). None of these
explicitly indicate that those who do not accept Christ will suffer eternal torment.

[49]Mt 7:13—destruction (many take this road); Mt 10:28—God is one who can destroy soul and
body in hell; Rom 9:22—objects of wrath made for destruction; Phil 3:19—destiny is destruction
(enemies of the cross); 2 Thess 1:9—punished with everlasting destruction, shut out from God's
presence (those who do not know God and do not obey the gospel—torment is not everlasting;
destruction is irreversible).

reconsider the illocutions of these passages. Options would include: threat, warning, deterrent, or instruction concerning metaphysical eschatology. Clearly we get the strong message that sin has consequences, and the most significant of these consequences has to do with not being coidentified with God. That in itself is death and destruction, regardless of what shape it takes. However, most descriptors of hell involve sensory attack or deprivation, and these are descriptions that are deeply embedded in the ancient Near Eastern cultural river.

When we turn our attention to the positive side of the ledger, we should follow the same pathways: the important issue is identity, not destiny. Many are now giving long-needed attention to the significance of the new heaven and new earth.[50] This is based on a bridge between Old Testament (Is 65) and New Testament (Rev 21). Even though the two texts each have their distinctive treatment of new creation, they are interrelated and should be considered together. The common bond and main point is that both of these passages are commenting not on personal destiny in the afterlife but on the idea that God's plan and purposes culminate in a fully ordered cosmos. This perspective can be helpful for us when we consider the emphases of our constructive theology.

---

[50]See the persuasive and accessible treatment in J. Richard Middleton, *A New Heaven and a New Earth: Reclaiming Biblical Eschatology* (Grand Rapids: Baker, 2014).

8

CONCLUSIONS

MODERN ISSUES AND CONTEMPORARY CONCERNS
IN OLD TESTAMENT THEOLOGY

These days it seems that the reaction to the Old Testament teeters between heated controversy and utter neglect. Controversies arise when God's actions or instructions seem either odd beyond comprehension or morally reprehensible. Neglect results when the Old Testament strikes readers as either irrelevant or so confusing that they throw up their hands in despair, frustrated at its perceived impenetrability. Yet amid the extremes of vitriol and dismissiveness, people continue to propose moral principles from its pages and garner proof texts to resolve the issues that arise in society by offering the "biblical view." The result is that both Christians and skeptics regularly abuse the Old Testament, as it is misrepresented and misunderstood, and its true message too often lies either fallow or trampled underfoot. In this concluding chapter, we will pick up a variety of issues that are sometimes only loosely related but that need to be addressed in an Old Testament theology for Christians.

Things God does or asks the Israelites to do that seem questionable (the compromised reputation of God). Over recent decades, the rise of strident attacks by neo-atheists and the antagonistic rhetoric of the blogosphere have contributed to increased accusations against the character of God as portrayed in the Old Testament. Christians have therefore been confronted more publicly about the questionable morality of the God they worship and have often responded with either defenses that prove inadequate or doubt about their own faith, which sometimes leads to the renunciation of Christianity. Our misunderstanding of the Old Testament and our inadequately developed hermeneutic have made us vulnerable, and we have been caught off guard and are reeling under the blows.[1] Admitting defeat and abandoning God, the faith, and the Old Testament is not the solution; instead, we should reinforce a proper understanding of the Old Testament.

We all know the most familiar accusations:

✦ What kind of God would command his people to commit genocide? (Deuteronomy, Joshua)

✦ What kind of God would tell someone to sacrifice his son? (Gen 22)

✦ What kind of God would wipe out the innocent firstborn sons of Egypt? (Ex 11–12)

✦ What kind of God would send bears to slaughter children (mockers though they be) in response to a prophet's overreactive curse? (2 Kings 2)

✦ What kind of God would mandate the execution of a son for rebellion against his parents? (Deut 21:18-21)

✦ What kind of God would judge all humanity guilty and worthy of eternal punishment because two people ate a piece of fruit?

✦ What kind of God would flood the world, killing innumerable innocents, rather than address situations on a case-by-case basis? (Gen 6–8)

The list goes on and on. Clearly, they say, such a God is unworthy of worship.

These accusations strike at the core of Christian belief, which maintains that the Bible is God's revelation of himself. If the God of the Old Testament does not even have the moral sensibilities of good people today, why should we be committed to him? Or perhaps the Old Testament is just a picture of God devised by Israelites, and we should reject it as primitive and in need of updating? This is not the place to present a treatment of each of these passages, but we can make some observations about response strategies.

---

[1]Described and discussed in Glenn Paauw, *Saving the Bible from Ourselves* (Downers Grove, IL: InterVarsity Press, 2016).

One of the most important responses is to analyze the form that the argument is taking in any particular attack. What do we *expect* God to do? What kind of God *would* be worthy of worship? At the same time, however, and more pertinent to this book, it is important to insist on an informed and careful interpretation of the passages. Since the Old Testament *is* an ancient text written to another culture, it is possible, if not likely, that we will misunderstand some of what is going on as we navigate ancient language and culture. Even when we deal with the people around us it is easy to misjudge their actions or motives, so we should not be surprised that we are inclined to jump to unwarranted conclusions when we read an ancient text.

Perhaps the best example of this misunderstanding exists in the ways that people today are inclined to think about the conquest of Canaan. On closer examination, however, we can discover that the people of the land were not being punished, and the Israelites were not commanded to commit genocide.[2] More care in translation and a deeper understanding of the ancient world and its literature cast these passages in a very different light.

Other strategies involve coming to a better understanding of the literature of the Old Testament in relation to that of the ancient world. In the list above, a number of the issues will be understood differently when we read them in light of the ancient genres such as law, narrative, and conquest accounts. Even so, however, the passages remain complicated.

One problem is that Christians tend to respond to attacks defensively with explanations developed from apologetics. This is a problem because skeptics, by their very nature, are not inclined to work hard at understanding the nuances of a text. When we approach the text this way (arguing against skeptics), too often we end up making it seem as though the Old Testament can be proven or that God can be vindicated (theodicy)—both futile pursuits. The Old Testament is to be believed, not proved. God is to be trusted. He doesn't need vindication from us, nor does he need to conform to our modern sensibilities.

The Old Testament is not trying to prove itself true or to justify the actions of God. It is presenting truth as it reveals God's plans and purposes, and it ultimately helps us to become acquainted with this God and to join

---

[2]Detailed treatment available in John H. Walton and J. Harvey Walton, *The Lost World of the Israelite Conquest* (Downers Grove, IL: InterVarsity Press, 2017).

him. Portraying him as a violent, immoral being is a distorted misreading of the text. But then again, it is also a distortion of the text to portray him as a beneficent, moral being. He transcends such classifications. Morality cannot be used as autonomous criteria to which God conforms or to which he fails to conform.

Issues that God seems to tolerate because he doesn't institute change. A second modern discussion is less concerned with what God *does* in the Old Testament than with what he *doesn't* do. Why does God not abolish slavery? Why does he not establish gender equality rather than reinforce patriarchy? To address this common concern, we have to begin with understanding what the law *is*.[3] The Torah is not legislation as we think of it today (see chapter five). The legal collections in the ancient Near East were wisdom treatises designed to help practitioners (in this case, judges) know how to make wise decisions. Such approaches are found in the list literature, whether they deal with language (lexical lists), divination, or disease.[4] The response to the pedagogical purpose of this type of literature was not obedience but comprehension (i.e., wisdom). What would order in society (or ritual) look like in this particular cultural context? The examples that occur in the list do not provide a comprehensive system; they are hypothetical as they circumscribe the discipline.

When we look at the Torah this way, we can see that it pertains to order rather than dictating legislation or morality. It was never the intention of the Torah to dictate an ideal society for Israel or for anyone else. We cannot use the lists in the Torah to infer or extrapolate abstractions. Even if numerous principles could be identified from the Torah, they would not really be the point of the text. I have elaborated on the nature of legal treatises elsewhere and summarized those findings in chapter five above. They were not canonized simply to preserve the record of their contents. As an analogy, we do not read historical narratives as merely a record of who did what, even though recording who did what is the purpose of the narrative genre. Just as the historical books were not preserved for the purpose of allowing posterity to

---

[3]For more information, see ibid.

[4]Jean Bottéro, *Mesopotamia*, trans. Zainab Bahrani and Marc Van de Mieroop (Chicago: University of Chicago Press, 1992), 161-69; Marc Van De Mieroop, *Philosophy Before the Greeks* (Princeton, NJ: Princeton University Press, 2015), 175; John H. Walton, *Ancient Near Eastern Thought in the Old Testament* (Grand Rapids: Baker, 2006), 287-88.

make accurate documentaries, so the legal wisdom of the Pentateuch was not preserved for the purpose of allowing posterity to reconstruct the governing principles of Israelite society. The literature in context is indeed supposed to shape Israelite society, but it is not supposed to provide a template by which anyone in any place or time can construct "God's ideal society."[5]

The value of Scripture as Scripture is found in its revelation of God and God's purposes. In the legal treatises, this revelation is not found in the demand for or prohibition of certain behaviors, and it does not seek to dictate the ideal shape of society. The Torah, then, is not approving slavery. Israel has slavery (far different from the institution in more recent history), and the Torah gives some guidelines about maintaining order in a society that has slavery. It dictates how slavery should function in a society where that particular function of slavery is indicative of a stable social order.

In a similar manner, the Torah does not privilege monarchy over democracy, agricultural economy over market economy, arranged marriages over marriages for personal preference, monogamy over polygamy, or patriarchalism over gender equality. It provides neither a portrait of nor a template for an ideal society, and since it is embedded as stipulations in a covenant, it provides no mandate for anyone else to construct such a society or base a society on it (see discussion in chapter four). We have been guilty of criticizing the Bible using a criterion that does not apply to the Bible and on the basis of objectives that it never intended. The purpose of the Torah is not to provide a moral system or a social system. Wisdom, not legislation, is its goal, and it serves Israel by instructing it in how it can reflect the identity that God has given it by conferring a holy status on it.

Once we establish what the Torah is and is not doing, we can still question why God did not do something different. For example, why did he not abolish slavery? Of course, we cannot enter the mind of God to examine his reasons, and we certainly cannot stand in judgment of his reasons, whatever they may have been. We trust his wisdom. God has created people in his image to work alongside him to bring order to the world. Just as he did not reveal remedies for bodily ills (e.g., antibiotics), he did not give a remedy to society's ills—he expects us to discover them.

---

[5]Adapted from Walton and Walton, *Lost World of the Israelite Conquest*, proposition 4.

Issues that arise today that we want the Bible to address (e.g., Bible and science, gender issues, moral questions): How to deal with modern discussions that invoke Old Testament theology. We have discussed our mistaken ideas of what God did and did not do, so we now turn our attention to the use of proof texts from the Old Testament, especially when they are invoked to support a position as "biblical" or condemn it as "unbiblical." Before we consider using the Old Testament this way, we need to ask ourselves an important question: Does the Old Testament anticipate the issues of today and provide answers to them? If we return to the "cultural river" analogy that we used earlier, we can draw the conclusion that the Old Testament does not anticipate the specific issues that face us today. To claim that it did, we would also have to contend that it anticipated the specific issues of every culture of every time and place. I don't know that anyone is prepared to make such a claim, and I cannot imagine how it would be defended.

Therefore, when we consider how to use the Old Testament in relation to modern issues, there are a few possibilities.

1. Some consider the entire Old Testament to be as valid today as it was for the ancient Israelites. These people want to build society on the "biblical" model and look for proof texts to address modern issues. In this scenario, nothing is considered irrelevant due to cultural relativity; everything is universally valid. The problem with this approach is in its all too obvious impracticality.

2. Some, since they do not consider the Old Testament God's Word, take the other extreme and conclude that nothing is valid for us today. The Bible is simply a document of antiquity, a cultural artifact that is not normative in any way.

3. A third group, and the majority of Christians, conclude that some parts of the Old Testament (as well as parts of the New Testament) are culturally relative and others are not. The problem with this approach is devising consistent criteria for deciding which is which. If we retain only what we think is appropriate, then we remove the transformative power of the text to lift us out of our comfort levels. Others try to use the New Testament as the guide. In this approach, something in the Old Testament retains its significance if it is repeated in the New Testament, or

it retains its significance if it is not discarded in the New Testament. However, either of these variations faces the difficulty that the New Testament does not explicitly have the role of screening the Old Testament. The absence of one discussion or another may simply be coincidental rather than determinative. The New Testament cannot be placed in the role of passing judgment on the Old Testament.

4. A fourth group, in sharp contradistinction to group two, maintains a high view of Scripture and yet concludes, based on a desire for hermeneutical consistency, that everything in the text must be considered culturally relative. In this view, none of the text provides normative propositions for us today. The problem with this lies in the desire to preserve the significance of the Old Testament as Scripture (unlike group two). If none of it actually addresses our world, then what good is it to us?

I have favored this last option and have tried to demonstrate how the Bible remains Scripture (contra group two) and retains relevance to a modern Christian audience. As laid out in chapter five, the Torah does not offer stipulations for all people of all times and cultures. It provides stipulations for the covenant between Israel and Yahweh that was designed to help them to survive and thrive in sacred space. These stipulations are therefore relative to both the covenant relationship and to the presence of God in the temple. None of these stipulations are directed to us, and therefore they cannot be used as proof texts to determine positions on modern issues. That is, they do not offer a "biblical" position; they offer a "covenant of Israel" position. This does not mean that such statements have no meaning to us at all—it only means that since they are culturally embedded, they cannot be used as proof texts to decide modern issues. The Old Testament cannot offer us the final word on homosexuality any more than on the mixing of linen and wool. It does not give us a position on abortion any more than it offers authoritative teaching on sexual contact with women in menstruation. The law does not function like that for us today. It cannot instruct us on the ethical acceptability or unacceptability of lying to save a life through narratives such as Rahab and the spies at Jericho. It is *all* culturally relative. We have to arrive at answers a different way.

How, then, can we determine a "biblical" stance on modern issues? We can't. But that does not mean that the Old Testament becomes irrelevant to us. The Old Testament has the role of instructing us concerning God's plans and purposes in the world. It illustrates the means that God used to carry out his work in the world. The specifics of that plan are now taking place under the new covenant, but familiarity with the old covenant can still help us to understand his plans and purposes and to participate in them. In the process we can become acquainted with the sort of God that he is. As we seek to be worthy partners, the Holy Spirit can transform us and help us to become more effective in our participation and in how we honor God as his representatives.

Then the question on any given modern issue concerns how a person transformed through the work of the Holy Spirit and participating in the plans and purposes of God for the world responds to such an issue. This is true whether it pertains to allegiance to political parties, reactions to immigration policies, questions of same-sex marriage, socialized medicine vis-à-vis abortifacients, stem cell research, conservation, climate change, and so on. Different Christians will arrive at different positions. We may find, however, that there are *perspectives* on these issues that are Christian more than *positions* that are Christian. Moreover, we may infer some Christian perspectives from our understanding about the cultural logic that was represented in Old Testament laws, but we will not thereby find hard and fast Christian positions.

Consequently, the Bible is not an answer book for modern issues, though its revelation can guide us to respond to them as faithful people of God. We want to represent him well, not follow the path of least resistance. Likewise, the Bible is not a book that provides a moral system, though its revelation can guide us to be morally responsible people as we seek to live into the identity that God has given us. When modern disputes invoke theology or biblical passages to offer a resolution, we must fall back on a consistent hermeneutic as we advocate for a proper role of Scripture. If the Bible is not designed to be a list of rules that provides a comprehensive moral system, we must refrain from treating it as one. If the Bible is not a science textbook, we must cease and desist from using the Bible to formulate or evaluate science.

Is the Old Testament primitive and obsolete? Has God changed? The Old Testament is ancient, but it is not primitive. In fact, it is startlingly sophisticated despite its antiquity. It is not obsolete, because God's plans and purposes have not changed; they have simply unfolded. Even speaking specifically of the law, it is not so much obsolete as particular in its focus. It pertains to Israel, but it retains its significance to us as God's revelation, even if not as a social system or as covenant stipulations. God has not changed; he has not learned anything over time; he has not improvised; and he has not experimented. His story is not filled with trial and error, and his purposes have remained fixed through the scope of time. He has not developed, and he has not grown more mature and sensible. These all-too-common perceptions about God at times reflect an inclination to make God in our own image, or at least may suffer from an overliteral reading of anthropopathic statements.

Is the Old Testament so culturally embedded that it is no longer relevant to us? As we have maintained and tried to demonstrate throughout this book, the Old Testament is culturally embedded but retains a message that transcends its cultural location. We dare not keep it at arm's length or read it only with antiquarian or academic interests. But likewise, we dare not be naive or casual about unpacking its continuing relevance. The message must be understood through the consistent application of sound principles of interpretation, principles committed to the authority of the text. The challenge has always been *how* we should identify its relevance—that transcendent message that was valid and understood by the original Israelite audience and can be understood and embraced by God's people today. This book has offered a proposal for such a reading.

MODERN THEOLOGY

The focus of this book on discovering the authority of the Old Testament based on discernment of the author's intentions has put its conclusions in a contrasting position to what we might find when we read some of the theological works of the church (from its earliest years until today). For some this raises worries: Is the dogma of the church at risk in this approach?

First we need to recognize the nature of the tasks that theologians have undertaken through the centuries. Often they did not restrict themselves to discerning the intentions of the original author in his context. In other words, theirs was not undertaken as a strictly analytical task. They were working at constructing theology: what Christians have believed and ought to believe. Good theology is always ostensibly rooted in the biblical text. But since the Bible is not by its nature a construction of theology (though it can be a source for theological ideas), the biblical foundation is only the beginning. Constructing theology requires reason and employs tradition and experience, among other things, in order to establish the shape of belief as it grows from that biblical foundation. Consequently, theologians are often, in the end, more interested in defining true beliefs for today than in exegetical determinations of an author's intention in context. They are at times more focused on the shape of the doctrine than on the communicative intentions of the human authors in their cultural and literary context. We may think those two should be related, but there are complications, which leads us to the next point.

Second, theologians focus on what our beliefs ought to be, and they therefore, of necessity, have to consider the whole of the canon. They examine the text in light of where we stand today, so, of course, all of the data from the entire canon, Old Testament and New Testament alike, must be considered as well as the deliberations of the ages. The discipline of historical theology is descriptive of Christian belief and theological developments of past ages; constructive theology brings the faith into conversation with other discourses for the sake of specific and targeted challenges: intelligibility, coherence, race relations, sexuality, and so on.

Consequently, and third, for the full scope of data to be brought to the construction of theology, the relationship of Christ to the Old Testament and the Old Testament to Christ would naturally be of interest. Certain aspects of the Old Testament receive illumination that would not have been available until the coming of Christ. Other aspects can be seen differently after the coming of the Holy Spirit and in light of the church. These are all legitimate perspectives to bring to the task of theology. At the same time, just as Christian writers throughout the centuries were not necessarily focused on identifying the contextual intentions of the author, so the New Testament writers, as often as they engaged with the Old Testament, were not generally seeking to unpack the contextual intentions of those ancient authors. Instead they were focused on the meaning of those texts in light of the coming of Christ.[6] That is a legitimate enterprise, but it is not the same objective that exegetes (who analyze the contextual intentions of the authors) are pursuing.

The question, then, is how these elaborated perspectives on which theology is constructed stand in juxtaposition to the author's intentions, on which we have been focusing. I propose that the solution is to be found in a both-and approach rather than in an either/or approach. We should be interested both in the authority of the original author's intention and in the construction of sound theology on the basis of the whole canon, the role of Christ, and the contributions of Christian thinkers throughout the ages. In the Protestant tradition, the former has authority, and the latter, the historical attempts to construct theology, does not. But while it does not have final authority, it still weighs quite significantly. And this is increasingly recognized, even by evangelical Protestants. The theological enterprise is of utmost importance, and careful exegesis of the author's intentions is not a threat to the final construction of theology. Neither contextual interpretation nor theological formulation has priority—they are equally necessary and significant parts of our Christian understanding of the text. Contextual interpretation must be retained because the Old Testament was not without meaning or authority before Christ came, and the coming of Christ did not change its meaning. Yet the Old Testament is insufficient for formulating theology today, though it has its unique contributions to make to our theological understanding.

The solution that I propose is that we give attention to each of the stages and recognize the role and significance of each. Study needs to begin with careful analysis of the text in its context—what the author intended to communicate and what it meant to the audience that received it. This message that we seek is the product of the work of the Holy Spirit and has authority. It cannot be neglected or overturned. As God's plan unfolds, theology must continue to be dynamically formulated. The work of Christ must be seen as taking its proper place. The remainder of the canon must be factored in appropriately, and the conversations concerning the development of doctrine (with all of its twists and turns, disagreements, and sometimes missteps) should be taken into consideration as theology is formulated.

---

[6]Richard B. Hays, *Echoes of Scripture in the Gospels* (Waco, TX: Baylor University Press, 2016).

In this approach, an interpreter can never stop with the technical, academic analysis of the language and context of the Old Testament. Given the belief that the text is indeed the living and active Word of God, we are under obligation to pursue all of the theological significance that develops and not only to understand the full theological teaching but also to embrace it as the basis for our faith and life. We move beyond the technical aspects of exegesis to the formulation of theology and accept that formulation as *our* theology, a theology characterized not just by affirmation but by the life we live. This takes us right back to the objective from the very beginning: the revelation of Scripture, the revelation of God's plans and purposes, is designed so that we may become participants in those plans and purposes. If that is not the outcome, we have failed to carry interpretation to its expected result.

To conclude this section, we should consider how we respond when the result of a contextual analysis of a text appears to stand in contradiction to how the text has been used to construct theology. We will use the example of the Holy Spirit to explore this conundrum.

The Israelites of the Old Testament did not have any revelation that led them to believe in the trinitarian nature of God. They knew nothing of the second or third persons of the Trinity. Even as messianic thinking developed, they did not consider the Messiah to be divine. They did not consider the "angel of the Lord" as the preincarnate Christ, and they did not think of the "spirit of the Lord" as the divine Holy Spirit. Furthermore, they had their own ideas about the identification of the angel of the Lord and the spirit of the Lord. Here we will focus on the on the example of the spirit of the Lord.[7]

In the Old Testament the "spirit of the Lord" (sometimes the "spirit of God") occurs with some frequency.[8] Scholarly contextual analysis concludes that it represents the immanent manifestation of God energizing and

---

[7]For an excellent treatment of the former, see H. D. McDonald, "Christology and the 'Angel of the Lord,'" in *Current Issues in Biblical and Patristic Interpretation*, ed. G. Hawthorne (Grand Rapids: Eerdmans, 1975), 324-35.

[8]For a thorough study see D. Firth and P. Wegner, eds., *Presence, Power and Promise: The Role of the Spirit of God in the Old Testament* (Downers Grove, IL: InterVarsity Press, 2011), including my chapter, "The Ancient Near Eastern Background of the Spirit of the Lord in the Old Testament," 38-67, from which the following comments are adapted.

motivating (usually select individuals) to execute his plan. By endowing life, authority, or strength, the Spirit effectuates the kingdom of God, including predominantly God's presence, power, and plan. In the ancient Near East no specific agent (i.e., a spirit of the gods) is identified, but the gods likewise are viewed as providing life, authority, and strength. Most consider the plans of deity in the ancient Near East to be of an ad hoc nature, but any king's role and any kingdom's success are understood as dependent on the presence and power provided through divine agency.

Given this contextual understanding of the spirit of the Lord in the Old Testament, we are now in a position to compare and contrast how the Old Testament occurrences are used in constructing theology. Christian theologians readily identify the spirit of the Lord with the Holy Spirit, since, as mentioned above, they are typically more concerned about a canonical view of theology than about contextual exegetical analysis.

Though there is no trinitarian perspective in Israelite theology, we will find both continuity and discontinuity when we compare the spirit of the Lord in the Old Testament to the Holy Spirit in the New Testament and Christian theology. Interestingly, we will also find continuity between the Holy Spirit and some of the ideas that we found in the ancient Near East that did not apply to the Old Testament spirit of the Lord.

Table 8.1. Portrayals of the spirit/Spirit

Functions	Ancient Near East	Spirit of the Lord—OT	Holy Spirit—NT
Embodiment	yes	yes	yes (more)
Energizing	yes	yes	yes
Essence	yes	no	yes
Emanation	yes	no	no
Personification	yes	no	yes
Qualified agency	no	yes	yes

Most notable from the comparison in table 8.1:

✦ The extent of the Holy Spirit's embodiment (indwelling) compares more favorably to the ancient Near East than to the spirit of the Lord.

✦ The spirit of the Lord does not confer the essence of deity, yet this essence is present in the ancient Near East and in the Holy Spirit.

✦ The Near Eastern—and especially Egyptian—literature personifies the
endowing agent of the gods. The Old Testament does not personify the
spirit of the Lord, though the New Testament presents the Holy Spirit as
a person of the Godhead.

Drawing these significant distinctions between the spirit of the Lord and the
Holy Spirit does not mean that the spirit of the Lord was never actually the
Holy Spirit. New Testament references, such as Peter's Pentecost sermon,
identify the work of the Holy Spirit with certain Old Testament passages
concerning the spirit of the Lord. But Peter is not doing contextual exegesis;
he is proposing an understanding of what he is witnessing that is informed
by knowledge of the Old Testament as well as by the assurances of Jesus that
he will send a Comforter. Here we have been discussing textual interpretation—that is, how the Old Testament audience would have understood the
spirit of the Lord in their context—not the ontological nature of the spiritual
entity. Old Testament authors occasionally refer to the spirit of the Lord as
the "holy" spirit (Ps 51:11; Is 63:10-11), not through a burst of trinitarian insight but because in those contexts the spirit of the Lord is the manifestation
of God's presence, which is intrinsically holy.

Even in the New Testament, we find that the Gospels portray the Spirit
more in the already-established pattern of the spirit of the Lord in the Old
Testament than in the yet-undeveloped trinitarian doctrine relating to the
Holy Spirit (in that time Christ had not yet ascended to send the Comforter).
Passages for consideration include Luke 1:35 (Mary); John 1:33 (Jesus); Luke
1:15 (John); Luke 4:1 (Jesus); and perhaps even John 20:22 (the disciples). Just
as the Spirit in the Old Testament functions much in the same way as the
endowment of divine power in the ancient Near East, while also demonstrating theological innovation and sophistication in its differences, so the
Holy Spirit (third person of the Trinity) functions much in the same way as
the endowment of the spirit of the Lord in the Old Testament, while also
demonstrating theological innovation and sophistication in its differences.

It is important to note that the theology of the Holy Spirit and its role as a
person of the Trinity are not undermined if we do not identify the spirit of
the Lord with the Holy Spirit. These doctrines (pneumatology) are not dependent on the identification of the spirit of the Lord as the Holy Spirit. That
interpreters through the ages made such a connection is of no consequence

for the meaning of the Old Testament text (though it has theological significance in terms of the continuity it provides for trinitarian theology throughout biblical history). When New Testament authors identify the spirit of the Lord in some Old Testament passage as the Holy Spirit, we readily accept that identification as inspired insight about the Holy Spirit's activity. However, that does not mean that every occurrence of the spirit of the Lord in the Old Testament is a manifestation of the Holy Spirit. The Holy Spirit's role and identity can be fully established on the basis of New Testament material and are worked out in the trinitarian discussions that permeate theological formulation throughout the history of the church.

The interpretation of the spirit of the Lord as simply an extension and manifestation of the power of God, rather than as the Holy Spirit, does not contradict theology, though it does offer an alternative interpretation of some passages. But remember that theologians are not as interested in the contextual interpretation of the human author's intentions as they are in theological truth. If the New Testament does not identify all occurrences of the spirit of the Lord in the Old Testament as manifestations of the Holy Spirit (which it doesn't), then only the occurrences of the spirit of the Lord that are specified in the New Testament as the work of the Holy Spirit can be safely and confidently so adopted as references to the Holy Spirit. But even then, the Old Testament author's intention is not represented in that adoption. Furthermore, the role of the spirit of the Lord as understood by the author and the audience should not be easily discarded, since it is embedded in authoritative text. Additional understanding is legitimate; replacement is more problematic. Ideally, to do justice to the whole of Scripture, it would be best for theology not to use the Old Testament passages of the spirit of the Lord to build the theology of the Holy Spirit. This will not change the theology, but it will result in different interpretations of some of the passages in the Old Testament.

If we restrict ourselves to building the theology of the Holy Spirit through the passages that speak specifically of the Holy Spirit, we will alleviate the risk of reading aspects of the Holy Spirit's work into Old Testament passages that concern the spirit of the Lord.

For example, in theology it is important to see the Holy Spirit as indwelling. In the Old Testament, the spirit of the Lord does not indwell. If we are not careful to distinguish the two, we may misinterpret Old Testament passages by thinking that the spirit of the Lord is engaged in indwelling. A quick comparison will help make the point (see table 8.2).

Table 8.2.

OT spirit of the Lord	Continuity/Discontinuity	Holy Spirit in NT and Theology
empowering (Samson)	continuity	empowering—Acts 1:8
authorizing (Saul and David)	continuity	authorizing
communicating (numerous prophets)	continuity	communicating—2 Pet 1:21
manifestation of divine action	discontinuity	personal
clothing, coming upon (numerous judges)	discontinuity	indwelling—Rom 8:9
involved in creation— Gen 1:2; Ps 33:6	no parallel	
	no parallel	sealing—Eph 1:13
	no parallel	convicting—Jn 16:8
	no parallel	regenerating—Jn 3:5-8
	no parallel	interceding—Rom 8:26
	no parallel	sanctifying—2 Thess 2:13

None of the Old Testament characteristics of the spirit of the Lord would cause difficulties if applied to the New Testament context. In contrast, however, nearly half of the New Testament/theological understandings of the Holy Spirit would be inappropriate to attach to the activity of the spirit of the Lord in the Old Testament. Caution with regard to "back-reading" the New Testament into the Old Testament does not impoverish or alter our theology, but this approach can satisfy both text analysts and theologians.

What Kind of God Is He?

The proposal of this book is that the most potent information supplied by the Old Testament is the revelation of God's plans and purposes as they are tracked through his plan as it unfolds. Through this revelation we can derive limited inside knowledge about the God whose purposes and plans are revealed, but it is sufficient to understand how we need to identify with him. This revelation comes with authority, and it is equally valid for both ancient Israelites and modern Christians. It can be understood within the Old

Testament revelation as far as it goes and is not changed by the New Testament (though our perspective is expanded).

We have noted that we are hampered by significant, essential limitations in any attempt to understand the depths of the nature of God and the consistent outworking of the attributes of God (his ways are not our ways, his thoughts not our thoughts, Is 55:8). But we can know him enough to participate with him in his plans and purposes insofar as he has revealed them to us. His plans and purposes bring order, and wisdom offers us ways to promote God's order. The fear of the Lord is the beginning of wisdom because the fear of the Lord leads us to submit to his authority as the center of order. It is not enough to love God; we must submit to him and trust him. We have learned enough to trust him even when we do not understand what he is doing or why; faith and trust kick in where knowledge and understanding fail. This premise is essential, and it is a concept that no skeptic can accept.

As we think about what it means to know God, let us consider the analogy of how we know one another. When we first meet people, we often exchange basic information that gives them a very small part of our story. In a college setting, this often includes items such as hometown, major, residence hall, activities, and so on. By sharing with one another these opening sentences of our story, we begin to know one another, and we gauge how well we know other people by how much of their story we know. People who are considered best friends have come to know each other's stories thoroughly and intimately. Our stories include not just our past but also our present (day-by-day activities) and our future (plans, aspirations, hopes, and dreams). Spouses typically begin their relationship with an insatiable desire to hear all of the other's stories. Unfortunately, that passion often wanes as marriage stretches on, and both lives and stories begin to seem more mundane. Similarly, in a healthy friendship the story of the other is important, not because the content of the story is of deep interest but specifically because it is the other person's story.

Nevertheless, no matter how intimately we know someone else's story, and no matter how passionate or insatiable we are about getting more of it, we often find the other person to still be enigmatic in significant ways. Someone may well be able to predict what his or her spouse will do or say in a given situation, but no matter how many years we have enjoyed a deep relationship, and no matter how many stories we have shared and repeated, we can still be surprised or mystified.

God has also given glimpses of himself to us by sharing his story: past, present, and future. We know God and what God does through his story, and the Bible has provided us with that story. In this way we know about many things he has done in the past and about what he plans for the future, and this story gives us a modicum of understanding of what he is like. But if people can remain enigmatic to one another even after a long and intimate life together in relationship, how much more will God's ways remain mysterious to us. Just as with the people who are close to us, we cannot know comprehensively who God is, but we can get a sense of what he is like as we learn what he does.

God's story may not always be scintillating to us, but it is important. It is his story, and he is sharing it as a means of communicating in the relationship that we share. We have come to understand that he likewise delights in hearing our stories as we communicate to him (prayer). It doesn't matter that he knows all the content already. It is the sharing of it that is important.

Consequently, we can say that since God has shared his story with us, we have become aware of his purposes and plans (to the extent that he has revealed them) and through that knowledge have come to believe that we have a sense of him—of what he is like, what he is inclined to do, and what he expects of us. He knows us comprehensively; we know him only in part. We know what he wants of us—to be partners with him in his Great Enterprise. We also know the sort of people that he expects us to be as we live out our identity in him.

We also have a good idea of what to expect of him. For example, we can recall the repeated affirmation of the way Israel perceived its God. It first appears in Exodus 34:6-7:

> And he passed in front of Moses, proclaiming, "The LORD, the LORD, the compassionate and gracious God, slow to anger, abounding in love and faithfulness, maintaining love to thousands, and forgiving wickedness, rebellion and sin. Yet he does not leave the guilty unpunished; he punishes the children and their children for the sin of the parents to the third and fourth generation."

The context is the aftermath of the golden calf incident. In Exodus 33:18, after Moses has interceded on behalf of the Israelites, he asks to see the glory of Yahweh. Yahweh indicates that he cannot show his face. But all his goodness (*ṭôb*) will pass before Moses, and he will proclaim his name (Ex 33:19-20). When that actually occurs in Exodus 34:6-7, his name is proclaimed as promised, and the "goodness" that passes in front of Moses is represented in that familiar list of attributes.

How is this list his "goodness"? In chapter six we briefly discussed the idea that "good" pertains to how something functions in our lives and experience. When God designated creation as "good" in Genesis 1, he was affirming that he had established order and that everything was functioning the way that he intended. "Goodness" (as represented by the Hebrew word *ṭôb*) pertains to a point of equilibrium, balance, stability, and the benefit that results. Yahweh's goodness is expressed in the list of attributes insofar as they comprise the two sides of the conundrum posed by God's observed work in the world; that is, how God decides when to be merciful, compassionate, forgiving, and patient, and when to judge sin and punish evildoers. At the fulcrum of that dilemma is the goodness of God. It is good and right that God should be compassionate; it is also good and right that wrongdoers should be punished. Mercy and justice must work hand in hand. The perfect balance of each is the measure of God's goodness, and these attributes of God work together in perfect harmony. That is the goodness of God. God demonstrates his goodness, and that is what we can know about him, even if we do not understand how it all works. As Paul affirms, "We know that in all things God works for the good of those who love him, who have been called according to his purpose" (Rom 8:28). Reading this, we need to understand that *good* does not mean "happiness"; it means "proper functioning in the created order." If the proper functioning doesn't make us happy, that's our problem.

In Psalm 86 the psalmist reiterates the list of attributes found in Exodus 34.[9] In this lament, the psalmist is praying for a restored equilibrium and for order to be returned to his life. We can see that even though he lacks understanding of why God has not acted on his behalf (i.e., his lack of understanding of God), he nevertheless trusts God (Ps 86:4) and relies on him

---

[9]Note that they also appear in Jon 4, though there the prophet assesses them negatively, disappointed that God has acted that way toward the Ninevites rather than choosing the proclaimed judgment.

(Ps 86:11), which is the appropriate response to a lack of understanding. The actual list of God's attributes in Psalm 86:15 is followed by a petition for mercy (based on the psalmist's claim that he has been faithful) and a request for a sign of God's "goodness" (the abstraction, *ṭôbâ*), which is also reminiscent of Exodus 33–34. In other words, this psalm offers further insight concerning the extent that we can and cannot know God. Relying on his faithfulness and trusting him are the responses of those with imperfect knowledge, yet these responses also imply that there is something to which God is expected to be faithful. That expectation is dependent on God teaching his "way" (Ps 86:11), and the expected result of God's teaching is that his people will walk in his paths (Mic 4:2).[10] In sum, when God teaches his ways, his people will discover how to be participants in what he is doing.

He is a God with plans for his people, for the world, for history, and for the cosmos. We can know this part of his plan as he reveals it both in the Old Testament and the New Testament, and we can trust him to fulfill that plan, though he often does so in surprising ways. He is a God who is worthy of our devotion and commitment, even when his ways are unclear to us. He is a God who defies definition, and any list of attributes is too limiting, any pretension of knowledge presumptuous. The extent to which we feel we have grasped the depths of his being is likely the extent to which we have made the mistake of crafting him in our own image.

CONCLUSIONS

To begin, we draw attention to some of the issues that have been raised throughout the book that help us to see the distinctions between Old Testament and New Testament theology, which will then lead us to consider the ways in which the Old Testament provides what the New Testament does not.

Brief summaries of ten ways in which Old Testament theology differs from New Testament theology.

✦ *No Trinity.* The understanding of the Trinity is entailed in the recognition of Christ as incarnate God, in consequence of which the Holy Spirit is understood as having been sent to indwell Christians. In the Old Testament, God's

---

[10]For other adumbrations see 1 Sam 12:23; Ps 25:8; 27:11; 32:8; 119:33; Is 28:26.

Prayer

Yahweh is a God who welcomes the prayers of his people. He is worthy of the worship we express, and he assures us that he listens and cares about the heartbreak of his people. Nevertheless, he does not gain anything through prayer. What, then, is prayer all about in the theology of the Old Testament? As we peruse the Psalms, we find the kinds of prayers that were well known in the ancient world, and these psalms have been extensively analyzed by type (e.g., praise, lament) in biblical scholarship. Unfortunately, the long-debated relationship between psalms and rituals or festivals has not been resolved and cannot be our guide. Therefore, instead of trying to identify the setting for these prayers, we should try to understand their theological content.

What do the psalmists pray for?[a] Asking the question that way already skews the discussion. The prayers of God's people are not always "for" something, and any question about "answers" to prayer only therefore addresses certain kinds of prayers. However, in general the lament psalms include petition. In these we note that the psalmists do not pray for some material good or personal advancement that they desire. They will occasionally pray for healing for themselves (not for others), but their petitions generally request that God restore order to their lives, often by resolving problems with their "enemies." They do not pray that warfare be ended, that poverty be relieved, or that injustice to someone else be requited. They do not pray for God to solve the problems of the world or for the spread of the kingdom. They do not pray that others come to the worship of Yahweh or join the covenant community. In sum, they do not pray for the things on which moderns are inclined to focus their prayers. Nevertheless, it is important to recognize that the book of Psalms is not in the canon (Israel's or the church's) to provide model prayers. When Jesus is asked for a model prayer, he neither points them to the book of Psalms nor offers one of the psalms. The role of the psalms in the Old Testament is theological; they reveal information about God and about prayers. It is not a "how to" book. Christians have traditionally drawn heavily from the book of Psalms for their hymns and prayers, and that is not misguided.

Such prayers and hymns are productive in our Christian life and worship. Even as we use them, however, we must not risk losing sight of the role they serve in the Old Testament.

What the Israelites do pray for is justice in their own experiences. In effect, they pray for God to be God (at least in accordance to their expectations about what God is like). The psalms reflect through many diverse genres the assertion that Yahweh rules, whether in a person's life circumstances, in the affairs of the nation, or in the cosmic realm. As a result, they ask that God teach them his ways and that he lead them in the right way. This suggests that their prayers are also concerned with the sort of person they are.

In keeping with this, we can evaluate the focus of our own prayers. Though psalms do not contain model prayers, the theology that they offer suggests that our prayers should perhaps reflect a greater concern for God's kingship and the identity we have in him. Being in partnership with God should transform us and give a different perspective. We should be less concerned with our personal success, achievements, attainments, comfort, or benefits, and more concerned with the sort of people we are. With respect to our prayers, then, we should recognize that God is God and call on him to play his role, and we should recognize that we are his people and that he makes us fit for our role. As those two results are manifested, order is maintained.

We conclude by turning brief attention to what apparently became the priestly blessing that Yahweh instructed Aaron and his sons to use to bless the people:

> The LORD bless you
>> and keep you;
> the LORD make his face shine on you
>> and be gracious to you;
> the LORD turn his face toward you
>> and give you peace. (Num 6:24-26)

This *is* given as a model prayer. We can see that it is a prayer for God's blessing on his people, for his favor and grace to be bestowed on his people, and for their enjoyment of the order that they experience in the absence of fear ("peace").

In other words, prayer represents the conversations of partners in a relationship. It is not about us wielding power by getting God to change our circumstances. Prayer is about stepping into God's perspective and plan and asking for him to change us.

---

[a]The prayers of the various ancient Near Eastern cultures are gradually becoming more available in English translation and analysis. Current important volumes include John L. Foster, *Hymns, Prayers, and Songs: An Anthology of Ancient Egyptian Poetry,* SBLWAW (Atlanta: SBL Press, 1995); K. A. Kitchen, *Poetry of Ancient Egypt* (Jonsered: Paul Åströms, 1999); I. Singer, *Hittite Prayers,* SBLWAW (Atlanta: SBL Press, 2002); Takayoshi Oshima, *Babylonian Prayers to Marduk* (Tübingen: Mohr Siebeck, 2011); A. Lenzi, *Reading Akkadian Prayers and Hymns* (Atlanta: SBL Press, 2011); K. van der Toorn, *Sin and Sanction in Israel and Mesopotamia* (Assen: Van Gorcum, 1985), including an appendix of *šigû* prayers; Uri Gabbay, *The Eršema Prayers of the First Millennium BC* (Wiesbaden: Harrassowitz, 2015); Uri Gabbay, *Pacifying the Hearts of the Gods: Sumerian Emesal Prayers of the First Millennium BC* (Wiesbaden: Harrassowitz, 2014). Substantial treatments of ancient Near Eastern psalms can also be found in W. Brown, *The Oxford Handbook of the Psalms* (New York: Oxford, 2014), and P. D. Miller, *They Cried to the Lord* (Minneapolis: Fortress, 1994).

---

revelation centered on the idea that there was one God as opposed to a community of gods. The metaphysical models that would make trinitarianism meaningful simply do not exist in the Israelite cultural context. In some passages in the Old Testament, Christians can look back and catch glimpses of some nascent trinitarianism, but such hindsight interpretations cannot be construed as a revelation of God in the Old Testament context and do not factor into the theology of the Old Testament.

✦ *No reward or judgment in the afterlife.* Israelites would have considered the afterlife to be the same for everyone regardless of their good or bad deeds, their covenant standing, or their holiness.

✦ *No concept of original guilt imputed to all.* Nothing in the Old Testament develops the idea that the plight of humanity is to struggle with a sin nature or with the result of original sin that spreads to all because of the actions of Adam and Eve. Sin is a pervasive reality, but it is seen more often in relation to a group than to an individual. Even when individuals commit offense, it often has an impact on the group to which they belong (e.g., Achan).

✦ *No developed Satan.* Due to the New Testament we are inclined to identify
Satan as the devil. However, there is no role for the devil in Old Testament
theology, and the Hebrew heavenly function of *śāṭān* consequently
should not be associated with the devil in Old Testament contexts. That
idea is not what the Old Testament authors intended to convey. In the Old
Testament, then, *śāṭān* is a much less significant character and really does
not figure in the Israelites' theology at all.

✦ *No mechanism for salvation from sin.* The Israelites did not even think
about being saved from sin. Their sacrifices maintained the sanctity of
the presence of God and allowed them to participate in the community.
They did not recognize sin as something from which they needed to be
saved, and they had no mechanism to do so. Jesus is the only way to be
saved from sin, and they did not see him (or even the Messiah) in that
role. Consequently, they had no hope of heaven. Spending eternity in the
presence of God was not an option that was revealed to Israelites, and it
was not a hope that they cultivated. No hope of heaven or fear of hell
motivated their behavior in this life.

✦ *No indwelling spirit.* The indwelling Holy Spirit can take place once
someone has been prepared for that presence through cleansing from sin.
But that cleansing from sin can only be accomplished through Christ. The
indwelling Spirit was the next stage in the understanding of God's
presence among his people as the temple metaphor concept shifted from
building to people.

✦ *Temple different from church.* The temple was God's dwelling place on
earth. Worship (mostly in the form of rituals) took place there because
he was there. Since the day of Pentecost, however, God's presence is in his
people. The building that they meet in is of little consequence and is not
the place of God's special dwelling. We gather together to worship in
community, but God dwells in his people, not in the church building.

✦ *No evangelism.* The Israelites were not expected to bring other people into
their covenant relationship with Yahweh. Others were allowed entry
under certain conditions, and the prophets anticipated that others would
come. But the role of being a light to the nations did not involve evangel-
izing and especially not proselytizing. Israel stood as the testimony to

Yahweh's plans and purposes, and it would be observed. For example, a book such as Jonah is badly misunderstood if it is interpreted as a call to go forth to bring others into relationship with God.

✦ *Identification of the people of God.* In the Old Testament, Israel is chosen to be the covenanted people of God. That identity is related to their ethnic identity, and circumcision is the marker of that identity. In contrast, the identification of the people of God in the New Testament is based on being "in Christ." This is a kingdom identity based in the new covenant rather than the first-covenant identity based on Torah and the presence of God in the tabernacle/temple. The new covenant has different identity markers.

✦ *God as spirit.* The Old Testament is more interested in divine activity than in the metaphysical descriptions of the divine being. Even though Israelites did not think of God as corporeal (despite the many anthropomorphisms such as hand or eye), they likewise did not classify him as "spirit." When the texts refer to the "spirit of Yahweh," they identify an extension of his person in spirit form, which suggests that the Israelites would not have identified him as spirit. They seemed uninterested in such metaphysical definitions.

Besides the necessity of the Old Testament for understanding the New Testament, and besides the use of the New Testament to shed additional light on the Old Testament, the Old Testament offers insights about what God is doing that cannot be gained from the New Testament alone. We will conclude with a sampling of such issues.

Brief summaries of what we gain from the Old Testament that would be difficult to gain from New Testament alone.

✦ *Nature of God's holiness (identity).* Holiness is discussed occasionally in the New Testament, but the focus is almost always human holiness. Little information is offered on the holiness of God (mostly attributed to God in Revelation). It is the Old Testament that gives us this information.

✦ *Importance of God's presence.* In the New Testament we encounter God's presence in the incarnation (Immanuel) and in the Holy Spirit's indwelling. Discussion of the temple as the place of God's presence is given less attention than all the ways that the temple was failing to play its role. Jesus is the temple, and the church is the temple. But these statements only pick up on the theme of the presence of God without giving the backstory.

✦ *Foundation of God's kingdom.* The kingdom of God in the New Testament grows out of the idea of the messianic kingdom. The messianic kingdom, in turn, has its roots in the Davidic kingdom. The connections are important for understanding what is going on in the teaching about the kingdom of God. The New Testament assumes that its audience has that background and thus does not provide it.

✦ *Scope of God's plan.* If it is on target to think of the Bible as primarily concerned with the revelation of God's plans and purposes (with the expectation that we will become involved as participants), the more we know about his plans and purposes, the better. The New Testament talks mostly about the role of Jesus in the plans and purposes of God, but much more is provided by the Old Testament. A few New Testament passages actually refer back to the Old Testament and recognize the transition:

> In the past God spoke to our ancestors through the prophets at many times and in various ways, but in these last days he has spoken to us by his Son, whom he appointed heir of all things, and through whom also he made the universe. (Heb 1:1-2)

> What advantage, then, is there in being a Jew, or what value is there in circumcision? Much in every way! First of all, the Jews have been entrusted with the very words of God. (Rom 3:1-2)

In such ways the New Testament writers confirm that they are building the superstructure on a foundation that was laid in the Old Testament. Without the Old Testament we would have a truncated view of what God is doing in the world and what he has done for us.

✦ *How God works through his people in the world.* We get a glimpse of this in the narratives of the book of Acts, but they are focused on just a few people. The broad scope of God's story is unfolded in the lives of his people, found in the narratives of the Old Testament. We come to know someone through his or her story, and in the Old Testament God has given us his story as well as the chance to enter into it. It will be difficult to know the God of the New Testament if we have not come to know him through the Old Testament.

✦ *Theology of creation.* Without the Old Testament, we would be able to identify Jesus' role in creation, but little else (Heb 1:2; 11:3 tell us little). Our theology of creation derives from the Old Testament. From it we learn that God has created the world to be sacred space as it receives his presence.

✦ *People as image of God.* Our identity as a human race and our relationship to God all relate to the image of God. Human dignity and human purpose derive from his image. We know who we are and why he has created us through the Old Testament, and none of this is available in the New Testament.

✦ *Ideas communicated through individual books.* Finally, certain Old Testament books contain specific messages that stand as significant perspectives revealed to us by God. Without the book of Job we would be given no guidance concerning how to think about God when we are suffering. Without Proverbs we would have no introduction to the fear of God as the foundation of wisdom, and we would have no instruction concerning all the aspects of wisdom that can guide us through life. Without Ecclesiastes we would not have the resetting of our expectations; without the power of its rhetoric to demonstrate that nothing in this world can bring self-fulfillment and that we should therefore stop seeking self-fulfillment, we would be left to flounder. Its message to enjoy the good things in life *and* adversity as gifts from God helps us to gain a perspective on life that the New Testament never offers.

Having identified these various areas of Old Testament contribution, we must nevertheless recognize that the Testaments are symbiotic. Neither can operate on its own. As in any symbiosis, each has its significant role to play. If the New Testament is not understood in continuity with the Old Testament, what we get from the New Testament is largely the result of the imposition of our own filter; we read it as if it were in our cultural river. If the Old Testament is not understood in its relationship with the New Testament, we risk entangling ourselves in that which, as part and parcel of the old covenant, is no longer descriptive of how our identity in Christ is to be understood. God has given us both Testaments, and we ignore either one at our peril.

Consequently, as Christians, we should read the Old Testament, and we should read it contextually as our first step. But we should not read it on its own. The shape and direction of our partnership with God is found in the new covenant and through Christ. The Old Testament does not provide us with that information, and we should not try to force it to do so. It has authority in what it provides, and it has value and relevance to us that will be available to us as we read the text contextually. But, as we have suggested, contextual reading is only the beginning of the process. Reading the Old Testament in the context of the whole canon will bring us to an understanding of our relationship to God.

In chapter one the analogy of a course syllabus was used to consider the nature of the Old Testament. The result of reading the Old Testament as Christians is that it helps us to grasp the wide range of God's plans and purposes, which will, by extension, help us to understand our role in those plans and purposes. It will not lead us into an understanding of all that God is, but it will provide some guidance concerning what and who he is not.

Above all, we discover what God has told us about what he has always wanted (at least as it pertains to us). We can infer that he created the world as a place for him to dwell, and he created us because he wanted to dwell among us. He did not need us or a place to live, but he embarked on a purposeful plan that involves us. He desires partners who reflect the identity that he has given them, and he wants us to fulfill the role that he has designed for us in his kingdom. We have been created for this, and it is what God expects and desires for us.

In the pages of this book, I hope that the reader has found a new energy, even a passion, for reading the Old Testament. As this book opened, I suggested that many people ignore the Old Testament because they don't know how to read it and don't understand its relevance for them. I hope that this book has remediated that for many readers. Most of all, however, I hope readers have found a focal point as they think about God's plans and purposes.

SUBJECT INDEX

Abram/Abraham, 2, 23, 31, 54,
61, 105-8, 110, 113-18, 122, 132,
134, 137-38, 142, 147, 152,
208, 227, 232, 257-60
Adam, 17, 90, 95, 100, 110, 205
and Eve, 100-102, 188, 205,
207, 214, 289
adultery, 164, 178
Adversary, the, 23, 78-79, 81, 198
afterlife, 13, 20, 89, 208, 225,
236-46, 250, 252, 254, 257,
265, 289
Akitu festival, 163
Akkadian, 43-44, 50, 52,
57-58, 78-79, 89-90, 92-93,
98, 119, 121, 129, 156, 175,
190-93, 238, 249
alienation, 187-88, 228
Amarna, 64
ʿAmmurapi, 58
Amun-Re, 36, 44, 57, 74, 184,
240. See also Re
ancient context, 4-6, 12, 14-15,
86-87, 102-3, 165, 213, 256.
See also cultural river,
ancient; cognitive
environment, ancient
angelology, 41
aniconism, 150-51, 162, 164
anthropology, 88, 91-92, 96,
98, 225
Anu, 54, 92, 208
Anzu, 55, 79
apologetics, 7, 269
Apophis, 79, 208
ark of the covenant, 124, 127,
150
aseity, 47, 49
Assyria(ns), 55, 80, 164,
234-35, 239
atonement, 128, 130, 141, 173,
226-28, 235
Atrahasis, 78, 89, 93-94
authority of God, 3, 75, 101,
125, 256, 283

authority of Scripture, 3-6,
10-11, 16, 22, 42-43, 233, 275,
277, 279, 282
of the New Testament, 11
of the Old Testament, 3,
10, 275
author's intention, 4, 11, 16,
146, 209, 275-77, 281
ba, 88-89, 240
Baal, 17, 79, 250
Babylon, 201, 203, 226-27
Babylonian(s), 27, 47,
53-54, 60, 75, 81, 92, 163,
184, 202, 221, 239
Belet-ili, 92
Bethel, 115, 148
biblical authority, 3. See also
authority of Scripture
biblical theology, 13, 20,
143-44, 195, 245
biology, 92, 94, 96, 98
blood rituals, 66, 157-58, 173,
228
Book of the Dead, 208, 226,
240-41
Canaanite(s), 55, 60, 75,
133-34, 136, 177, 210, 237,
250, 253
challenger, 197-98, 201, 213,
216. See also Adversary;
devil; Satan
chaos, 55, 77, 82, 104, 145, 210,
216-17, 223
creature(s), 78, 185, 194,
208, 211-13, 218
Chaoskampf, 55, 78-80, 82
cherub(im), 147, 203-6, 211
Christ, 2-6, 8-11, 21-23, 26, 28,
53, 56, 68-70, 88, 98-99, 101,
104, 108, 113-14, 128, 130-32,
142, 152, 154-55, 167, 172-75,
181-82, 206, 217-18, 226-31,
235, 237, 247, 256, 258-64,
276-78, 280, 286, 290-91,
293-94. See also Jesus, Christ

Christology, 6, 143
church, 9, 20, 25-26, 28, 74,
131-33, 151, 171, 180, 182, 218,
231, 256, 275-76, 281, 287,
290, 292
fathers, 207-8
history, 16, 22, 103, 201,
255
circumcision, 12, 119, 291-92
clan deity, 37-38, 54
Coffin Texts, 48, 93-94, 244
cognitive environment, 16, 18,
33, 218-19, 244
ancient, 14-16, 18-19, 31,
66, 78, 81-82, 91, 143, 195,
245. See also ancient
context; cultural river,
ancient
Greco-Roman, 215
of Israel, 31, 61
See also cultural river
cosmic deity, 38, 54
cosmogony, 55, 78-80, 82
cosmology, 15-16, 20, 77, 83, 146
See also worldview
covenant, 13, 24, 26-28, 51, 60,
61, 65, 67, 69, 85, 98-99,
104-9, 111-22, 126, 128-30,
132-36, 138-42, 149-51, 157,
159-62, 165-66, 168-71,
173-74, 177, 179-81, 215, 218,
220, 223, 228, 245, 259-62,
273-75, 289-91
Abrahamic, 61, 105, 107,
114-17, 142, 227, 258
ancient, 119-20
benefits/blessings, 109, 118,
259-60
community, 155, 161, 173,
179, 229, 233, 236, 287
curses, 188, 229, 252
Davidic, 107, 124-26, 128,
142, 232
disorder, 217, 227-29, 233
faithfulness, 60

SCRIPTURE INDEX

Finding the Textbook You Need

The IVP Academic Textbook Selector
is an online tool for instantly finding the IVP books
suitable for over 250 courses across 24 disciplines.

---

ivpacademic.com